Jury Ethics

Jury Ethics
Juror Conduct and Jury Dynamics

Edited by
John Kleinig and James P. Levine

Paradigm Publishers
Boulder • London

Copyright © 2006 Paradigm Publishers

Published in the United States by Paradigm Publishers, 3360 Mitchell Lane Suite E, Boulder, CO 80301 USA.

Paradigm Publishers is the trade name of Birkenkamp & Company, LLC, Dean Birkenkamp, President and Publisher.

Library of Congress Cataloging-in-Publication Data

Jury ethics : juror conduct and jury dynamics / edited by John Kleinig and James P. Levine.
    p. cm.
  Papers presented at the workshop on jury ethics, held September 12-13, 2003 at John Jay College of Criminal Justice.
  Includes bibliographical references and index.
  ISBN 1-59451-148-9
    1. Jury ethics—United States. I. Kleinig, John, 1942- II. Levine, James P.

  KF8980.A5J87 2005
  347.73'752—dc22

                                    2005054455

Printed and bound in the United States of America on acid free paper that meets the standards of the American National Standard for Permanence of Paper for Printed Library Materials.

10 09 08 07 06   1 2 3 4 5

Contents

Prologue: Toward a Jurisprudence of Jury Ethics

This book is about jury ethics—primarily norms of conduct that jurors are expected to heed as they go about their profoundly important business. Examined superficially, the jury's function in reaching verdicts is a mechanical one devoid of moral choices: they simply apply the law as explained by the judge to the facts revealed by the evidence. The reality is otherwise; their participation in the trial process is fraught with ethical questions that require judgment rather than formulaic processes. Jurors are to a considerable degree driven and constrained by a code of conduct;[1] for the most part they must rely on their own consciences in drawing the limits of proper behavior.

From the time a person is summoned for jury service to the end of the trial and beyond, jurors are confronted by a host of moral questions about proper conduct. Jurors must decide whether to try to avoid jury service altogether and what strategies to use should they choose to do so. They must consider how much information about themselves to reveal or withhold during the voir dire process. In reaching a decision about verdicts, jurors sometimes must ponder whether the interests of justice may warrant an acquittal even when the accused appears to be guilty on the basis of facts. Deep-seated matters of conscience almost invariably enter the decision-making crucible when jurors must inflict the death penalty. During deliberations, jurors must think about proper etiquette and decorum in the deliberations process as they try to persuade their co-jurors. And after the verdict is in, they must concern themselves with the sanctity of the discussion—whether and under what conditions to divulge what transpired in the jury room.

Both trial and appellate courts have been perplexed about the moral contours of jury decision making, as was revealed by an ethical predicament confronting the Colorado Supreme Court in March 2005. Jurors considering whether to sentence a man to death for raping and murdering a cocktail waitress were told by the presiding trial judge to make an "individual moral assessment" in deciding whether the convicted defendant should live or die. The jurors consulted various passages in the Bible to clarify their thinking, and the resulting death sentence was challenged on appeal on the grounds that such guidance from religious sources represented undue outside influence on the jury. The three to two split on the Colorado Supreme Court keenly illustrates the moral conundrums about appropriate jury behavior. The majority, which voted to overturn the verdict, ruled that "jurors must deliberate" without the reliance on "higher authority" and "without the aid or distraction of extraneous texts." The minority vehemently disagreed, claiming that "the biblical passages the jurors discussed constituted either a part of the jurors' moral and religious precepts or their general knowledge and thus were relevant to their court-sanctioned moral assessment."[2] If the highest court of a state is so divided about the limits of proper jury behavior, one can only imagine the confusion in the mind-set of jurors who lack the jurisprudential grounding of judges and who are often at sea about what conduct is permissible.

Several of these ethical dilemmas came to light in a *New York Times* investigation of jury behavior in the case of those accused of the 1998 terrorist bombing of the American embassies in Tanzania and Kenya in which 224 were left dead.[3] Four men were accused of the crime, and the federal government asked for the death penalty for two of them. All four were convicted, but the request for execution requiring unanimity among the jurors was denied by the jury, which split nine to three in favor of capital punishment.

One of the jurors who voted against the death sentence later revealed to reporters that he was vehemently against the death penalty despite having said during the pre-trial screening that he had an open mind and that the propriety of imposing death "depends on the occasion." His obstinance was all the more glaring given the fact that when asked on a pre-trial questionnaire to rank his views on capital punishment from 1, "strongly oppose," to 10, "strongly favor," he circled "6." Query: Was it legitimate for this juror to be less than forthright when questioned about his beliefs before the trial in order to get on the jury and prevent what he thought was an unconscionable outcome?[4]

Another matter of controversy revolved around jurors seeking spiritual guidance. Despite the fact that the judge had instructed jurors not to communicate with *anyone* about the trial, two of the jurors consulted their pastors during the deliberation process to get advice on whether the scriptures permitted execution. Although these jurors had initially said they could vote for capital punishment, when confronted with the actual decision to impose death they felt compelled to get reassurance that they would not be violating any religious proscriptions. Both were ultimately part of the majority opting for the death penalty, having been reassured that such an action was morally sound. Query: Is it wrong for jurors to get clarification on their beliefs before agreeing to a decision that would terminate someone's life?

Yet another juror confessed that he considered the possible ramifications of executing the terrorists. He wound up voting to spare the defendants partially on the grounds that an execution would be provocative, perhaps inciting another attack again the United States. Also worthy of note was his expressed concern for his own personal safety as the only Jew on the jury should the verdict be for death; he was not convinced that the anonymity of the jury would prevent his identity from being discovered. Query: Is it *ever* legitimate for a juror to vote for leniency because of worries about retaliation from vengeful supporters of the defendants?

Finally, what about the matter of nine jurors talking openly to the press about jury room dynamics? There is no doubt that this probing piece of journalism provided valuable information about jury decision making and furthered the ideal of transparency regarding the judicial process. But there is a downside: although no names were revealed in the *New York Times* story, it is always possible to pierce the wall of anonymity, as was made abundantly clear by the very fact that the reporters were able to discover and track down all but one juror on what was purportedly an anonymous jury. Query: If jurors fear that what they say in what is supposed to be a confidential setting might later be made public, will it have a chilling effect on the openness of discourse?

The problematic behaviors occasioned by the terrorist case are but a sampling of normative issues that jurors face. Over one million Americans serve on juries annually,[5] and those so engaged are often taking part in the most momentous public decisions of their lives. By all accounts, they take their responsibilities very seriously; they want to do the right thing. And though they are generally inclined to follow the instructions announced by presiding judges, their role is inherently discretionary; and reliance on personal beliefs and values is an inescapable part of the decision-making ordeal.

This is what Alexis de Tocqueville meant when, in his classic volume *Democracy in America,* he said that the "jury is, *above all* a political institution and it must be regarded in this light to be duly appreciated."[6] It is also what sociologists Harry Kalven and Hans Zeisel meant decades ago when they wrote in their seminal empirical study of the jury that the jury is "non-rule minded" and "will move where the equities are."[7] And it is what psychologist Norman Finkel meant when, after reviewing experimental research involving mock jurors, he concluded that jurors are and should be embarked on a search for "the deeper roots of justice."[8] Although the quest for truth is an inherent part of the pursuit of justice, it is not the only facet of sound jury behavior. Like police, prosecutors, defense attorneys, and judges, in reaching verdicts jurors bring in quintessentially moral criteria in fashioning their behavior; they are not robots.

The purpose of this volume is to explore the dimensions of jurors' moral quandaries. Some aspects of this ethical terrain, although complex, have been studied extensively. One such is jury nullification: under what conditions (if at all) should jurors set the law aside in pursuit of a just outcome?[9] Other issues are less apparent but perhaps more pervasive. Consider the legitimacy of compromise verdicts: Is it right for the jury to achieve unanimity through an arrangement whereby in search of middle ground tough jurors wanting conviction on the most serious charges and lenient jurors wanting acquittal consent to conviction on lesser charges, a gambit somewhat analogous to the plea bargain?[10] This issue raises a related one concerning the behavior of "holdout" jurors who refuse to go along with colleagues to achieve a verdict: Are they independent persons of conscience to be admired for their courage or stubborn fanatics who shamefully blind themselves to the wisdom of their colleagues?

In the following pages we highlight and analyze such questions. In quest of a jurisprudence of jury behavior, this volume's contributors attempt to clarify the merits of different models of juror conduct—what is gained and what is lost through alternative specifications of appropriate "jurying." Whereas many judicial systems produce practical handbooks for jurors that try to simplify the nature of juror tasks, we will be doing just the opposite: examining the ethical nuances of the complex decision-making process. In pinpointing and deciphering the subtleties of the juror's role, it is our hope to bring intellectual clarity to what has heretofore been rather uncharted waters—a differentiation between good and bad jury behavior.

The jury is deeply embedded in the American legal system, and the right to a jury trial is enshrined in the Sixth Amendment to the U.S. Constitution.[11] Yet some celebrated cases and dubious verdicts in recent years have called this vaunted institution into question and even led to calls for the attenuation of the jury's role as has occurred in the United Kingdom. It is our hope and intent that by more clearly specifying the rights and wrongs of jury conduct, we can help preserve the jury's integrity and fortify its continued vitality. There are no easy answers about how juries ought to behave, but posing the questions carefully and proposing sensible prescriptions about jury ethics will help maintain and enhance the American jury system.

NOTES

1. Most likely an informal code of conduct, though some formal codes exist: see <http://216.29.61.4/CourtWeb.nsf/Jury_CodeofConduct.htm?OpenPage&charset=iso-8859-1> (2/4/2005); <http://co.hancock.oh.us/commonpleas/juryservice/jurorconduct. aspx> (2/4/2005).

2. Kirk Johnson, "Colorado Court Bars Execution Because Jurors Consulted Bible," *The New York Times*, March 29, 2005, A1.

3. Benjamin Weiser, "A Jury Torn and Fearful in 2001 Terrorism Trial," *New York Times*, January 5, 2003, 1, 28.

4. The issue of excluding jurors opposed to capital punishment in capital cases is a highly controversial one, both as policy and in regard to its effects. For court decisions, see *Witherspoon v. Illinois*, 391 U. S. 510 (1968); *Wainwright v. Witt*, 469 U. S. 412 (1985); *Lockhart v. McCree*, 476 U. S. 162 (1986). See also "In the Supreme

Court of the United States: *Lockhart* v. *McCree*; Amicus Curiae Brief for the American Psychological Association," *American Psychologist* 42 (January 1987): 59–68; William J. Bowers, "The Capital Jury: Is It Tilted toward Death?" *Judicature* 79 (5) (March–April 1996): 220–23.

5. Interview with Tom Munsterman, National Center for State Courts, March 25, 2005.

6. Alexis de Tocqueville, *Democracy in America*, trans. Henry Reeve, rev. Francis Bowers, ed. Phillips Bradley (New York: A. A. Knopf, 1946), vol. I, 282 [emphasis added].

7. Harry Kalven Jr. and Hans Zeisel, *The American Jury* (Boston: Little Brown, 1966), 495.

8. Norman Finkel, *Commonsense Justice: Jurors' Notions of the Law* (Cambridge, MA: Harvard University Press, 1995).

9. Clay Conrad, *Jury Nullification: The Evolution of a Doctrine* (Durham, NC: Carolina Academic Press, 1998).

10. James P. Levine, "Jury Room Politics," *Trial Lawyers Quarterly* 16 (1984): 21–33.

11. Although the ethical questions surrounding this right do not provide the main theme for the volume, the editors have addressed them in the first chapter.

Acknowledgments

The chapters included in this volume had their beginnings in a two-day intensive workshop on jury ethics that took place on September 12–13, 2003, at John Jay College of Criminal Justice. The workshop was sponsored by the Institute for Criminal Justice Ethics. We acknowledge two greatly valued sources of support—first, the City University of New York and the provost of John Jay College, Dr Basil Wilson, and second, the Criminal Justice Research Center and its director, Dr Nancy Jacobs. We are grateful to the cluster of scholars at John Jay College who were excited by the idea of examining jury ethics and who encouraged us to focus on the largely unexamined terrain of ethical issues associated with juror conduct and jury dynamics. To accommodate some of the broader, traditional ethical questions about the jury, we have provided an introductory chapter that reviews some of those larger debates and frames the chapters that follow.

We are, in addition, grateful for the enthusiasm of those who participated as presenters and respondents. Sequestering many of the top jury scholars in the country for two days showed how productive democratic deliberation can be. Although we did not seek or expect to get a unanimous view on the many issues we covered, we were able to see how the simple process of focusing a "jury of diverse minds" on an issue could result in a progressive articulation and enrichment of understanding that would have been less likely to occur if left to a single—albeit trained—mind.

Conferences do not come into being automatically. As with previous institute ventures, Margaret Leland Smith showed herself to be the consummate manager and valued academic gadfly. Not only would the conference not have occurred without her, it would not have been the same without her. We are also appreciative of the early assistance of Kim Reeves. Much of the preparation of this material for publication was carried out while John Kleinig was working in the Centre for Applied and Public Ethics, Charles Sturt University, Australia, and gratitude is expressed for its support along with that of Stephen Coleman.

In preparing the materials for publication, we are indebted to Liza Yukins for her acute compositional and copyediting eye. We are, in addition, greatly appreciative of the faith that Dean Birkenkamp and Mike Peirce have shown in this project, and we have also benefited from the ready assistance provided by Dianne Ewing and Melanie Stafford.

1

Introduction: Ethical Foundations of the American Criminal Jury

John Kleinig and James P. Levine

> The jury invests each citizen with a kind of magistracy; it makes them all
> feel the duties which they are bound to discharge towards society and the
> part which they take in its government. By obliging men to turn their
> attention to other affairs than their own, it rubs off that private selfishness
> which is the rust of society.[1]

Jury trials have ancient roots; evidence of their existence is found in Egyptian, Greek, and Roman writings. But for the jury system as we now know it, the most instructive starting point is probably the Norman Conquest of England in 1066, which imported into English law a system of grand and petit juries initially developed in eighth-century France by Charlemagne. It was not until the thirteenth century, however, that determination of guilt became the jury's primary role. In 1215 the Magna Carta provided for trials by peers, and, with the Fourth Lateran Council's condemnation of trial by ordeal later that same year, trial by jury became a major tool for resolving the issue of criminal guilt.[2] Nevertheless, early jury trials relied heavily on the oath of jurors familiar with the defendant, and the practice of calling witnesses was not well established until a few centuries later. As the English Bill of Rights (1689) made clear, jury trials were sometimes circumvented and frequently corrupted, thus constituting an uncertain safeguard against overweening authority. Therefore, although the traditions of English law were formally observed in its American colonies, they provided inadequate protection against judicial and administrative tyranny. In these circumstances, it is not surprising that the writers of the Declaration of Independence (1776) accused George III of, inter alia, "depriving us in many cases of the benefits of Trial by Jury."

In 1791, with the ratification of the Bill of Rights appended to the U.S. Constitution (1787), it was guaranteed that "in all criminal prosecutions, the accused shall enjoy the right to a . . . trial, by an impartial jury of the State

1

and district wherein the crime shall have been committed, which district shall have been previously ascertained by law."[3] Originally formulated for federal criminal trials, in 1968 this constitutional right was formally extended to all state criminal trials (though by then many state constitutions had already established such a right).[4]

The final wording of the Sixth Amendment was not decided without vigorous debate, and it incorporates elements that have remained in tension ever since. The requirement of an *impartial* jury is problematically linked with the requirement that the jury be *drawn from the district in which the crime was committed*. One can easily imagine how the latter requirement might jeopardize achievement of the former, because of local partiality with respect to either the victim or alleged perpetrator—a problem that has been subsequently aggravated by the media feeding frenzies that frequently accompany serious crimes. That of course was not intended. Early advocates of vicinage argued for the importance of a jury's reflecting the competence of *local* knowledge, its shared understanding of the law, and the protection it provided against prosecutorial tyranny.[5] But the balance has often been hard to maintain, and in high-profile cases, such as those that followed the bombing of the Oklahoma City federal building, the impartiality requirement has sometimes sustained an argument for transferring a trial to a distant venue. This latter option, however, has usually been pursued only when it has been determined prior to voir dire that the local atmosphere has been so tainted by publicity that selecting a jury capable of judging fairly would be impossible.[6]

The impartiality requirement is not itself controversial. Controversy has centered on what it requires so far as jury selection and decision making are concerned. And here the implicit presumption of competent local knowledge has been a sticking point. There is, of course, a possibility that the alleged perpetrator may not be from the place in which the crime is committed, thereby weakening the contextualizing presumption of vicinage. But a more serious concern is that local jurors will have been exposed to tainting opinions about the crime. Should an impartial juror therefore know nothing about the case? Even though it may not be easy to disentangle fact from opinion, should we presume that all local knowledge is tainted? Or should we assume that all jurors who have been exposed to opinions that tend to prejudge the case will be so uncritical as to be persuaded by them, or, even if they have formed some opinion as a result, that those opinions will not be open to revision on acquaintance with court testimony? If minimal exposure to opinion about the case is required, is there not a heightened probability that those selected won't care too much about what is going on about them in contrast to those who take an active and intelligent interest in what goes on in their community? Although the presumption behind the requirement of relative ignorance is that what needs to be known about a case will be presented at trial, the danger will be that those who qualify will not be socially prepared to rise to the challenge that is put to them.[7]

More abstract than the problems posed by the local knowledge requirement is the suggestion that impartiality requires indifference on the part of
the juror. Indifference is not necessarily synonymous with impartiality.
Indifference has to do with caring, impartiality with preference. Someone
who is indifferent may also be impartial in that he does not care which way
a verdict goes. But uncaring indifference may also compromise impartial
judgment by undermining its conditions. Jury determinations are not
mechanical operations on a complex array of data, but judgments that
embody not only intellectual but also certain moral virtues—integrity and a
passionate concern for truth. Were this not so, the pretension that the law is
an instrument of *justice* would be hollow.

I. FOUNDATIONS

Why have a jury trial? Is its advocacy anything more than the ideological
residue of anti-colonial feeling, a symbolic rejection of monarchical
concentrations of power? Are not judges better trained and able to make the
determinations that jurors are sometimes asked to make? These are serious
questions. Many liberal democratic theorists have argued against the value
of jury trials.[8] Most liberal democratic countries make significantly less—or
no—use of jury trials, and even in the United States defendants may, except
in capital cases, choose to waive their right to one.[9] More challenging, over
ninety percent of criminal cases in the United States are now resolved through
some form of plea bargaining, and about half of the remainder are decided
by means of a bench trial.[10] It is unlikely that any argument for jury trials
will be decisive and exclusive.

Nevertheless, even though the jury predates liberal democratic
institutions, its *contemporary* expressions can be anchored in liberal
democratic and republican theory, in the foundational rationale for the
"American experiment." The Declaration of Independence affirmed that
the "unalienable Rights" to life, liberty, and the pursuit of happiness with
which all humans have been endowed are secured through the operation of
governmental authority that derives its "just powers from the consent of the
governed." In doing so, it reflected the social contract tradition that under-
scores most liberal democratic thinking.

In John Locke's *Second Treatise of Civil Government* (1689), long considered
the classic of social contract theory and a major resource for American
political ideology, a state of nature—social life unregulated by civil
government—is said to suffer from three crucial institutional deficiencies:
legislative, judicial, and (to put into effect the determinations of the first
two) executive.[11] In the unlikely event that people in a state of nature would
be able to agree on the formal content of the law of nature (social morality),
they would still disagree about how to interpret and apply it. It is a manifest
fact of human experience (Locke writes) that those who need recourse to

law are likely to exhibit bias in interpreting its provisions and, in cases in which their own interests are not involved, their commitment to its application is likely to be half-hearted. And so *"a known and indifferent Judge, with Authority to determine all differences according to established Law"* needs to be instituted.[12]

In Lockeian social contract theory, the purpose of government is limited to the protection of limited fundamental rights. Although that now generally strikes us as too limited an understanding of the functions of government, it nevertheless indicates, in a general way, that the appropriate role of government and its institutions is to secure certain kinds of justice (protection of rights; corrective justice; perhaps distributive justice). Governmental processes, including those of the courts, should seek to maximize the likelihood that appropriate justice is done. The rule of law, understood in part as the exclusion of arbitrariness from social life, plays a key role in securing that justice.

At first blush, this does not appear to offer much space for a jury, and may even be taken to exclude it. Unlike a jury, the "known and indifferent Judge"—presumably skilled in matters of law and in asking the right questions of fact,[13] and without a stake in the outcome—possesses the requisite knowledge and impartiality that judicial judgment requires. Ensuring equal protection of the laws is a central judicial function. Not only is the law a complex social tool but the understanding of fact patterns is also a sophisticated task.[14] Not only an open court but consistency of judgment appear to be demanded.

However, pressing the idea a bit harder, juries might be considered as good an expression of Lockeian ideals, if not better, than judges ruling on their own. Underlying Lockeian social contract theory is the idea that each person has a right to determine the conditions under which his or her life is to be lived, subject, of course, to others being enabled to make similar determinations with respect to their own lives. Civil society is a strategic (and morally sensitive) attempt to implement that foundational understanding. One might argue that this consensual strategy anticipates each person's input into an understanding of the various conditions necessary for an orderly social life—the formation, application, and enforcement of social rules. Taken literally, such an expectation would be too strenuous and difficult to manage. And so, instead of a fully participatory political and legal order, we settle for a representative one in which we choose those who will act on our behalf. Because the resulting system is imperfect, however, we institute further measures to minimize or counteract its imperfections. Jury trials can be construed as one of those measures. Instead of having a single detached judge determining how a particular law is to be interpreted and applied in a particular place and set of circumstances, we use a form of decision making that places important determinations back into the hands of the people who are the ultimate agents of the conditions of their social life. The point of having a plurality of jurors is that through their deliberative engagement with each other they will come to a decision that better expresses the will of those whose system it ultimately is. Such a plurality is more likely to judge correctly the facts of the case at hand than would have been the case had the decision been left entirely in the hands of judges.[15] Even if the decisions are no better than those of judges, it may be, as Tocqueville observed, good for the vitality of a liberal democratic community if its members play such a role: civic education as well as republican virtue are fostered through jury participation.

II. COMPOSITION

The theory behind the jury trial has significant implications for issues of jury eligibility and jury selection. Should some people be excluded from jury service altogether? The history of exclusionary policies is mixed and instructive.[16] In the United States, early juries consisted exclusively of white male owners of property. African Americans began to be added to juries in some states from about 1860 and women from 1898,[17] although as recently as the 1960s African Americans were routinely excluded from Southern jury pools by administrative fiat. Even then discrimination was often perpetuated through the use of blue-ribbon juries and jury lists that excluded daily wage earners or were disproportionately skewed to favor white males. Until recently, eligibility lists were also restricted in other ways—for example, they did not include those who were not registered voters, thus disproportionately omitting the young, Hispanics, Native Americans, and those of low socioeconomic status.[18] Some people are still ineligible for jury service: those who are under a certain age, illiterate, mentally or physically incapacitated; those who fail to meet residency or citizenship requirements; and those deemed to lack good moral character by virtue of their felony status.[19] The legitimacy of some of these exclusions and how they are to be interpreted is a matter of ongoing debate.

Even if the issue of eligibility is resolved, the underlying rationale of a jury trial can be subverted in other ways. The longstanding practice known as peremptory challenge, whereby potential jurors can be excluded for no articulated reason, has often been used to exclude jurors who are judged unfriendly to a particular outcome. The justifying claim is that those with interests at stake ought to have some say in determining those who make the judgment, and that leaving such decisions in the hands of a single, fallible judge does not sufficiently secure those interests. More likely, however, is their use to "stack the deck" with a jury that is partial to the prosecution or the defense. Although use of the peremptory challenge has been curbed in recent years,[20] mainly to inhibit the exclusion of people solely on account of their race or gender, it remains a problematic entitlement.[21]

Backing up peremptory challenges and voir dire questioning has been the use of jury consultants to "craft" juries that will underplay or overemphasize certain social factors considered to be relevant to the ways in which jurors will deliberate. Their use in the trial of El Sayyid A. Nosair for the murder of Rabbi Meir Kahane enabled the defense lawyer to include in the jury people who would not only lack sympathy for Israel but also be sympathetic to claims about Nosair's marginalized social status.[22] Although the adversary system itself calls on the defense and prosecuting lawyers to do what they can for those they represent, zealous advocacy can subvert fairness in the name of victims' or defendants' rights.[23] Whether defense attempts to make "scientific" selections succeed in sufficient numbers to make them worthwhile is a moot point.[24]

In addition to diminishing the discriminatory use of peremptory challenges, other efforts have been undertaken to make the jury better fitted for its purpose. Some of these efforts might be criticized for losing sight of the theory that underlies a jury trial. Jury diversity ought not to be understood as a response to identity politics but rather as an expression of John Stuart Mill's contention that truth and the assurance thereof are most likely to be achieved when the available data are exposed to those with varying opinions and perspectives.[25] The purpose of jury decision making is not democratic majoritarianism, but consensus or at least concurrence achieved after a situation has been scrutinized from a suitably diverse set of perspectives. The end is truth, not cross-sectional representation.[26] It is, moreover, not easy to decide in advance what groups should be included: Should gay-bashing cases include homosexual jury members? Should jury selection in cases of violence against abortion clinics include both pro-choice and right-to-life supporters? And so forth. Only at its best will some form of cross-sectional representation increase the likelihood that in the search for truth salient dimensions of a situation will not be left out of account or excluded.[27]

III. DELIBERATION

Behind the problematic idea of a demographically structured jury there nevertheless lies a valid recognition that even if those who become jurors can be presumed free from certain kinds of disqualifying prejudice, they cannot be expected to shed all past beliefs, preconceptions, values, and ways of thinking. Moreover, they may suffer from certain kinds of prejudicial ignorance. Prejudice varies greatly in its subtlety. Even though jurors may not be interest-group representatives, they are not tabulae rasae. The deliberative ideal of juror engagement is that each will enrich the others' perceptions in ways that will lead to a common or at least integrated understanding that might not have been available to them individually. Via their deliberative engagement, the truth of a matter is more likely to emerge than would have been the case had the decision been left to a single individual or determined through an interest-based poll.

As a matter of policy, however, that may not be the last word on this issue. If, despite attempts to ensure jury openness, practice suggests a persisting bias, quotas may appear to offer a pragmatic solution. When prosecution and defense both have an interest in a partisan jury, prejudice may veil itself in ways that are manifest only in aggregate outcomes. That, certainly, is the continuing danger posed by peremptory challenges.

At its best, trial by a local jury might be seen as an attempt to secure the consensual account of governmental power that underlies the American tradition.[28] Although those who pass the laws are elected representatives of the people, there is no guarantee that their legislative decisions will always reflect the nuanced understanding of those who elected them; furthermore, although judges are supposed to be impartial interpreters of law, there is no guarantee that they will always be sensitive to the ways in which local knowledge impacts on its interpretation and application. Determinations by a local jury have the potential for ensuring that the judgments of civil society are products of consensus rather than of an elite.[29] As Andrew Hamilton put it, it is the task of jurors "to see with their own eyes, to hear with their own ears, and to make use of their own consciences and understandings in judging of the lives, liberties or estates of their fellow subjects."[30]

A jury also serves the more pragmatic purpose of diminishing the temptations of judicial misconduct. Despite the high ideals of judicial office, the potential for bribery and other perversions of justice remains strong, and judicial power is legitimately balanced by a jury of twelve rotating individuals.[31] Of course, the benefits of this pragmatic corrective are at best only relative, as is made clear by the history of racial prejudice displayed by juries and occasional scandals of jury tampering.[32]

IV. SCOPE AND NULLIFICATION

As Jeffrey Abramson makes clear, although the shell of vicinage has been retained, it has been increasingly emptied of substance. On the one hand, the claims of impartiality have led to a growing demand that jurors possess relatively little prior knowledge of the defendant or victim and the circumstances of the crime. On the other hand, juries have been increasingly expected to confine their determinations to factual matters and to yield their understanding of the law to judges. They have not been prevented from making legal determinations—as is evidenced by their indefeasible *practical power* to nullify—but judicial directives have been a significant practical deterrent and later judicial decisions have made it clear that juries that take matters of law into their hands have neither a (legal) *right* nor a *privilege* to do so.[33]

Jury nullification entered the criminal courts a century before American independence, in the trials of William Penn and Edward Bushell, one of the jurors in Penn's case. That chaotic episode provided stark evidence of the value of jury trials as well as a vivid example of the kind of occasions for which jury nullification might be deemed an ethically appropriate option. The charges brought against Penn and his associate, William Mead, reflected governmental tyranny as well as judicial collusion. The bench's attempt to confine the jury to matters of fact showed how interrelated matters of fact and law could be. Fining the jurors for making their own judgment magnified that wrong by "depriving" them of their voice regarding the justice of a law, its application, or its consequences in a particular case.

The classic American case involved Peter Zenger, publisher of *The New York Journal*, who in 1735 was charged with committing seditious libel for printing articles critical of the British colonial government. Because the judge had ruled as a matter of law that the articles were libelous, the jurors' only task, it seemed, was to determine whether Zenger had in fact printed them. But the colonists' antipathy toward the British politicization of the law prompted the jury to acquit Zenger. Although American history books celebrate this as a triumph of press freedom, it also involved a jury "taking the law into its own hands." Zenger's jury did not take the law into its own hands by abandoning the rule of law. Rather, it eschewed an understanding of the rule of law as a mechanical application of statutes or unquestioning acceptance of judicial directive, and saw it as an agent of social justice.

Despite the potential that jury nullification has for countering government oppression, it is a double-edged sword. As an unchecked power, it can also be a vehicle of injustice. Such has notoriously been the case in the United States in its long struggle with racial prejudice; moreover, in the interest of tough law enforcement, it has also been used to exonerate police officers palpably guilty of using excessive force.

Jury nullification is also theoretically problematic. The foregoing comments on the Zenger jury notwithstanding, the "rule of law, not men," a pillar of liberal democratic order, arguably requires that social life be regulated by means of previously determined and transparent procedures, and, further, that procedures for determining and applying law be stated in advance. Such practices are intended to prevent the arbitrary judgments of a single individual (or group). Jury nullification appears to fly in the face of the notion that if we do not like the way things are done, change must be brought about through established procedures.[34] Not only would the right of a jury to make legal (as against factual) determinations leave it unclear how a person might order his life to conform with the law, but it would also litter the judicial landscape with decisions lacking precedential value.

And yet like civil disobedience, with which it is frequently compared, jury nullification may appear to be a morally necessary option in a less than perfect world. Even in democratic societies, legislative power can be used to enforce the morally suspect interests of a particular group of people, particular laws may be too coarse to exclude from their purview certain actions that are justified, and the sanctions attached to certain breaches may be unconscionable.[35] The problem is to keep such a power from getting out of hand. In the case of civil disobedience, there is usually the recognition that disobedients will or should suffer the consequences of their disobedience. That will give pause to those contemplating it, as they weigh the cause against the costs. But there are no sanctions against jurors who nullify.[36]

In point of fact, however, it is rare for juries to consciously disregard judges' instructions and to acquit those who are unmistakably guilty. For the most part, it is a power that is conscientiously exercised. This has led to the suggestion that in some cases—such as those in which horribly brutalized women have killed their abusive husbands—jurors be given nullification instructions that explicitly permit them to acquit in order to avert injustice.[37] But others have condemned such license, arguing that it opens the door to jury arbitrariness and caprice.[38] In the words of one appeals court, when it rejected the request of a defendant in a Vietnam War protest case that jurors be told explicitly that they had no obligation to follow the law: "What makes for health as an occasional medicine would be disastrous as a daily diet.... An explicit instruction to the jury [of their right to set laws aside] conveys an implied approval [of such a practice] that runs the risk of degrading the legal structure."[39]

The scholarly consensus is apparently to leave well enough alone on the ground that juries will nullify when they have "damn good reason" to do so, sparing defendants from overly harsh application of the law in cases in which defendants are truly deserving of special consideration.[40] If a 2002 vote in South Dakota is any indication, the body politic agrees. Voters overwhelmingly rejected a proposal to explicitly permit jurors to acquit defendants who admit guilt should the jurors conclude that the law under which they were charged is misguided or draconian.[41] It is likely that the status quo that permits jurors to nullify without telling them they can do so will continue indefinitely.[42]

The nullification option is further complicated by the fact that even if, as Locke claimed, the law of nature is clearly "discernible to the eye of reason," the criminal law in complex industrial and postindustrial societies is no longer so transparent. In addition, fact patterns may be exceedingly complex, demanding a great deal of those who must make sense of them. These considerations may be taken to strengthen the argument for a division of labor, allocating to judges the responsibility for determining applicable law and interpreting it and burdening the jury with no more than responsibility for judging the unique factual situation of the case before it. It is not simply that the criminal law in industrial and postindustrial societies has become increasingly complex, but also that the Lockeian "eye of reason" no longer possesses argumentative appeal. In a homogeneous community one might presume that reasonable people will have a shared perception of right and wrong. In diverse modern societies that presumption is questionable, and so the contours of criminal law result from social compromise as much as from any "natural law." Although criminal law has not completely abandoned its moorings in moral judgment, the high seas of diversity have left its determinations increasingly in the hands of experts. Although we may not like that, we may have to come to terms with it.

That said, the division of labor between judge and jury is not altogether helpful to the practice and standing of the jury trial. Just because criminal jurors are called to pronounce on questions of *guilt*, it is important that they see themselves as engaging with the substance of the law and not simply with neutral determinations of fact. As triers of fact, their task is ultimately a normative one, and any suggestion that they are merely passive appliers of law places them in a morally impossible position. There is probably a practical middle way. If the division of labor is seen as tactical—one that gives primary responsibility for matters of law to the judge and for matters of fact to the jury, and it is recognized that this does not constitute a strict division—jurors will not be prevented from appreciating the normative and moral dimensions of their task and even, in rare instances, from legitimately exercising a nullifying power.[43]

Indeed, empirical studies have demonstrated rather convincingly that jurors' reliance on their own values is far more subtle than the purposeful abandonment of the law involved in true jury nullification.[44] Although most jurors make sincere attempts to follow the law and base verdicts on evidence, legal ambiguity and factual uncertainty give them ample opportunities for incorporating personal sentiment and exercising conscientious judgment. The adversary process itself, with its presentation of opposing arguments and evidence, permits the jury such leeway. There is always some fragment of evidence, some line of argument, or some legal definition that will enable jurors to justify the outcome they consider to be preferable. People can see the same things differently and draw different inferences from the same information. Thus jurors who desire acquittal can take a "merciful view of the facts,"[45] and those wanting conviction can look at the facts vindictively.

The O. J. Simpson case was a striking example of this phenomenon. Although a majority of Americans who followed the televised trial thought that the football star and sportscaster was guilty of murdering his wife and her friend, the jury that acquitted him thought otherwise. Many critics of the verdict claimed that the predominately black jury showed favoritism toward a hero in the black community. As *New York Times* columnist Maureen Dowd put it: "Mr. Simpson's jury in the criminal trial had plenty of evidence, but made a decision based on race."[46] But the jurors themselves disavowed such a contention, claiming that the police investigation was muddled, that the evidence was inconclusive, and that the forensic experts were divided.

As one of the jurors emphatically defended the verdict: "I was brought up to love everyone. I'm not for anyone, yellow, black, blue, green. I'm just for justice. . . . We were fair. It wasn't a matter of sympathy. It wasn't a matter of favoritism. It was a matter of evidence."[47]

Such differences of opinion should not be exaggerated. The one value to which virtually all jurors subscribe is a commitment to truth, and so when the law and evidence are crystal clear, they seldom distort reality to reach a preferred verdict. Even though there are exceptions, they rarely convict those who are patently innocent or acquit those who are clearly guilty.

V. SIZE AND UNANIMITY

The desire to maximize the probability of reaching a correct assessment of the situation has implications for two other questions, one concerning the size of a jury and the other concerning the kind of conclusion that it reaches— whether it should be unanimous, super-, or simple-majoritarian. There are probably no timelessly correct answers to such questions, though the development of jury practice has to some extent reflected the exigencies of the times.

We are accustomed to think of juries of twelve, though that has recently been changing, as some states have opted for juries of six, at least for less serious criminal trials and for civil cases. Trials that might result in a death penalty have continued to have juries of twelve, even where smaller juries are used in other cases. Is there any magic to the number "twelve"? The legal cases that address the issue suggest that it was simply happenstance that arrived at the number twelve.[48] One might suspect, given the environment in which the modern jury developed, that the number tapped into a certain Judaeo-Christian fondness for the number twelve—the original twelve tribes of Israel and the twelve disciples chosen by Jesus, a number restored by the early church after the defection of Judas.[49] It was certainly more workable than the jury of 501 that convicted Socrates.[50]

There is probably no more magic to twelve than there is to the age of majority. It is a workable convenience that bears some reasonable relation to the purposes for which it is designed. Having fixed on it, it then exercises its own influence on public consciousness. Just as recognition of eighteen as the age of majority has subsequently influenced the nurturing and educational process by providing a socially determinate "cutoff" point, so the need to have twelve persons agreeing on an outcome has provided a certain operational framing of our deliberative processes. Getting three people to agree is not the same as getting thirty people to agree. Getting twelve to agree has acquired a certain conventional weight.

Fixing on a number influences the kind of rationale that might be presented. In a fairly diverse community, we might consider that twelve is a sufficiently large number to represent that diversity in a relatively fair manner.[51] It is also large enough for us to draw reasonably firm conclusions about systematic bias when it occurs. If we begin to observe a pattern in which members of certain groups (and, along with that, an appropriate diversity of perspective) are being regularly excluded from jury service, it is easier to argue that this is due to bias more than bad luck if the number of people on the jury is twelve rather than six.

Other factors may also be relevant to the likelihood of a jury's decision representing a genuinely deliberative outcome. Having too many on a jury will make it difficult for all jurors to have a proper say. Having too few might deny a jury the insights that come from a diversity of initial perspectives.

None of these arguments has "twelve" as its necessary conclusion, though together they make a reasonable case for the number being as it is. As has been the case with the age of majority, we might think that for certain cases a different cutoff would be acceptable. As we may allow consent to medical procedures at an earlier age, we may also think that a smaller jury is adequate for certain kinds of cases. In any event, the U.S. Supreme Court has determined that six is the lower limit of jury size.[52]

What about unanimity? Once again, certain religious considerations may have originally influenced such a requirement. The "one mind" that was said to characterize the early church was seen in part as assurance that its mind was the mind of God,[53] and those acting as his earthly agents might have sought similar assurance.

Although unanimity has been the dominant tradition, since the 1970s a number of states have qualified it.[54] For many cases some jurisdictions require only majority or supermajority decisions. A unanimity requirement has seemed costly and inefficient. Drawn-out jury deliberations, hung juries, and, no doubt, unconvicted offenders have disposed some jurisdictions to loosen the requirement. And even where the unanimity requirement has been formally observed, it has sometimes reflected a jury-room compromise in which, in order to secure a conviction, an offender has been dealt with more lightly than might otherwise have appeared to be warranted.[55]

But even if one might want to make some concessions to less-than-unanimous decision making, there are strong reasons for pursuing unanimity as an ideal. If the point of a jury is to seek, through a deliberative process, an outcome that is sensitive to the diversity of considerations that might be brought to bear on the case—an outcome that might be said to have taken adequate cognizance of the various perspectives and understandings of its members—then unanimity might reasonably be seen as the goal of, and expectation in, such deliberations. A significant danger, should the unanimity requirement be compromised, is that jury decision making will take on the character of political decision making, with its members seeking to persuade each other to their side rather than focusing on the deliberative challenge posed by a diversity of understandings. A jury must attempt to give such diverse views their due weight in the process of arriving at a factual conclusion that is not predetermined by or merely reflective of interests. It is the fact of a jury trial that reflects liberal democratic values—an opportunity for those who are under law to participate in its determinations. But the jury process is directed to the establishment of certain factual conclusions—concerning guilt or innocence—and not merely to the representation of preexisting interests in a political process.

There is another factor of moment. The outcome of a decision to convict, particularly in a criminal trial, is the imposition of some penalty on a human being, and governmental authority needs strong justification for that. Otherwise it subverts the very purpose of a civil order—the preservation of a person's life, liberty, and projects. Thus a high level of concurrence should be expected before the power to penalize is exercised.[56]

In upholding a less-than-unanimous decision, it was Justice Lewis Powell's contention that the unanimity requirement forced juries into compromises that were unsatisfactory to all.[57] No doubt that is one possibility. But not every compromise need create dissatisfaction, and there is no more reason to seek a compromise that is unsatisfactory than to acquiesce in a hung jury.[58] Although retrials may be costly and inconvenient, they provide a socially acceptable option.[59]

To some degree, the issue of unanimity may be a tempest in a teapot. In point of fact, small minorities on juries rarely hold out, capitulating instead to the majority will. A study of 225 cases that compared first ballot breakdowns with final verdicts showed that initial majorities almost always prevailed.[60] A complex peer-pressure process operates that prompts dissident jurors to reexamine their opinions and conform to the dominant viewpoint. In reality, what the unanimity requirement normally accomplishes is an extension of debate rather than a change in the ultimate outcome.

It may well turn out that the deliberative ideal of jury decision making is sometimes breached —an outcome likely to be of greater media interest than its opposite—but this is no reason for abandoning it. If anything, indeed, it warns of the perils of abandonment.[61] The expectation that twelve people will contribute their varied understandings and perspectives to a conversation in which they are expected to reach a consensus or at least a concurrence affirms the seriousness of the responsibility they have as well as the fundamental commitments of a liberal democratic polity. Their goal is truth not numbers. And each has standing as a rational being equal with others, respected and respecting.

The deliberative and democratic ideal that informs jury service is an ideal and it can be subverted in many ways. The underlying premise of this volume is that the ideal is important enough both to warrant our identification of the ways in which its realization is impeded and to seek ethically acceptable strategies for improving the likelihood of its realization. In the final analysis, the merit of the jury hinges not simply on abstract notions about its salutary role in the legal system but on the exposition of norms of proper conduct that maximize the jury's contribution to social jurisprudence. The noble concept of trial by jury stands or falls on the articulation of a generally accepted code of jury ethics and a willingness of jurors to subscribe to such a code. The fate of the jury system may well hang in the balance.

NOTES

1. Alexis de Tocqueville, *Democracy in America*, trans. Phillips Bradley (1833; New York: Vintage, 1945), 1: 295.

2. Ironically, Lateran IV repudiated the Magna Carta, though it was later reinstated. The dispute reflected the awkward relations between (English) temporal and (Roman) spiritual authority.

3. U.S. Constitution, amend. 6. This almost redundantly expands on article 3, section 2 of the Constitution, which provides that "The trial of all crimes, except in cases of impeachment, shall be by jury; and such trial shall be held in the State where the said crimes shall have been committed; but when not committed within any State, the trial shall be at such place or places as the Congress may by law have directed." Note, though, that what seems to be presented as a requirement in article 3 is posited only as a (waivable) right in the Sixth Amendment.

4. *Duncan v. Louisiana*, 391 U.S. 145 (1968).

5. A modern version of this latter unseemliness can be found in federal Attorney General John Ashcroft's decision to have the alleged Washington snipers tried in the state in which they were most likely to face the death penalty. See further, Jeffrey Abramson, *We, the Jury: The Jury System and the Ideal of Democracy* (New York: Basic Books, 1994), chap. 1.

6. Even then a problem may arise since supporters of the defendant and victim may vary over where a fair trial is likely to be possible. Depending on one's point of view, the decision to locate the original Rodney King trial in Simi Valley, California, might have been seen as an effort to ensure a jury less likely to be prejudiced by public reactions to the videotaping of his beating or as a strategy for securing a jury likely to be unusually sympathetic to the police. See Abramson, *We, the Jury*, 242–45.

7. This is a problem that—albeit for different reasons—has dogged the jury from its earliest days. Mark Twain acidly observed that "we have a criminal jury system that is superior to any in the world; and its efficiency is only marred by the difficulty of finding twelve men every day who don't know anything and can't read." "Fourth of July Speech in London," in *Collected Tales, Sketches, Speeches, and Essays 1852–1890* (1873; New York: Library of America, 1992), 556.

8. The judiciary has always had its skeptics. Thus, Jerome Frank scathingly observed: "While the jury can contribute nothing of value so far as the law is concerned, it has infinite capacity for mischief, for twelve men can easily misunderstand more law in a minute than the judge can explain in an hour." *Skidmore v. Baltimore and Ohio Railroad*, 167 F.2d 54 (1948). Among contemporary scholars who oppose it, see Penny Darbyshire, "The Lamp That Shows That Freedom Lives—Is it Worth the Candle?" *Criminal Law Review* (1991): 740–52.

9. In some countries traditionally committed to jury trials (e.g., Great Britain), there have recently been efforts to narrow their use. These moves have arisen out of Lord Justice Auld's September 2001 *Review of the Criminal Courts of England and*

Wales. For the text, supporting documents, and commentary, see http://www.criminal-courts-review.org.uk/ (accessed January 6, 2005).

10. See John H. Langbein, "The Myth of Written Constitutions: The Disappearance of Criminal Jury Trial," *Harvard Journal of Law and Public Policy* 15 (1992): 119–27. However, we probably should not be overly sanguine about the practice of plea bargaining. See especially Albert W. Alschuler, "Plea Bargaining and Its History," *Law and Society Review* 13 (1979): 211–45. Assuming, though, that plea bargaining can be justified, it should be noted that expectations of the way in which a jury would decide a case greatly influence the nature of the plea agreements arrived at by prosecutors, defense attorneys, and their clients.

11. See especially, John Locke, *Two Treatises of Government,* ed. Peter Laslett (Cambridge: Cambridge University Press, 1960), *Second Treatise,* chap. 9.

12. Locke, *Second Treatise,* section 125.

13. "Presumably" is the operative word. Whatever we may wish from judges, practices of judicial selection frequently give much greater weight to political and partisan connections. This was true at the beginning of the American republic, when few judges had a professional knowledge of the law, and remains true in a society in which many lower court judges are not attorneys and in which the processes of judicial selection have become highly politicized. See Doris Marie Provine, *Judging Credentials: Nonlawyer Judges and the Politics of Professionalism* (Chicago: University of Chicago Press, 1986). For a valuable historical overview that provides a sense of judge-jury dynamics, see Albert W. Alschuler and Andrew G. Deiss, "A Brief History of the Criminal Jury in the United States," *University of Chicago Law Review* 61 (1994): 867–928.

14. This is perhaps a reason why, in civil cases, jury trials are declining in certain jurisdictions and have never been popular in European jurisdictions. There is also the silent rebuke to jury trials in the plea bargaining of criminal charges. Plea bargains require judicial but not juror approval.

15. In any case, as Justices Holmes and Cardozo recognized long ago, judges are not simply "oracles of the law" (as Blackstone idealistically supposed) but the proponents of particular ideologies and policies, however benign they may sometimes be. Judicial decision making is about judgment, not the discovery of some Platonic form of law.

16. For a useful brief history, see Alschuler and Deiss, "A Brief History," 876–901.

17. This is when Utah authorized the admission of women. There were earlier cases, but they were not routinized and they often involved "female issues." Only in 1975 did the Constitution give women equal jury status, *Taylor v. Louisiana,* 419 U.S. 522 (1975).

18. There is of course an argument for using registered voter lists, namely, that registration reflects a certain level of commitment to public affairs. But that reads too much into why people do or do not register, and fails to take account of the fact that levels of voting registration vary considerably among different demographic groups. In recent years much has been done to expand the lists of those broadly eligible for jury service. Voter lists have been replaced by lists created from several sources—driver's licenses, utilities customers, telephone directories, tax rolls, public assistance rosters, and so forth, and many "routine" exemptions (of lawyers, doctors, teachers, etc.) have been eliminated.

19. Although there are obvious practical problems about including the incarcerated, many states permanently exclude *ex*-felons from jury service, an administrative source of bias in jury pools.

20. See *Batson v. Kentucky*, 476 U.S. 79 (1986) and a line of subsequent cases— e.g., *Powers v. Ohio*, 499 U.S. 400 (1991); *Georgia v. McCollum*, 112 S.Ct. 2348 (1992).

21. Indeed, because of its inherent potential for bias, Justice Marshall, in his concurring opinion in *Batson*, stated his general opposition to peremptory challenges, and not just to those that were race-based. His concerns have been borne out by subsequent decisions in which courts have allowed "thin" rationales for exclusion.

22. Abramson, *We, the Jury*, 144. A corollary of such attempts will be the heightened intrusiveness of the jury-selection process, raising important ethical questions about juror privacy. How deeply may a judge or lawyer inquire into the personal history and predilections of a juror? See *United States v. Payne*, 962 F.2d 1228, 1233 (6th Cir. 1992), where a potential juror was excluded for favoring civil rights. When should a voir dire examination be carried out in private?

23. According to some lawyers—most notably Monroe Freedman—the task of a defense lawyer is circumscribed by the defendant's rights and, provided the law is not transgressed, this is the limit of the lawyer's duty to the court and community.

24. On the use of social science methodologies to discover jurors' predilections, see James P. Levine, *Juries and Politics* (Belmont, CA: Wadsworth, 1992), 55–57; Franklin Strier and Donna Shestowsky, "Profiling the Profilers: A Study of the Trial Consulting Profession, Its Impact on Trial Justice and What, if Anything, to Do about It," *Wisconsin Law Review* (1999): 441–99; Neil Kressel and Dorit F. Kressel, *Stack and Sway: The New Science of Jury Consulting* (New York: Perseus Books Group/Westview Press, 2002). Abramson also considers other "scientific" techniques for jury manipulation—e.g., the use of shadow and mock juries. Although he is generally skeptical of their efficacy, that may simply reflect our current state of knowledge (or, just as likely, the simplistic approaches of jury consultants). In any case, all that may be needed in a case that could go either way is an "edge." No less problematic than the possibility that scientific techniques are efficacious is the *perception* that they are, for this reinforces the belief that one gets the justice one pays for.

25. John Stuart Mill, *On Liberty*, ed. Elizabeth Rapaport (1859; Indianapolis: Hackett, 1978), chap. 2.

26. Once we start down the road of "cross-sectional representation" we are faced with the representativeness of the representatives. In a divided society, the jury predicament goes very deep. Because the judicial system is embedded in the broader political system, it is not only subject to the demand that it *be* fair but that it *be seen to be* fair. The demand that the jury be seen to be fair is a *political* demand whose satisfaction may be at odds with its capacity to be fair.

27. One might of course express postmodernist skepticism about whether there is such a thing as "the truth of the matter." That arises out of a theory that itself must withstand rational scrutiny, and cannot simply be concluded from the troubling diversity of perspectives that we encounter in our day-to-day lives. For a penetrating critique, see Bernard Williams, *Truth and Truthfulness: An Essay in Genealogy* (Princeton, NJ: Princeton University Press, 2002).

28. Note Alexander Hamilton's much-quoted observation on the different valuations of trial by jury by Federalists and Anti-Federalists: "The friends and adversaries of the plan of the convention, if they agree in nothing else, concur at least in the value they set upon the trial by jury; or if there is any difference between them it consists in this: the former regard it as a valuable safeguard to liberty, the latter represent it as the very palladium of free government." *The Federalist Papers*, No. 83 (1788) <http://www.law.ou.edu/hist/federalist/federalist-papers>. More recently, Lord Devlin observed: "No tyrant could afford to leave a subject's freedom in the hands of twelve of his countrymen. So that trial by jury is more than an instrument of justice . . . it is the lamp that shows that freedom lives." *Trial by Jury* (London: Methuen, 1956), 164.

29. The contrast is relative rather than absolute, since eligibility for jury service in the early republic was restricted. Those who proclaimed that we were created equal also kept slaves.

30. James Alexander, *A Brief Narrative of the Case and Trial of John Peter Zenger*, ed. Stanley Nider Katz, 2nd ed. (Cambridge, MA: Harvard University Press, 1972), 93.

31. Although the judiciaries of many democratic countries have now developed strong professional cultures of independence, impartiality, and integrity, they are still vulnerable to political and other kinds of influence, especially in their lower courts.

32. Some forms of jury tampering might be diminished by using anonymous jury panels. But this generates its own perceptual and accountability problems. In any case, it does not resolve many other ethical problems that jury trials encounter. It is to these latter issues that most of the chapters in the current volume are addressed.

33. See *Sparf and Hansen v. U.S.*, 156 U.S. 51 (1895). For an account of the evolutionary shift from juries as determiners of both law and fact to their predominantly fact-finding role, see Alschuler and Deiss, "A Brief History," 902–21.

34. Nevertheless, jury nullification differs from other post facto legislation in exempting a person from what might otherwise be the constraining requirements of the law rather than subjecting him to unanticipatable requirements. This makes nullification much less threatening to the underlying concerns of the rule of law.

35. A study of jury behavior in draft evasion cases involving the prosecution of conscientious objectors accused of feigning pacifism showed a direct correlation between the unpopularity of the war into which people were being conscripted and the unwillingness of juries to convict. See James P. Levine, "The Legislative Role of Juries," *American Bar Foundation Research Journal* 9 (1984): 605–34.

36. No doubt the fact that jury nullification (in practice) imposes no legal sanction diminishes its social and institutional costs. Nevertheless, when the nullification option has been used in prejudicial ways (as in the acquittals of Ku Klux Klansmen), its effects have been grossly demeaning and unfair to victims and their loved ones.

37. See James P. Levine, "The Role of Jury Nullification Instructions in the Quest for Justice," *Legal Studies Forum* 18 (1994): 473–95.

38. See Candace McCoy, "If Hard Cases Make Bad Law, Easy Juries Make Bad Facts: A Response to Professor Levine," *Legal Studies Forum* 18 (1994): 497–508.

39. *U.S. v. Dougherty*, 473 F.2d 1113 (D.C. Cir., 1972).

40. Mortimer Kadish and Sanford Kadish, *Discretion to Disobey: A Study of Lawful Departures from Legal Rules* (Stanford, CA: Stanford University Press, 1973), 62.

41. "Drug Policy Alliance: Election Results 2002," http://www.drugpolicy.org/statebystate/election2002/initiatives2002.cfm (accessed January 9, 2005).

42. In this volume the issue is developed at length in the chapters authored by Michael Dann (pp. 93–117) and Shari Seidman Diamond (pp. 119–30). See also the discussion in Alan Scheflin's chapter (pp. 131–72).

43. For further discussion, see Scheflin's contribution to the present volume.

44. This has been a constant theme of Norman Finkel, developed in *Commonsense Justice: Jurors' Notions of the Law* (Cambridge, MA: Harvard University Press, 1995), and *Not Fair! The Typology of Commonsense Unfairness* (Washington, D.C.: American Psychological Association, 2001) and further in this volume. See also Harry Kalven Jr. and Hans Zeisel, *The American Jury* (Boston: Little, Brown, and Co., 1966), 163–67, 286–301; Irwin Horowitz, "The Effects of Jury Nullification Instructions on Verdicts and Jury Functioning in Criminal Trials," *Law and Human Behavior* 9 (1985): 25–36; Irwin Horowitz and Thomas Willging, "Changing Views of Jury Power: The Nullification Debate, 1787–1988," *Law and Human Behavior* 15 (1991): 165–82; and Martha Myers, "Rule Departures and Making Law: Jurors and Their Verdicts," *Law and Society Review* 13 (1979): 781–97.

45. Patrick Devlin, "Morals and the Criminal Law," in *The Enforcement of Morals* (London: Oxford University Press, 1965), 21.

46. Maureen Dowd, "The Sound and the Fury," *New York Times*, November 21, 1996, A29.

47. L. Adams, "Simpson Jurors Cite Weak Case, Not Race," *The Washington Post*, October 5, 1995, A1, A26.

48. See discussion in *Williams v. Florida*, 399 U.S. 78 (1970); *Colgrove v. Battin*, 413 U.S. 149 (1973).

49. Acts 1:15–26.

50. He was convicted by a majority vote (281 voting for his conviction).

51. It would not, of course, be a sufficient number were we to insist on cross-sectional representation of the jury and not just the jury pool.

52. *Ballew v. Georgia*, 435 U.S. 223 (1978).

53. Acts 1:14, 4:32.

54. See *Johnson v. Louisiana*, 406 U.S. 356 (1972); *Apodaca v. Oregon*, 406 U.S. 404 (1972). An easing of the unanimity requirement occurred in England at about the same time. See Richard A. Primus, "When Democracy Is Not Self-Government: Toward a Defense of the Unanimity Rule for Criminal Juries," *Cardozo Law Review* 18 (1997): 1417–57.

55. James P. Levine, "Jury Room Politics," *Trial Lawyers Quarterly* 16 (1984): 21–33.

56. Given that split votes would more likely favor conviction than acquittal, this is a salient consideration. It is for much the same reason that we also require a high standard of proof: "beyond reasonable doubt." Such a demand is not exclusive to jury decision making. There is not only a presumption of innocence—which places on the prosecution whatever burden of proof there is—but also the ancient maxim that, as Blackstone formulates it, "it is better that ten guilty persons

escape than that one innocent suffer." *Commentaries on the Laws of England*, bk. 4, chap. 27 (1765–1769; Boston: Beacon Press reprint, 1962), 420.

57. *Johnson v. Louisiana*, 406 U.S. at 377 (1972).

58. We should not necessarily see compromises as departures from an ideal of truth. Human behavior is sometimes too complex to fit neatly into the categories provided for it by law, and the compromise position may better reflect the awkwardness of fit than a majority decision would have.

59. About six percent of juries are hung, though not evenly across all jurisdictions. See Paula L. Hannaford, Valerie P. Hans, and G. Thomas Munsterman, "How Much Justice Hangs in the Balance? A New Look at Hung Jury Rates," *Judicature* 83 (September/October 1999): 65.

60. Kalven and Zeisel, *The American Jury*, 481–92.

61. Whether many decisions would be different were super-majority decisions to be accepted is not clear. What would change is the way in which the deliberative process is conceived.

2

Ethical Reciprocity: The Obligations of Citizens and Courts to Promote Participation in Jury Service

Paula L. Hannaford-Agor and
G. Thomas Munsterman

I. INTRODUCTION

Ask the proverbial man on the street his opinion about jury service and you are likely to hear one of two diametrically opposite views—sometimes from the same person, depending on his frame of mind when the question is posed. The first will be a heartfelt tribute to the glory of the American jury, its role as a bulwark of American democracy, and the honor and civic virtue of those individuals who serve without ambition through their participation as jurors in the administration of justice.[1] The second will be a diatribe against the same institution as a waste of citizens' time and taxpayer monies, a burden to be avoided if at all possible, and if not, to be dispensed with as quickly and with as little effort as possible. In the words of one such character, "jury duty is a pain in the butt."[2]

Why is there this bipolar approach to jury service? Several possible explanations come to mind, many of which involve the distinction between being one of many individuals in the jury pool versus being one of the twelve[3] jurors sworn to serve in a particular trial, the latter of whom are generally accorded far more respect than the former. Consider, for example, how the justice system traditionally views citizens in the earliest stages of the jury trial process:

- Prospective jurors are *summonsed*—that is, they are legally compelled—to appear for jury service and are subject to criminal penalties if they fail to appear;

- Prospective jurors are expected to shoulder the financial burden and inconvenience of jury service with only marginal compensation or accommodation from the justice system;
- Prospective jurors place themselves at the disposal of judges, lawyers, and court staff for an indeterminate period of time[4] and are expected to follow unquestioningly the court's directions as to where to go, where to sit, and for how long;
- Prospective jurors are required to answer all questions posed by judges, lawyers, and court staff candidly and completely, no matter how private the subject matter or how seemingly irrelevant they are to the task of jury service.

The unmistakable image of prospective jurors at this point in the trial process is one of largely fungible objects.[5] This is a far cry from the image of indepen-dent, autonomous citizens selflessly undertaking the collective task of ren-dering fair and impartial justice, which comprises the former view of jury service.

Placing citizens' participation in jury service in the context of theoretical ethics presents a formidable challenge. First and foremost, ethics is the study of conduct and moral judgment,[6] which by definition implies the possibility of autonomous decision making on the part of an individual. As Lord Moulton explained, ethics is the "domain of Obedience to the unenforceable" in which "there is no law which inexorably determines our course of action, and yet we feel that we are not free to choose as we would."[7] Yet those who work regularly in or with the courts tend to view jury service as a legally enforceable obligation rather than a voluntary contribution to the justice system.[8] The relative inability of prospective jurors to dictate the terms of their participation was the first of several conceptual challenges that we grappled with as we responded to this request to write a chapter on the ethics of jury service.

A second difficulty was that the ethical conduct of most critical import in the context of the jury system is not that of individual behavior or moral judgment, but rather the collective decision making of a group. Indeed, the nature of the jury system as a collective decision-making process is purported to be its greatest strength: The process of collective deliberation exposes and neutralizes inappropriate—that is, unethical—influences that might otherwise dominate individual judgments. The 1957 MGM movie *Twelve Angry Men*, starring Henry Fonda, is perhaps Hollywood's most famous dramatization of this process in which the integrity and moral courage of a single juror is sufficient to overcome the other jurors' preexisting prejudices and raise the quality of the deliberative process to an ethically appropriate level.[9]

The fact that jury verdicts rely on a collective rather than individual ethos for their legitimacy can be unsettling for some observers in that it implies the need for a certain number of ethically motivated jurors within each jury—a critical mass—to guard against the possibility of an unjust verdict resulting from unethical deliberations. These concerns have become more pronounced as recent studies document that jury verdicts often fail to reflect a completely unanimous consensus on the verdict.[10] Indeed, growing support for the traditional twelve-person jury (as opposed to a six-person jury)[11] is premised on the principle that larger juries are more diverse—demographically and attitudinally—and their deliberations are likely to be more thorough, robust, and (presumably) ethically defensible.

A third challenge was the historical emphasis on the role of trial-by-jury in upholding individual liberties. Judicial opinions and critical commentary tend to view the jury as a means of protecting the rights of criminal defendants, but they traditionally pay little attention to the mechanics of impaneling a "fair and impartial jury" or the underlying motivations of citizens to participate in such a system. Even the early judicial opinions that prohibit the intentional exclusion of certain classes of citizens from the jury pool (for example, on the basis of race, gender, or socioeconomic status) are premised on criminal defendants' Sixth Amendment right to a fair and impartial jury.[12] Only recently has case law expanded the legal reasoning to include the Equal Protection rights of citizens not to be excluded from participation in the jury system.[13] Both lines of jurisprudence make the unspoken assumption that all citizens who are given the opportunity to serve as jurors will do so willingly and conscientiously for the good of the community.

The final challenge was one of professional competence to consider and comment on the ethical dimensions of jury service. Neither of us is a trained ethicist, so we were reluctant even to attempt to frame the issues related to citizen participation in the jury system in a theoretical or philosophical context. For the purpose of this chapter, we have adopted a more user-friendly conceptual framework, expounded in a 2002 Chautauqua Institution lecture by Rushworth M. Kidder, president of the Institute for Global Ethics. We use Kidder's framework to examine the various components of citizen participation in the jury system, and the subtle adaptations that are necessary to accommodate the changes in the role of the jury as citizens pass through each successive stage of the trial process—summoning and qualification, voir dire, presentation of evidence, and deliberations. We then look at the extent to which citizens live up to these expectations for ethical conduct, and consider some of the underlying reasons that citizens might not always live up to these ideals. Finally, we consider whether the courts have a reciprocal set of ethical obligations to the citizens who report for jury service.

II. MORAL JUDGMENT AND ETHICAL CONDUCT IN THE EARLY STAGES OF THE JURY TRIAL

Our task here is to discuss the ethical obligation of jurors during the initial summoning, qualification, and jury selection stages of the trial. To do so, we begin by noting a critical difference between the summoning and qualification stage of jury service and subsequent stages of the trial process including the voir dire.

Beginning with the voir dire and throughout the remainder of the trial process, jurors' ethical obligations are focused on specific, identified parties—the judge, the lawyers, and most importantly, the litigants. In contrast, the ethical obligation required of citizens during summoning and qualification is relatively diffuse. The identity of the parties and the legal and factual bases for their cases are not yet apparent, making it difficult for jurors (and judges and court staff, for that matter) to view the process as more than a tedious bureaucratic exercise with little connection to the grander mission of the justice system. Indeed, those citizens who are aware that their likelihood of being selected to serve on a jury is actually quite low— typically less than 30 percent of citizens who report for jury service are impaneled[14]—may be even less enthusiastic about making this particular contribution to their communities given that it is hard for most people to imagine that their mere presence in the jury pool is a particularly valuable service to the community.

The ethical obligation of citizens to report when summonsed for jury service is owed therefore to the larger community.[15] It is a duty of mutuality in that the various benefits of the American justice system, such as the protection of individual rights, can be secured only if citizens support the system through individual contributions of time, finances, and respect for the rule of law.[16] These contributions are also made as gestures of honor and respect for the sacrifices of those who contributed much more to support and strengthen the justice system—sometimes even their lives—so that we might enjoy its benefits.

But what is the difference between the summoning and qualification stage of jury service and the jury selection, the trial, and the deliberation stages? For one, the primary objectives differ—summoning and qualification involve preparation for an indeterminate number of future events (trials) that may or may not occur. This preparatory stage exists to create a pool of prospective jurors who are statutorily qualified to serve as jurors in the jurisdiction[17] and to ensure that those individuals who comprise the jury pool collectively reflect a fair cross section of the community.[18] Jury qualification statutes typically require that prospective jurors be citizens of the United States, residents of the jurisdiction in which they will serve, over the age of eighteen, not subject to a legal disability (for example, convicted of a felony or adjudicated incompetent), and that they speak and understand the English language sufficiently to comprehend the evidence presented at trial and to engage in meaningful jury deliberations.[19]

In essence, this stage of the jury system is a screening process that results in a legal presumption that members of the jury pool have the capacity to exercise moral judgment and ethical conduct as trial jurors. Their status as U.S. citizens and residents in the community implies their familiarity with the cultural values of their country and their communities; their status as mentally competent adults indicates cognitive and intellectual maturity; and the absence of felony convictions signals a record of acceptable moral conduct.[20]

The fair cross-section requirement, in contrast, is not focused on individual members of the jury pool, but on the demographic characteristics of the collective jury pool. Implemented as a legal requirement in federal courts in 1968[21] and extended to state courts in 1975,[22] it eliminated the possibility of intentional exclusion of women and minorities from the jury pool characterized by "key-man" systems of jury administration.[23] The intent, as Jeffrey Abramson has written, was to "silence expressions of group prejudice" and "to enhance the quality of deliberation by bringing diverse insights to bear on the evidence, each newly evaluating the case in light of some neglected detail or fresh perspective that a juror from another background offered the group."[24]

The fair cross-section requirement implicitly foreshadows an expectation of impartiality (fairness) for the ethical conduct of the collective jury by assuming that individual biases or unethical motivations will not survive the process of vigorous debate among demographically and attitudinally diverse jurors. It does, however, send a decidedly mixed message with respect to its expectations of ethical conduct and moral judgment of individual jurors. It replaced the key-man system criteria that individual prospective jurors "be honest and intelligent and . . . esteemed in the community for their integrity, good education, and sound judgment"[25] with a system that assumes that individual jurors harbor bias and partiality and are incapable of setting them aside during deliberations. The underlying reasoning marked a dramatic shift from the common-law requirement that jurors be impartial not only with respect to the parties and issues adjudicated at trial, but also with respect to their own interests and preconceptions.[26] Thus, the possibility of an impartial jury only occurs "when group differences are . . . invited, embraced, and fairly represented"[27] in the jury pool.

In the jury selection phase (voir dire), the focus shifts abruptly from general presumptions about individuals' ethical capacity to intense attention on the individual and his or her ability to be fair and impartial in the context of a specific trial. The extent of the individual examination of jurors varies substantially from jurisdiction to jurisdiction, but the general process is fairly standard. Typically, a court clerk or bailiff administers an oath to the assembled jurors that they will answer all questions honestly and completely. The judge then briefly describes the case to be tried; introduces the parties, lawyers, and courtroom staff; and discloses the names of potential witnesses. The judge then questions the jurors, either individually or as a panel, about their personal knowledge of the case; their relationships with the parties or witnesses; and their personal experiences, attitudes, and biases concerning material aspects of the case that might impair an individual juror's ability to judge fairly and impartially. The judge may also inquire about the possibility of financial hardship or inconvenience, especially in longer trials, as well as each juror's willingness to adhere to the applicable law. In many jurisdictions, the trial judge then permits the lawyers to pose supplemental questions to the jurors to ascertain their suitability for the case.

Based on potential jurors' responses to these questions, the judge may determine that some individuals cannot serve fairly and impartially and will excuse them for cause, or one of the attorneys may exercise a peremptory challenge to remove them from the panel of potential jurors. After the requisite number of individuals has been deemed acceptable by the judge and lawyers, they are sworn in as the jury panel. Individuals remaining in the jury venire are excused from further service in that trial, although they may be assigned to another courtroom to be considered for a different trial.

At first blush, none of the objectives of either the summoning and qualification stage or the voir dire stage appears to require moral judgment or ethical action on the part of the summonsed jurors; they merely receive their summonses and report to the courthouse, and obey further directions as ordered. Prospective jurors are largely passive, acted upon by judges, lawyers, and court staff. Independent moral judgment or action is neither expected nor desired of them; the only requirements at this stage are obedience to the summonses and candid disclosure of requested information.[28] It is not until individuals are sworn in as jurors and the evidentiary stage of the trial begins that the expectations of ethical decision making and behavior attach to the role. Yet the relatively passive role of citizens during these early stages of the jury trial should not be confused with the absence of ethical obligations, as we now discuss.

III. AN ETHICAL FRAMEWORK FOR CITIZEN PARTICIPATION IN THE JURY SYSTEM

One of the primary attractions of Kidder's framework is its general ease of application. Ethics, he contends, is characterized by the presence of five core values: honesty, respect, responsibility, fairness, and compassion.[29] Of critical importance is the simultaneous presence of all five values in ethical conduct. That is, conduct must be honest, respectful, responsible, fair, and compassionate to be viewed as ethical. The absence of any one of the values detracts from the ethical quality of the conduct. For example, conduct that is respectful, responsible, fair, and compassionate, but dishonest cannot be described as completely ethical. These are familiar value concepts that do not require intensive theoretical study, although there may be cases in which their application requires a careful understanding of their rationales and boundaries. More importantly, they provide a consistent framework for examining the ethical obligations of citizens participating in the jury system at all of the stages of the trial process. For the purpose of this chapter, we discuss how this framework applies only at the summoning and qualification stage, but we are confident that it extends easily to other stages of the jury trial.

- **Honesty** at the summoning and qualification stage of a jury trial requires that citizens answer candidly and completely all questions related to their qualifications and ability to serve as jurors. False or incomplete answers may result in the inclusion in the jury pool of a person who should be disqualified (for example, a noncitizen or nonresident, a minor, or a convicted felon) or the exclusion of a qualified person from the jury pool. In either case, the demographic characteristics of the jury pool are distorted by the absence of qualified individuals or by the presence of individuals who should be excluded, which undermines the fair cross-section requirement and jeopardizes litigants' ability to select a fair and impartial jury.[30]

  And if the deception is not discovered and the person is improperly impaneled on a jury, the justice system in most jurisdictions presumes as a matter of law that an injustice has occurred and will either declare a mistrial or vacate the jury's verdict. This needlessly wastes valuable time and resources of the parties, the witnesses who testified at trial, the lawyers, the judge and courtroom employees, and the other jurors who participated in jury selection in the case. On the other hand, if the deception results in an otherwise qualified person being excluded from the jury pool, the burden of jury service is unfairly distributed on those individuals who remain in the pool.

- **Respect** requires that citizens accept the legitimate authority of the court to summons citizens for jury service, but in addition anticipates civility toward the judges and associated court staff as they carry out their jobs.[31] All complex social systems—and especially the system of representative democracy that exists in this country—rely extensively on the acceptance of societal norms and deference to governmental authority. When citizens fail to respond to a court's demand to report for jury service, they show little respect for the system of government under which they live. The result is a disproportionate burden on those who observe legitimate court orders. When citizens' behavior upon reporting is disrespectful, it can undermine the ability of judges and court staff to do their jobs as well as encourage more widespread public disrespect.

- **Responsible conduct** requires that one complete one's jury service obligations as instructed—that is, by arriving at the courthouse on time, by completing paperwork fully and legibly, by paying attention during announcements and orientation instructions by court staff, and, generally, by not interfering with the ability of other prospective jurors to do the same.

- In contrast to later stages of the jury trial process, **fairness** at this early stage concerns citizens' conduct toward their fellows. Because jury service is a responsibility shared by all citizens, those who shirk that responsibility place an unfair burden on others.[32] Thus, citizens who request to be excused from jury service alleging medical or financial hardship when, in fact, jury service is simply inconvenient or perceived to be "not worth their time" are behaving unfairly to those individuals who do report for service (even though they likewise are inconvenienced or could be engaged in activities that are more personally productive or fulfilling).

- Like fairness, **compassion** at this early stage of jury service does not require sympathy for individual litigants but an appropriate understanding of the logistical complexity of the justice system that occasionally creates inconvenience for citizens who are summoned to serve. Compassionate conduct therefore manifests itself in forbearance toward the unintentional or minor discomforts imposed on prospective jurors, and perhaps an obligation to assist others in the jury pool to cope with those discomforts.

As we noted earlier, one obvious feature of how these five core values play out in the summoning and qualification stage of the jury trial is the relatively diffuse nature of prospective jurors' ethical obligations. Here, the obligations are owed generally to the larger community to ensure that the burden of jury service is distributed fairly among all qualified members of the community. At later stages of the jury trial, these obligations will be owed directly to the litigants as well as to other jurors serving in that trial.

Considering to whom jurors owe an ethical duty raises an important question about the relative weights that should be assigned to each core value at each stage of the jury trial. Although ethical conduct requires that all of the values be honored, in the context of a particular situation, one value may play a more prominent role than others. For example, in the context of summoning and qualification, respect appears to be the controlling value—respect for the rule of law, respect for the authority of the judicial system, and respect for the institutional role of the jury system in American democratic governance. All the other core values are secondary to this central recognition—that is, citizens should be honest because they understand and respect the importance of a fair cross section in the jury pool; citizens should be fair to others by shouldering their share of jury service out of respect for the importance of a broadly inclusive jury pool that reflects the values of the community; and so on. In later stages of the jury trial, other values will play a more prominent role. For example, honesty may be the prevailing value during voir dire, responsibility (e.g., paying careful attention) may be the dominant value during the evidentiary portion of the trial, and fairness toward the litigants is certainly the crux of jury deliberations.

IV. RECIPROCITY: THE ETHICAL OBLIGATIONS OF COURTS TO CITIZENS

Assuming for the purposes of this chapter that our application of the core values in Kidder's framework constitutes an appropriate expression of citizens' ethical obligation to participate in the jury system, is there evidence that citizens are failing to live up to this expectation? And if so, why? With respect to the former question, the good news is that compliance with jury summonses is fairly high. In most jurisdictions, if the summons is actually received, individuals do respond to qualification questionnaires and report as directed to the courthouse,[33] albeit sometimes grudgingly. The relative lack of enthusiasm is likely due to temporary inconvenience more than any inherent disrespect for the jury system itself, and those individuals who actually serve as trial jurors tend to leave jury service with more positive views of their experience than those who do not serve.[34]

The extent to which prospective jurors fulfill their obligations during the voir dire and beyond is a bigger question, however. Certainly, there is widespread concern within the judicial community that jurors routinely fail to disclose key information related to their ability to serve fairly and impartially.[35] Reports of juror misconduct—for example, jurors who disregard judicial admonitions not to conduct their own investigations or to refrain from discussing the case with others during the trial—are the bane of judges hearing post-verdict motions. Even the most banal reports of jurors acquiescing in the majority viewpoint simply to avoid prolonging deliberations cause considerable consternation.[36]

The explanation for jurors' failure to consistently live up to ethical obligations in jury service may be related to a whole host of factors, only one of which is the perception that adherence to a common set of ethical standards related to civic duty is no longer highly valued by society.[37] Another possibility, however, is that through their treatment of citizens, courts have left the impression that they do not value citizens' participation as an important component of the justice system. Instead, by becoming excessively reliant on a seemingly inexhaustible supply of largely obedient citizens, courts have not often felt the need to insist that citizens adhere to the highest ethical standards at every stage of jury service, which is itself an ethical failure on their own part. If this is the case, then part of the solution will be for courts to recognize that they have a reciprocal obligation to act in an ethically appropriate way toward the citizens they summons for jury service. The same five core values apply to courts and their personnel as well as to prospective jurors. Again, these values extend through all stages of the jury trial.

- **Honesty:** Courts have an ethical obligation to provide citizens with complete and accurate information about the practical demands of jury service including the amount of time that citizens can reasonably expect to dedicate to it, the amount of compensation (juror fees, transportation reimbursement) that will be provided, and information about procedures for requesting to be excused or to defer service until a more convenient date.

- **Respect:** Courts have an ethical obligation to demonstrate that they value citizens' contributions to the justice system by providing appropriate facilities in which to serve. That is, parking for jury service should be reasonably convenient to the courthouse, jury assembly rooms should be furnished with reasonably comfortable seating including work space (tables or carrels), and courts should provide access to dining facilities (or at least beverage and snack vending machines) and leisure activities (current issues of magazines, books, television, card or board games) to use while waiting.

- **Responsibility:** Courts have an ethical obligation to use citizens' time wisely by improving calendar management and juror utilization practices. These improvements include predicting actual jury trial rates more accurately, implementing appropriate panel size restrictions based on actual past experience of the number of citizens needed for jury service, summoning only those citizens necessary to meet panel size needs, and reducing the amount of time citizens spend waiting to be sent to a courtroom for jury selection through better judicial pretrial management practices.

- **Fairness:** Courts have an ethical obligation to distribute the burden of jury service fairly among the citizenry by ensuring that the juror source list is broadly inclusive and accurate,[38] that the automated selection procedures are functioning as intended,[39] and that excusal and deferral policies are administered in a consistent manner.

- **Compassion:** Courts have an ethical obligation to recognize that jury service is, in fact, burdensome on many of the citizens who are summoned to appear and should take appropriate steps to relieve that burden. Examples of such policies are implementing shorter terms of service (ideally, one day/one trial), eliminating broad-based occupational exemptions from jury service that unfairly impose the burden on nonexempt citizens, reimbursing citizens for the reasonable out-of-pocket expenses incurred as a result of serving, providing citizens with the option to postpone their service date to a more convenient time if desired, and granting requests for excusal for citizens whose service would cause a genuine hardship (something more than mere inconvenience).

V. CONCLUSIONS

The duty that courts and citizens owe one another is relatively easy to discharge, at least for the purposes of assembling the jury pool. Except for a few rare situations, it is not a hardship for citizens to contribute the occasional day that is necessary for the justice system to continue functioning. Similarly, with advances in jury system technology and improved case management practices, ethical behavior from judges and court staff consists of little more than basic courtesy and consideration for fellow citizens. Perhaps this is one of the reasons why we tend not to think about ethics at this early stage in the jury trial process.

As Kidder observed in his Chautauqua Institution lecture, behaving ethically is not difficult when the decision is between right and wrong; the difficulty arises when the decision is between one right and another equally valid right, such as when two of the core values come into conflict. Since there is no great moral conflict to resolve in the case of jury summoning and qualification, the ethical components get passed over in favor of more immediate concerns about efficiency, cost effectiveness, and convenience. The more familiar difficulties arise at later stages of the jury trial process, when jurors must grapple with the possibility of conflicts between responsibility and honesty to their communities, compassion to victims, fairness to litigants, and respect for the institutional strictures of the justice system. Likewise, courts must find the balance between honesty to and respect for jurors, fairness and compassion for litigants, and responsibility for upholding the institutional framework. These are the more difficult challenges, and we leave those to others. What we emphasize here is how important it is for citizens and courts (and lawyers and litigants) to acknowledge the ethical dimensions of jury service at the outset, before opportunities for major conflicts among the core values are likely to arise. By doing so, we hope that all of the trial participants will strive to uphold the core values of ethical behavior and find appropriate (ethical) balances when they conflict.

NOTES

1. American Bar Association, *And Justice for All: Ensuring Public Trust and Confidence in the Justice System* (Chicago, IL: American Bar Association, Standing Committee on Judicial Independence, Coalition for Justice, 2001).

2. State of New York Unified Court System, *Your Turn*, juror orientation film (1998).

3. The number of jurors impaneled for trial varies according to jurisdiction and trial type (civil or criminal). See David B. Rottman, Carol R. Flango, Melissa T. Cantrell, Randell Hansen, and Neil LaFountain, *State Court Organization 1998*, Table 42 (June 2000) for a state-by-state list of jury size and verdict rules, available at http://www.ojp.usdoj.gov/bjs/pub/pdf/sco98.pdf.

4. All courts place a limit on the amount of time a citizen is required to make himself available for jury service, which is generally referred to as the "term of service." This period has become shorter over time such that a large proportion of American jurisdictions now use a "one day/one trial" term of service. Within the frame of the defined term of service, however, the juror has no control over how long he or she will spend on jury service.

5. Indeed, the basis for most of jury system administration is essentially inventory control—that is, ensuring that a sufficient number of "bodies" are available to meet the demand as determined by the number of trials and the "quality" of jurors (in terms of perceptions of fairness) required by judges and lawyers.

6. *Webster's New World Dictionary,* 3rd college ed. (New York: Simon and Schuster, Inc., 1988), 466.

7. Right Honorable Lord Moulton, "Law and Manners," *The Atlantic Monthly* 1 (July 1924), 1–2.

8. As a practical matter, this view does not receive much in the way of resistance. Failure to appear (FTA) rates are relatively modest, usually less than 5 percent of all qualified jurors summonsed. Those citizens who actually receive their jury summonses and are statutorily qualified to serve usually do so, albeit grudgingly.

9. *Twelve Angry Men,* dir. Sidney Lumet (MGM/United Artists, 1957). Whether this movie is merely a well-crafted Hollywood drama or a realistic description of jury deliberations has been the focus of American drama and literature classes for decades. Although it is not clear what types of arguments will persuade jurors to change their votes, the rate at which small minorities of jurors (one or two in a twelve-person jury) successfully convert the majority that initially favors conviction to vote for an acquittal is surprisingly high—approximately one in eight trials. Paula L. Hannaford-Agor, Valerie P. Hans, Nicole L. Mott, and G. Thomas Munsterman, *Are Hung Juries a Problem?* (Final Report to the National Institute of Justice, September 30, 2002), available at http://www.ncsconline.org/WC/Publications/Res_Juries_HungJuriesPub.pdf.

10. The 2001 Civil Justice Survey of State Courts, which examined civil jury and bench trials in forty-six large, urban jurisdictions, revealed that as many as one-third of civil verdicts in jurisdictions that permit non-unanimous verdicts are not unanimous. The Civil Justice Survey of State Courts is a joint project of the National Center for State Courts (NCSC) and the Bureau of Justice Statistics (#2002-BJ-CX-K001). Similarly, a study of nearly four hundred felony jury trials in four large, urban courts found that 13 percent of jurors reported that, if the verdict had been entirely up to them, they would have made a different decision than the jury as a whole. Nearly half of the juries in the study included at least one juror who was either undecided about his or her personal verdict preference or who personally disagreed with their jury's verdict. Hannaford-Agor, Hans, Mott, and Munsterman, *Are Hung Juries a Problem?*

11. The U.S. Supreme Court ruled that juries comprised of as few as six persons were constitutionally permissible in criminal trials in 1970 and in civil trials in 1973. *Williams v. Florida,* 399 U.S. 78 (1970); *Colgrove v. Battin,* 413 U.S. 149 (1973).

12. See, e.g., *Duncan v. Louisiana,* 391 U.S. 145, 151–57 (1968)

13. *Duren v. Missouri,* 439 U.S. 357 (1975); *Batson v. Kentucky,* 476 U.S. 79 (1986). Efforts to protect citizens' rights to participate also underlie operational modifications to the jury selection process, such as random selection from a broadly inclusive master jury list. Upon implementing these changes, however, courts had to contend with a greatly expanded jury pool that included people who did not necessarily have the financial wherewithal to serve. See Paula L. Hannaford, G. Thomas Munsterman, and B. Michael Dann, "Administrative, Structural Reforms of the American Jury in the Past Thirty-Five Years," in American Bar Association, *The Improvement of the Administration of Justice,* 7th ed. (2001), 146–50.

14. Susan Saulny, "Jury Duty? Prepare for Rejection," *New York Times*, September 8, 2003, B1.

15. The concept of jury service as a civic duty is premised on the assumption that the American justice system, including the jury trial component, is itself an ethically legitimate institution. By ethical legitimacy, we refer to a broad-based social consensus that the American justice system is a fair and effective mechanism for determining guilt or innocence in criminal cases and in resolving civil disputes.

16. Although studies of American political philosophy have tended to promote the criminal jury as more important for legitimizing the judicial branch, it is noteworthy that de Toqueville viewed the civil jury as the more important component of civic education. Alexis de Tocqueville, *Democracy in America*, trans. Phillips Bradley (1833; New York: Vintage, 1945), I, ch. 16. In making this observation, de Toqueville may have implied that most people are reluctant to imagine themselves as criminal defendants, but can more easily seen themselves as potential plaintiffs or defendants in a civil case. Consequently, the duty of mutuality to the community may be more salient for citizens in the context of the civil justice system, even though the stakes are typically higher in criminal cases.

17. See generally G. Thomas Munsterman, *Jury System Management* (Williamsburg, VA: National Center for State Courts, 1996), 21–42.

18. *Taylor v. Louisiana*, 419 U.S. 522 (1975)

19. Rottman et al., *State Court Organization*, Table 39.

20. The ability to speak and understand English today is largely a pragmatic requirement to ensure that prospective jurors can participate as jurors without the assistance of a foreign language interpreter. New Mexico is the only state that explicitly prohibits the disqualification of individuals from jury service on this ground. New Mexico Constitution art. 7, sec. 3.

21. *Jury Selection and Service Act*, 28 U.S.C. §§ 1861–78.

22. *Taylor v. Louisiana*, 419 U.S. 522 (1975).

23. Hannaford et al., "Administrative, Structural Reforms," 146–50.

24. Jeffrey Abramson, *We, the Jury: The Jury System and the Ideal of Democracy* (Cambridge, MA: Harvard University Press, 2000), 101. It is important to note, however, that the fair cross-section requirement only guarantees that the jury pool will be broadly representative of the community, but places no such requirement on a particular jury impaneled for a specific trial. *Strauder v. West Virginia*, 100 U.S. 303 (1880).

25. *Carter v. Jury Comm'n*, 396 U.S. 320, 323 (1970). The literal meaning of these statutes notwithstanding, it is now widely recognized that such subjective criteria helped to create and maintain a highly discriminatory jury selection system.

26. Abramson, *We, the Jury*, 100.

27. Abramson, *We, the Jury*, 101.

28. A nominal amount of griping from citizens is tolerated, provided that it does not interfere with the routine business of the court.

29. Rushworth M. Kidder, "You Said What? Ethics in the Information Age" (lecture, Chautauqua Institution, Chautauqua, NY, July 22, 2002). According to studies conducted by the Institute for Global Ethics, these five components are universally recognized, without regard to differences in language, culture, gender, or socioeconomic status. Some of Kidder's more recent work suggests a possible sixth component: moral courage. See http://www.globalethics.org/.

30. The purpose of the fair cross-section requirement is to ensure that the jury pool reflects a sample of the local population that is sufficiently diverse so that individual biases, life experiences, or other attitudes that might prompt a juror to behave unethically toward a litigant are likely to be challenged by other jurors with different viewpoints.

31. This value implicitly assumes that jury service itself is a legitimate function of the justice system. Citizens are not obligated to acquiesce to governmental authority where tasks are illegitimate and, in fact, a large body of literature on the topic of civil disobedience discusses the ethical requirement that citizens actively oppose the illegitimate acts of government.

32. Fairness to the parties is also implicated, albeit indirectly to the extent that lower participation rates by citizens can deprive the parties of a fair cross section of the community from which to select the jury.

33. A large proportion of summonses—in fact, the majority in many jurisdictions—are returned as undeliverable due to inaccurate addresses on the jury source list. Robert G. Boatright, "Why Citizens Don't Respond to Jury Summonses and What Courts Can Do about It," *Judicature* 82 (1999): 156; G. Thomas Munsterman, *Jury System Management*, 44–50.

34. Shari S. Diamond, "What Jurors Think: Expectations and Reactions of Citizens Who Serve as Jurors," in *Verdict: Assessing the Civil Jury System,* ed. Robert E. Litan (Washington, D.C.: Brookings Institution, 1993).

35. See Gregory E. Mize, "On Better Jury Selection: Spotting UFO Jurors Before They Enter the Jury Room," *Court Review* 36 (Spring 1999): 10.

36. An unsettling finding from the NCSC study of hung juries was that over 20 percent of jurors from a sample of 372 felony trials in four large, urban jurisdictions reported being undecided about their personal verdict preferences or in disagreement with the verdict delivered by the jury, even though those verdicts were reported as unanimous. Moreover, these "dissenting" jurors were distributed across nearly half (46%) of the cases in the study. Hannaford-Agor et al., *Are Hung Juries a Problem?* 69–70.

37. A number of social factors may be responsible including increased demand for business productivity leading to less disposable time for individuals to devote to community activities, the delegation of responsibility for social welfare to government agencies, and the rise in consumerism, to name a few.

38. See G. Thomas Munsterman and Paula L. Hannaford-Agor, *The Promise and Challenges of Jury System Technology* (Williamsburg, VA: National Center for State Courts, 2003).

39. A large portion of technical assistance provided to state and local courts by the NCSC in the area of jury system management involves identification and corrections of computer malfunctions that result in non-random selection procedures, which effectively disenfranchise some portion of the potential jury pool and place the burden on those individuals who remain in the jury pool.

An Ethical Framework for Jury Selection: Enhancing Voir Dire Conditions

Julie E. Howe

I. INTRODUCTION

Ask the proverbial man on the street to outline the components of ethical conduct and you may very well hear words like honesty, responsibility, fairness, and respect, or a reference to doing the right thing. Yet applying these concepts to specific contexts such as jury duty is easier said than done. Ethical behavior cannot always be described as the difference between right and wrong. There are often competing obligations within and between individuals that complicate the analysis. Nonetheless, society does expect its citizens to behave ethically. Professional organizations expect that their members behave ethically and they have developed codes of professional conduct that incorporate concepts of honesty, respect, responsibility, fairness, and compassion. Professionals such as doctors, lawyers, and psychologists often rely on their professional code for guidance when they find themselves in situations where there are competing obligations.

In our justice system, society expects citizens to set aside their personal lives and participate in jury service. Yet there is no code of ethics for jurors to follow when they find their obligation to jury service competes with their obligation to their families, employers, and others. Nor is there a code of ethics for jurors to rely upon when they become obligated to honestly answer questions about their personal lives, and when their ability to be fair and impartial is judged.

In an attempt to fill this void, Paula Hannaford-Agor and G. Thomas Munsterman adopted Rushworth M. Kidder's "user-friendly" ethical framework[1] to examine how the core values of honesty, responsibility, respect, fairness, and compassion might impact citizen participation in jury service. This framework is coupled with the notion of ethical reciprocity as a vehicle for promoting participation in jury service. If the justice system expects citizens to behave ethically and to participate in jury service, then the courts need to reciprocate and examine their treatment of prospective jurors. If jurors perceive that they are not a valued part of the justice system, they, in turn, may not perceive themselves as important and may not take their participation seriously. On the other hand, if courts communicate the belief that juror participation is highly valued and jurors are treated in accordance with the core values of ethical behavior, they are likely to rise to the occasion.

Hannaford-Agor and Munsterman apply their analysis of ethical reciprocity and its relationship to jury service to the summoning and statutory qualification stage. This chapter extends their analysis of ethical reciprocity by applying Kidder's framework to the jury selection stage of trial. Suggestions for enhancing voir dire conditions are discussed in terms of ethical conduct of those participating at this stage of trial. That is, how jurors, judges, and attorneys (and their trial consultants) might exhibit the core values of honesty, responsibility, respect, fairness, and compassion as they maintain the integrity of the jury system.

II. JURY SELECTION PROCESS

Prospective jurors who are statutorily qualified remain for further questioning under oath (voir dire) during jury selection. A few, or many, will be excused before the actual jury is seated. In New York State, 82 percent of those called for jury service never serve as trial jurors.[2] These excused jurors will not benefit from the knowledge and understanding that jurors gain from actually serving at the trial stage.[3] There is speculation that jurors who have not had an opportunity to serve on a jury might be less satisfied with the judicial process and, therefore, be less likely to participate in the future. The relatively limited research that focuses on jurors who are excused has not found this to be the case.[4] Nonetheless, it is important that all jurors, whether or not they ultimately serve on a jury, receive ethical treatment as embodied in Kidder's five core values. These jurors can communicate to their com-munities a positive experience that might translate into greater participation and greater respect for the jury system.

As important as increasing the numbers of citizens responding to their summons and participating in jury service is increasing the quality of participation in the jury selection process. The role of the jury and individual juror conduct has come under greater scrutiny with the increasing number of high-profile cases in both the civil and criminal arenas.[5] The right to a fair trial requires uncovering biases that impact jurors' abilities to be fair. This requires an extensive jury selection process that demands ethical conduct from not only prospective jurors, but also from attorneys and judges. Of critical importance are the conditions under which prospective jurors are questioned. An atmosphere that inhibits candor and honest responses limits jurors' abilities to participate ethically. The courts, via judges and attorneys, can provide more optimal conditions for jurors to respond in an ethical manner—with honesty, responsibility, respect, fairness, and compassion.

Improvements in voir dire conditions have been studied and proposed by the legal community including judges, attorneys, trial consultants, and social psychologists. There have been significant jury-trial innovation efforts in thirty states.[6] Additionally, trial consultants who have hands-on experience developing questions for juror questionnaires and in-court voir dire, observing and talking to jurors in and out of court, and participating in jury selection can offer distinct insights into voir dire conditions that encourage jurors to respond in the ethical manner society expects.

III. EXPECTATIONS OF INDEPENDENT MORAL JUDGMENT

Ethics are standards of conduct and moral judgment governing the making of decisions. Reconciling jury service as a legally mandated requirement with autonomous decision making at the summoning and statutory qualification stage is an aspect of ethical conduct with which Hannaford-Agor and Munsterman struggle. They suggest that prospective jurors are largely passive at the summoning and qualification stage and that "independent moral judgment or action is neither expected nor desired" and that "it is not until individuals are sworn as jurors and the evidentiary stage of the trial begins that the expectations of ethical decision making and behavior attach to the role."[7] A different perspective is that the independent moral judgment of prospective jurors *is* expected and desired during the jury selection stage. Rote responses to requested information are problematic. Just as we expect jurors to engage actively in evaluating evidence during the trial, and have developed trial innovations to facilitate this process,[8] we should expect prospective jurors to participate actively in the jury selection process by carefully listening to the questions and information presented about the case, asking clarifying questions, and conscientiously considering their responses to questions. Juror responses impact directly on whether or not they remain in the jury pool from which the actual jury will be selected, and such responses indirectly affect the rendering of verdicts.

In practice, there is opportunity for autonomous decision making by prospective jurors who respond to their summons, but choose not to serve, by the way in which they respond to questions. Similarly, there is opportunity for prospective jurors who want to serve on particular cases (for various reasons that are not always ethical) to remain in the pool of prospective jurors. Many citizens believe that they know what to say and do to "get out of jury duty" as well as to "get on a jury." Jurors with ulterior motives contravene ethical codes entailing honesty and fairness. However, a majority of jurors do not have ulterior motives and do attempt to answer all questions honestly. This is easier said than done. There are a number of factors that inhibit candid responses from prospective jurors. A major inhibitor is the obligation to reveal information about their private lives, not only in front of a group of other prospective jurors, but also in open court where there is elevated emphasis on the standard of "fair and impartial."[9] Such an atmosphere limits opportunities for candid responses and encourages more "politically correct" responses, for example, "I can be fair."[10]

Three lines of inquiry require ethically significant responses to determine whether a juror is qualified for a specific trial: undue hardship, ability to follow the law, and ability to be fair and impartial.

Hardship: Although there are statutes defining exemptions and hardship excusals,[11] judges and attorneys rely on jurors' responses to determine whether an expressed hardship is legitimate or merely an inconvenience. For example, the prospective juror must assess how much of a financial hardship it would be to lose days of work, pay for a babysitter, and survive on the minimal daily pay rate for jury service. Is it unethical to require a prospective juror, who will not be paid by his employer, to sit for a two- to four-week trial that makes it impossible for him to pay his rent?

Following the law: Prospective jurors who report that they cannot follow the law will be excused.[12] For example, jurors who indicate their religious beliefs preclude them from applying the law are excused. Prospective jurors who indicate that their opposition to the death penalty is so strong that they would never consider the death penalty in a capital trial will be excluded because of their inability to follow what the law allows.[13] Attorneys and judges generally must accept the answers to these questions as true, yet the context in which these questions are asked may hinder honest and candid responses.

Fair and impartial: The purpose of jury selection is to seat jurors who can fairly and impartially evaluate the evidence, or, to put it another way, to ferret out and excuse prospective jurors who have biases that prevent them from being fair to both sides. Answers to questions about jurors' backgrounds, experiences, and attitudes enable judges and attorneys to evaluate a juror's ability to be fair and impartial in a given trial. In practice, prospective jurors are routinely asked: "Given what you've just told us, do you think you can be fair to both parties?" The voir dire questions and conditions under which they are asked can influence juror responses, and the answers are often decisive in determining whether the juror remains in the pool of prospective jurors. However, the legal definition of "fair and impartial" can be different from a prospective juror's interpretation of "fair and impartial."[14] People, including prospective jurors, naturally want to present themselves in the most positive light. They are more likely to portray themselves as fair rather than unfair. Thus, in some respects it would be unethical, if not illegal,[15] for courts to rely solely on a prospective juror's self-assessment of his or her ability to be fair. In-depth questioning and candid responses from prospective jurors are required.

Certainly jurors have an ethical obligation to be forthright during voir dire. They should honestly reveal information bearing on their ability to serve as fair and impartial jurors given what they have learned of the case and what they know about themselves. Anything less threatens the integrity of the jury system. However, jurors generally find the courtroom to be intimidating—they are uncomfortable, they want to make a good impression, and they know that their "performance" during the interview will affect whether they ultimately serve. Public conditions under which prospective jurors are questioned subject them to what social psychologists identify as evaluation apprehension: group pressures and social comparisons lead them to make socially desirable responses that are often contrary to their true beliefs and feelings.[16]

Thus, the courts, via judges and attorneys, have a duty to help prospective jurors fulfill their obligations to be honest and candid. Trial consultants, hired by counsel, provide important assistance in this process. Social psychologists, trial consultants, and other jury researchers understand that the quality of information obtained in any interview is dependent on the conditions of the interview and they are in a unique position to offer suggestions to enhance voir dire conditions.[17]

Treating jurors ethically is complicated by the nature of the adversary process. The primary obligation of attorneys is to their clients, not to the prospective jurors who may decide their clients' cases. Further, in the process of treating litigants fairly, judges may have to treat jurors in an ethically suboptimal manner. For example, they may need to push prospective jurors to explore and explain painful experiences relevant to their jury service. That said, there should and can be opportunities to enhance the process that encourage Kidder's ethical concepts of honesty, responsibility, respect, fairness, and compassion.

IV. A TRIAD OF ETHICAL OBLIGATIONS AND RECIPROCITY DURING JURY SELECTION

The ethical obligations of the key participants during jury selection can be thought of as a triad. It is reasonable to expect that, within a universal ethical framework such as Kidder's, jurors, attorneys, and judges will exhibit core ethical values toward each other. We can examine how prospective jurors, attorneys, and judges might exhibit the values of honesty, responsibility, respect, fairness, and compassion. Improvements that exemplify and encourage ethical conduct are promoted by the American Bar Association[18] and are taking hold in various state courts.[19] Most recently, New York State's "Commission on the Jury" has put significant effort into "promoting efficient and dignified voir dire proceedings."[20] The American Society of Trial Consultants also promotes the ethical treatment of jurors.[21] Trial consultants routinely recommend to their clients procedures to enhance voir dire conditions.

The following framework highlights a few of the many ways in which ethical reciprocity might be developed during the jury selection stage. Ethical reciprocity using Kidder's five core values provides an added dimension to enhance citizen participation in jury service within the constraints of an adversarial process and legally mandated procedures. Implementing the suggestions below will allow jurors to return to their communities with positive perceptions of the process and to fulfill their civic duty by being honest, responsible, respectful, fair, and compassionate; thereby enhancing the integrity of the jury system.

A. Honesty

The purpose of jury selection is to draw out bias and evaluate jurors' abilities to be fair and impartial. Honesty is of greatest importance. Judges and attorneys must make all reasonable efforts to provide conditions that promote honesty. Attorney-conducted voir dire, as opposed to court-conducted voir dire, is just one example of a way to elicit more honest responses.[22] Experience and research have shown that attorney-conducted voir dire elicits more candid responses from jurors because there is less "social distance" between the questioner and prospective juror, minimizing evaluation apprehension and tendencies to please the questioner.[23]

Judges in the courtroom play a very important role as authority figures. Judges must be honest with both attorneys and jurors and be clear about their expectations for ethical conduct. As judges make preliminary remarks to prospective jurors at the beginning of jury selection, they should, even at this early stage, incorporate a discussion of the importance of jury service—emphasizing to prospective jurors that even if not selected for this specific trial they have participated in a very important civic duty. Judges' comments should stress the importance of candid responses, explain that there are no right and wrong answers, and acknowledge that everyone has biases—indeed, that bias is a normal result of life experience. Jurors should understand that the goal of voir dire is to make sure that their biases will not make it difficult for them to be impartial.[24]

Attorneys could use, and judges should allow, pre-voir dire statements to provide prospective jurors a better sense of the case issues. A clearer understanding of the specific case might prompt prospective jurors to reveal more relevant information. At least one judge, Judge Connor in Los Angeles County, believes that pre-voir dire statements lead to more complete and candid responses in voir dire as well as to a more complete understanding among jurors as to why they may be excused.[25]

Attorneys have an ethical obligation to represent their case accurately, avoid deception, be clear in their questioning, and use lay language. Trial consultants often assist attorneys in drafting respectfully worded, straightforward questions that are easy to understand and that elicit clear and concise answers that relate to a juror's ability to be fair and impartial. Pretrial jury research and preparation assist attorneys in conducting a focused voir dire.

Because jury selection is part of an adversarial process, there are instances of conflicting ethical obligations in which attorneys and judges cannot be completely honest with prospective jurors. They cannot, for example, disclose previous criminal conduct of the parties at trial. Yet jurors often want to know this and other types of information that cannot legally be revealed. Judges should make clear to the prospective jurors the legal basis for not disclosing certain information. After such explanation, jurors' answers to questions about their ability to adhere to the law are more meaningful. For example, in criminal cases, defendants are afforded the presumption of innocence and the right not to testify, and the prosecution must prove its case beyond a reasonable doubt. For prospective jurors to honestly answer questions about their ability to follow these principles, they must first be educated on the law and be afforded opportunities to candidly express their agreement or disagreement. The question "can you follow the law?" cannot be answered honestly without context.

B. Responsibility

Prospective jurors have a responsibility (an ethical obligation) to reveal all experiences, attitudes, or beliefs they are asked about, no matter how personal the information may be. Additionally, even if not directly asked by the attorneys or judge, prospective jurors should volunteer information they feel might negatively impact their ability to be fair and impartial.[26] Reciprocally, attorneys and judges have an ethical responsibility to provide a comfortable atmosphere for prospective jurors to share private information about themselves. The very nature of a case may require that jurors be questioned about personal experiences and beliefs. Jurors may be asked about their political or religious affiliations, or about their personal experiences with the justice system, chemical dependencies, mental health professionals, and various types of discrimination, or about other sensitive topics they might prefer to be kept private. Jurors may be reluctant to be completely honest about their experiences and attitudes in a public setting. They also may hesitate to express their personal views if they find their views are different than the majority of the other prospective jurors. This social-comparison information may hinder them from revealing beliefs different from those expressed by fellow jurors. Attorneys and judges have responsibilities to provide—and inform prospective jurors of—opportunities to respond to questions in private.

Supplemental juror questionnaires and procedures for individual voir dire provide effective ways to promote candor and evaluate a juror's ability to be fair and impartial. Supplemental juror questionnaires can be drafted and submitted to the court by counsel for each side or in agreement by both sides. These efforts are often supported by trial consultants who have experience in creating supplemental juror questionnaires that include well-worded, relevant questions that uncover biases related to the case on trial. Written juror questionnaires allow for more efficient voir dire practices including reduced juror waiting time, focused follow-up questions for prospective jurors, and the quick identification of jurors who should either be excused for cause or questioned in more detail. Answering questions in private, whether in a questionnaire or during individual voir dire, promotes honesty and minimizes evaluation apprehension and social comparisons that hinder full disclosure among prospective jurors when questioned in group settings.[27]

C. Respect

As citizens respond to their summons out of respect for the justice system so should they show respect by honestly answering *all* questions. Attorneys and judges can reciprocate by respecting the privacy of prospective jurors, even though in an adversarial system they must question extensively and touch on all areas of potential bias that might unfairly impact the parties. The extent to which attorneys can and should delve into the private lives of jurors is debatable.[28] Delving into private lives should be done only if it is necessary to ferret out bias. Attorneys should not ask irrelevant questions about the lives of prospective jurors.

It should be left to the attorneys who know the intricacies of the case facts to determine what questions to ask. For this, attorneys often rely on trial consultants both to give insight into the case issues that might elicit bias among prospective jurors and to create questions that elicit reliable and valid responses. Trial consultants advocate using open-ended questions to encourage prospective jurors to express their opinions using their own words, rather than a closed-ended question in which the correct response is embedded. For example, the often-asked question, "Can you set aside your opinion and be fair to both sides?" actually hinders a prospective juror's ethical obligation to be honest. First, the question elicits a yes/no response without an explanation. Second, people's tendencies to perceive themselves as fair will lead to positive responses—yes, they can be fair. Third, when the question is asked by an authority figure such as a judge, the answer is likely to be "yes." Thus, under typical voir dire conditions most jurors will report that they can be fair and impartial, when in fact many of them may have underlying biases that keep them from being fair within the context of a particular case.

Judges, in an adversarial process, have ethical obligations to ensure a fair trial to both parties. In their client's interest, attorneys may be tempted to conduct pretrial, out of court investigations to help identify jurors with strong biases.[29] The judge must decide what depth of inquiry into a juror's background is warranted, and balance this against the juror's right to privacy.[30]

Attorneys and judges should protect sensitive information and inform jurors how that information will be kept private. Efforts should be made to keep personal information like jurors' addresses and telephone numbers confidential. This information is important for administrative purposes but has little to do with a juror's ability to be fair and impartial, and therefore it is not relevant to the voir dire process. All sensitive materials, such as juror questionnaires, should be returned or disposed of. Such safeguards will assure jurors that their privacy is being treated with respect. In return, jurors may be more willing to share private information.

An added complication is the public's right to juror information. Because our system of justice is public, judges and the courts must often balance the rights of the individual jurors with the public's right to know. Given the greater scrutiny in high-profile trials, there seems to be increasing emphasis on obtaining juror information. The tension between the goals of juror privacy and jury accountability is not easily resolved.

D. Fairness

Citizens who take their dispute to the legal arena expect that they will receive a fair hearing. This core value of fairness holds particular importance for the jury system. Prospective jurors, attorneys, and judges all have ethical obligations to uncover and disclose juror biases that might impact a juror's ability to be fair. Jurors also have a right to expect that they will be treated fairly.

It has been suggested that peremptory challenges do not treat jurors fairly. On the supposition that peremptory challenges are used to discriminate against individual jurors, proposals have been made to reduce or eliminate these challenges.[31] Attorneys, who should demonstrate the core value of fairness, have ethical and legal obligations not to exclude prospective jurors solely on the basis of such characteristics as race and gender. Despite legal safeguards against such discriminatory peremptory challenges,[32] some argue that citizens may feel they have been personally discriminated against based on their demographics. Although there has been no research supporting hypotheses that jurors are insulted, offended, or disappointed when removed by peremptory challenge,[33] concerns about peremptory challenges can nonetheless be addressed when attorneys and judges educate jurors about the purposes of jury selection.

Concerns about prospective jurors' perceptions of the jury selection process are valid and should be addressed via preliminary remarks made by the judge. They should also be addressed at the time prospective jurors are excused. Citizens who understand that screening prospective jurors is important to ensure a fair and impartial jury may feel more positive about the process and ultimately be more candid when participating in the selection process. Additionally, attorneys and judges might consider excusing individuals from the pool only when the jury selection process is complete. After all the cause and peremptory challenges have been exercised, the names of jurors who will remain to be sworn in as trial jurors could be read, thereby excusing remaining individuals as a group. Singling out prospective jurors suggests that they cannot be fair and impartial or have otherwise done something wrong.

E. Compassion

An adversarial system that requires the fair and impartial evaluation of evidence and that instructs jurors not to rely on sympathy in their decision making makes it difficult to suggest that jurors, attorneys, and judges should show compassion. Yet there are a number of subtle ways in which compassion might enhance the jury selection process. Prospective jurors might extend compassion to the attorneys and judges by understanding that attorneys and judges are working hard to formulate voir dire questions and argue/decide legal issues that will help jurors participate in an ethical manner. Judges can address this in their preliminary remarks to prospective jurors. Reciprocally, attorneys and judges should show compassion to jurors who are actively participating in the process and struggling to respond honestly to very difficult and private questions by using pre-voir dire statements, preliminary judicial instructions, supplemental juror questionnaires, attorney-conducted voir dire, individual voir dire, and other procedures that make jurors more comfortable.

It is difficult to know the level of compassion that attorneys should have when seeking to examine jurors whom they believe to be biased against their clients. Attorneys as advocates for their clients must rigorously question jurors whom they believe to be biased against their clients and challenge responses they believe to be untrue. However, attorneys would be wise to show compassion toward prospective jurors who will decide their case. Additionally, the parties may be interested in selecting jurors who are themselves compassionate. Judges must make judgments about the "truthfulness" of a juror's response and ultimately that juror's ability to be fair and impartial. Both attorneys and judges should be careful about putting words in a juror's mouth and jurors should not be encouraged to deny or ignore their biases.

Judges might also show compassion toward prospective jurors when deciding whether to excuse them for hardships. For example, excusing prospective jurors for hardship on a particular case and asking them to serve at a different time is reasonable and compassionate. Most judicial systems, such as New York's, allow at least one automatic postponement of service to a date more convenient for the prospective juror.

Judges may be available at the end of a trial to answer any questions or concerns of the trial jurors. Yet, there appears to be little in the way of debriefing prospective jurors who are excused during the jury selection process. Courts might establish procedures to talk with dismissed jurors about their experiences at this stage. The dismissed juror should be assured that participating in this process is an important aspect of the justice system and fulfills a civic duty. At a minimum, all jurors should be thanked by the presiding judge for their participation.

Striving for ethical conduct on the part of all participants in jury selection is a necessary means of assuring the integrity of the jury system. The adversarial nature of a jury trial demands that the attorney's primary obligation be to the clients he or she represents. Judges must balance not only the interests of those on trial but also those of prospective jurors. What is important is that jurors be provided the means by which they can fulfill their obligations to participate ethically in the jury selection process. That is, they can share information about their background, life experiences, attitudes, and beliefs in an environment conducive to open and candid disclosure. Trial consultants contribute to the ethical treatment of jurors by working with attorneys to allow prospective jurors to participate fully in an honest and candid manner.

V. TRIAL CONSULTANTS

It is reasonable to expect other members of a trial team to exhibit the same core values of ethical behavior expected of attorneys, judges, and jurors. Trial consultants are typically hired by one side or the other and work under the direction of the hiring attorney. Trial consultants who belong to the American Society of Trial Consultants (ASTC) agree to a professional code that includes ethical principles as well as professional standards and guidelines for various practice areas including jury selection, small group research, witness preparation, and posttrial juror interviews.[34] Trial consultants should also exhibit the core values of honesty, responsibility, respect, fairness, and compassion.

In addition to working with attorneys to improve voir dire conditions, trial consultants conduct pretrial jury research and posttrial juror interviews.[35] Like other jury researchers, trial consultants must balance ethical obligations for sound social science research against ethical obligations to their research participants (real and mock jurors) and to their clients.

Trial consultants routinely conduct pretrial research to help their attorney clients to communicate their case effectively and to prepare for jury selection. Pretrial jury research often includes focus groups and mock trials in which jury-eligible citizens ("mock jurors") evaluate a specific case in small groups.[36] Mock jury research is an example of how ethical obligations might conflict and need to be addressed. While conducting focus groups and mock trials, the consultant must balance obligations of informed consent and confidentiality to both the participants and the attorney clients. For example, unlike the purely academic researcher, trial consultants are not "neutral" and are typically hired by one side in the litigation, arguably having an "interest" in the outcome of the research. However, trial consultants behave as "disinterested" facilitators of the research. Trial consultants typically do not reveal who is sponsoring the research as it introduces a confounding variable that would make it difficult to interpret the results. There may also be additional reasons related to the specific litigation, such as court orders or proprietary client information, that prevents full disclosure to participants. Similarly, trial consultants preserve mock jurors' confidentiality by not disclosing the names and addresses of participants to their clients.

Like other jury research, it is standard for trial consultants to gain informed consent and assurances of confidentiality from participants as well as measure any preexisting knowledge or experiences that might preclude them from participation. Trial consultants routinely disclose to mock jurors the purpose of the research exercise—that the information they will learn during the research exercise is based on a real case, that the exercise including their deliberations will be videotaped, and that it is essential that they agree to keep everything they learn during the research confidential so that the actual case is not jeopardized in any way. After being informed of the conditions of the research, mock jurors are given an opportunity to decline participation. If they choose to participate, each participant is required to sign a confidentiality form.

Trial consultants typically recruit participants who are representative of the pool of jurors in the venue in which the trial will take place, while simultaneously working to protect the integrity of the actual jury pool. For example, trial consultants may decide not to conduct research in a small venue where there is a chance that citizens summoned for jury service may be recruited inadvertently. Participants who themselves, or someone close to them, have been called for jury duty are routinely excluded. Participants are usually told that if they are by chance called for jury duty, they should let the judge know that they know something about the case. Trial consultants exercise the same level of care with their research participants as other jury researchers.

As with prospective jurors summoned by the courts, mock jurors recruited for mock jury research should receive treatment aligned with the core values of ethical behavior. Mock jurors may form impressions of the court system through their experiences on a mock jury. Consultants should work to make that experience positive.

Critics have suggested that trial consultants intrude on the jury process, tinker with the jury, and ultimately change the process and/or outcome.[37] However, there is no empirical support for this complaint, nor is there evidence that a consultant's advice provides an unfair advantage.

Often it is the case that both sides in litigation have retained trial consultants to support counsel. The consultant's role is to provide advice, based on research and experience, to the attorney client. Indeed the consultant's role is to help attorneys be better advocates for their clients. Trial consultants assist attorneys in preparing an effective and persuasive case; they assist in identifying jurors who are biased against their client, they offer advice in terms of juror-friendly trial strategies, and they help attorneys learn through posttrial juror interviews. There is nothing new about advocacy. Arguably, advocacy skills improve with the assistance of a trial consultant. Neither trial consultants nor attorneys have control over the case facts, legal standards, the jury pool or others involved in the litigation process, and so on. They work together to advocate for the client, given the circumstances of a specific case. Indeed, success cannot be measured by the outcome of the trial, but more appropriately by the consultant's ability to help the attorney be a more effective advocate for his or her client. Thus, the trial consultant offers a different expertise than the attorney, and involving a consultant early in the litigation process, not just at trial, can be useful.

Nonetheless, perceptions of the trial consultants' role and their impact on perceived legitimacy of the trial process are worth further exploration. Dennis P. Stolle, Jennifer K. Robbennolt, and Richard L. Wiener applied procedural justice theory to empirically test the perceived fairness of the use of trial consultants. They hypothesized that "regardless of trial consulting's effectiveness or legality, if scientific trial consulting is perceived by the public as being a fundamentally unfair trial tactic, then the practice carries the potential to undermine the legitimacy of legal authorities and proceedings."[38] However, initial research results reveal that a consultant's presence alone does not affect judgments of perceived fairness. Further research and investigation into perceptions of trial consultants and their role in litigation would be informative and useful for all involved in the justice system.

VI. CONCLUSION

Reflecting on the ways in which the core values of ethical behavior can be emphasized during the trial process should raise the bar for ethical behavior within the justice system. It is particularly important to focus on the jury selection stage. Many citizens who are summoned to jury service but ultimately do not have an opportunity to serve as jurors nevertheless communicate their experience to others in their communities who may be prospective jurors. A framework of ethical reciprocity among prospective jurors, attorneys, and judges during jury selection highlights ways in which all involved might enhance ethical participation in jury service. There are specific trial innovations that can be put in place during jury selection to

48   *Julie E. Howe*

create an atmosphere that allows prospective jurors to be as candid and honest as possible, and enables all involved in the jury selection to evaluate prospective jurors' abilities to be fair and impartial in a specific case.

NOTES

1. Paula Hannaford-Agor and G. Thomas Munsterman, "Ethical Reciprocity: The Obligations of Citizens and Courts to Promote Participation in Jury Service," in this volume, pp. 21–34, citing Rushworth M. Kidder, "You Said What? Ethics in the Information Age" (lecture, Chautauqua Institution, Chautauqua, New York, July 22, 2002); Rushworth M. Kidder, "There's Only Ethics" (keynote speech, Human Services Council of Northeast Florida, 1992), revised and copyrighted by the Institute for Global Ethics, 2001: <http://www.globalethics.org>.
2. Susan Saulny, "Jury Duty? Prepare for Rejection," *New York Times*, September, 8, 2003, A21.
3. James P. Levine, "The Ethics of Jury Room Politics: A Response to Jeffrey Abramson," in this volume, 209–18
4. Mary Rose, "A Voir Dire of Voir Dire: Listening to Jurors' Views Regarding the Peremptory Challenge," *Chicago Kent Law Review* 78 (2003): 1061; Ken Broda-Bahm and Samantha Schwartz, "Those Who Might Have Served: The Attitudes of Excused Venire Members of the Baltimore County Circuit Court" (paper presented, annual conference of the American Society of Trial Consultants, Reno, NV, June 6, 2003).
5. See the court cases of O. J. Simpson, Timothy McVeigh, Jayson Williams, Martha Stewart, Michael Jackson, Scott Peterson, and Dennis Kozlowski as examples.
6. See Gregory E. Mize and Christopher J. Connelly, "Jury Trial Innovations: Charting a Rising Tide," *Court Review* 41 (Spring 2004): 4–10, for a history of jury trial innovations. Also the "National Program to Increase Citizen Participation in Jury Service through Jury Innovations" has been initiated. This program is a collaboration of the National Center for State Courts, the Council for Court Excellence, and the Trial Court Leadership Center in Maricopa County, and it stems from the National Jury Summit 2001 led by the National Center for State Courts and Chief Judge Judith Kaye of the New York Unified Court System.
7. Hannaford-Agor and Munsterman, "Ethical Reciprocity," 26.
8. B. Michael Dann and Valerie P. Hans, "Recent Evaluative Research on Jury Trial Innovations," *Court Review* 41 (Spring 2004): 12–19; B. Michael Dann, "Learning Lessons and Speaking Rights: Creating Educated and Democratic Juries," *Indiana Law Journal* 68 (1993): 1229; Valerie P. Hans, "U.S. Jury Reform: The Active Jury and the Adversarial Ideal," *St. Louis Law Review* 21 (2002): 85.
9. Research and experience have shown that statements made during voir dire call for responses that are consistent with ideal norms of fairness and impartiality. See Gary Giewat, "Juror Honesty and Candor during Voir Dire Questioning: The Influence of Impression Management" (PhD diss., University of Nevada, Reno, 2001); R. W. Balch, C. T. Griffiths, E. L. Hall, and L. T. Winfree, "The Socialization of Jurors: The Voir Dire as a Right of Passage," *Journal of Criminal Justice* 4 (1976): 271–83.
10. For additional social science research on the voir dire process see: D. Broeder, "Voir Dire Examinations: An Empirical Study," *Southern California Law*

Review 38 (1965): 503–28; D. Suggs and B. D. Sales, "Juror Self-Disclosure in Voir Dire: A Social Science Analysis," *Indiana Law Journal* 56 (1980): 245–71; R. Seltzer, M. A. Venuti, M. A. Lopes, and G. M. Lopes, "Juror Honesty during Voir Dire," *Journal of Criminal Justice* 19 (1991): 451–62; C. Johnson and C. Haney, "Felony Voir Dire: An Exploratory Study of Its Content and Effect," *Law and Human Behavior* 18 (1994): 487–506; R. W. Shuy, "How a Judge's Voir Dire Can Teach a Jury What to Say," *Discourse and Society* 6 (1995): 207–22.

11. Most state and U.S. district courts outline specific exemptions in their jury plans. For example, in some courts members of the armed services, fire or police departments, or public officials are exempt. With regard to hardship, prospective jurors who are self-employed, required at home to take care of children or the aged, are over the age of seventy, or volunteer safety personnel may be excused upon request. The specific exemptions vary by venue.

12. For a discussion of jury nullification, see Alan W. Scheflin, "Mercy and Morals: The Ethics of Nullification," in this volume, 131–72.

13. *Witherspoon v. Illinois* 391 U.S. 510 (1986); *Wainwright v. Witt* 469 U.S. 841 (1985).

14. Martha Minow, "Stripped Down Like a Runner or Enriched by Experience: Bias and Impartiality of Judges and Jurors," *William and Mary Law Review* 33 (1992): 1201–18.

15. *United States v. Battle*, 979 F. Supp. 1442 (N.D. GA 1997) held that "the question sought by defense counsel 'could you set aside your beliefs and follow the court's instructions,' while meaningful to judges and lawyers, is ambiguous and possibly misleading to a lay person. A prospective juror may not know to what instructions the question is referring and may be reluctant to state unwillingness to follow the law of the court's instructions. Also some jurors are more prone to feeling pressured and confused by leading voir dire questions than others." See also *Morgan v. Illinois*, 112 S. Ct. 2222 (1992) which generally says that "follow-the-law" questions and questions that simply ask the jurors to self-assess whether they can be fair and impartial are not adequate to elicit bias.

16. See generally, Elissa Krauss and Beth Bonora, "Improving Voir Dire Conditions," *Jurywork: Systematic Techniques*, 2nd ed. (New York: Thomson West, 2003) for a summary of relevant research. See more specifically: L. L. Marshall and A. Smith, "Effects of Demand Characteristics, Evaluation Anxiety and Expectancy on Jurors' Honesty during Voir Dire," *Journal of Psychology* 120 (1986): 205–17; M. J. Rosenberg, "When Dissonance Fails: On Eliminating Evaluation Apprehension from Attitude Measurement," *Journal of Personality and Social Psychology* 1 (1965): 28; M. J. Rosenberg, "The Conditions and Consequences of Evaluation Apprehension," *Artifact in Behavior Research*, ed. R. Rosenthal and R. Rosnow (New York: Academic Press, 1969), 279–349; David L. Roth, C. R. Snyder, and Lynn M. Pace, "Dimensions of Favorable Self-Presentation," *Journal of Personality and Social Psychology* 51 (1986): 867; Robert Zajonc, "Social Facilitation," *Science* 149 (1965): 269; Bibb Latane, "Psychology of Social Impact," *American Psychologist* 36 (1981): 343; and J. M. Levine, "Reaction to Opinion Deviance in Small Groups," in *Psychology of Group Influence*, ed. P. B. Paulus (Hillsdale, NJ: Lawrence Erlbaum, 1980).

17. Elissa Krauss and Beth Bonora, *Jurywork: Systematic Techniques*, 2nd ed. (New York: Thomson West, 2003); M. Snyder and W. Ickes, "Personality and

Social Behavior," in *Handbook of Social Psychology,* ed. G. Lindsay and E. Aronson (New York: Random House, 1985).

18. American Bar Association, *Principles for Juries and Jury Trials* (2005): http://www.abanet.org/juryprojectstandards/principles.pdf .

19. Dann and Hans, "Recent Evaluative Research on Jury Trial Innovations," 12; G. Thomas Munsterman, Paula L. Hannaford, and Marc Whitehead, *Jury Trial Innovations* (Williamsburg, VA: National Center for State Courts, 1997).

20. The New York State Unified Court System, *Commission's Report* (2004): http://www.jurycommission.com/pr2004_11.pdf. See also http://www.nycourts.gov; and Elissa Krauss, "Jury Trial Innovations in New York State: Improving Jury Trials by Improving Jurors' Comprehension and Participation," *New York State Bar Association Journal* (May 2005): 22–27.

21. http://www.astcweb.org.

22. Generally speaking, the practice in federal courts has been for the judge to conduct voir dire; while attorney-conducted voir dire has been accepted in most, but not all, state courts. However, the amount of attorney-conducted voir dire varies by state and is often left to the judge's discretion. In some states—such as New York—a judge may not be present at all, while in other states the judge does all of the questioning. For example, New Jersey does not currently allow attorney-conducted voir dire, although a recent Special Committee on Voir Dire and Peremptory Challenges appointed by the New Jersey Supreme Court is studying the issue.

23. Susan Jones, "Judge versus Attorney Conducted Voir Dire: An Empirical Investigation of Juror Candor," *Law and Human Behavior* 11 (1987): 131; Michael Neitzel and Ronald Dillehay, "The Effects of Variations in Voir Dire Procedures in Capital Murder Trials," *Law and Human Behavior* 6 (1982): 1.

24. See Los Angeles County Superior Court Judge Judith Chirlin's sample preliminary remarks to jurors as a good example. Presented during a symposium on "Jury Innovations: Research and Practice" at the annual conference of the American Society of Trial Consultants (June 2003).

25. Robert Boatright and Elissa Krauss, "Jury Summit 2001," *Judicature* 86 (2002): 145–65.

26. Some participants at the workshop at which this paper was delivered discussed an opposing viewpoint as to whether jurors are obligated to offer anything other than answers to the questions asked, believing that the burden of asking the questions should be on the attorneys. Alan Scheflin's "Mercy and Morals: The Ethics of Nullification," chapter 5 in this volume, also raises the issue of jurors with agendas.

27. For discussions of the use of supplemental juror questionnaires and individualized voir dire to assist jury selection, see Munsterman, Hannaford, and Whitehead, *Jury Trial Innovations*; and Krauss and Bonora, "Improving Voir Dire Conditions" and "Supplemental Juror Questionnaires," *Jurywork: Systematic Techniques.*

28. As a starting point, see Principle 7 of the American Bar Association's *Principles for Juries and Jury Trials,* which states: "Courts should protect juror privacy insofar as consistent with the requirements of justice and the public interest": http://www.abanet.org/juryprojectstandards/principles.pdf.

29. See Jonathan Redgrave and Jason J. Stover, "Juror Investigation in the Information Age: Looking at the Internet as a Private Investigator—Implications for the Trial Lawyer" (paper, Conference on Patent Litigation, The Sedona Conference, November 9, 2000), for a more detailed analysis of juror investigations. The American Bar Association, *Principles for Juries and Jury Trials,* expressly prohibits surveillance of jurors. Principle 7B states: "Without express permission, surveillance of jurors and prospective jurors outside the courtroom by or on behalf of a party should be prohibited."

30. For more on juror privacy see Mary R. Rose, "Expectations of Privacy? Jurors' Views of Voir Dire Questions," *Judicature* 86 (2001): 10; Paula L. Hannaford, "Safeguarding Juror Privacy: A New Framework for Court Policies and Procedures," *Judicature* 86 (2001): 19; Karen Monsen, "Privacy for Prospective Jurors at What Price? Distinguishing Privacy Rights from Privacy Interests; Rethinking Procedures to Protect Privacy in Civil and Criminal Cases," *Review of Litigation* 21 (2002): 285. See also Munsterman, Hannaford, and Whitehead, *Jury Trial Innovations,* for a discussion of privacy considerations in voir dire.

31. Morris B. Hoffman, "Abolish Peremptory Challenges," *Judicature* 82 (1999): 202; Gregory E. Mize, "A Legal Discrimination," *The Washington Post,* October 8, 2000, B8. See also Munsterman, Hannaford, and Whitehead, *Jury Trial Innovations,* for a discussion of the issues surrounding the reduction or elimination of peremptory challenges.

32. See *Batson v. Kentucky,* 476 U.S. 79 (1986); *J.E.B. v. Alabama,* 114 S. Ct. 1419 (1994); *Hernandez v. New York* 500 U.S. 352 (1991).

33. Rose, "A Voir Dire of Voir Dire," 106; Broda-Bahm and Schwartz, "Those Who Might Have Served." See also American Society of Trial Consultants, "Position Statement of the American Society of Trial Consultants Regarding Efforts to Reduce or Eliminate Peremptory Challenges" (2004), available at: http://www.astcweb. org.

34. For the American Society of Trial Consultants' professional code, see http://www.astcweb.org. ASTC is currently finalizing practice standards and guidelines for posttrial juror interviews.

35. See Valerie P. Hans, "Jury Research Ethics and the Integrity of Jury Delibera-tions," and Nancy J. King, "Ethics for the Ex-Juror: Guiding Former Jurors after the Trial," in this volume, pp. 247–64 and 219–36, respectively.

36. The specific format of focus group and mock trial research depends on a number of factors, including, but not limited to, the area of expertise of the consultant, the type of case and specific case issues, and the goals of the research as identified by the consultant in partnership with his or her client.

37. Neil Kressel and Dorit Kressel, *Stack and Sway: The New Science of Jury Consulting* (Boulder, CO: Westview Press, 2002).

38. See Dennis P. Stolle, Jennifer K. Robbennolt, and Richard L. Wiener, "The Perceived Fairness of the Psychologist Trial Consultant: An Empirical Investi-gation," *Law and Psychology Review* 20 (1996): 239.

3

Jurors' Duties, Obligations, and Rights: The Ethical/Moral Roots of Discretion

Norman J. Finkel

I. INTRODUCTION: A DILEMMATIC PROBLEM AT THE EMPIRICAL/NORMATIVE NEXUS

I plan to cultivate a wide swath of ground at the empirical/normative nexus around the topic of "jurors' discretion." My purpose is to unearth some of discretion's distal ethical/moral roots whose rhizomes lie far removed from the obvious, visible, and audible one which the law sanctions in its jury instructions—and which jurors swear to uphold in their oath. These distal roots, be they "avowed or unconscious," to borrow Justice Oliver Wendell Holmes's phrase,[1] feed the jurors' notions of "commonsense justice" and "commonsense fairness."[2] These notions not only give "life" to the "Law" jurors invoke but also help them resolve the knottiest of moral and ethical conflicts in their verdict deliberations—the kind E. J. Lemmon calls "dilemmatic,"[3] which oftentimes arise in "hard cases," as Justice Holmes knew well from experience.[4] However, some of the jurors' resolutions in these hard cases may appear as "wrong verdicts"—verdicts that should not have been rendered had the jurors been simply following the instructions and their oath. The most popular suspect for the outcome I just described has been "jury nullification." But in digging for those distal roots a curious thing happened once I brushed away a legal fiction, two embarrassments, and some overlaying simplisms. When the ground was cleared so was jury nullification, and what was revealed was juror discretion, my topic, with its roots and complexities.

By examining juror discretion more closely, my aim is to draw connections between the jurors' "empirical life" and the "normative law" they invoke; but going further, I also seek to draw connections between "jurors' discretion" and "judicial discretion," for both involve an interplay between the empirical and the normative. These connections will not take the form of syllogisms, though not for the obvious reason that empirical facts cannot prove normative propositions. Rather, it is because "life" and "Law" do not fall neatly on their respective sides of the is/ought divide, but are *admixtures*, blending the empirical and the normative in complex ways. To explicate, as soon as we try to hold fast to certain mutually exclusive dichotomies—empirical versus normative, is versus ought, life versus law—we run into problems. Modern cognitive psychologists would have little difficulty in empirically affirming what Immanuel Kant would have been quick to point out conceptually—that jurors' perceptions of the empirical world have to be affected by their normative conceptions and values.[5] Alternatively, the law's normative answers to questions of rights and duties often rest on empirical grounds, which take, in Jean-Jacques Rousseau's words, "men as they are."[6] Put another way, airy laws may embody lofty principles, but they are enacted by earthy human beings, who interpret them through psychological processes.

In terms of the criminal law, we have laws about human actions and intentions that cross the law's normative culpability line. These normative laws return to empirical ground when an actual case goes to trial, where a defendant contests the charges, and where ordinary citizens-turned-jurors, the conscience of the community, must find the facts and, as the simple prescription dictates, must follow the ethical oath they swore to uphold and apply the law as the judge instructs. At times, however, particularly when jurors confront dilemmatic moral/ethical problems in a case, this simple dictate becomes an inconvenient fiction. More importantly and broadly, this fiction is a simplism, for it ignores the jurors' sanctioned discretionary room—which may lead them, in their search for a fair and just process and outcome, to invoke the deepest ethical/moral roots in resolving the dilemma they confront.

The dilemmatic conflict of greatest concern here is the one between their duty *to follow the law as the judge instructs them*, which jurors have sworn to uphold, and their *individual sense of what is just and fair*, which may lead them to follow what they believe is the "Law." When jurors appear to yield to the latter it is oftentimes labeled "jury nullification," a catchall term that is replete with pragmatic holes and overlaying confounds. It is my contention, however, that "nullification" frequently masks the wider and deeper topic of "jury discretion," the subject of this chapter, and so my "dig" to clear away the fictive begins here.

In section II, I begin with "jury nullification," already the "convicted suspect" in the minds of many, about which much hyperbole exists. But once we mute the hue and cry, and examine the essential elements of nullification in the light of psychological literature regarding "conformity versus rebelling to rules and norms," this preliminary analysis points to the *infrequency* of nullifications. I show that this "convicted suspect" could not be the likely cause of all those "wrong verdicts" that the media so frequently and confidently report. Then, going to a more fine-grained analysis, once we scrutinize the more common misinformation and consider alternative hypotheses,[7] the finger begins to point to the more likely suspect: jurors' discretion.

Section III begins with the law's ambivalence about jurors' discretion in death penalty adjudication as it has manifested itself in various U.S. Supreme Court decisions. Despite periodic vacillations over jurors' competence to do this weighty, final, and sometimes fatal job, the overall trend of thirty years of court decisions reveals that jurors' discretion has become more firmly and centrally entrenched in this process. I then turn to a first "embarrassment," one that was raised by James Madison in *The Federalist Papers*. I examine a problem endemic to the *construing* of language: reasonable people can construe words in different ways, to mean different things.[8] This psychological point reveals that variance cannot be removed from jurors' decision making and adjudication. This telling point and problem, of course, transcends death penalty adjudication, for it runs throughout the construing of all the legal instructions that judges give jurors, whatever the crimes.

But this construing and variance problem also transcends jurors, for it affects judges and justices as well, and this leads into section IV, where the empirical/normative nexus becomes more entwining and complex. Here I draw a series of connections between commonsense decision making and judicial decision making, and here we find a contentious normative debate about the place of community sentiment in legal adjudication. When the connections are made and the debate is portrayed, a second "embarrassment" emerges—about an "objective jurisprudence." I begin this part by reviewing a distinction I first put forth in *Commonsense Justice: Jurors' Notions of the Law*, where I stated that there are two kinds of law, the familiar "black-letter law" (BLL) and "commonsense justice" (CSJ), which "reflects what ordinary people think is just and fair . . . [and what they] think the law ought to be."[9] To sharpen this distinction, I briefly review how CSJ differs from BLL, and from subsequent work, *Not Fair! The Typology of Commonsense Unfairness*, I review how commonsense unfairness is broader than the law's notions, and what the import of these distinctions may be.[10] For good measure, I toss in Justice Holmes's empirical claims, put forth in *The Common Law*, that community sentiment, be it "avowed or unconscious," exerts a powerful influence on judges' decision making, and thus strongly affects the law.[11]

I then shift to Holmes's normative argument, where he takes an extreme position that the law "should correspond with the actual feelings and demands of the community, whether right or wrong."[12] Anchoring the other extreme of this debate on the place of CSJ within the law is Justice Antonin Scalia, who has been the most vociferous critic of both his fellow brethren on the Supreme Court and the citizenry regarding the intrusion of community sentiment into legal decision making (e.g., *Planned Parenthood of Southeastern Pennsylvania v. Casey* [1992]).[13] Scalia presses for an "objective law," a strict interpretation, and "legal reasoning" untainted by the intrusions of community sentiment. Here we meet the second "embarrassment"—the seeming impossibility of obtaining an objective law, for, according to jurisprudes of the left and right (e.g., Dworkin[14] and Posner),[15] the specie "legal reasoning" does not exist, as judges disagree as to the major and minor premises. As Holmes recognized long ago, legal decision making is not syllogistic, but is, rather, pragmatic, psychological, legal, and moral, all rolled into one.[16]

In section V, I begin with one of Justice Holmes's aphorisms—that "great cases, like hard cases, make bad law."[17] In Holmes's explication of his aphorism, he relied on a series of empirical assertions about how great cases stir the community's passions. They affect judicial decision making, because they generate an "immediate overwhelming interest which appeals to the feelings and distorts the judgment."[18] In this section, I review some recent empirical data on how ordinary citizens adjudicate such hard cases, and the reasons they offer to support their decisions, and then compare CSJ and Supreme Court decision making (BLL) on the very same cases.[19] As it turns out, ordinary citizens engage in a "moral analysis," in contrast to the Court's "legal analysis," and they invoke deontological (constitutive) considerations more frequently than the Court, while embracing, as judges and justices do, an ethical duty to be fair in adjudication.[20] But beneath the differences a similar "moral reading" may be discerned, which means that both justices and citizens, at times, have to reach for roots and sources beyond those found in "the law."

We now reach the critical part of the chapter. In sections II and III, I have merely cleared the ground of some overlays, fictions, embarrassments, and simplisms. The empirics in sections IV and V, including a comparison of jurors' and justices' decision making, can be seen to be akin to a "scientific study of morality," one of the non-normative subdivisions of ethics.[21] In this type of study the two groups are treated as if they are two different societies, and the researcher compares whether they differ in their moral attitudes and codes; furthermore, by examining how each group analyzes the meaning of crucial ethical terms, such as "right," "obligation," and "responsibility," the researcher may be doing something akin to "metaethics," a second non-normative subdivision of ethics. Still, these comparisons and connections, while laying the ground, largely work the *is* side of the is/ought divide.

In section VI, I cross the is/ought divide to make conceptual distinctions between "law" (in the lower case) and "Law" (with a capital letter) and between direct (proximal sources) and distal (indirect) ethical/moral roots of jury discretion. My concern here is to bring to the surface those distal roots which lie deep within the psychic ground, oftentimes at great distances from the obvious, visible, and audible ethical root of the jurors' oath, which jurors ritualistically enact and conscientiously swear to uphold. My argument is that these deeper roots help jurors solve certain dilemmatic conflicts—not by nullifying the law—but because, in their minds, they have found "the Law," and their duty, obligation, and right.

In the concluding section VII, I return briefly to those "embarrassments" regarding "discretion" in jurors' and justices' decision making—embarrassments endemic to the psychological process of construing and interpreting that make variance among jurors and judges inevitable. I underscore the point that there is nothing to be embarrassed about, unless this reaction is but a sad and realistic recognition that psychological beings, and the Law, are human. In my final comments I return to the ways in which ordinary citizens typically exercise their discretion, and conclude that they need not be embarrassed about too many of their decisions or the supporting ethical/ moral roots of their decisions. Moreover, the evidence suggests that justices should not fret too much over the CSJ these citizens sometimes invoke, for their effects appear more likely to ease the headaches of justices when they confront "hard cases."

II. WEEDING OUT NULLIFICATION AND FINDING JUROR DISCRETION

A. Beneath the Hue and Cry over Nullifications . . . Some Lingering Doubts

A "jury nullification," if we pare it down to its bare-bones essence, seems to show CSJ and BLL to be "so fundamentally apart"[22] that jurors will: (1) disregard the fact that the prosecution has proved all the elements of the crime, (2) disregard the law that is given to them by the judge, and (3) disregard the oath they took to follow the law—in order to bring in a *wrongful* "not guilty" verdict. Historically, alleged nullifications, particularly in high-profile cases, have exerted a powerful pull on politicians, the press, and the populace.[23] And why not? Metaphorically speaking, these are "black hole" decisions—emitting no light, making no sense, threatening the law's enterprise, and showing CSJ to be untrustworthy.[24]

Alleged nullifications often trigger a hue and cry, with maligning the jurors a common feature.[25] Consider, for example, responses of the press and politicians to M'Naghten's insanity verdict.[26] The *Illustrated London News* decried "the natural tendency of society to refuse to contemplate them [assassinations] in any other light than as acts of madness," while an editorialist for *The Times* of London voiced the hope that the "soft headed" would not "twist and torture" minor incidents of peculiar behavior in the accused's background into "symptoms of insanity." Lord Cooper suggested that jurors simply retire and ask themselves: "Is this man mad or is he not?" no matter what instructions the judge provided.[27] In the present era, similar refrains have been heard in the wake of John Hinckley's insanity verdict, the first Rodney King verdict, and the O. J. Simpson verdict.[28]

But not only do today's critics raise the nullification claim loudly and often,[29] they also do so in new ways, for we live in an age in which pundits on Court TV predict and post-dict, and in which "armchair jurors" dial in

their "verdicts," and their "verdicts of the verdicts," even before the real
verdict is rendered.[30] Yet despite the frequency, amplitude, and certainty of
these pronouncements, skepticism remains as to whether these decisions
are, in fact, nullifications. For example, were we to press the pundits and
armchair jurors who confidently pronounce that the jury nullified, could
they tell us *why* the jurors nullified? Did the jurors nullify because they
found the law objectionable, or because the punishment attached was too
draconian, or because they found either the law or the punishment ill-fitting
for the particular defendant? In sum, whether a nullification has in fact
occurred, we are generally imprisoned in a veil of ignorance, and if one has
indeed occurred, we are reduced to guessing, based on how we frame the
case, as to why the jurors may have nullified. And this may not be the way
the jurors framed the case at all.

B. The Psychology and Pragmatics of Nullification

But let us proceed differently now, first, by muting the hue and cry and
silencing the prejudicial characterizations of jurors so we can proceed in
quiet detachment to conduct something of an autopsy and preliminary
analysis. What I am suggesting is that we use the bare-bones essence of
nullification that I laid out at the start of section II to examine the available
psychological evidence regarding rebellion versus compliance, an issue,
after all, that is at the heart of nullification. A first question worth asking is:
"What is the likelihood that a jury of six or twelve people would, individually
and collectively, decide to disregard the facts, including the fact that the
prosecution has apparently proved all elements of the crime beyond a
reasonable doubt?"

The social-psychological literature on conformity, compliance, and rebellion
informs this question. Whether we look at the old literature on conformity,
where the work of Solomon E. Asch and Stanley Milgram stand out,[31] or the
newer, normative approaches to social behavior,[32] we find that people generally
follow the norms and rules. Despite the portrayal of America's "rugged
individualism," as a people we turn out to be no more nonconformist than
many other societies.[33] When we look at the social science literature as it relates
to law, we find that people generally obey the law, even when outcomes go
against them, if they perceive the process as fair.[34] And when we look at Harry
H. Kalven Jr. and Hans H. Zeisel's classic study, *The American Jury*, the jury, in
the main, does not turn out to be a wildcat operation.[35] These findings, when
taken together, suggest that nullifications are likely to be quite rare, certainly
rarer than what many critics of juries allege.

A second question worth asking is: "If the jurors, individually and
collectively, decided to disregard the law given to them by the judge, how
would that disregarding process likely have come about?" Most probably,
the process would involve a majority of jurors who favor nullification pulling

a minority to its side, even though this majority had sworn the oath to follow the law, as did the minority. If the minority was not a lone juror yielding to overwhelming majority pressure, but a minority of allied jurors helping each other anchor their beliefs, the greater likelihood is for a hung jury, rather than a nullification.

A third question worth asking is: "What is the likelihood that these jurors—who have been vetted through voir dire and who have sworn an oath to follow the law, an oath made in the courtroom, before a judge, amid all the trappings and symbols of the law—would decide, individually and collectively, to violate consciously and willfully the oath they just took?" Again, the broad psychological literature on rule-and-norm following, cited above, suggests that this phenomenon would not be all that likely.

C. The Confoundings That Overlay Nullification

I now turn to a number of confoundings that overlay the nullification hypothesis, for each confounding suggests an alternative explanation.[36] Sustaining the nullification claim means ruling out these alternatives, which involve (1) the verdict, (2) reasonable doubt, (3) verdict options, and (4) jury instructions. In regard to the verdict, there is a transcendent problem confronting the nullification claimants, for the assertion that the jurors rendered the "wrong" verdict presupposes that we know the *right and true* verdict. Were the right and true verdict known, there would of course have been no need for a trial at all. Cases that go to trial begin with doubt about the true verdict. Moreover, we are aided in our search for the "true" verdict neither by divine revelation, as God seldom answers a *subpoena duces tecum* to tell us what really happened, nor by claims of the media, media experts, or call-in citizens that they *know the true verdict*,[37] for such claims can be challenged as no more than a shared delusion. Furthermore, armchair jurors and commentators cannot be sure that jurors have set aside the proven facts of a case, for "facts" are not uniformly perceived, but must be construed or inferred from other facts. This is most clear with respect to circumstantial facts and facts relating to the defendant's "intent": in the former, jurors must make inferences from certain objective facts, whereas in the latter, they must enter the subjective mind and motives of a defendant—matters visible to no one. In the process of construing and inferring, jurors are likely to bring their prototypes of crimes to the task, particularly if the legal definition of the crime is less than precise.[38] Thus, we cannot be sure, given all the inferences that jurors are legally sanctioned to make, that their not guilty verdict is not a true "not guilty" that has been arrived at through the legitimate exercise of their discretion, rather than through the disregard of the facts, the law, and their oath as the nullification hypothesis posits.

The second alternative involves "reasonable doubt," which represents a legitimate and sanctioned area for jurors to exercise their discretion.

Definitions of "reasonable doubt" not only vary in different jurisdictions, but research findings reveal that these definitions are construed differently by different jurors.[39] Moreover, the various "operative phrases" of these definitions—like "firmly convinced," "to a moral certainty," "but which wavers and vacillates," and "left with a real doubt"—certainly create Rorschach-like room for variance to occur. Yet to sustain a nullification claim the reasonable doubt hypothesis must be ruled out.

To sustain a claim of nullification also requires that we rule out a third hypothesis: Did the jury get the verdict *option* it wanted? The nullification claim presupposes that jurors had an appropriate array of choices, including the "right" choice, and then defiantly chose the wrong "not guilty" choice. But what if, in trying to do justice, they did not have the choice that made "best sense" to them? That is what the *Hinckley* jury foreperson told the Senate Subcommittee on Criminal Law.[40] From mock juror work, where it is possible to manipulate case vignettes and get not only the participants' verdicts but their reasons for their verdicts, this "absence" of the verdict they wanted occurs not only in cases of insanity,[41] but also in cases of self-defense,[42] accessory felony-murder,[43] euthanasia,[44] infanticide,[45] mistake,[46] and manslaughter.[47] In such instances, jurors may fashion a compromise verdict, but this may be the jurors' "best-fit solution" to the verdict option constraints imposed by the judge, rather than an outright nullification.

The fourth alternative, the broadest of all, involves jurors using their discretion to construe and interpret the words of the instructions to find the law's embedded meanings. This is a far deeper task than merely "remembering" and "comprehending" the literal instructions, which are the typical dependent measures used in the jury instruction comprehension literature.[48] To "get" to the deeper meanings that the law intends them to find, jurors must interpret those words and, as James Madison pointed out, reasonable people can disagree about what these words mean.[49] This can be illustrated by any number of bitterly divided Supreme Court opinions, though I am mentioning only one. In *Smith v. United States* (1993), the word "used" divided the majority and the dissent: John Angus Smith offered to trade an automatic weapon to an undercover officer for cocaine, and was charged with a drug trafficking crime in which a weapon was "used."[50] To Justice O'Connor, writing for the majority who upheld Smith's conviction, this meaning of "used" fell within Congress's intent, which did not specify a particular manner of use, but to Justice Scalia, in his dissent, he argued for the ordinary meaning of "used." My point here is that if jurors are merely interpreting words in different ways, at times, and coming to a different interpretation from the law's intended meaning, this would be something quite distinct from a nullification.

In most cases of alleged nullification, we cannot rule out these four alternatives, and juror discretion is central to these alternatives. Weighing nullification against juror discretion, I would argue that juror discretion has the stronger case, all things considered. Proceeding on this greater likelihood, I move to the law and juror discretion.

III. JURORS' DISCRETION GROWS, WHILE AN ENDEMIC EMBARRASSMENT REMAINS

A. Initial Flip-Flopping over Discretion, Yet a Discernible Trend

In the modern era, the Supreme Court's initial holdings regarding jury discretion and the death-penalty decision reveal not consistency, but vacillation.[51] In 1971, in *McGuatha v. California*, the Court ruled that the jury's absolute and untrammeled discretion in imposing the death penalty did not violate any provision of the Constitution, and that using "jurors' discretion"—the "judgment and the consciences of the jury"—seemed to be the best way to proceed, in the context of many worse ways.[52] But just one year later, in its decision in *Furman v. Georgia*, the Court reversed itself on untrammeled jury discretion, describing such discretion with words like "wanton," "freakish," "capricious," and "arbitrary," as it called a halt to all death sentences in the United States until the problem could be statutorily fixed.[53] Yet, when the high Court had the opportunity four years later to remove jury discretion completely from the death decision in *Woodson v. North Carolina* (1976), the Court ruled that North Carolina's proposed fix was unconstitutional, holding that individualized sentencing was necessary to discriminate the death-worthy from those who warranted only life imprisonment.[54]

We also find ambivalence more than a decade later in a line of cases dealing with "victim-impact" statements, where the question was whether the jurors' discretion ought to be exposed to this highly emotional testimony in the death-penalty decision. In *Booth v. Maryland* (1987) and *South Carolina v. Gathers* (1989) the Court ruled that victim-impact testimony was too inflammatory and prejudicial, but two years later, in *Payne v. Tennessee* (1991), the Court reversed course and sanctioned this testimony, seeming then to trust the jurors' discretion.[55]

But in the longer and broader pattern of cases, a trend is discernible, revealing an expansion and entrenchment of juror discretion. The implication of *Furman* was that to pass Supreme Court muster, states needed to design death penalty schemas that would limit discretionary excesses but not shackle discretion with too much restraint, and in 1976 the Supreme Court approved a number of different schemas. Georgia's schema (e.g., *Gregg v. Georgia*)—the prototype most commonly used in states employing the death penalty—requires jurors to find that at least one of the statutorily fixed aggravating factors was present, and also to find that aggravating factors outweigh any mitigating factors.[56] This schema gives discretion wide latitude—perhaps too much latitude—because how jurors find these factors, and how they weigh and balance them, are left to the jurors to decide, as no formula is given. Moreover, as the Supreme Court's subsequent decision in *Lockett v. Ohio* (1978) made clear, mitigating factors could not be fixed in number, as the jurors' discretion is given even greater room to find, weigh, and balance as they will.[57]

Another schema that passed Supreme Court muster in 1976 was that of Texas (*Jurek v. Texas*), which channeled jury discretion narrowly—perhaps too narrowly—into three specific questions that all had to be answered with "12 yes votes" for a death penalty to result, but which, in a real sense, boiled down to one question dealing with a prediction of future dangerousness.[58] Subsequent challenges to this schema raised questions about whether discretion was restrained too severely by not affording jurors sufficient outlet to register all of their mitigating concerns.[59]

Still, the case that may yet have the greatest impact, affecting those states in which the judge does the sentencing, is *Ring v. Arizona* (2002), which concerned both the judge's and the jurors' discretionary orbit.[60] As background, Arizona's death-penalty statutory scheme (which the Supreme Court endorsed in *Walton v. Arizona* [1990]),[61] like those in Idaho and Montana, had the judge making the final death versus life decision without any input or recommendation from the jury (this is similar to schemes in Colorado and Nebraska, where a panel of judges decides without jury input). In *Ring*, the jurors were deadlocked over whether this was premeditated murder, but they found Timothy Stuart Ring guilty of felony murder occurring in the course of armed robbery. The judge conducted a sentencing hearing in which Ring's accomplice testified (though he had not testified before the jury in the culpability phase of the trial) that Ring was the triggerman who had also planned the robbery. The judge, finding two aggravating factors and one mitigating factor, the latter not calling for leniency, sentenced Ring to death.

But the Supreme Court upheld Ring's argument and ruled that the judge's decision and Arizona's scheme were unconstitutional. Ring argued that Arizona's sentencing scheme violated the Sixth Amendment's jury-trial guarantee, as the jury neither heard nor made judgment on the accomplice's claim, which occurred solely in the sentencing phase before the judge. The Supreme Court held that the Court's earlier *Apprendi v. New Jersey* (2000) decision was in conflict with *Walton*, and that *Apprendi* was controlling.[62] *Apprendi* dealt with a weapons offense, where the judge determined that racial animus was an aggravating factor making this a "hate crime," which called for an increased penalty. The Supreme Court ruled that it was not an aggravating factor but a specific element of the offense that needed to be proved beyond a reasonable doubt by the jury, under the Sixth Amendment. Similarly, in *Ring*, this was the jury's decision to make, for the triggerman's allegation was a specific element of the charge, rather than an aggravating factor about which the judge could exercise discretion.

The import of this case is that it places even greater emphasis on jury discretion at the expense of the judge's discretion, enhancing the scope of the jury's powers, as *Apprendi* did. While the *Ring* holding did not mandate shifting the final decision from the judge to the jurors, that was what the Arizona legislature did. What the Supreme Court did in *Ring* was to affirm in a firmer and more secure way the place of jurors' discretion in death-penalty adjudication. The recent and highly controversial decision regarding Ralph Howard Blakely Jr. continues this trend.[63]

B. A First Embarrassment

"Jury discretion" is not just in death penalty adjudication, but in every case, for in all cases judges give jurors instructions that must be construed and interpreted. This brings us to an embarrassment that James Madison recognized in *The Federalist Papers*:

> Besides the obscurity arising from the complexity of objects and the imperfection of the human faculties, the medium through which the conceptions of men are conveyed to each other adds a fresh embarrassment. The use of words is to express ideas. Perspicuity, therefore, requires not only that the ideas should be distinctly formed, but that they should be expressed by words distinctly and exclusively appropriate to them. But no language is so copious as to supply words and phrases for every complex idea, or so correct as not to include many equivocally denoting different ideas. Hence it must happen that however accurately the discrimination may be considered, the definition of them may be rendered inaccurate by the inaccuracy of the terms in which it is delivered.[64]

We know that the Bill of Rights—those amendments to the Constitution which convey many of our fundamental notions of justice, fairness, rights, and duties—can be construed differently by our most learned hands, and this is no less true of lesser laws and statutes. It would be almost a certainty that variance would occur in the jurors' construing of instructions about the law given to them by judges—not just because they are neither justices nor judges, but because the psychological processes of construing and interpreting produce variance among those doing the construing and interpreting whether it is done by justices, judges, or jurors.

IV. COMMONSENSE JUSTICE (CSJ) VERSUS BLACK-LETTER LAW (BLL)

A. CSJ's Differing Perspectives on Justice and Fairness

In *Commonsense Justice: Jurors' Notions of the Law*, I wrote:

> There are two types of "law." There is the type we are most familiar with, namely "black-letter law," the "law on the books." This is the law that legislators enact, the law that was set down by the Founding Fathers in the Constitution, the law that evolves through common-law cases and through

appeals decisions. It is the law that law school students study, judges interpret, and jurisprudes analyze. But there is another law—although "law" may be too lofty or lowly a term to describe it: I call it "commonsense justice," and it reflects what ordinary people think is *just and fair*. It is embedded in the intuitive notions jurors bring with them to the jury box when judging both a defendant and the law. It is what ordinary people think the law ought to be.

These commonsense notions are at once legal, moral, and psychological. They provide the citizen on the street and the juror in the jury box with a theory of why people think, feel, and behave as they do, and why the law should find some defendants guilty and punishable and others not. Black-letter law also has its theories of human nature, culpability, and punishment. But there is mounting and persuasive evidence that the "law on the books" may be at odds with commonsense justice in many areas.[65]

Empirical evidence strongly suggests that CSJ brings a different perspective to bear on "culpability."[66] For example, CSJ will generally widen the law's "moment of the act" *context* to consider a fuller story that is richer in history. CSJ will also accent *subjectivity* more significantly than BLL and reject extreme objectivism.[67] When it comes to judging *mens rea*, CSJ see types and degrees, including culpability for bringing about a disability of mind, rather than seeing simple dichotomies.[68] When it comes to punishment, CSJ favors proportionalism over equalism.[69] The empirical evidence shows that citizens' notions of "unfairness" tend to be wider and more nuanced than the law's.[70] Moreover, citizens, particularly as they age, blame most severely those unfairnesses they see being perpetuated by society, and particularly by the law, and they want them redressed.

B. If Not an Empirical/Normative Connection, Then Certainly a Contentious Debate

The empirical connection between CSJ and BLL was drawn most clearly by Holmes in *The Common Law*, when he noted that community sentiment, be it "avowed or unconscious," exerts a powerful influence on judges' decision making, and thus strongly affects the law.[71] This was one of his many psychological insights, grounded in his own experiences and his observations of fellow judges. Holmes, though, went beyond his "empirical facts" and seemed to take a normative position on the relationship between community sentiment and law. It turns out to be an extreme position, for he claimed that the law "should correspond with the actual feelings and demands of the community, whether right or wrong."[72]

What, we may ask, is the justification for Holmes's claim? Just because something *is* so does not mean that it *ought* to be so. In *The Common Law*, Holmes held that community sentiment generally exerts a "sound" force on judges and the law,[73] and Roscoe Pound subsequently spoke to community sentiment's strength, predicting that in "all cases of divergence between the standard of the common law and the standard of the public, it goes without saying that the latter will prevail in the end."[74] But does this argument collapse the empirical/normative (is/ought) divide merely because judges live and decide cases within community sentiment's "powerful gravitational/ psychological force field," making resistance futile? If this is the basis for why the is/ought divide must fall, then Holmes's argument is a psychological one, not a normative one.

But not everyone is either in favor of CSJ's sway over BLL or resigned to its inevitability and ready to throw in the towel and concede. Moreover, very few scholars, even those most sympathetic to the "life" in Holmes's "law," are persuaded by the "logic" of his argument. At the other extreme of this debate is Justice Antonin Scalia. In his dissenting opinion in *Planned Parenthood of Southeastern Pennsylvania v. Casey*, Scalia wrote: "How upsetting it is, that so many of our citizens . . . think that we Justices should properly take into account their views, as though we were engaged not in ascertaining an objective law but in determining some kind of social consensus."[75] Yet Scalia reserved his sharpest criticisms for "a few of the more outrageous arguments in today's opinion, which it is beyond human nature to leave unanswered."[76] Scalia focused his ire on the majority's concern for community sentiment, the justices' attempt, by not overturning *Roe*, to call "the contending sides of a national controversy to end their national division by accepting a common mandate rooted in the Constitution," and the Court's concern that its "legitimacy" will be subverted if the decision does not rest on community sentiment.[77] Scalia argued that it was the Court's attention to community sentiment that inflamed the controversy to begin with, and the "Court's description of the place of *Roe* in the social history of the United States is unrecognizable . . . [and] to portray *Roe* as the statesmanlike 'settlement' of a divisive issue . . . is nothing less than Orwellian."[78]

C. On the Illusive Quest for an Objective Law, and a Second Embarrassment

The way out of this mess, for Justice Scalia, was clear, and he cited approvingly Justice Curtis's warning in *Dred Scott v. Sandford* (1857). Scalia[79] said Curtis's dissent, quoted below, was "as timely today as it was 135 years ago":

> [W]hen a strict interpretation of the Constitution, according to the fixed rules which govern the interpretation of laws, is abandoned, and the theoretical opinions of individuals are allowed to control its meaning, we have no longer a Constitution; we are under the government of individual men, who for the time being have power to declare what the Constitution is, according to their own views of what it ought to mean.[80]

Yet jurisprudes from the left and right of the political spectrum seem to agree that this "objective law" that Justice Scalia yearns for cannot be ascertained by hermetically sealed "legal reasoning," for there are no "fixed rules" of interpretation.[81] For example, justices may disagree about either the major or minor premise, and if that happens, there is no syllogism; and if that is the case, then there appears to be no distinct specie called "legal reasoning," a notion that becomes but a legal fiction. So here is our second "embarrassment": that discretion, endemic to psychological processes of construing and interpreting, and its by-product of variance, cannot be removed from judicial decision making. Thus, the textualist's holy grail of a strict interpretation appears to give way to the sort of pragmatism Holmes argued for more than a century ago when he began *The Common Law* with that now famous aphorism, that "the life of the law has not been logic, but experience."[82]

Although Scalia wants to bar community sentiment from entering judicial decision making, this is psychologically impossible. Scalia's "want" is also thwarted by the Supreme Court, which has opened the door to community sentiment through its Eighth Amendment jurisprudence. The Court has committed itself to doing proportionality analysis, because the Court has hinged the very meaning of "cruel and unusual" punishment to the community's "evolving standards of decency that mark the progress of a maturing society."[83] Thus, despite Scalia's objections, an empirical gauging of community sentiment enters and affects the highest reaches of BLL, as it affects the bottommost reaches: When citizens meet the law at the very beginning of a case, they bring their CSJ notions to the courtroom to judge both fact and law—as they have for centuries.

Although a normativist may wish this phenomenon away, the empiricist chooses to study it, for empirical research on CSJ can inform the law in at least two ways.[84] First, it may reveal disparities between BLL and the community's views, identifying those topics on which the law is most likely to be nullified, reconstrued, disrespected, or disregarded, and on which the institutional legitimacy of the court is likely to be called into question. And second, it may be able to offer the law answers to those "hard cases" in which empirical and normative issues likely mix—answers, in the words of George P. Fletcher, that seek "not to defeat the law, but to perfect the law, to realize the law's inherent values."[85] We now turn to such "hard cases."

V. "HARD CASES": A MORAL VERSUS A LEGAL ANALYSIS

A. Some General Comparisons That Point to Sharp Differences

Here I begin with another memorable aphorism from Justice Holmes—"great cases, like hard cases, make bad law"—penned in his dissent to *Northern Securities Company v. United States*. In Holmes's explication, he made a series of empirical assertions about how these great cases generate an "immediate overwhelming interest which appeals to the feelings and distorts the judgment . . . a kind of hydraulic pressure which makes what previously was clear seem doubtful, and before which even well-settled principles of law will bend."[86] In reference to these hard cases, Holmes seems to have "reversed and remanded" his earlier opinion about community sentiment, for he is now singing a different tune about the community's sentiment—for its "sound" now produces headaches for the justices while its questionable soundness may produce bad law for the nation.

In some recent empirical work and analysis, I examined how ordinary citizens decided such "hard cases" and compared CSJ and BLL decisions and their decision-making processes.[87] Regarding the decision *outcomes*, CSJ and the Supreme Court's decisions (BLL) were oftentimes not only different, but widely divergent. To take but one example out of many, in a homosexual sodomy case that we cast as *Hardwick v. Georgia* (the original case was *Bowers v. Hardwick* [1986]),[88] where the Supreme Court ruled 5–4 (56%) in favor of Bowers (Georgia), the lay citizens ruled overwhelmingly (93%) in favor of Hardwick.[89]

In terms of the *process* of adjudicating, participants began their analyses by *de-abstracting* the respondents' claims, which were typically cast in abstract principles, and then attaching these claims to *concrete unfairnesses* in the case. They then *contextualized, nuanced,* and *weighted* these unfairnesses with certain *mitigating* factors (for example, whether the claims were limited or overreaching, whether the motives propelling the claims were legitimate or impure, and whether distributive justice or injustice would result), and then they used both *instrumental* and *constitutive* reasons to reach fair and just solutions. What did not enter CSJ decision making as a determinative factor was *stare decisis*, which is quite different from BLL decision making. But surprisingly, on *constitutive* grounds, CSJ seemed to hold the high ground, citing these reasons more frequently than in Supreme Court decision making. Looked at broadly, citizens did "moral decision making" rather than "legal decision making." Finally, there was evidence that participants embraced an ethical duty to be fair in their adjudicating much like judges and justices embrace.

B. An In-Depth Look at a Hard-Wick Case, and a Sequela

The participants' determinative reasons in the *Hardwick* case turned out to be not only instructive, but also prescient. Many of the research participants were deeply offended about the state being in anyone's bedroom, and further offended by the state's use of what they saw as a nonsense pretext of crime control for being there; but their ire was compounded by the state's discriminating against one group (homosexuals), and "equal rather than discriminatory treatment" was one of their constitutive reasons for supporting Hardwick. Still, many participants went deeper in their constitutive analysis, recognizing that beyond the "equal justice under law" issue of discriminatory treatment (that is, the motto which is etched atop the Supreme Court building) lay the more fundamental issues of privacy, autonomy, basic human dignity, and liberty, which the Georgia law threatened. Moreover, this normative principle seemed tied to an empirical fact: Many participants wrote that the Georgia law had taken leave of its moral base—because community sentiment had shifted the moral base—which left the Georgia law standing on an anachronism.

To cast this case in sharper relief, the 1986 Supreme Court's decision in *Bowers* was close and contentious, and after his retirement, Justice Powell, who voted with the majority, said in a speech that he had changed his mind and thought the decision was wrong.[90] Seventeen years after *Bowers*, Justice Kennedy, writing the 6–3 majority opinion in *Lawrence & Garner v. Texas* (2003), acknowledged that the *Bowers* Court did not "appreciate the extent of the liberty at stake" for it framed the case in a way that demeaned Hardwick's claim. He further acknowledged that the community's sentiment had changed, concluding that the Court's former decision "was not correct when it was decided, and it is not correct today. It ought not to remain binding precedent. *Bowers v. Hardwick* should be and now is overruled."[91]

Justice Kennedy's opinion went beyond Justice O'Connor's concurring equal treatment argument to the deeper constitutive issue that many of my participants reached. Justice Kennedy also recognized (and apologized for the fact) that the *Bowers* Court did not value the deeper issues then, but rather dismissed them. And he acknowledged, in a way, that CSJ was ahead of BLL at the time of *Bowers*. In this *Lawrence* opinion, Justice Kennedy clearly registered and relied on the emerging changes in community sentiment.

But Justice Scalia, in his dissent, chafed at Justice Kennedy's opinion, particularly at Kennedy's reference to "an emerging awareness." Scalia noted that "an 'emerging awareness' is by definition not 'deeply rooted in this Nation's history and tradition[s],' as we have said 'fundamental right' status requires." He believed that the Court's opinion resulted from "a law-profession culture signing on to the so-called homosexual agenda," seeking to eliminate the "moral opprobrium that has traditionally attached to homosexual conduct," and seeking to expand fundamental rights, while it overturns its duty to "the 'societal reliance' on the principles confirmed in *Bowers* and discarded today."[92] But Scalia's argument *is not a normative one—*for it is not based on a finding of the "objective law"; rather, he is seeking to place the law on still older empirical ground (which Scalia labels as the nation's "tradition"), where the community's sentiment was different. But the label of "tradition" confers no deontological status, for someone, in ages past, no doubt called that tradition a "new agenda," and raised questions about whether the older traditions should be discarded so fast.

Yet if we return to Scalia's concurring opinion in *Ring v. Arizona*, we find him admitting "that he had made a mistake in *Walton* when he voted to uphold Arizona's judge-based capital sentencing. Specifically, Scalia explained at some length that he had 'acquired new wisdom' in the years since *Walton* that had led him to understand, as he had not before, that the right to jury trial must trump a state's discretion in creating a system of capital punishment."[93] Edward Lazarus comments:

> Supreme Court Justices rarely confess error. That is a shame because it is often a noble and courageous act. . . . Yet doing so is an affirmation of the fact that good judging is a never-ending process of deliberation on the interplay of new facts and new thinking with all that has come before. Ironically, Scalia, a proponent of originalist interpretation that is often faulted for being frozen in time at the Founding, proved in *Ring* that the Constitution is very much alive, and very much the product of individual Justices' evolving understandings of the document and the Court's precedents.[94]

C. The Herculean Task of Adjudication

In *Law's Empire*, Ronald Dworkin considers the following problem: What principle shall a judge use in order to reach the best decision, when harmonizing the three principles of majoritarian fairness, justice, and due process fairness does not yield a clear answer?[95] Dworkin concludes that the judge, in such a hard case, needs a superordinate principle, which he calls the principle of integrity. Assume, says Dworkin, that all our laws were created "by a single author—the community personified—expressing a coherent conception of justice and fairness."[96] Integrity seeks to find the interpretation that best fits with the deeper coherence of the ongoing story. It is not just a "vertical" consistency, in terms of past decisions, but a "horizontal" consistency "across the range of the legal standards the community now enforces."[97] Furthermore, integrity is not just some expedient solution for reconciling conflicting virtues, but is itself a distinct virtue. It has a political integrity that embodies the "community's conception of justice" and the underlying moral justifying principles, woven into "a single, coherent scheme of justice and fairness in the right relation."[98] This principle of integrity is not found *in the law*, but elsewhere.

In *Freedom's Law: The Moral Reading of the American Constitution*, Dworkin puts forth a view that serves to connect what I believe my research participants were doing in those hard cases with what Dworkin alleges judges and justices do in hard cases. According to Dworkin, the "moral reading proposes that we all—judges, lawyers, citizens—interpret and apply these abstract clauses [of the Constitution, and particularly the Bill of Rights] on the understanding that they invoke moral principles about political decency and justice."[99] But this raises the question, "In what are these moral principles rooted?"

VI. FROM A SIMPLISTIC ANSWER TO A MORE COMPLEX ONE

The stock and simple answer to dilemmatic problems locates the *ought* in the Supreme Court's 1895 decision in *Sparf and Hanson v. United States*, in which the Court, acknowledging that the jury had the power to nullify the law, held that it had no *right* to do so.[100] Put in terms of their *duty*, this simplistic answer holds that jurors have but one duty which they swear to in their oath—to follow the judge's instructions. And if that's "the be all and end all" of this story, then the case is closed.

In the following section, I reopen the question and advance the argument that the stock, simplistic answer is a fiction—not on the *realpolitik* grounds that jurors have the power to do otherwise—but because the stock answer ignores certain ethical/moral roots. These roots, once exposed, provide the justification for a more complex answer to the dilemmatic problem jurors confront, and to a fuller understanding of the duties, obligations, and rights jurors believe they have.

A. "Direct" and "Indirect" Sources, within the "law" and within the "Law"

I make two distinctions that are critical to my argument: the first separates "direct" and "indirect" ethical/moral roots, and the second distinguishes between "law" (in the lower-case) and "Law" (with a capital letter). A "direct" ethical/moral root is proximal to the decision making, being visible, specific, and concrete. The oath is emblematic of a "direct" root—it comes shortly before the decision-making process begins, it has a specific ritualistic form and patterned content, and it is easily seen and heard within the courtroom. Moreover, this oath is situated within the "law" in the lower-case, for the duty it ordains results from the citizens' role as "jurors," which they assume for this specific legal case.

But there are ethical/moral roots to one's duties, obligations, and rights that are not easily seen and heard in the courtroom, for they, like rhizomes, abstractions, and walking spirits, are active below, above, or behind the scene. Although these sources may be distal from the courtroom, time and distance do not still their effects. Though I call these "indirect" sources, this does *not* imply that they are in any sense weaker than "direct" sources; in fact, I argue that they may be more powerful and empowering sources. These indirect sources can be found in the "Law," with a capital letter. Before considering those distal roots that jurors may invoke, it is instructive, at this point, to consider where justices, Founding Fathers, and other learned hands find such sources.

B. From "law" to "Law"

Typically, when "hard cases" come before the Supreme Court, they are thoroughly briefed, as the appellants have cited the cases and the law that are on point. Still, in deciding such cases, justices may cite cases and law that were not cited in the appellants' briefs but that they find determinative. While reaching within the wider boundaries of the "law," they have nonetheless gone outside the parameters of the case as the appellants have framed it. Moreover, the justices may reach for constitutional amendments which were not cited, or clauses that are not invoked, or "readings" of such clauses that are novel, yet which the justices find dispositive. Perhaps we are in a gray area here, where a justice is doing Dworkin's Herculean task via the principle of integrity, operating at the boundary between "law" and "Law."[101] But when a justice moves deeper into the past—past the actual words of the Constitution and Bill of Rights that gave legitimacy to the federal government, the Court, and rights—let us say by invoking something from Jefferson's *Declaration of Independence*, *The Federalist Papers*, or one of Madison's unenumerated Rights—we have entered the "Law."

C. From Jefferson's Declaration and Madison's Unratified Right, to Biblical and Natural Law

From the vantage point of King George III, Thomas Jefferson and those Founding Fathers who put their signatures to the *Declaration of Independence* were treasonous rebels; staying with the term that opened this chapter, they were "nullifiers," for the law of the land was British law, which they had a duty to obey, and they were defiantly disregarding it with their *Declaration*. If this act of nullification was merely based on their *power* to do so, a *realpolitik* argument, the declaration could have been much shorter, and without any justificatory rhetoric. Jefferson could simply have written: "Just try to stop us, for if you do, we'll meet and beat your armies on the battlefield."

But in this most revolutionary of foundational doctrines, Jefferson tells us that "when a long train of abuses and usurpations . . . evinces a design to reduce them under absolute Despotism, *it is their right, it is their duty*, to throw off such Government, and to provide new Guards for their future security" (emphasis added). So Jefferson offers justifications. But from where comes this "right," and from what source does Jefferson derive this "duty"? The "right" cannot be from our government and its laws, which were not yet established, and it certainly does not derive from British law. As for Jefferson's "duty," as subjects of the British crown we had a duty to obey the sanctioned laws. So the question still stands.

Jefferson situates the right among the "unalienable Rights" with which the Creator endows us *qua* human beings. Legitimate duties derive from God and, as Jefferson tells us, from those governments "deriving their just powers from the consent of the governed." In other words, Jefferson dips into biblical and natural law, invoking both the Creator and a natural law theory about just governments. These are governments whose moral basis derives from the consent of the people, in which rights, duties, and obligation flow from the governed to the government and back to the governed because they are all part of the same compact, grounded not only on shared political values, but on fundamental moral values about persons, liberty, and laws.

Paul Finkelman recounts the history of James Madison's "reluctant paternity" as "father of the bill of rights." Infrequently remembered about that great debate is that when Madison finally got around to introducing the amendments, he proposed not ten but twelve, and he was most passionate about the one that was ultimately rejected, which would have prohibited the states from infringing "the equal right of conscience . . . freedom of speech or the press, . . . [and] the right of trial by jury in criminal cases."[102] Now, if the "equal right of conscience" had been adopted, and connected to "the right of trial by jury in criminal cases," and invoked by jurors in deciding matters of law as well as fact . . . well, then the right to set aside the oath and nullify would have been rooted in the Constitution. Oh, how things would have been different! (Minimally, I would have had no need to write this chapter.)

One of the arguments against including the Bill of Rights—one that Madison agreed with—was that they "might actually be dangerous," for as James Wilson asked, "who would 'be bold enough to undertake to enumerate all the rights of the people?' He thought no one could, but warned that 'if the enumeration is not complete, everything not expressly mentioned will be presumed to be purposely omitted.' "[103] More to the point, what if some modern jurors, like Madison and many others, believe that the equal right of conscience is a fundamental right, though not an enumerated right, and invoke this distal root source?

There are other indirect sources as well. Think of the Bible, the Ten Commandments, and religious precepts; then think of "in God we trust" on our money, "under God" in our Pledge, the gay marriage issue, and Supreme Court justices saying their prayers before the first Monday in October; and then think of the Establishment Clause, and try to find the line that neatly separates law and morality. Recently, the Third Circuit Court of Appeals took up the case of *United States v. Jerry DeJesus* (2003), and affirmed, as permissible, the prosecution using two of its peremptory challenges to strike two African American prospective jurors (over *Batson* challenges by the defense) for "heightened religious involvement," behavior that was taken as a sign that these individuals might be more likely to inject their morality into the legal issues, and possibly mercifully nullify the verdict.[104] In the same year, but at a higher level, the Supreme Court refused to consider an appeal filed by suspended Alabama Chief Justice Roy Moore over a controversial monument of the Ten Commandments, but this did not stop Representatives Tom DeLay and Robert Aderholt from introducing legislation that would nullify the power of federal courts to review cases in which governments permit the display of religious slogans and symbols on public property—a response, as DeLay put it, to out-of-control "judicial activism."[105] In historical context, absolute religious freedom was one of the amendments James Madison and many Virginians wanted to push for, but Madison knew that "New Englanders would oppose absolute religious freedom."[106] The "divide" among citizens and states is still there, though "red" and "blue" states seem to have flip-flopped since Madison's time, for the presidential race of Bush versus Kerry revealed that "moral values" were cutting issues dividing both states and voters. The main point here is that the moral guidance found within biblical sources, one of the most distal of roots, has been among the most influential for ordinary and extraordinary citizens in solving the dilemmatic. For example, it served as a source for President Lincoln, who bypassed the secular Constitution (that made no mention of the Creator) in going back "four score and seven years ago" in his Gettysburg Address, in order to set this country and our Constitution on a new basis.[107]

That formal law is derived from moral law has been a belief of many citizens throughout the world, and a tenet of natural law theorists.[108] However, the logical positivists anchor the other end of this debate, and they put forth the counterargument "that it is in no sense a necessary truth that laws reproduce or satisfy certain demands of morality."[109] But the fact that logical positivists can and do point out that we have some laws that have no relationship to any underlying moral principle, such as customary laws (for example, making driving on the left illegal in the United States and driving on the right illegal in Britain; or making barbering without a license an offense), turns out to be a weak and unconvincing argument for many learned hands, who find that most laws—our most important laws, such as those regarding the serious crimes of murder, rape, and robbery—are tied quite directly to moral laws deriving from older natural law and biblical sources. But to natural law proponents, the larger point is *normative*, and not about whether the empirical facts concerning most laws support their position; their point is that laws *ought* to be tied to morality. As Lloyd Weinreb states:

> [N]atural law's subject is the moral analysis of the positive law . . . [for the] law has moral content. One way or another, explicitly or not, they [natural law theorists] assert that a rule of positive law that fails to conform to overriding, fully general moral principles, and is for that reason not obligatory, is not truly *law* at all. Law is different from threats or commands; the difference is of the essence of law and is manifest in its obligatory character.[110]

But we literally see in Weinreb's words, via his use of italics, two different meanings to "law," which correspond to my distinction between "law" and "Law." About the former, John Finnis concludes that laws that violate general standards of justice do not have the obligatory character of Law, though they may be law and may be enforced as legally obligatory.[111] If these distinctions between "law" and "Law" are clear to some philosophers, learned hands, Founding Fathers, and justices—and they are willing to act, enact, and decide on this discretionary basis—then in this light it is now time to return to ordinary citizens caught in the dilemmatic between "law" and "Law," and to a consideration of the root sources they are likely to invoke.

D. Commonsense Justice and Fairness

To gain entrée into the thinking of ordinary citizens, let us resume with Jefferson's *Declaration of Independence* at that point in the document following the memorable second paragraph in which he makes his claim to certain "self-evident . . . unalienable Rights." Jefferson goes on, in twenty-seven short paragraphs, to list the King's unjust actions and unfair procedures. In the words of the title to one of my works, Jefferson cries "Not Fair!"—twenty-seven times.[112] And let us also consider Sophocles' *Antigone*, in which the heroine recognizes the dilemmatic, for she is caught in one: Antigone invokes and follows "the gods' unwritten and unfailing laws," rather than determining her duty from Creon's all too human law, devoid as that law is of a moral basis.[113] I suggest that ordinary citizens may do much the same when they face dilemmatic conflicts, although they may have neither Jefferson's eloquence nor Antigone's/Sophocles' conscious ability to cite the source.

People do "commonsense justice" and "commonsense fairness," and they can give reasons for doing so when the methodology affords them the means for doing so, though most (but not all) people are unable to trace their reasons back to their moral/ethical roots. In my work on unfairness, for example, we learn that individuals' notions and instantiations of "unfairness" are clearer, more elaborated, and more differentiated than their construct of "fairness," as there seems to be a *primacy* to unfairness.[114] And we parents hear it, for our small children, long before they get to grade school (let alone law school), cry out their unfairness claims before they learn about those root sources cited above, such as the *Declaration of Independence*, the Constitution, biblical law, or natural law. Yet, for them to utter, whine, or screech their plaintive (and plaintiff) cries, there must first have been a *judgment* made on the part of these children that some actions, rules, or edicts violated some standards of fairness, in their minds. To make that judgment means that they already have in place certain *standards* of what is right, just, and fair. These standards, then, are their "root-sources." And, as it turns out, they complain about arbitrary rules, unfair punishments, disproportionate punishments, wrongful acts not punished, lack of due process, discriminatory treatment when it should be equal treatment, and uniform treatment when it should be individualized treatment. Put another way, they complain about some of the same types of unfairnesses that Jefferson and Antigone cried out about.

As I said, in order to do "commonsense justice" in the face of perceived injustices, or to cry out to the gods their "commonsense unfairness" woes, citizens, even the smallest of citizens, need to summon these root-sources. But if their unfairness claims were bogus, imagined, or had no basis in fact, or if their root-sources were petty or selfish, eventually continued education would quell these cries. However, empirical evidence shows that these unfairness claims are not vacuous, in the main, and that their root-sources (that is, commonsense justice and commonsense fairness) have an ethical/ moral grounding.

Now, considering children and adults of all ages, and the data previously presented, I could make the case, using empirical findings, that these ethical/ moral root-sources ought to be taken seriously for (1) citizens regard these root-sources as their most highly valued sources and (2) they reach for and use these sources when deciding "hard cases" at the deepest and highest constitutive levels. But my argument does not rest solely on empirical grounds. These normative principles that citizens invoke look quite similar, perhaps identical at certain places, to the deep values that Jefferson and Antigone summoned.

From these root-sources of commonsense justice and commonsense fairness, we find or infer certain "duties," "obligations," and "moral principles." As Lemmon states:

> [D]uty-situations are status-situations [like being a juror] while obligation-situations are contractual situations. Both duties and obligations may be sources of "ought's," but they are logically independent sources. And a third source, independent of the other two, is that it is right to do something in view of a moral principle.[115]

What happens, then, when the explicit or implied duties, obligations, and moral principles from these indirect sources conflict with the specific duty of the oath? This may come about because the conflict involves that duty with another, an obligation with that duty, or a moral principle with that duty. One solution, offered by the utilitarians, stresses instrumental/ consequential solutions to these dilemmatic conflicts. As Paul Taylor states:

> [U]tilitarians ask us to consider how the principle of utility would apply to situations of social conflict . . . [where] the principle of utility requires social rules which enable people to resolve their disagreements and live in harmony with one another. To live in harmony means, not that no social conflicts occur, but that whenever they do occur, there is a set of rules everyone can appeal to as a fair way to resolve them. Such rules will (a) take everyone's interests into account, (b) give equal consideration to the interests of each person, and (c) enable all parties to a dispute to decide issues on grounds freely acceptable by all.[116]

Deontologists, in contrast to utilitarians, go in a different direction. As William Frankena states:

> They assert that there are other considerations that may make an action or rule right or obligatory besides the goodness or badness of its consequences—certain features of the act itself other than the *value* it brings into existence, for example, the fact that it keeps a promise, is just, or is commanded by God or by the state.[117]

These considerations may involve actual duties or prima facie duties (that is, exceptionless rules) that lead to constitutive reasons, or they may spring from a right, a "valid claim" (in Joel Feinberg's terms) to follow such a duty or obligation.[118] But not all rights lead to a valid claim to follow such a duty, and here Feinberg distinguishes moral rights from legal or institutional rights, where the former "are held to exist prior to, or independently of, any legal or institutional rules." "Moral rights" may involve a *conventional right*, which "is derived from established customs and expectations, whether or not recognized by law," or an *ideal right*, one that *"ought* to be a positive (institutional or conventional) right, and would be so in a better or ideal legal system or convention," or a *conscientious right*, whose validity is given "by the principles of an enlightened individual conscience."[119]

In summary, these indirect roots are the sources of our most revered moral principles, and they generate certain rights, duties, and obligations. If these roots are invoked by jurors in their decision making, they are likely to create a moral dilemma for jurors—a conflict between the specific duty contained in the oath and the duties and obligations explicit or implicit in these deeper roots. And when jurors apply these ethical/moral principles to solve the dilemmatic conflict they perceive, as they believe they have a right to do, either a teleological or a deontological application may end up favoring those indirect duties and obligations, and the moral principles they reflect. Empirically, or in terms of what happens literally "on the ground," those indirect sources may come to trump the duty contained in the oath; but more importantly, on psychological and normative grounds, jurors may believe that those sources *ought* to trump.

VII. CONCLUDING THOUGHTS ABOUT AN EMBARRASSMENT NEEDING NO APOLOGY

When the autopsy was performed on "nullification," "juror discretion" was found to be operative. This "discretion" turns out to be a psychological process, for when a judge gives jurors instructions as the "law," jurors must construe and interpret those words. But in the light of Madison's first "embarrassment"—that words can be construed in different ways—this means that the "law" can be construed in light of the "Law," such that conflicting duties may arise and a different course may be followed. This process is not fundamentally different from the discretion that judges and justices exercise when they do their decision making, though to those espousing an "objective jurisprudence," this is a second "embarrassment."

These embarrassments, I submit, call for neither apology nor redress, for "discretion"—and its elements of construing and interpreting, and the variance that will follow as night follows day—is part and parcel of the ontology of decision making. In terms of what modern psychologists understand, or in terms of what Kant or Madison understood, these are not truly embarrassments at all, but an admission: that the psychological, the all too human, necessarily intrudes into life and Law and prevents strictly syllogistic, normative decision making—thus forever pinning life and Law at the empirical/normative divide. Some may react to this with sadness, embarrassment, or rage, which are all human emotions, wishing that legal decision making could be logical or mathematical . . . but wishing does not make it so. If life and Law are thus tied at the empirical/normative divide, then what potentially enhances both life and Law is the possibility that each can inform and better the other.

This interaction and informing function has played out over the topic of "jurors' discretion" for quite some time now. On one side, the law chooses to guide that discretion, as it *ought* to do. Yet the law's guidance or reins need not severely restrain for, on the other side, empirical findings have shown that the jury is generally not a "wildcat operation," as the normative *ought* seems firmly established in the jurors' minds as well.[120] However, the jurors' *ought* is likely to align with the "Law" rather than the "law," particularly at those dilemmatic points in "hard cases." Perhaps this was Madison's faith and the *McGautha* decision's faith, too—that citizens using their discretion, conscience, and commonsense justice would find the "Law." Given what these citizens-turned-jurors have generally done with their discretion in "hard cases" across centuries, there is, in my opinion, no need for either embarrassment or apology, and that goes for the ethical/moral roots they sometimes invoke. And as for justices fretting over jurors invoking commonsense justice and fairness, or other justices taking this factor into account in their decision making, my guess is that this intrusion is more likely to ease rather than add to the headaches of justices—when they confront "hard cases."

NOTES

1. Oliver Wendell Holmes, *The Common Law*, ed. M. D. Howe (1881; repr. Cambridge, MA: Harvard University Press, 1963), 32.

2. Norman J. Finkel, *Commonsense Justice: Jurors' Notions of the Law* (Cambridge, MA: Harvard University Press, 1995).

3. E. J. Lemmon, "Moral Dilemmas," in *Contemporary Issues in Bioethics*, ed. Tom L. Beauchamp and Leroy Walters (Belmont, CA: Wadsworth Press, 1978), 6–11.

4. *Northern Securities Company v. United States*, 193 U.S. 197 (1904).

5. Immanuel Kant, *Kant Selections*, ed. Theodore Meyer Greene (New York: Charles Scribner's Sons, 1957), 57.

6. Jean-Jacques Rousseau, *The Social Contract and Discourses*, trans. G. D. N. Cole (New York: Dutton, 1950), bk.1, p. 3.

7. Norman J. Finkel, "Commonsense Justice and Jury Instructions: Instructive and Reciprocating Connections," *Psychology, Public Policy, and Law* 6, no. 3 (2000): 591–628.

8. Alexander Hamilton, James Madison, and John Jay, *The Federalist Papers* (New York: Mentor, 1961), No. 37, 229.

9. Finkel, *Commonsense Justice*, 2.

10. Norman J. Finkel, *Not Fair! The Typology of Commonsense Unfairness* (Washington, D.C.: American Psychological Association, 2001).

11. Holmes, *The Common Law*, 1.

12. Holmes, *The Common Law*, 36.

13. *Planned Parenthood of Southeastern Pennsylvania v. Casey*, 505 U.S. 833 (1992).

14. Ronald Dworkin, *Law's Empire* (Cambridge, MA: Harvard University Press, 1986).

15. Richard A. Posner, *The Problems of Jurisprudence* (Cambridge, MA: Harvard University Press, 1990).

16. Holmes, *The Common Law*, 1.

17. *Northern Securities Company v. United States*, 193 U.S. 197 (1904).

18. Holmes, *The Common Law*, 1.

19. Norman J. Finkel, "When Principles Collide in Hard Cases: A Commonsense Moral Analysis," *Psychology, Public Policy, and Law* 7 (2001): 515–60; Norman J. Finkel, "On the Commonsense Justice and Black-Letter Law Relationship: At the Empirical-Normative Divide," in *The Psychology of Rights and Duties: Empirical Contributions and Normative Commentaries*, ed. Norman J. Finkel and Fathali M. Moghaddam (Washington, D.C.: American Psychological Association, 2004).

20. Finkel, "When Principles Collide in Hard Cases."

21. Tom L. Beauchamp, "Ethical Theory," in *Contemporary Issues in Bioethics*, ed. Tom L. Beauchamp and LeRoy Walters (Belmont, CA: Wadsworth, 1978), 1–5.

22. Finkel, "Commonsense Justice and Jury Instructions," 596.

23. Norman J. Finkel, *Insanity on Trial* (New York: Plenum Press, 1988); Finkel, *Commonsense Justice*; Thomas A. Green, *Verdict according to Conscience: Perspectives on the English Criminal Trial Jury, 1200–1800* (Chicago: University of Chicago Press, 1985); Valerie P. Hans and Neil Vidmar, *Judging the Jury* (New York: Plenum Press, 1986).

24. Finkel, "Commonsense Justice and Jury Instructions," 596.

25. Norman J. Finkel, "Maligning and Misconstruing Jurors' Insanity Verdicts: A Rebuttal," *Forensic Reports* 1 (1988): 97–124.

26. *R. v. M'Naghten*, 10 Cl. & Fin. 200, 8 Eng. Rep. 718 (1843).

27. Richard Moran, *Knowing Right from Wrong: The Insanity Defense of Daniel McNaughtan* (New York: Free Press, 1981).

28. Finkel, *Insanity on Trial*; Finkel, *Commonsense Justice*.

29. Jeffrey Abramson, *We, the Jury: The Jury System and the Ideal of Democracy* (New York: Basic Books, 1994); Stephen J. Adler, *The Jury: Trial and Error in the American Courtroom* (New York: Times Books, 1994).

30. Norman J. Finkel and Bruce D. Sales, "Commonsense Justice: Old Roots, Germinant Ground, and New Shoots," *Psychology, Public Policy, and Law* 3 (1997): 227–41.

31. Solomon E. Asch, "Studies of Independence and Conformity: A Minority of One against a Unanimous Majority," *Psychological Monographs* 70, no. 416 (1956): 9; Stanley Milgram, *Obedience to Authority* (New York: Harper & Row, 1974).

32. Fathali M. Moghaddam, *Social Psychology* (New York: Freeman, 1998).

33. Moghaddam, *Social Psychology*; Fathali M. Moghaddam, Donald M. Taylor, and Stephen C. Wright, *Social Psychology in Cross-Cultural Perspective* (New York: Freeman, 1993).

34. Tom R. Tyler, *Why People Obey the Law* (New Haven: Yale University Press, 1990).

35. Harry H. Kalven Jr. and Hans H. Zeisel, *The American Jury* (Chicago: University of Chicago Press, 1971).

36. Finkel, "Commonsense Justice and Jury Instructions."

37. Daniel W. Shuman and Anthony Champagne, "Removing the People from the Legal Process: The Rhetoric and Research on Judicial Selection and Juries," *Psychology, Public Policy, and Law* 3, nos. 2/3 (1997): 242–58.

38. Norman J. Finkel, "Commonsense Justice, Psychology, and the Law: Prototypes That Are Common, Senseful, and Not," *Psychology, Public Policy, and Law* 3 (1997): 461–89; Norman J. Finkel and Jennifer L. Groscup, "Crime Prototypes, Objective vs. Subjective Culpability, and a Commonsense Balance," *Law and Human Behavior* 21 (1997): 209–30; Vicki L. Smith, "Prototypes in the Courtroom: Lay Representations of Legal Concepts," *Journal of Personality and Social Psychology* 61 (1991): 857–72; Vicki L. Smith, "When Prior Knowledge and Law Collide: Helping Jurors Use the Law," *Law and Human Behavior* 17 (1993): 507–36; Vicki L. Smith and C. A. Studebaker, "What Do You Expect? The Influence of People's Prior Knowledge of Crime Categories on Fact-Finding," *Law and Human Behavior* 20 (1996): 517–32; Loretta J. Stalans, "Citizen's Crime Stereotypes, Biased Recall, and Punishment Preferences in Abstract Cases: The Educative Role of Interpersonal Sources," *Law and Human Behavior* 14 (1993): 199–214.

39. Irwin A. Horowitz, "Reasonable Doubt Instructions: Commonsense Justice and Standard of Proof," *Psychology, Public Policy, and Law* 3 (1997): 294.

40. Senate Subcommittee on Criminal Law of the Committee of the Judiciary, *Limiting the Insanity Defense*, ser. no. J–97–122, (Washington, D.C.: U.S. Government Printing Office, 1983).

41. Norman J. Finkel, "The Insanity Defense: A Comparison of Verdict Schemas," *Law and Human Behavior* 15 (1991): 533–55; Norman J. Finkel and Kevin B. Duff, "Felony Murder and Community Sentiment: Testing the Supreme Court's Assertions," *Law and Human Behavior* 15 (1991): 405–29; Norman J. Finkel and Christopher Slobogin, "Insanity, Justification, and Culpability: Toward a Unifying Schema," *Law and Human Behavior* 19 (1995): 447–64.

42. Norman J. Finkel, "Haute Couture, Poorly Tailored Crimes, and Ill-fitting Verdicts," *Duke Journal of Gender Law & Policy* 10 (2003): 173–223; Norman J. Finkel, Kristen H. Meister, and Deirdre M. Lightfoot, "The Self-Defense Defense and Community Sentiment," *Law and Human Behavior* 15 (1991): 585–602; Diane R. Follingstad, Darlene S. Polek, Elizabeth S. Hause, Lenne H. Deaton, Michael W. Bulger, and Zanthia D. Conway, "Factors Predicting Verdicts in Cases Where Battered Women Kill Their Husbands," *Law and Human Behavior* 13 (1989): 253–69; Jessica P. Greenwald, Alan J. Tomkins, Mary Kenning, and Dennis Zavodny, "Psychological Self-Defense Jury Instructions: Influence on Verdicts for Battered Women Defendants," *Behavioral Sciences & the Law* 8 (1990): 171–80.

43. Norman J. Finkel, "Capital Felony-Murder, Objective Indicia, and Community Sentiment," *Arizona Law Review* 32, no. 4 (1990): 819–913; Finkel and Duff, "Felony Murder and Community Sentiment"; Norman J. Finkel

and Stefanie F. Smith, "Principals and Accessories in Capital Felony-Murder: The Proportionality Principle Reigns Supreme," *Law & Society Review* 27 (1993): 129–56.

44. Norman J. Finkel, Marie L. Hurabiell, and Kevin C. Hughes, "Competency, and Other Constructs, in Right to Die Cases," *Behavioral Sciences & the Law* 11 (1993): 135–50; Norman J. Finkel, Marie L. Hurabiell, and Kevin C. Hughes, "Right to Die and Euthanasia: Crossing the Public/Private Boundary," *Law and Human Behavior* 17 (1993): 487–506.

45. Finkel, "Haute Couture, Poorly Tailored Crimes, and Ill-fitting Verdicts"; Norman J. Finkel, John E. Burke, and Leticia J. Chavez, "Commonsense Judgments of Infanticide: Murder, Manslaughter, Madness, or Miscellaneous?" *Psychology, Public Policy, and Law* 6, no. 4 (2000): 1113–37.

46. Norman J. Finkel and Jennifer L. Groscup, "When Mistakes Happen: Commonsense Rules of Culpability," *Psychology, Public Policy, and Law* 3, no. 1 (1997): 1–61.

47. Norman J. Finkel, "Achilles Fuming, Odysseus Stewing, and Hamlet Brooding: On the Story of the Murder/Manslaughter Distinction," *Nebraska Law Review* 74 (1995): 742–803; Finkel, *Commonsense Justice*; Norman J. Finkel, "Culpability and Commonsense Justice: Lessons Learned betwixt Murder and Madness," *Notre Dame Journal of Law, Ethics & Public Policy* 10 (1996): 11–64.

48. Joel D. Lieberman and Bruce D. Sales, "What Social Science Teaches Us about the Jury Instruction Process," *Psychology, Public Policy, and Law* 3 (1997): 589–644.

49. Hamilton, Madison, and Jay, *The Federalist Papers*, No. 37, 229.

50. *Smith v. United States*, 508 U.S. 223 (1993).

51. Finkel, *Commonsense Justice*.

52. *McGuatha v. California*, 402 U.S. 183 (1971).

53. *Furman v. Georgia*, 408 U.S. 238 (1972).

54. *Woodson v. North Carolina*, 428 U.S. 280 (1976).

55. *Booth v. Maryland*, 482 U.S. 496 (1987); *South Carolina v. Gathers*, 490 U.S. 805 (1989); *Payne v. Tennessee*, 501 U.S. 808 (1991).

56. *Gregg v. Georgia*, 428 U.S. 153 (1976).

57. *Lockett v. Ohio*, 438 U.S. 586 (1978).

58. *Jurek v. Texas*, 428 U.S. 262 (1976).

59. *Penry v. Johnson*, 532 U.S. 916 (1999).

60. *Ring v. Arizona*, 536 U.S. 584 (2002).

61. *Walton v. Arizona*, 497 U.S. 639 (1990).

62. *Apprendi v. New Jersey*, 430 U.S. 466 (2000).

63. *Blakely v. Washington*, 125 S.Ct. 21 (2004).

64. Hamilton, Madison, and Jay, *The Federalist Papers*, No. 37, 229.

65. Finkel, *Commonsense Justice*, 2 (emphasis added).

66. Finkel, *Commonsense Justice*.

67. Norman J. Finkel, Stephen T. Maloney, Monique Z. Valbuena, and Jennifer L. Groscup, "Lay Perspectives on Legal Conundrums: Impossible and Mistaken Act Cases," *Law and Human Behavior* 19 (1995): 593–608.

68. Finkel, *Commonsense Justice*.

69. Finkel and Smith, "Principals and Accessories in Capital Felony-Murder"; Norman J. Finkel, Stephen T. Maloney, Monique Z. Valbuena, and

Jennifer Groscup, "Recidivism, Proportionalism, and Individualized Punishment," *American Behavioral Scientist* 39 (1993): 474–87.

70. Finkel, *Not Fair!*

71. Holmes, *The Common Law.*

72. Holmes, *The Common Law*, 35.

73. Holmes, *The Common Law*, 35.

74. Roscoe Pound, "The Need of a Sociological Jurisprudence," *Green Bag* 19 (1907): 615.

75. *Planned Parenthood of Southeastern Pennsylvania v. Casey*, 505 U.S. 833, 999–1000 (1992).

76. *Planned Parenthood of Southeastern Pennsylvania v. Casey*, 505 U.S. 981 (1992).

77. *Planned Parenthood of Southeastern Pennsylvania v. Casey*, 505 U.S. 866–67 (1992).

78. *Planned Parenthood of Southeastern Pennsylvania v. Casey*, 505 U.S. 995 (1992).

79. *Planned Parenthood of Southeastern Pennsylvania v. Casey*, 505 U.S. 984 (1992).

80. *Dred Scott v. Sandford*, 60 U.S. 393 (1857).

81. Dworkin, *Law's Empire*; Posner, *The Problems of Jurisprudence.*

82. Holmes, *The Common Law*, 1.

83. *Trop v. Dulles*, 356 U.S. 86, 102 (1958).

84. Finkel, *Commonsense Justice*; Finkel, *Not Fair!*; Finkel, "When Principles Collide in Hard Cases."

85. George P. Fletcher, *A Crime of Self-Defense: Bernhard Goetz and the Law on Trial* (Chicago: University of Chicago Press, 1988).

86. *Northern Securities Company v. United States*, 197.

87. Finkel, "When Principles Collide in Hard Cases"; Finkel, "On the Commonsense Justice and Black-Letter Law Relationship."

88. *Bowers v. Hardwick*, 478 U.S. 186 (1986).

89. Finkel, "When Principles Collide in Hard Cases," 531–32.

90. Ronald Dworkin, *Freedom's Law: The Moral Reading of the American Constitution* (Cambridge, MA: Harvard University Press, 1996).

91. *Lawrence & Garner v. Texas*, 539 U.S. 558 (2003).

92. *Lawrence & Garner v. Texas*, 539 U.S. 558 (2003).

93. Edward Lazarus, "A Surprise from Scalia: The Justice Votes for the Sixth Amendment, and for the Death Row Prisoner, in *Ring v. Arizona*," *FindLaw's Legal Commentary Writ* (June 27, 2002): http://writ.news.findlaw.com/lazarus/20020627.html.

94. Lazarus, "A Surprise from Scalia."

95. Dworkin, *Law's Empire*, 164.

96. Dworkin, *Law's Empire*, 225.

97. Dworkin, *Law's Empire*, 227.

98. Dworkin, *Law's Empire*, 166, 219.

99. Dworkin, *Freedom's Law*, 2.

100. *Sparf and Hanson v. United States*, 156 U.S. 51 (1895).

101. Dworkin, *Law's Empire.*

102. Paul Finkelman, "James Madison and the Bill of Rights: A Reluctant Paternity," in *1990: The Supreme Court Review*, ed. Gerhard Casper, Dennis J. Hutchinson, and David A. Strauss (Chicago: The University of Chicago Press, 1991), 344.

103. Finkelman, "James Madison and the Bill of Rights," 311.

104. *United States v. Jerry DeJesus*, 347 F.3d 500 (3d. Cir. 2003).

105. "Supreme Court Denies Moore Appeal: Legal, Political Issue of Ten Commandments Displays Linger," American Atheists, Inc., http://www.atheists.org/fash.line (2004).

106. Finkelman, "James Madison and the Bill of Rights," 331.

107. George P. Fletcher, *Our Secret Constitution: How Lincoln Redefined American Democracy* (Oxford: Oxford University Press, 2001).

108. G. J. Hughes, "Natural Law," in *Contemporary Issues in Bioethics*, ed. Beauchamp and Walters, 30–32; Lloyd L. Weinreb, *Natural Law and Justice* (Cambridge, MA: Harvard University Press, 1987).

109. H. L. A. Hart, *The Concept of Law* (Oxford: Clarendon Press, 1961), 181.

110. Weinreb, *Natural Law and Justice*, 99.

111. John Finnis, *Natural Law and Natural Rights* (Oxford: Clarendon Press, 1980), 351.

112. Finkel, *Not Fair!*

113. David Grene and Richmond L. Lattimore, eds., *Greek Tragedies (Sophocles, Antigone)* (Chicago: University of Chicago Press, 1954), 363–92.

114. Finkel, *Not Fair!* 6.

115. Lemmon, "Moral Dilemmas," 7.

116. Paul Taylor, "Utilitarianism," in *Contemporary Issues in Bioethics*, ed. Beauchamp and Walters, 21.

117. William K. Frankena, "Deontological Theories," in *Contemporary Issues in Bioethics*, ed. Beauchamp and Walters, 23.

118. Joel Feinberg, "Rights," in *Contemporary Issues in Bioethics*, ed. Beauchamp and Walters, 38–39.

119. Feinberg, "Rights," 39.

120. Kalven and Zeisel, *The American Jury*.

Who's the We? Toward a Framework for Understanding and Evaluating Critiques of the American Jury

Adina Schwartz

We live in a society marked by increasing income gaps, major differences between blacks' and whites' experiences with and attitudes toward the criminal justice system, and "blue" and "red" states whose populations differ markedly in their political, cultural, moral, and religious outlooks. Norman J. Finkel abstracts from these divides within American society, and deploys the concepts of "ordinary people," "commonsense justice," and "community sentiment" in an attempt to dispel fears of jury nullification and wildcat juries. On the basis of a critical analysis of Finkel's defense of the jury, I will suggest that attention to the socioeconomic, racial, and cultural divides in the United States is a prerequisite to understanding and evaluating critiques of jurors' decision making.

In defending jury decision making, Finkel employs an idiosyncratic definition of jury nullification. As standardly defined, nullification occurs whenever a person who has been proved guilty beyond a reasonable doubt is acquitted because the jury has deliberately disregarded the evidence or the judge's instructions on the law.[1] According to Finkel's definition, however, a nullification occurs only if the jury has disregarded the evidence or the law "in order to bring in a *wrongful* 'not guilty' verdict."[2] It follows from Finkel's definition that juries do not nullify, but instead legitimately exercise their discretion, when they rightfully acquit someone whose guilt has been proved beyond a reasonable doubt. The central thesis of Finkel's chapter is that most alleged instances of jury nullification in fact amount to legitimate exercises of jury discretion.

According to Finkel, critics of the jury tend to overestimate the frequency of nullifications because they subscribe to an overly narrow conception of the law. Properly understood, the law includes "commonsense justice" as well as "black-letter law" and "'Law' (with a capital letter)'" as well as "'law' (in the lower-case)."[3] Commonsense justice "reflects what ordinary people think is *just and fair*" and "is what ordinary people think the law ought to be."[4] "[T]he jurors' *ought* [or commonsense justice] is likely to align with the 'Law' [that is, basic moral and ethical principles] rather than the 'law.'"[5]

Finkel contends that when an acquittal results from a jury's decision to follow commonsense justice rather than a judge's instructions on the black-letter law, jurors have not acted wrongfully. Therefore, a nullification has not occurred. To support this position, Finkel advances an "ought implies can" argument: Jurors cannot be criticized for relying on commonsense justice because, as a matter of human psychology, this will inevitably occur. In addition, he seeks to dispel embarrassment about the jury's resort to commonsense justice by showing that judgments based on it tend to be morally superior to those based on black-letter law.

The view that legal language is radically indeterminate is the basis for Finkel's "ought implies can" argument. From a psychological point of view, the resort to commonsense justice is inevitable, Finkel claims, because it "is no less true of lesser laws and statutes" than of the Bill of Rights that "the psychological processes of construing and interpreting produce variance among those doing the construing and interpreting."[6] Hence, "'[j]ury discretion' . . . [must be exercised] in every case, for in all cases judges give jurors instructions that must be construed and interpreted."[7]

The problem, however, is that Finkel does not merely want to defend the jury's discretion to use commonsense justice to interpret a judge's instructions. He contends, much more radically, that it is within the jury's discretion to decide that the basic moral obligations embedded in their conceptions of the Law and commonsense justice trump or override their legal obligation to follow the judge's instructions. Finkel blurs the distinction between using commonsense justice to interpret a judge's instructions and following commonsense justice rather than a judge's instructions, when he advances his thesis about the psychological necessity of interpreting legal language.

> This "discretion" turns out to be a psychological process, for when a judge gives jurors instructions as the "law," jurors must construe and interpret those words. But . . . [since] words can be construed in different ways[,] . . . the "law" can be construed in the light of the "Law," such that conflicting duties may arise and a different course may be followed.[8]

Contrary to Finkel's implication, his thesis about the indeterminacy of legal language does *not* support the claim that it is psychologically inevitable for jurors to follow the Law rather than the law. Instead, if all legal language is subject to interpretation, any rule that jurors follow can count as an interpretation of a judge's instructions. In other words, if legal language is radically indeterminate, it is impossible to distinguish between following and not following a judge's instructions. By thus eliminating the possibility of any conflict between law and Law, Finkel's radical indeterminacy thesis makes it nonsense to claim that jurors have disobeyed the law in the name of a higher Law. It is equally incoherent to defend their doing so.

It might seem that Finkel's "ought implies can" argument can be rescued by distinguishing between reasonable and unreasonable interpretations of the law. Making viable distinctions appears to go hand in hand, however, with recognizing that some types of legal language are vaguer and more open to interpretation than others. For instance, a statute prohibiting the execution of anyone under twenty-one is less vague in regard to the permissible age of execution than the Eighth Amendment's prohibition of cruel and unusual punishment. Therefore, it is less reasonable to interpret the statute than the Constitution to permit the execution of a twenty-year-old. A jury instruction not to count a person as twenty-one unless his or her twenty-first birthday has passed would leave still less room than the statute for reasonable, interpretative disagreement about the permissible age of execution.

This places Finkel on the horns of a dilemma. On the one hand, unless he acknowledges that different types of legal language are more or less open to interpretation, it seems impossible to distinguish between reasonable and unreasonable interpretations or between juries who obey and disobey a judge's instructions. On the other hand, Finkel cannot acknowledge the existence of degrees of interpretability without granting that jury instructions tend to be more concrete and less open to interpretation than statutory provisions, which in turn bear the same relationship to provisions of the Bill of Rights. If Finkel grants this, however, questions arise about his generalization that "'[j]ury discretion' . . . [must be exercised] in *every* case, for in *all* cases judges give jurors instructions that must be construed and interpreted."[9] In sum, it is illogical for Finkel to equate criticizing the jury for following commonsense justice with railing against psychological necessity. Consistency requires that he abandon either the claim that the exercise of jury discretion is psychologically inevitable or the claim that it is within the jury's discretion to disobey the law in the name of the Law.

Finkel's argument that it is psychologically necessary for jurors to appeal to commonsense justice is distinct from his argument that jury decisions to follow commonsense justice rather than a judge's instructions on the law are almost always justified. In articulating the latter position, Finkel ignores the distinction between subjective and morally justifiable conceptions of justice. He states, for example, that the jury's discretion is likely to encompass following "their *individual sense of what is just and fair,* which may lead them to follow what they believe is the 'Law,'" instead of "*follow[ing] the law as the judge instructs them,* which jurors have sworn to uphold."[10] Would it count as a legitimate exercise of discretion, however, for a jury to acquit a defendant of murder if, according to "their *individual sense of what is just and fair*," deliberately killing an abortion provider is not a crime, but a vindication of the "culture of life"?

Finkel suggests that empirical work has shown that there is no need to be concerned about the substance of ordinary people's conceptions of justice. He claims to have found, through presenting lay subjects with scenarios based on Supreme Court decisions, that in deciding hard cases, ordinary people "*contextualized, nuanced, and weighted* . . . unfairnesses," and "used both *instrumental* and *constitutive* reasons to reach fair and just solutions."[11] In particular, when they were presented with a scenario based on *Bowers v. Hardwick*, "the lay citizens ruled overwhelmingly (93%) in favor of Hardwick."[12] Their reasoning anticipated Justice Kennedy's reasoning in *Lawrence v. Texas*. On this basis, Finkel concludes that "CSJ [commonsense justice] was ahead of BLL [black-letter law] at the time of *Bowers*," and that "[i]n [his] *Lawrence* opinion, Justice Kennedy clearly registered and relied on the emerging changes in community sentiment."[13] The results of the 2004 elections, including voters' passage of anti-gay marriage amendments to the constitutions of eleven states,[14] raise the question of whether Finkel relied (albeit unconsciously) on a selective definition of the community in recruiting participants for his studies.

At a minimum, these criticisms show that more work is needed before such abstractions as "ordinary people," "community sentiment," and "commonsense justice" can be used as a basis for either empirical or normative analysis of jurors' decision making. However, it seems more promising to ask: Who is the "we" who worry about jury nullification? Who is the "they" whom "we" fear may nullify if they are selected as jurors?[15] Hand in hand with this, it seems important to dig beneath the topic of nullification and ask why criticisms of the jury tend to focus on the prospect of acquittals despite proof beyond a reasonable doubt of guilt. Why, when DNA evidence has shown that significant numbers of innocent people are wrongly convicted, are critics not at least as concerned that juries may convict despite reasons to doubt defendants' guilt?[16]

A route to answering these questions is to consider the concept of reasonable doubt. Finkel briefly remarks that the possibility of different definitions of "reasonable doubt" creates room for jury discretion. Contemporary fears of jury nullification seem to be rooted, however, in more radical disagreement about the place of the reasonable doubt requirement in the American criminal justice system. The tensions are revealed by analyzing Justice Brennan's majority opinion and Justice Harlan's concurrence in *In re Winship*, the 1970 decision in which the Supreme Court constitutionalized the reasonable doubt requirement.

Both Justice Brennan's and Justice Harlan's opinions are grounded in the recognition that the possibility of factual mistakes cannot be eliminated from litigation. "[I]n a factual proceeding in which there is a dispute about the facts of some earlier event, the factfinder cannot acquire unassailably accurate knowledge of what happened."[17] However, as Justice Harlan's opinion explains particularly well, the desire to prevent erroneous fact finding *does not by itself* dictate a choice between the reasonable doubt and the preponderance of the evidence standards. Instead, the choice depends on the relative values accorded to avoiding convictions of the factually innocent and acquittals of the factually guilty. "If . . . the standard of proof for a criminal trial were a preponderance of the evidence, rather than proof beyond a reasonable doubt, there would be a smaller risk of factual errors that result in freeing guilty persons, but a far greater risk of factual errors that result in convicting the innocent."[18] Therefore, choosing the reasonable doubt standard amounts to choosing to decrease the likelihood of convictions of the factually innocent *at the cost* of increasing the likelihood of acquittals of the factually guilty. According to Justice Harlan, the Due Process Clause requires this tradeoff because "a fundamental value determination of *our society* [is] that it is far worse to convict an innocent man than to let a guilty man go free."[19]

In ascribing these values to "our society" in 1970, Justice Harlan implicitly relied on a selective definition of *our* society. In 1964, "law and order" had become an issue for the first time in a presidential campaign. Since Richard Nixon's 1968 campaign, national as well as local political campaigns have successfully exploited voters' fear of crime.[20] If most Americans in fact subscribed to the values that Justice Harlan considers *"fundamental"* to *"our society,"* politicians would not win elections by claiming to be tough on crime. Nor would it be the case that, as Finkel claims, "the media, media experts, [and] call-in citizens" are all inclined to assume that a guilty verdict is "the *right and true* verdict."[21] The anxiety about jury nullification becomes understandable once one recognizes, contrary to Justice Harlan, that many Americans do *not* believe that it is far worse to convict the innocent than to let the guilty go free.

To explain the hue and cry over nullification, it is also necessary to identify the "they" whom "we" think of as likely to nullify. Here, the candidate is race. Mainstream ire over jury nullification seems directed toward the prospect of nullification by black jurors. In 1999, an article in the *Washington Post* stated that "the phrase 'jury nullification' burst into the mainstream media" with the O. J. Simpson verdict.[22] "Some of the most sensational cases [of nullification], or at least most publicized, arise when the subject of race does."[23]

In 1989, the Fully Informed Jury Assocation was formed to lobby for laws allowing jury nullification. Its members included NRA members, anti-logging environmentalists, advocates for legalizing marijuana, and bikers opposed to mandatory helmet laws.[24] The advocacy of nullification by these groups of (primarily, if not exclusively) white Americans makes it necessary to explain why popular culture identifies blacks as *the* potential nullifying jurors.

A hypothesis that would explain the identification of blacks as the nullifying "other" is that black Americans are much more likely than whites to subscribe to the values underlying the reasonable doubt requirement.[25] If this hypothesis is correct, the mainstream media and white Americans should be less inclined than black jurors to believe there are reasons to doubt a defendant's guilt. To the extent that the media and white Americans do not grasp black jurors' reasons for doubt, they are likely to criticize these jurors for acquitting in the face of the law and facts.

The hypothesis of racially differentiated attitudes toward the reasonable doubt standard accords with the well-known existence of "substantial racial differences in opinion about criminal justice."[26] Further support for the hypothesis comes through considering Justice Brennan's reasoning in *In re Winship*. According to Justice Brennan:

> [U]se of the reasonable doubt standard is indispensable to command the respect and confidence of *the community* in applications of the criminal law. It is critical that the moral force of the criminal law not be diluted by a standard of proof that leaves people in doubt whether innocent men are being condemned. It is also important in our free society that every individual going about his ordinary affairs have confidence that his government cannot adjudge him guilty of a criminal offense without convincing a proper factfinder of his guilt with utmost certainty.[27]

This account of the legitimating effects of the reasonable doubt standard can be criticized for resting on a selective definition of "the community." As of 2001, the disparity in the odds of incarceration for black and white Americans had risen to 8:1.[28] Consequently, one would expect blacks to be much more likely than whites to experience the concerns that Justice Brennan identifies as leading people to insist on the reasonable doubt standard.[29]

A factor related to the racial differences in attitudes toward the reasonable doubt standard may further explain the hue and cry over jury nullification. Finkel plausibly contends that a failure to realize that "'facts' are not uniformly perceived, but must be construed or inferred from other facts" leads "armchair jurors and commentators" to overestimate the frequency of jury nullification.[30] He fails to recognize, however, that the public is preoccupied with the specter of nullification by *black* jurors. This racially tinged concern is partially explained by the fact that experiences and perceptions of police encounters are *racially patterned*.[31] According to Henry Louis Gates Jr., "[b]lacks—in particular, black men—swap their experiences of police encounters like war stories, and there are few who don't have more than one story to tell."[32] Gates concludes that to understand the racially differentiated response to the O. J. Simpson verdict, "you need nothing so grand as an epistemic rupture to explain why different people weigh the evidence of authority differently. . . . It's a commonplace that white folks trust the police and black folks don't. Whites recognize this in the abstract, but they're continually surprised at the *depth* of black wariness."[33]

In this response I have suggested, but not proved, that we can better understand and evaluate criticisms of the jury if we abandon such abstractions as "ordinary people," "commonsense justice," and "community sentiment," and consider the social divisions within our society. This approach strongly indicates that the hue and cry over jury nullification is a symptom of a much more fundamental social problem: the existence of "two nations: black and white, separate, hostile, unequal."[34]

NOTES

1. See, e.g., *United States v. Thomas*, 116 F.3d 606, 614 (2d Cir. 1997) ("Nullification is, by definition, a violation of the juror's oath to apply the law as instructed by the court."); Paul Butler, "Racially Based Jury Nullification," *Yale Law Journal* 105 (1995): 677, 700 ("When a jury disregards evidence presented at trial and acquits an otherwise guilty defendant, because the jury objects to the law that the defendant violated or to the application of the law to that defendant, it has practiced nullification."); James P. Levine, "The Role of Jury Nullification Instructions in the Quest for Justice," *Legal Studies Forum* 18, no. 4 (1994): 473 ("Jury nullification, defined as the deliberate decision of jurors to acquit those who are presumably guilty because jurors have moral compunctions about convicting, is an endangered species.").

2. Norman J. Finkel, "Jurors' Duties, Obligations, and Rights: The Ethical/ Moral Roots of Discretion," in this volume, 57.

3. Finkel, "Jurors' Duties, Obligations, and Rights," 55–56.

4. Finkel, "Jurors' Duties, Obligations, and Rights," 64 (footnote omitted).

5. Finkel, "Jurors' Duties, Obligations, and Rights," 77.

6. Finkel, "Jurors' Duties, Obligations, and Rights," 63.

7. Finkel, "Jurors' Duties, Obligations, and Rights," 63.

8. Finkel, "Jurors' Duties, Obligations, and Rights," 76.

9. Finkel, "Jurors' Duties, Obligations, and Rights," 63 (emphasis added).

10. Finkel, "Jurors' Duties, Obligations, and Rights," 54. Finkel also fails to distinguish between subjective and morally justifiable views about what is right, when he states:

> And when jurors apply these ethical/moral principles to solve the dilemmatic conflict they perceive, as they believe they have a right to do, either a teleological or deontological application may end up favoring those indirect duties and obligations, and the moral principles they reflect. Empirically, or in terms of what happens literally 'on the ground,' those indirect sources may come to trump the duty contained in the oath; but more importantly, on psychological and normative grounds, jurors may believe that those sources *ought* to trump.

Finkel, "Jurors' Duties, Obligations, and Rights," 76.

11. Finkel, "Jurors' Duties, Obligations, and Rights," 67.

12. Finkel, "Jurors' Duties, Obligations, and Rights," 67.

13. Finkel, "Jurors' Duties, Obligations, and Rights," 68.

14. See Associated Press, "Voters Pass All 11 Bans on Gay Marriage," November 3, 2004, http://www.msnbc.msn.com/id/6383353.

15. For a related attempt to show the significance of the "who is the 'we'" question, see Adina Schwartz, "Homes as Folding Umbrellas: Two Recent Supreme Court Decisions on 'Knock and Announce,'" *American Journal of Criminal Law* 25 (1998): 545, 566–94 (analyzing how the Supreme Court's articulation of Fourth Amendment doctrine has been intertwined with the development of different narratives about who "we" are in relation to criminal defendants and the police).

16. I thank Jacob D'Eustachio for framing this question. See http://www.innocenceproject.org (stating that as of April 29, 2005, postconviction DNA testing had exonerated 158 prisoners in the United States).

17. *In re Winship*, 397 U.S. 358, 370 (1970) (Harlan, J., concurring). Similarly, Justice Brennan states that "there is always, in litigation, a margin of error, representing error in factfinding" (citation omitted; 397 U.S. at 364).

18. 397 U.S. 371 (Harlan, J., concurring). Justice Brennan also recognizes that constitutionalizing the reasonable doubt standard involves decreasing the risk of factually erroneous convictions at the cost of increasing the risk of factually erroneous acquittals. "Where one party has at stake an interest of transcending value—as a criminal defendant his liberty—this margin of error is reduced as to him by the process of placing on the other party the burden of . . . persuading the factfinder at the conclusion of the trial of his guilt beyond a reasonable doubt" (397 U.S. 364, citation omitted).

19. 397 U.S. 372 (1970) (emphasis added).

20. For an overview of the politics of crime and race in the 1960s, *see* Adina Schwartz, "'Just Take Away Their Guns': The Hidden Racism of *Terry v. Ohio*," *Fordham Urban Law Journal* 23 (1996): 317, 326–27.

21. Finkel, "Jurors' Duties, Obligations, and Rights," 59.

22. Joan Biskupice, "In Jury Rooms, a Form of Civil Protest Grows," *Washington Post*, February 8, 1999, http://www.erowid.org/freedom/jury_ nullification/jury_nullification_media1.shtml.

23. Biskupice, "In Jury Rooms, a Form of Civil Protest Grows."

24. See Candace McCoy, "If Hard Cases Make Bad Law, Easy Juries Make Bad Facts: A Response to Professor Levine," *Legal Studies Forum* 18, no. 4 (1994): 497, 503.

25. See Edward W. Said, *Orientalism* (New York: Vintage Books, 1978), for a discussion of how "we" define ourselves in relation to the "other."

26. Lawrence D. Bobo and Devon Johnson, "A Taste for Punishment," *Du Bois Review* 1, no. 1 (2004): 151, 153.

27. *In re Winship*, 397 U.S. 364 (1970) (emphasis added).

28. Bobo and Johnson, "A Taste for Punishment," 152.

29. This expectation accords with findings that "Blacks [are] more skeptical [than whites] of the equal application of law [and] more critical of the police and their tactics." Bobo and Johnson, "A Taste for Punishment," 156 (citations omitted).

30. Finkel, "Jurors' Duties, Obligations, and Rights," 59. See Adina Schwartz, "A 'Dogma of Empiricism' Revisited: *Daubert v. Merrell Dow Pharmaceuticals, Inc.*

and the Need to Resurrect the Philosophical Insight of *Frye v. United States,"* *Harvard Journal of Law and Technology* 10 (1997): 149, 171–75, for an overview of philosophical arguments for the claim that facts are theory-laden.

31. In his dissent from the Supreme Court's holding in *Illinois v. Wardlow,* 528 U.S. 119, 126 (2000), that flight from the police in a high crime neighborhood is sufficient to justify a stop and frisk, Justice Stevens recognized that race shapes experiences with and attitudes toward the police:

> Among some citizens, particularly minorities and those dwelling in high crime areas, there is also the possibility that the fleeing person is entirely innocent, but, with or without justification, believes that contact with the police can itself be dangerous.

528 U.S. 119, 132. See also 528 U.S. 119, 132–33 and nn. 7–10 (citing empirical studies showing that blacks are both more likely to be stopped and frisked than whites and more likely to be suspicious of the police). Further, see Schwartz, "'Just Take Away Their Guns,'" 373–74 (discussing racial differences in the likelihood of being stopped and frisked and in attitudes toward the police).

32. Heny Louis Gates Jr., "Thirteen Ways of Looking at a Black Man," in *Thirteen Ways of Looking at a Black Man* (New York: Random House, 1997), 109.

33. Gates, "Thirteen Ways of Looking at a Black Man," 109.

34. This is the title of a book by Andrew Hacker, originally published in 1992 by Macmillan. Interestingly, the Amazon.com web site advertises that the expanded and updated 1995 edition of the book "includ[es] a new chapter in which the foremost expert on race in America analyzes the O. J. Simpson verdict." http://www.amazon.com/exec/obidos/tg/detail/-/0345405374/103-0998706-2755830?v=glance).

4

The Constitutional and Ethical Implications of "Must-Find-the-Defendant-Guilty" Jury Instructions

B. Michael Dann

I. INTRODUCTION

I presided over jury trials of felony cases during my twenty years on Arizona's trial bench. I routinely instructed juries at least twice, once before trial and once at the end, regarding the reasonable doubt standard and the jury's "duty" to convict the defendant if the jurors were satisfied that the prosecution had carried its burden. The operative language of the pattern instruction read something like this:

> If, based on your consideration of the evidence, in light of the law that applies, you are satisfied that the defendant's guilt has been proven beyond a reasonable doubt, then you *must* find him/her guilty.[1]

As time passed, I became increasingly uncomfortable reading this instruction to juries. It was a feeling akin to intruding—going where I had not been invited and was not welcome. Telling the jurors they "must" convict when all the elements of the crime had been established beyond a reasonable doubt seemed too strong and provocative a direction from the judge regarding their ultimate responsibility. But I never could articulate, to others or to myself, the legal or normative reasons for my unease. Now, having reflected on the question from a greater distance, I feel I can.

In this chapter I explain why this kind of mandatory instruction invades the jury's constitutional prerogative to "bring in a verdict in the teeth of both law and facts"[2] for reasons of conscience. Indeed, the power of the American jury to return a verdict based on mercy or leniency, or to check abusive prosecutions, is "one of the peaceful barricades of freedom."[3] The refusal of jurors to enforce the law in a particular case because their consciences would

93

not allow a guilty verdict is a central feature of our criminal justice system and is a component and incident of the Sixth Amendment right to trial by jury. I also argue that judges' instructions that mandate, coerce, or direct a conviction by the jury under these (or any) circumstances invade the province of the jury and violate the constitutional guarantee of an "impartial jury." These "must-find-the-defendant-guilty" instructions mislead jurors concerning their power and role in the criminal process and raise serious ethical questions. Last, I consider alternative solutions from revising the current jury instruction by removing the command "must" to affirmative jury instructions informing jurors of their limited power of nullification and making suggestions for the wise exercise of their power.

II. THE CONSTITUTIONAL POWER . . . AND RIGHT . . . TO ACQUIT FOR "REASONS OF CONSCIENCE"

Nullification, or what is often confused with nullification, takes a number of forms.[4] Two types of nullification power associated with juries in the rather distant past were (1) the power to decide all legal questions, including the interpretation and application of law; and (2) resolving constitutional issues. Some still advocate for this form of jury power, contending that juries should be told that they can accept or reject the judge's instructions on the law.[5] I do not believe jurors have, or should have, such broad powers.

The remaining type of nullification assumes that the judge, not the jury, resolves all legal questions at trial, and that the jury applies the court's legal instructions to the facts. However, the final step of reaching a verdict in light of the law and the facts is the sole province of the jury. The jury's deliberate decision to acquit for reasons of conscience, despite the judge's instructions, is the only form of nullification that is the subject of current serious legal debate.[6] Some authorities that recognize and celebrate this role of the jury argue that since this power finds its source in the Constitution, such decisions by juries are within the law and do not constitute unlawful nullifications of the law at all.[7]

Many others have ably recounted the history of jury nullification—both its exercise and the debates it has engendered[8]—and accordingly I will not repeat it here. Examples of the narrow form of nullification on which I will focus, practiced by both English and American juries, dot our legal, political, and social landscapes. Some typically are celebrated—for example, acquittals of political dissidents, social activists, Prohibition-era liquor law violators, peaceful war protestors, and those accused of aiding slaves in violation of fugitive slave laws, to name just a few. Other examples are embarrassments and are widely condemned—the frequent refusals of all-white Southern juries to convict whites who murdered or assaulted African Americans and civil-rights workers being the cases most often mentioned.[9]

The constitutional status of the criminal jury's "decisive negative"[10] has not been squarely recognized by the U.S. Supreme Court. Indeed, some of the Court's references to this discretionary power of the jury have been less than endearing. For example, the jury's disregard of the evidence and law in order to acquit has been called "lawless,"[11] "an assumption of a power which [the jury has] no right to exercise,"[12] resulting in "unreasonable"[13] verdicts returned for "impermissible reasons."[14] On the other hand, the Court has repeatedly characterized the jury's ability to return a verdict against the weight of the evidence for reasons of conscience as a central feature of our criminal justice system and an essential bulwark against overreaching, tyrannical, or otherwise errant government officials, including prosecutors and judges.[15] An oft-cited example of the American jury's "control over the ultimate verdict" is the case of John Peter Zenger, a celebrated press freedom case.[16]

One of the most complete explications of this role of the jury is found in *Duncan v. Louisiana* (1968), in which the Court held that the Sixth Amendment right to jury trial is applicable to the states through the Due Process Clause of the Fourteenth Amendment. After noting that the jury trial right in serious criminal cases is ensured by both Article III, Section 2, of the Constitution and the Sixth Amendment, the Court agreed that the jury "is more than an instrument of justice and more than one wheel of the constitution: it is the lamp that shows that freedom lives."[17] The majority observed that the Constitution's framers clearly intended the right as a defense against arbitrary law enforcement:

> Providing an accused with the right to be tried by a jury of his peers gave him an inestimable safeguard against the corrupt or overzealous prosecutor and against the compliant, biased, or eccentric judge. If the defendant preferred the common-sense judgment of a jury to the more tutored but perhaps less sympathetic reaction of the single judge, he was to have it. Beyond this, the jury trial provisions . . . reflect a fundamental decision about the exercise of official power—a reluctance to entrust plenary powers over the life and liberty of the citizen to one judge or to a group of judges. Fear of unchecked power, so typical of our State and Federal Governments in other respects, found expression in the criminal law in this insistence upon community participation in the determination of guilt or innocence.[18]

Duncan alluded to, but did not explicitly address, the legal status of the jury's prerogative to return a verdict of not guilty against the weight of the evidence and the court's instructions.[19] It is fair to say that the Court did not find it necessary to be so explicit, for if judges could compel verdicts of guilty then the jury would no longer serve as the intended safeguard.

The Court also has emphasized the importance of juror conscience—as representative of community conscience—to the jury's ability to play its role as a check on the abuse of the criminal sanction.[20] Prohibiting "discretionary act[s] of jury nullification," the Court has stated, "would be totally alien to our notions of criminal justice."[21]

Moreover, constitutional history does not limit the jury to the "mechanical and deadening" act of fact-finding.[22] The Supreme Court's 1895 decision in *Sparf v. United States*, which is most often cited in support of this limited view of the jury's role at trial, cannot be read so broadly.[23] *Sparf* put an end to the "lawmaking" power of juries by declaring that the source of law in federal criminal trials is the trial judge, and that the jury is bound to follow the law. More recently, the Supreme Court made it clear that *Sparf* does not negate the separate responsibility of the jury to decide upon its verdict *after* applying the law in the judge's instructions to the facts found.[24] Students of the role of the modern criminal jury in the democratic process also agree that the Court's century-plus-old decision in *Sparf* does not bear on the constitutional right of the jury to reject the received law and vote its conscience.[25] As the Court stated in 1995, "After all, it is one thing to tell the jury what the applicable law is; it is quite another for the judge to require the jury to apply the law."[26]

Throughout our history, all legal attempts to cabin jury decisions based on conscience have failed, in large part because, at bottom, this role of the jury is political, not legal in nature.[27] Of course, this truism has not discouraged modern-day judges and lawyers and some academics, too many of whom would like to straightjacket the jury, from trying to do so.[28] Only by giving explicit constitutional standing to the jury's role to vote its conscience, and giving the criminal defendant the right to invoke the principle, will these efforts to "subjugate the jury"[29] subside.

III. COERCIVE JUDICIAL INSTRUCTIONS AND THE CONSTITUTION

I return to where I started: the issue of instructing juries to convict upon finding the requisite proof of legal guilt. Current efforts to constrain decisions of conscience assume various forms, but they all have this much in common: They seek to impose the government's will (as spoken by the judge) on the jurors in an unconstitutional manner and prohibit the jury's free exercise of its prerogative to check the government's particular use of the powerful criminal sanction.

Most state and federal trial judges use the strongest term "must" when instructing the jury on its duty to convict if all the jurors agree that the law's definition of the crime has been met by proof beyond a reasonable doubt. This direction is frequently found at the conclusion of the reasonable doubt instruction. The usual instruction is along the lines of the model suggested for use by the Federal Judicial Center (FJC):

> If, based on your consideration of the evidence, you are firmly convinced that the defendant is guilty of the crime charged, you *must* find him guilty.[30]

Almost all of the appellate opinions dealing with use of the word "must" in this context have rejected arguments that it unduly constrains jurors' discretion.[31] Trial judges frequently use similar mandatory language—for example, "duty"—to eliminate, confine, or steer juror discretion regarding the verdict, and these instructions have likewise been upheld.[32] The use of "should" to describe the jury's duty to find guilt, assuming the requisite amount of proof, has also been approved on the theory that it lacks the compulsion of "must."[33]

From a purely logical point of view, it is difficult to square these instructions with the constitutional role mandated for juries. Clearly, the instructions reduce the independence of the jury, channel verdicts according to the judge's substantive instructions, and eliminate, or at least discourage, considerations of conscience. In short, they deprive defendants of an impartial jury, one free of judicial pressure to return a guilty verdict. What about the jury's ability to check the overreaching government official? The answer: "Put simply, the right to be tried by a jury of one's peers finally exacted from the king would be meaningless if the king's judges could call the turn."[34]

Similar attempts to steer or influence jury verdicts in favor of guilt have consistently been condemned on Sixth Amendment grounds. For example, the jury-control measures that are available to the judge in civil cases—motions for summary judgment, a directed verdict of guilty, a new trial following a defense verdict, judgment notwithstanding the verdict, and appeal from a defense verdict—are not available in criminal cases for constitutional reasons.[35] Partial directed verdicts of guilty, on just one of several elements of the offense,[36] even where the defendant stipulates to the underlying facts,[37] are also prohibited. The reason? Such rulings invade the province of the jury.[38] The same must be said about the use of special verdicts or interrogatories that require the jury to answer factual questions before or after a general verdict is reached.[39] The First Circuit left no doubt that the rationale for precluding the use of devices that would "restrict [the jury's] historic function" is constitutionally based:

> Uppermost . . . is the principle that the jury, as the conscience of the community, must be permitted to look at more than logic. . . . The constitutional guarantees of due process and trials by jury require that a criminal defendant be afforded the full protection of a jury unfettered, directly or indirectly.[40]

A. Supreme Court Case Law

Appellate courts, including the U.S. Supreme Court, have clearly struggled in their efforts to reconcile trial judges' attempts to steer juries toward guilty verdicts with the guarantee of an impartial jury. In *Horning v. District of Columbia*, the Court was confronted with a case in which the trial judge told the jury that since all the evidence pointed to legal guilt, the only lawful verdict was one of guilt. Justice Holmes disposed of the defendant's objection in short shrift, noting that when the evidence is all one way "the function of the jury, if they do their duty, is little more than formal."[41] The jurors, he said, "were allowed the technical right, if it can be called so, to decide against the law and the facts—and that is all there was left for them after the defendant and his witnesses took the stand."[42] Justice Brandeis, writing for four dissenters, concluded that the trial judge "usurped the province of the jury."[43]

> What the judge is forbidden to do directly, he may not do by indirection. . . .
> [H]e may not command or coerce. He does coerce when without convincing
> the judgment he overcomes the will by the weight of his authority.[44]

Lower courts were left to struggle with *Horning*[45] until 1995, when the Supreme Court effectively repudiated its 1920 decision, calling it an "unfortunate anomaly" in the court's jurisprudence about the right to trial by jury.[46]

Prior to the Supreme Court's repudiation of *Horning*, a federal appeals court, in *United States v. Hayward* (1969), expressly held that a "must-find-the-defendant-guilty" instruction violated the Sixth Amendment jury trial guarantee:

> While the judge in this case did not direct a verdict of guilty in form, that is
> the substantive effect of the instruction given. The rule against directed
> verdicts of guilt includes perforce situations in which the judge's instructions
> fall short of directing a guilty verdict but which nevertheless have the
> effect of doing so by eliminating other relevant considerations.[47]

Although the "anomalous" decision in *Horning* would not likely loom large in the Supreme Court's consideration of the Sixth Amendment arguments raised here, another opinion in an analogous area of jury decision making, sentencing in death penalty cases, will pose a problem. In *Blystone v. Pennsylvania* (1990),[48] a divided Court upheld the constitutionality of a state death penalty statute and jury instruction that read, in part:

> [T]he verdict *must* be a sentence of death if the jury unanimously finds at
> least one aggravating circumstance . . . and no mitigating circumstance or
> if the jury unanimously finds one of more aggravating circumstances which
> outweigh any mitigating circumstances.[49]

The majority concluded that the mandatory language did not offend the Court's death penalty jurisprudence and properly "channeled" jury discretion and avoided "arbitrary and capricious capital sentencing."[50] The majority relied heavily on the Court's earlier decision upholding a Texas statute requiring the *judge* to impose the death penalty if the jury answered a series of questions in a certain fashion.[51]

The four-justice minority in *Blystone* claimed that the majority erred by equating the Texas procedure, which limited only the sentencing judge's discretion, with the Pennsylvania procedure that operated to deprive the jury of needed discretion and the ability to determine for itself the penalty in the particular case.

I choose to deal with and limit *Blystone's* reach and impact in the following manner:

(1) It is not a Sixth Amendment right to impartial jury case. None of the Court's opinions mention the jury provisions, just the Eighth Amendment limitations on the imposition of the death penalty. For all one can tell, no right to jury claim was raised or briefed.

(2) No reference to *Blystone* has been found in the numerous Supreme Court and lower court decisions or in the literature on the jury's role under the Sixth Amendment, the subject of jury "nullification" generally, or the ability of the jury to find contrary to the law and according to conscience.

(3) Death and cases dealing with the death penalty are different.

B. Lower Court Case Law

Although the entire language used by the trial judge in *Billeci v. United States* (1950) to direct the jury to return a guilty verdict was more coercive than a "must-find-the-defendant-guilty" instruction, the court plainly disapproved of the direction that the jury "must" find the defendant guilty if it found certain facts true:

> [G]uilt or innocence must be decided by twelve laymen and not by the one judge. A judge cannot impinge upon the right any more that he can destroy it. He cannot press upon the jury the weight of his influence any more than he can eliminate the jury altogether.[52]

Many appellate court rulings on such mandatory directions to the jury confuse the jury's exclusive control over its own verdict of acquittal with the larger question of the jury's power to decide all questions of law. An example is *State v. Ragland* (1986)[53] in which the New Jersey Supreme Court, by a four-to-three vote, approved an instruction that the jury "must" convict upon finding certain facts true. After surveying state and federal authority on the propriety of using such mandatory language to describe the jury's duty, the majority concluded:

> What emerges from this authority is that the United States Constitution does not appear to invalidate such a charge; that state authority is divided— although, on balance, sustaining its propriety.

> We conclude that the power of the jury to acquit despite not only overwhelming proof of guilty but despite the jury's belief, beyond a

reasonable doubt, in guilt is not one of the precious attributes of the right to trial by jury. It is nothing more than a power.[54]

The New Jersey court's description of the many different ways courts' jury instructions have curtailed the jury's constitutional prerogative is revealing:

> To summarize what we found in this review of recent [jury] charges, we shall refer to the "standard" charge as taking the form "if you find a, b and c beyond a reasonable doubt then you ____ find the defendant guilty; but if you do not find a, b and c beyond a reasonable doubt, then you ____ find defendant innocent." The most common forms of this standard charge use either must-must (in other words "must find defendant guilty" and "must find defendant innocent") or should-should. There is also a liberal sprinkling of will-will, and a whole combination of mixes (should-must, must-should, shall-shall, will-would, would-will, etc.). The phraseology "it would be your duty" is also sometimes used, as is "entitled to be acquitted." These different forms are sometimes found in the same case. In the cases we reviewed, some judges never used "must," some used "must" and "will," and aligned them with "must" and "will" on the innocent side, some mixed it up with "should" for guilty and "must" for innocent and then "must" for guilty and "should" for innocent. The combinations and permutations are obviously numerous.[55]

This "Tower of Judicial Babel" would be humorous were the stakes not so high. The existence of so many variations reveals judicial uncertainty and unevenness from court to court and from jurisdiction to jurisdiction. Only a clear constitutional resolution can curb this confusion. A bit of candor from the courts is called for as well.

> In the final analysis, the best answer to all this nonsense was written long ago by Justice Cardozo. He observed in a related context that he had no objection to giving a jury greater latitude with their verdict in a case that "seems to call irresistibly for the exercise of mercy, but it should be given to them directly and not in a mystifying cloud of words."[56]

The three-justice minority in the New Jersey court's decision in *Ragland* correctly observed that the right to an impartial jury—one free to reach its own verdict on guilt or innocence—is plainly undercut:

> [T]his so-called must-charge implicated not simply the jury's independent role in making findings of fact, but its singular responsibility for determining ultimate criminal guilt or innocence.[57]

> An instruction possessing this compulsive connotation stands at variance with the fine discretion that a jury must exercise when considering the myriad factors, definable and indefinable, obvious and subliminal, that bear upon the ultimate determination.[58]

To the minority, the issue was not whether to tell the jury of its nullification power; instead, the three dissenting justices found that the "must" instruction was clearly coercive:

> [I]t simply does not follow, from the absence of a right to an instruction that the jury may nullify the law, that no compulsion results from an instruction that the jury must convict.[59]

The opinions in *Ragland* frame the issues well: (1) whether the discretionary power to acquit against the facts and the law should be accorded constitutional status (apart from the question of "nullification at large"); and (2) whether judges can, consistent with the jury's constitutional role, instruct the jury in ways that compel a guilty verdict.

C. Legal Commentators

Many students and observers of the modern jury agree that the jury's prerogative to acquit is an important component of the criminal defendant's Sixth Amendment right to trial by jury.[60] I will highlight three recent defenses of this critical function. Jeffrey Abramson traces the history of the jury's power to defy judges' instructions to acquit and describes the important political role that jurors play (or at least should play) in the uniquely American democratic process. He writes that the fact-law distinction that judges have constructed to describe the roles of jurors and judges has weakened the jury as an institution, producing "deadening" and "mechanical" descriptions of the jury that defy history and the Constitution.[61] Emphasizing the role of individual and collective conscience in judging guilt, Abramson concludes:

> To permit juries to show mercy by not enforcing the law in a given case is hardly to destroy the fabric of a society under law. Indeed, putting pressure on jurors to convict against their conscience would seem to threaten the integrity of the law far more seriously. Our current system, in which we tell jurors they must apply the law in every case no matter how unjust the results seem to them, opens the chasm between law and popular beliefs that the jury system exists to prevent.[62]

Rejection of jurors' power to acquit solely as a matter of conscience causes Abramson to wonder whether it is not "a rejection of the idea of the jury altogether."[63]

Nancy Marder, who has written extensively about juries, offers two different conceptions of the modern jury in her recent article on jury nullification.[64] Her first model is the "traditional" jury, the view most compelling to judges and attorneys, in which jurors are restricted to finding the facts and applying the law. The broader role, the "process" view, envisions a jury that does more than find facts and apply the law—it also plays a political role. The jury's process function includes interpreting facts and law, and engaging in a dialogue with political actors "through which it informs them when they have overstepped their bounds, and it does this through nullification. Under this view, when the jury nullifies, it provides feedback to the other branches, rather than usurping their functions."[65]

> To ask [the juror] to vote contrary to his conscience would make jury duty into a more burdensome task that it already is. Also, to ask citizens to serve as jurors because they introduce a community sense into the decision-making, and then to say that they are to act "like a computer" and simply follow the law and not bring their own notions of justice to the process is to undercut one of the reasons for calling upon ordinary citizens rather than professional judges to make these decisions.[66]

According to Marder, "the conventional view offers a parsimonious view of the jury"; the process view is one "that is consistent with how the jury works in practice."[67]

The third piece I want to highlight is by a well-known federal trial judge.[68] Senior Judge Jack B. Weinstein, of the Eastern District of New York, is a recognized authority on federal procedure and evidence. Judge Weinstein states his premise at the outset of a 1993 article:

> Nullification is but one legitimate result in an appropriate constitutional process safeguarded by judges and the judicial system. When juries refuse to convict on the basis of what they think are unjust laws, they are performing their duty as jurors. Once judges and courthouse personnel have set the stage and parameters for fair decision-making, the result is not nullification but vindication of the process.[69]

His views are buttressed by his faith in both jurors and the group decision-making process in which they participate:

> Juries are charged not with the task of blindly and mechanically applying the law, but of doing justice in light of the law, the evidence presented at trial, and their own knowledge of society and the world. To decide that some outcomes are just and some are not is not possible without drawing upon personal views. . . . Given the procedural safeguards and requirements of group decision-making, we can remain confident that, first, instances of nullification will continue to be rare, and, second, if twelve individuals decide to "nullify," they will have a good reason for so doing.[70]

Jurors are able to make the nuanced kind of moral judgments that legislators, who enact laws of general applicability, cannot. Judge Weinstein concludes by characterizing nullification as "one of the peaceful barricades of freedom."[71]

IV. THE ETHICAL ISSUES RAISED BY THE "MUST CONVICT" INSTRUCTION

No thoughtful observer of the American jury can deny that jurors have the raw power to acquit despite judicial instructions to the contrary. How, then, can one justify judges consistently telling jurors the contrary, that they have no choice but to convict when the proof is evident?

As we have seen, judges can point to an abundance of case law in support of their position, and there is no contrary holding from the Supreme Court. But the judiciary cannot claim that their message to jurors comports with reality. From the founding of the nation to the current day, the instruction and the judicial rationalizations behind that instruction have variously been described as absurd, dishonest, deceptive, and discreditable.[72] This ubiquitous, but mistaken, practice has caused many to question the integrity and credibility of the entire criminal justice system.[73]

I do not intend to suggest that individual judges (including this former trial judge) should be disciplined for continuing to charge juries in this manner. Even if they are not on the side of angels on the issue, judges must follow the case law that sanctions the instruction's use. Moreover, conventional rules of judicial ethics distinguish between legal errors correctable on appeal and sanctionable misconduct.[74] Nevertheless, judges have been disciplined for a pattern of rulings that deny criminal defendants their constitutional rights and thereby bring the judiciary into disrepute.[75] Interestingly, a California trial judge was removed from the bench for telling a jury to find a defendant guilty.[76]

Although individual judges should not be deemed personally culpable for helping perpetuate the myth that jurors can not find contrary to the evidence and the law, one is left to consider the potential, if not real, corrosive effects the practice has on the public's faith and trust in a judicial system that tolerates the falsehood.[77] Judges, of all public officials, should be especially concerned with, and be seen being faithful to, the truth.[78] Those in positions of public power must remain mindful of the effects of deception "upon the deceived and social trust."[79] Judges who see themselves as protecting against the certain anarchy that would result were jurors told the truth about their power are behaving much like other public officials, who (too often) choose not to level with the public out of concern that the latter could not, or would not, understand the stakes involved and would lack the judgment to respond correctly to the truth.[80] In addition, neither history nor research supports judges' concerns about the "anarchy" that would follow from jurors being dealt with honestly on the subject.[81] As a result, judges arrogate constitutional power to themselves that an informed public would not likely give up voluntarily. If the judiciary does not trust the jury to exercise its constitutional prerogative wisely, then "we must re-examine a great deal more than just the nullification doctrine."[82]

V. CREATING SPACE FOR THE EXERCISE OF
COMMUNITY CONSCIENCE

(1) A Minimalist Approach to Resolving the Problem

If one agrees with my second proposition—that when jurors hear "must" in describing their duty to return a guilty verdict, their constitutional independence and power are compromised and the right to an impartial jury is denied—the question arises how best to instruct the jury at trial. One approach is to say nothing, or next to nothing, about the jury's option of finding the defendant guilty. However, since no one seriously suggests that juries should not be instructed concerning their verdict options, I will first look at an instruction that communicates the reasonable doubt standard while avoiding the dangerous semantic jungle of "must," "duty," "should," and so forth. Why not simply tell the jury, after explaining the presumption of innocence and the reasonable doubt standard, "Before returning a verdict of guilty, all of you must agree that the guilt of the defendant for the crime charged has been proven beyond a reasonable doubt," and leave it at that? This is the course chosen by the instruction suggested in a popular federal practice manual.[83] A similar instruction would inform the jury that "A verdict of guilty is authorized only if all of you agree that the defendant's guilt has been proven beyond a reasonable doubt."

These "minimalist" approaches to instructing juries on their constitutional prerogative hardly seem fitting to the occasion. Their principal short-coming is that they fail to inform the jurors that they *do* have the power. However, these alternatives may be better than affirmatively misleading the jury on the question.[84] That is about all that can be said for telling the jury so little on the subject.

(2) A More Elaborate Instruction Can Safely Provide Jurors with Needed Guidance

The "minimalist" approach fails to inform jurors explicitly of their prerogative and offers them no guidance whatsoever for its wise exercise. Jurors deserve better and need more regarding the role the Constitution had in mind for them. The case law on the necessity and propriety of explicitly instructing juries regarding this form of nullification power is, of course, almost uniformly opposed to dealing with the subject openly and honestly. The leading case on the question is *United States v. Dougherty.*[85] The two opinions, the majority by Judge Leventhal and the dissent by Judge Bazelon, constitute a tour de force on the historical and modern (as of 1972) views toward jury power and the role of the court in dealing with it.

The majority in *Dougherty* rejected a broader form of nullification charge that would have informed the jurors they could disregard the trial judge's instructions because (1) it feared that the number of jury nullifications would increase to the point of anarchy, (2) it viewed jury nullification as anti-democratic, and (3) it felt an instruction unnecessary because the jurors would likely know of this power anyway. Judge Bazelon, in his dissent, dealt rather convincingly with the majority's positions. Specifically, he observed that there is not such a serious disconnect between the public and the law that nullifications would rise to the level feared by the majority; nullifying juries can make positive contributions to law-making; and one cannot safely assume that jurors will know or learn of their constitutional verdict options absent an explicit instruction.[86]

Although *Dougherty* involved a defense request for an instruction on "the jury's nullification power," and the court did not expressly address a narrower instruction regarding the residual nullification power to acquit out of conscience, the arguments for and against such an instruction are fully articulated in the two opinions. The same arguments—pro and con— are made regarding the narrower question addressed in this chapter.

One of the majority's contentions—that anarchy would result if juries were told of their power—warrants special mention here. Substantial social science research has been done and reported on the question since *Dougherty* was decided, and the data collected on this phenomenon do not support opponents' worst fears. Studies of mock juries that are given affirmative nullification instructions report that while jurors who are given affirmative nullification instructions are more likely to discuss issues of conscience in deliberations—and acquittals increase in cases in which strong appeals to conscience might be expected—overall rates of acquittals and hung juries do not increase dramatically.[87]

Anarchy did not materialize in England following the 1792 passage of Fox's Libel Act, which enlarged the jury's nullification role in cases covered by the law.[88] Nor is there reason to believe that the American public is "at war" with the law.[89] In most cases that are tried, where jurors' self-interest in seeing the law enforced is apparent, they will convict.[90] Even when rules departures occur, and judges cannot explain the verdicts by reference to the instructions, "it is usually because [juries] are serving some of the very purposes for which they were created and for which they are now employed."[91] Two prominent students of the contemporary jury have noted this important role of the jury:

> The jury is an instrument of the formal legal structure—law does matter— and jury decisions generally mirror those of its judicial counterpart. But much of the value and vitality of the jury, embedded in the legal rules and structures that only partially restrain it, lies in the jury's power to, and indeed in the expectation that it will on occasion, deviate from formal doctrinal paths or from what a judge would do. In that role, the jury acts as a safety valve able to respond to the particulars of an individual case without disturbing or creating legal precedent.[92]

Given the many suggestions that have been made, it is possible to craft an honest, straightforward—not to mention constitutional—instruction that reflects our trust in the jury and gives jurors some needed guidance when they struggle to resolve tensions between law and conscience. There are some who do not favor giving such affirmative instructions generally, but would reserve them for "exceptional cases," where issues of conscience are most likely to arise.[93] Some would bifurcate the trial to accommodate such instructions,[94] while others would allow nullification only as an affirmative defense.[95] Among the problems posed by these latter suggestions are the obvious definitional ones (for example, what is an "exceptional" case?). There are also problems related to process (for example, who decides?), and concerns about complexity. If left to trial judges to decide, this power of the jury to acquit as a matter of conscience will most likely remain caged.

Instructing jurors in a manner consistent with the Constitution would be an admirable step and would seem to be reward enough. But there are other important benefits as well. Removing jurors' "blindfolds" regarding the law and the effects of their decisions can have beneficial consequences, not the least of which is the demonstration of respect for the jury.[96] An instruction telling the jury of its constitutional power and giving jurors some guidelines for its wise exercise will also strengthen jurors' respect for the criminal justice system and assist them in reaching more rational, thoughtful, and deliberate verdicts.[97] The equity function of the jury will be enhanced and confusion, caprice, and bad faith reduced.[98] The knowledge gained by jurors will promote equal justice across equally well-informed juries and among cases with similar appeals to conscience.[99]

Last, if the court doesn't instruct the jury concerning its powers in ways consistent with the Constitution, interest groups may well fill the vacuum with their own versions of the jury's prerogatives framed in ways to suit the particular group's aims.[100]

An explicit instruction should be truthful, comprehensible, helpful, and constitutionally and legally accurate. Such an approach will resonate well in Alexis de Tocqueville's "peoples' classroom," where, it is said, jury service "raises the people itself . . . to the bench of judicial authority [and] invests the people . . . with the direction of society," making them "all feel the duties which they are bound to discharge towards society."[101] Finally, the instruction should impress upon jurors that the law applicable to the case comes from the judge, that the law should be given serious consideration, and that the power to acquit despite the law should be reserved for the exceptional cases that present jurors with strong issues of conscience.[102] Obviously, the determination whether a particular prosecution rises to that level should be the jury's.

A number of such jury instructions are suggested in the recent literature about jury nullification.[103] Each has its own strengths and weaknesses. Some stress the role of juror conscience, some do not; some might be read to allow frequent departures from the instructions given the jurors, others focus more narrowly on their verdict option of guilty. The instructions I recommend for consideration borrow heavily from at least two of these recent studies.[104] My recommendations are also influenced by the other recent literature and contain some further editing to suit my style for communicating with jurors:

1. A suggested short form:

> To reach a verdict that you believe is just, each of you must consider all the evidence presented at trial along with the law as I have given it to you. In addition, you may rely on your own common sense, your conscience, and your knowledge of your larger community. If you determine that the defendant has been proven guilty beyond a reasonable doubt, but you cannot in good conscience support a guilty verdict, you cannot be required to do so. However, you should exercise with great caution your power to find not guilty a defendant whose legal guilt has been proven.

2. A somewhat more elaborate suggestion:

> It is presumed by our system of criminal justice that juries are the best judges of the facts. Accordingly, you are the sole judges of whether, considering all the evidence, the defendant's guilt has been proven beyond a reasonable doubt.
>
> Because judges are presumed to be the best judges of the law, you must accept my instructions as being correct statements of the generally accepted legal principles that apply in a case of this type.
>
> These principles are intended to help you in reaching a fair result in this case. You are also entitled to act upon your conscientious feeling about what is a fair result in this case and acquit the defendant if you believe strongly that conscience and justice require a verdict of not guilty. No one can require you to return a verdict that does violence to your conscience.
>
> However, you should exercise with great caution your power to find not guilty a defendant whose legal guilt has been proven. Give due regard to the letter of the law as the expression of intention by lawmakers that persons proven to have violated the law be found guilty of the crime. Only in the most unusual case, where a verdict of guilty would offend strongly held notions of justice, should you acquit an otherwise guilty person.
>
> You should exercise your judgment and examine your conscience without passion or prejudice, but with honesty and understanding. Give respectful consideration to my instructions on the law, as they will help you in arriving at a conscientious determination of justice in this case. This is your highest duty as a juror, as representatives of the public, and as officers of this court.

The second and longer instruction was based in part on one approved by the Kansas trial judges and printed in the handbook of pattern instructions for use in criminal trials in that state.[105] It was accompanied by the following official comment:

> Arguably, the above instruction should bring into play the underlying value of trial by jury: The application of community conscience. If extenuating circumstances make an otherwise culpable act excusable, a jury should feel empowered to so find. Community standards are more apt to be applied if the jurors are told they are free to do what, overall, seems right to them.[106]

This Kansas instruction was short-lived. The Kansas Supreme Court disapproved of it just two years after it was published.[107] The court adopted the orthodoxy on jury nullification followed by almost all other state and lower federal courts:

> The administration of justice cannot be left to community standards or community conscience but must depend upon the protections afforded by the rule of law. The jury must be directed to apply the rules of law to the evidence even though it must do so in the face of public outcry and indignation. Disregard for the principles of established law creates anarchy and destroys the very protections which the law affords an accused.[108]

Both the instructions I have suggested appear to satisfy the requirements of truthfulness, comprehensibility, helpfulness, and legal accuracy. Both convey the idea that jury nullification by returning a not guilty verdict contrary to the court's instructions should be the exception. Their use should be followed by rigorous empirical evaluation, so that their effects can be assessed scientifically rather than left to guesses, assumptions, and anecdotes.

VI. OTHER CHALLENGING ISSUES REMAIN

Considerations of time and space require me to leave for future discussion and resolution several important and difficult issues that arise should the views expressed here prevail. Many of these problems are addressed by others and deserve further serious consideration by still more friends of the jury. Chief among the remaining problems are: (1) whether potential jurors should be disqualified from serving because of their views on nullification;[109] (2) whether, how, and when counsel will be permitted to advocate for and against nullification;[110] (3) whether rules of evidence ought to be revised to admit evidence relevant to the jury's nullification power;[111] (4) whether deliberating jurors who declare an intention to consider nullifying the law after hearing the case should be removed for cause;[112] (5) whether "race-based" nullification should be accommodated;[113] (6) how to instruct juries that decide sentencing issues,[114] including if not especially those that impose death sentences;[115] (7) how to accommodate "sentencing nullification" itself;[116] (8) whether and how nullification works to the detriment of crime victims and how to ameliorate that;[117] and the application of jury nullification at the grand jury stage.[118]

A less difficult issue is presented by some jurors' oaths that require a verdict "according to the evidence and the law."[119] If jurors are told of their power and right to return a verdict of not guilty despite the evidence and the law's definition of the crime, there may be confusion because of the oath. If conflict persists, the oath's language and purported requirements must give way to accommodate the Constitution.

VII. CONCLUSION

A different conception of the jury is offered by the discussion here. Consistent with the several procedural reforms proposed for the jury trial in the past decade,[120] I have offered a view of the jury that is based on trust in jurors and in the institution of trial by jury, one that sees jurors as thoughtful citizens capable of playing a larger and more effective role at trial and in the democratic process.[121] It rejects the views of many judges and lawyers—and some academics—who "too frequently develop an ahistorical, vocational understanding of trial by jury."[122]

Instructing jurors that they do not have the limited power of nullification the Constitution grants them is not the first attempt by judges and lawyers to assume power at the expense of the jury, [123] and it probably will not be the last. From the fourteenth century and the emergence of professional judges and lawyers to modern times, legal administrators have sought to impose controls on the jury and jury trials that would constrain the jury and enhance the power of those trained in the law. Some of the measures were blatant grabs for power that did not survive the test of time—for example, the imprisonment of jurors until they returned a "correct" verdict. Many other forms of jury control proved to be of such utility that they persist as standard practices today: rules of evidence, jury selection procedures, and instructions on the law and review of the verdict by appeal. Still other controls—for example, enforced juror passivity during trial—are being questioned and modified in light of new knowledge and experience.

At least three factors distinguish judicial efforts to prevent verdicts of conscience from most of the earlier attempts by judges and lawyers to constrain lay jurors: (1) arguably, a constitutional violation is involved when jurors are told they "must" convict; (2) this refusal to accommodate jury power restricts jury prerogatives precisely where they are needed most—where the government invokes the powerful machinery of the criminal justice system; and (3) the judiciary's insistence on misleading the jury and the public at large concerning their power and responsibilities in our democracy.

We revere the institution of trial by jury and greatly value the right. We should trust ourselves and our fellow citizens enough to move the reality closer to the constitutional ideal.

NOTES

This essay was prepared for and delivered at the conference, "Jury Ethics: Juror Conduct and Jury Dynamics" sponsored by the John Jay College of Criminal Justice and held in September 2003. I am indebted to the conference organizers, Professors James P. Levine and John Kleinig of John Jay, and the other conference attendees for their insightful comments and suggestions as well as their needed encouragement. I am also grateful to Professor Shari Seidman Diamond, who responded so ably to this essay.

1. *Recommended Arizona Jury Instruction* 5 (1989) (RAJI Crim. 5), emphasis added. In 1995, the Arizona Supreme Court disapproved of the definition of reasonable doubt in RAJI Crim. 5, but left intact language mandating a guilty verdict upon proof satisfying the reworded standard. *State v. Portillo*, 182 Ariz. 592, 898 P.2d 970.

2. *Horning v. District of Columbia*, 254 U.S. 135, 138 (1920).

3. Jack B. Weinstein, "Considering Jury 'Nullification': When May and Should a Jury Reject the Law to Do Justice," *American Criminal Law Journal* 30 (1993): 239, 254.

4. William L. Dwyer, *In the Hands of the People* (New York: St. Martin's Press, 2002), 62–63, 73; Alan Scheflin and Jon Van Dyke, "Jury Nullification: The Contours of a Controversy," *Law and Contemporary Problems* 43 (1980): 55–56.

5. For example, the Fully Informed Jury Association (FIJA) advocates for the broadest possible form of jury authority to decide questions of law. See http://www.fija.org/. For a discussion of FIJA's views and activities and judicial reactions to them, see, generally, Nancy J. King, "Silencing Nullification Advocacy Inside the Jury Room and Outside the Courtroom," *University of Chicago Law Review* 65 (1998): 433. The role and history of jury nullification in trials of civil cases are beyond the scope of this chapter. Useful accounts include Larry Alexander, Robert P. George, and Frederick Schauer, "Developments in the Law: The Civil Jury," *Harvard Law Review* 110 (1997): 1408, 1429–32; Lars Noah, "Civil Jury Nullification," *Iowa Law Review* 86 (2001): 1601; and Noel Fidel, "Preeminently a Political Institution: The Right of Arizona Juries to Nullify the Law of Contributory Negligence," *Arizona State Law Journal* 23 (1991): 1.

6. Jeffrey Abramson, *We, the Jury: The Jury System and the Ideal of Democracy* (New York: Basic Books, 1994); Dwyer, *In the Hands of the People*; Mark DeWolfe Howe, "Juries as Judges of Criminal Law," *Harvard Law Review* 52 (1938): 582; Scheflin and Van Dyke, "Jury Nullification," 55.

7. See, e.g., Abramson, *We, the Jury*, 68; Weinstein, "Considering Jury 'Nullification,'" 253; Darryl K. Brown, "Jury Nullification within the Rule of Law," *Minnesota Law Review* 81 (1997): 1149. Some "inexplicable" acquittals may result from the jury's misapprehension of the law or resolution of issues of mixed fact and law. These are not examples of nullification either. See Norman J. Finkel, "Commonsense Justice and Jury Instructions," *Psychology, Public Policy, and Law* 6 (2000): 591, 599–600; Joel D. Lieberman and Bruce D. Sales, "What Social Science

Teaches Us about the Jury Instruction Process," *Psychology, Public Policy, and Law* 3 (1997): 589, 620–22.

8. E.g., Abramson, *We, the Jury*, 57–88; Howe, "Juries as Judges of Criminal Law"; Scheflin and Van Dyke, "Jury Nullification"; Weinstein, "Considering Jury 'Nullification'"; Albert W. Alschuler and Andrew G. Deiss, "A Brief History of the Criminal Jury in the United States," *University of Chicago Law Review* 61 (1994): 867; Finkel, "Commonsense Justice and Jury Instructions."

9. It has been suggested that these race-based acquittals are not proper examples of nullification because the juries were not validly constituted on account of systematic exclusion of African Americans. Brown, "Jury Nullification within the Rule of Law," 1192–93.

10. Fidel, "Preeminently a Political Institution," 56 n. 379, citing diary entry, February 12, 1771, in *Life and Works of John Adams*, ed. Charles F. Adams, vol. 2 (Boston: Little, Brown & Co., 1850), 253–55.

11. *Strickland v. Washington*, 466 U.S. 668, 695 (1984).

12. *Dunn v. United States*, 284 U.S. 390, 393 (1932).

13. *Jackson v. Virginia*, 443 U.S. 307, 317 n. 10 (1979).

14. *Harris v. Rivera*, 454 U.S. 339, 346 (1981).

15. E.g., *Duncan v. Louisiana*, 391 U.S. 145, 155–56 (1968); *Williams v. Florida*, 399 U.S. 78, 100 (1970) (this interpositional role is the "essential function of the jury"); *United States v. Martin Linen Supply Co.*, 430 U.S. 564, 572 (1977) (their "overriding responsibility"); *Sullivan v. Louisiana*, 508 U.S. 275, 281–82 (1993) (the "right reflects . . . a profound judgment"); *Jones v. United States*, 526 U.S. 227, 245–48 (1999) (historically, attempts to limit opportunities for juror nullification have failed); *Apprendi v. New Jersey*, 530 U.S. 466, 477–78 n. 5 (2000) (power to acquit in the face of guilt finds its origins in common law tradition; called "'pious perjury' on the jurors' part" by William Blackstone).

16. *Jones v. United States*, 246–47; see, generally, Abramson, *We, the Jury*, 73–75.

17. *Duncan v. Louisiana*, 155–56, citing Patrick Devlin, *Trial by Jury* (London: Stevens & Sons, 1956), 164.

18. *Duncan v. Louisiana*, 156.

19. "[T]he most recent and exhaustive study of the jury in criminal cases concluded that juries do understand the evidence and come to sound conclusions in most of the cases presented to them and that when juries differ with the result at which the judge would have arrived, it is usually because *they are serving some of the very purposes for which they were created and for which they are now employed.*" *Duncan v. Louisiana*, 157 n. 26, citing Harry Kalven Jr. and Hans Zeisel, *The American Jury* (Boston: Little, Brown, 1966), 4 (emphasis added).

20. E.g., *In re Winship*, 397 U.S. 358, 363 (1970) (jurors render verdict "upon their consciences"); *United States v. Gaudin*, 515 U.S. 506, 514 (1995) (jurors' ultimate duty is to reach a verdict "as their own consciences may direct," citing Chief Justice Marshall's jury charge in the trial of Aaron Burr).

21. *Gregg v. Georgia*, 428 U.S. 153, 199–200 n. 50 (1976).

22. Abramson, *We, the Jury*, 60, 90. See Wayne R. LaFave, Jerold H. Israel, and Nancy J. King, *Criminal Procedure* (St. Paul, MN: West Group, 1999), Sec. 22.1(g).

23. *Sparf v. United States*, 136 U.S. 51 (1895).

24. *United States v. Gaudin*, 515 U.S. 506, 511–15 (1995) (*Sparf* does "not support [the] . . . concept of the criminal jury as mere factfinder.").

25. E.g., Abramson, *We, the Jury*, 90–92 ("Conscientious acquittals" are "in fact the time-honored way of permitting jurors to leaven the law with leniency."). See LaFave, Israel, and King, *Criminal Procedure*.

26. *United States v. Gaudin*, 513 ("Our decision [in *Sparf*] in no way undermined the historical and constitutionally guaranteed right of criminal defendants to demand that the jury decide guilt or innocence on every issue, which includes application of the law to the facts."). See Abramson, *We, the Jury*, 68.

27. Clay S. Conrad, *Jury Nullification: The Evolution of a Doctrine* (Durham, NC: Carolina Academic Press, 1998), 298–99; Norman J. Finkel, *Commonsense Justice: Jurors' Notions of the Law* (Cambridge, MA: Harvard University Press, 1995), 336–37; Abramson, *We, the Jury*, 95; and James P. Levine, *Juries and Politics* (Pacific Grove, CA: Brooks/Cole, 1992).

28. See text accompanying notes 30–35 *infra*; Abramson, *We, the Jury*, 90.

29. Alschuler and Deiss, "A Brief History of the Criminal Jury in the United States," 916–17. See Conrad, *Jury Nullification*, 301–2 ("The distinction between jury 'rights' and jury 'powers' is nonsensical and should be discarded. A legal power that can be exercised with legal impunity is a legal right.").

30. *Federal Jury Practice & Instructions, Pattern & Model Jury Instructions* (Criminal) Sec. 21 (Federal Judicial Center, 1988). Cited approvingly in a concurring opinion in *Victor v. Nebraska*, 511 U.S. 1, 27 (1994) (Ginsburg, J.), this instruction has been adopted by some state courts, e.g., *State v. Portillo*, 182 Ariz. 592, 898 P.2d 970 (1995). Importantly, neither the FJC's commentary nor these opinions addressed use of the word "must" in the FJC instruction. It does not appear that the precise question was raised in the two cases.

31. E.g., *Farina v. United States*, 622 A.2d 50 (D.C. App. 1993); *People v. Goetz*, 73 N.Y.2d 751, 536 N.Y.Supp.2d 45, 532 N.E.2d 1273 (1988) ("It is well settled that the jury's function is to apply the legal definition of the crime to the evidence and convict if it is satisfied that each of the elements of the crime has been established."); *State v. Ragland*, 105 N.J. 189, 519 A.2d 1361 (1986) (same; case collected).

32. E.g., *United States v. Hanley*, 974 F.2d 14 (4th Cir. 1992)("duty to convict" instruction upheld); *United States v. Pierre*, 974 F.2d 1355 (D.C. Cir. 1992) (same). The instruction approved for use in the Sixth Circuit suggests the "middle course" by adopting the "say so" approach, as in, "if satisfied that the government has proved the defendant guilty beyond a reasonable doubt, *say so* by returning a guilty verdict." *Federal Jury Practice & Instructions, Pattern Criminal Jury Instructions: Sixth Circuit*, 1.03 (1991), emphasis added.

33. E.g., *Watts v. United States*, 362 A.2d 706 (D.C. App. 1976).

34. *United States v. Spock*, 416 F.2d 165, 181 (1st Cir. 1969). See Conrad, *Jury Nullification*, 301 (An impartial jury is lost if the judge can direct jurors concerning their verdict.).

35. *United States v. Martin Linen Supply Co.*, 572–73; *Standefer v. United States*, 447 U.S. 10, 23 (1980).

36. *United States v. Gaudin*.

37. *United States v. Muse*, 83 F.3d 672, 679–80 (4th Cir. 1996).

38. *United States v. Muse; United Brotherhood of Carpenters & Joiners of America v. United States*, 330 U.S. 395, 408 (1947) (citing, with approval, the dissent in *Sparf*, at n. 21); *United States v. Garaway*, 425 F.2d 185 (9th Cir. 1970). See, generally, Chaya Weinberg-Brodt, "Jury Nullification and Jury-Control Procedures," *New York University Law Review* 65 (1990): 825.

39. *United States v. Spock*, 180–83 ("There is no easier way to reach, and perhaps force, a verdict of guilty than to approach it step by step."); *State v. Surrette*, 130 N.H. 531, 544 A.2d 823, 825 (1988) ("Any such direction to the jury, however subtle, denies the defendant an impartial jury.").

40. *United States v. Spock*, 181–82.

41. *Horning v. District of Columbia*, 138.

42. *Horning v. District of Columbia*, 139.

43. *Horning v. District of Columbia*, 140.

44. *Horning v. District of Columbia*, 139.

45. Compare *Brasfield v. United States*, 8 F.2d 472, 473 (9th Cir. 1925) (conviction affirmed, citing *Horning*, despite the presiding judge's stated preference for a guilty verdict) with *Billeci v. United States*, 184 F.2d 394 (D.C. Cir. 1950) (*Horning* distinguished; reversal where verdict followed "must find guilty" instruction to jury).

46. *United States v. Gaudin*, 520.

47. 420 F.2d 142, 144 (D.C. Cir. 1969).

48. 494 U.S. 299 (1990).

49. 42 Pa. Cons. Stat. 9711(c)(1)(iv) (emphasis added).

50. *Furman. v. Georgia*, 428 U.S. 238 (1972)

51. *Jurek v. Texas*, 428 U.S. 262 (1976).

52. 184 F.2d 394, 403 (D.C. Cir. 1950).

53. 105 N.J. 189, 519 A.2d 1361 (1986).

54. 105 N.J. 199, 204–5, 519 A.2d 1366, 1369.

55. 105 N.J. 200 n. 4, 519 A.2d 1366 n. 4.

56. James J. Duane, "Jury Nullification: The Top Secret Constitutional Right," *Litigation* 22 (1996): 6, 11, citing Benjamin Cardozo, "What Medicine Can Do for Law," in *Law and Literature* 70, 100 (1931) (quoted in *McGautha v. California*, 402 U.S. 183, 199 [1971]).

57. 105 N.J. 217, 519 A.2d 1375.

58. 105 N.J. 220, 519 A.2d 1377. Can there be a serious question whether jurors will treat "must" and "duty" other than as a mandatory direction? Jurors naturally defer to the professional judge, who is an expert in the law and the singular authority figure in the courtroom. See Nancy S. Marder, "The Myth of the Nullifying Jury," *Northwestern University Law Review* 93 (1999): 877, 944.

59. 105 N.J. at 222, 519 A.2d at 1378. See Weinstein, "Considering Jury 'Nullification,'" 252 (favors instruction that the jury "should (not must) find the defendant guilty if all the elements of the case have been proved beyond a reasonable doubt.").

60. See, generally, Abramson, *We, the Jury*, 57–67, 85–95 ("timeless strategy of bringing law into line with their consciences"); Finkel, "Commonsense Justice and Jury Instructions," 337; Conrad, *Jury Nullification*, 297–303; Levine, *Juries and Politics*, 101–8; Marder, "The Myth of the Nullifying Jury"; Darryl K. Brown, "Jury Nullification within the Rule of Law"; Duane, "Jury Nullification"; Weinstein, "Considering Jury 'Nullification'"; Lisa Kern-Griffin, "The Image We See Is Our Own: Defending the Jury at the Heart of the Democratic Process," *Nebraska Law Review* 75 (1996): 332, 348–52, 361–65; Coleen P. Murphy, "Integrating the Constitutional Authority of Civil and Criminal Juries," *George Washington Law Review* 61 (1993): 723, 769; Alschuler and Deiss, "A Brief History of the Criminal Jury in the United States"; David C. Brody, "*Sparf* and *Dougherty* Revisited: Why

the Court Should Instruct the Jury of Its Nullification Right," *American Criminal Law Review* 33 (1995): 89. See LaFave, Israel, and King, *Criminal Procedure*, sec. 24.10 (the power of the jury to acquit despite the facts and law "may be of constitutional dimension").

61. Abramson, *We, the Jury*, 90.

62. Abramson, *We, the Jury*, 92.

63. Abramson, *We, the Jury*, 93.

64. Marder, "The Myth of the Nullifying Jury."

65. Marder, "The Myth of the Nullifying Jury," 925–26. On occasion, juries add their own unsolicited thoughts and desires to the verdict form to inform the other branches and the public at large. Jerry Markon, "MS-13 Jury Hoped to Deter Others," *Washington Post*, June 16, 2005, B05.

66. Marder, "The Myth of the Nullifying Jury," 933–34. Others have drawn an analogy between the jury's political role and the voters' repudiation of candidates' unpopular policies at the ballot box, e.g., Robert F. Schopp, "Verdicts of Conscience: Nullification and Necessity as to Crimes of Conscience," *Southern California Law Review* 69 (1996): 2039, 2055; Joseph L. Sax, "Conscience and Anarchy: The Prosecution of War Resisters," *Yale Review* 57 (1968): 481, 494.

67. Marder, "The Myth of the Nullifying Jury," 956.

68. Weinstein, "Considering Jury 'Nullification,'" 239, 254. See, in addition, Jack B. Weinstein, "The Many Dimensions of Jury Nullification," *Judicature* 81 (1998): 168.

69. Weinstein, "Considering Jury 'Nullification,'" 240.

70. Weinstein, "Considering Jury 'Nullification,'" 244–45.

71. Weinstein, "Considering Jury 'Nullification,'" 254.

72. *Legal Papers of John Adams*, ed. L. Kinvin Wroth and Hiller B. Zobel (Cambridge, MA: Harvard University Press, 1965), 230 (it is "an absurdity to supose that the law would oblige [jurors] to find a verdict according to the direction of the court, against their own opinion, judgment, and conscience"); Howe, "Juries as Judges of Criminal Law," 616 (this "deceptive ingenuity" by judges is "discreditable" to the profession); Abramson, *We, the Jury*, 67 (instruction can deceive jurors); Brody, "*Sparf* and *Dougherty* Revisited," 110–11 (a "dishonest and irresponsible" judicial practice); *United States v. Dougherty*, 473 F.2d 1113, 1139 (D.C. Cir. 1972) (a "deliberate lack of candor" by judges) (Bazelon, J., dissenting).

73. Conrad, *Jury Nullification*; Duane, "Jury Nullification" (hypocritical to refuse to instruct jurors truthfully regarding their verdict options); Bradley J. Huestis, "Jury Nullification: Calling for Candor from the Bench and Bar," *Military Law Review* 173 (2002): 68.

74. Jeffrey M. Shaman, Steven Lubet, and James J. Alfini, *Judicial Conduct and Ethics*, 2nd ed. (Charlottesville, VA: Michie Law, 1995), Sec. 2.02, 32–37.

75. Shaman, Lubet, and Alfini, *Judicial Conduct and Ethics*, Sec. 2.02, 32–37.

76. *McCullough v. Commission on Judicial Performance*, 49 Cal.3d 186, 776 P.2d 259 (1989).

77. Schopp, "Verdicts of Conscience," 2046–47.

78. Sissela Bok, *Lying: Moral Choice in Public and Private Life* (New York: Vintage Books, 1979), 89 ("When judges . . . are caught in a fraud, the sense of betrayal is great.").

79. Bok, *Lying*, 172–73.

80. Bok, *Lying*, 177.

81. See text accompanying footnotes 87–92 *infra*.

82. Weinstein, "Considering Jury 'Nullification,'" 244 (quoting Judge Bazelon's dissent in *United States v. Dougherty*, 1142).

83. Kevin F. O'Malley, Jay E. Grenig, and William C. Lee, *Federal Jury Practice and Instructions, Criminal*, 5th ed. (St. Paul, MN: West Group, 2000), sec. 12.10.

84. See Abramson, *We, The Jury*, 64; Marder, "The Myth of the Nullifying Jury," 958; Scheflin and Van Dyke, "Jury Nullification," 105–6. "I see no justification for, and considerable harm in, this deliberate lack of candor" (Judge Bazelon, dissenting in *United States v. Dougherty*, 1139.

85. 473 F. 2d 1113 (D.C.Cir. 1972).

86. See, in addition, John Guinther, *The Jury in America* (Washington, D.C.: Roscoe Pound Foundation, 1988), 226 ("When jurors are told they *must* do something by the . . . judge, the probability is that under this judicial compulsion they are not very likely to remember John Peter Zenger or similar lessons in freedom they may have learned in their history classes.") (emphasis in original).

87. E.g., Irwin A. Horowitz, Norbert L. Kerr, and Keith E. Niedermeier, "Jury Nullification: Legal and Psychological Perspectives," *Brooklyn Law Review* 66 (2001): 1207; Dennis J. Devine, Laura D. Clayton, Benjamin B. Dunford, Rasmy Seying, and Jennifer Pryce, "45 Years of Empirical Research on Deliberating Groups," *Psychology, Public Policy, and Law* 7 (2001): 622; Lieberman and Sales, "What Social Science Teaches Us about the Jury Instruction Process," 622; and Irwin A. Horowitz, "The Effect of Jury Nullification Instruction on Verdicts and Jury Functioning in Criminal Trials," *Law and Human Behavior* 9 (1985): 25.

88. Sax, "Conscience and Anarchy," 488.

89. Valerie P. Hans and Neil Vidmar, *Judging the Jury* (New York: Plenum Press, 1996), 154–55, 163 ("The hard facts indicate that on the whole the jury behaves responsibly and rationally."); Levine, *Juries and Politics*, 105–8; Guinther, *The Jury in America*, 226; Paula L. Hannaford-Agor and Valerie P. Hans, "Nullification at Work? A Glimpse from the National Center for State Courts' Study of Hung Juries," *Chicago-Kent Law Review* 78 (2003): 101, 118; Shari Seidman Diamond and Jason Schklar, "The Jury: How Does Law Matter?" in *How Does Law Matter*, ed. B. Garth and A. Scott (Evanston, IL: Northwestern University Press, 1998): 191, 211–13.

90. Sax, "Conscience and Anarchy."

91. *Duncan v. Louisiana*, 391 U.S. 145, 157 n. 26 (1968).

92. Diamond and Schklar, "The Jury," 215.

93. E.g., John C. Coughenour, "Canary in the Coal Mine: The Importance of the Trial Jury," *Seattle University Law Review* 26 (2003): 399, 423–25; David N. Dorfman and Chris K. Iijima, "Fictions, Faults, and Forgiveness: Jury Nullification in a New Context," *University of Michigan Journal of Law Reform* 28 (1995): 861, 918–25.

94. Dorfman and Iijima, "Fictions, Faults, and Forgiveness," 919–23 (they separate fact-finding from issues of conscience).

95. Andrew D. Leipold, "Rethinking Jury Nullification," *Virginia Law Review* 82 (1996): 253, 312–23.

96. See Stephan Landsman, "The Jury's Role in Administering Justice in the United States: Of Mushroom and Nullifiers," *St. Louis University Public Law Review*

21 (2002): 65, 79–80 ("For the jury to fulfill . . . [its constitutional] roles, it must be treated with respect. Respect seems ever harder to secure the more jurors are consigned to the fate of mushrooms."). Cf. Shari Seidman Diamond and Neil Vidmar, "Jury Room Ruminations on Forbidden Topics," *Virginia Law Review* 87 (2001): 1857, 1907–14 (given the likelihood that the subject of insurance will arise in and may affect jurors' deliberations when nothing is told them on the subject, a sounder behavioral approach is to treat the jury collaboratively and instruct them in a straightforward manner on the subject).

97. Dorfman and Iijima, "Fictions, Faults, and Forgiveness," 925–27; Scheflin and Van Dyke, "Jury Nullification," 114–15.

98. John Clark, "The Social Psychology of Jury Nullification," *Law & Psychology Review* 24 (2000): 39.

99. Schopp, "Verdicts of Conscience," 2046–47.

100. Nancy Marder, "Juries, Drug Laws, and Sentencing," *Journal of Gender, Race, and Justice* 6 (2002): 337, 372–77.

101. Alexis de Tocqueville, *Democracy in America* (New York: Shocken, 1961), 1334–37. This is probably the most frequently mentioned observation of Tocqueville's evaluation of the American jury. See, e.g., *Powers v. Ohio*, 499 U.S. 400, 406–7 (1991).

102. Clark, "The Social Psychology of Jury Nullification."

103. E.g., Conrad, *Jury Nullification*, 135; Marder, "The Myth of the Nullifying Jury," 957–58; Duane, "Jury Nullification," 10; Robert E. Korroch and Michael J. Davidson, "Jury Nullification: A Call for Justice or an Invitation to Anarchy?" *Military Law Review* 139 (1993): 131, 147–48; Brody, "*Sparf* and *Dougherty* Revisited," 121–22; Scheflin and Van Dyke, "Jury Nullification," 53–55, 64–65.

104. Korroch and Davidson, "Jury Nullification"; Scheflin and Van Dyke, "Jury Nullification," 64–65.

105. *Pattern Instructions for Kansas* (1971), 51.03, at 36. The last sentence in the third paragraph is my addition. (The original instruction is quoted and discussed in Scheflin and Van Dyke, "Jury Nullification," 64.)

106. *Pattern Instructions for Kansas* (1971), 51.03, at 36.

107. *State v. McClanahan*, 212 Kan. 208, 510 P.2d 153 (1973).

108. 212 Kan. at 216, 510 P.2d at 159.

109. Compare King, "Silencing Nullification Advocacy Inside the Jury Room and Outside the Courtroom" and Marder, "The Myth of the Nullifying Jury."

110. Compare King, "Silencing Nullification Advocacy Inside the Jury Room and Outside the Courtroom" and Marder, "The Myth of the Nullifying Jury."

111. Weinstein, "Considering Jury 'Nullification'"; Elizabeth Stoffelmayr and Shari Seidman Diamond, "The Conflict between Precision and Flexibility in Explaining Beyond a Reasonable Doubt," *Psychology, Public Policy, and Law* 6 (2000): 769, 782–84. Cf. Robert D. Bartels, "Punishment and the Burden of Proof in Criminal Cases: A Modest Proposal," *Iowa Law Review* 66 (1981): 899 (sentencing range relevant to jury's determination of "guilt beyond a reasonable doubt").

112. See Note, "The Second Circuit's Attack on Jury Nullification in *United States v. Thomas*: In Disregard of the Law and the Evidence," *Cardozo Law Review* 20 (1999): 1275.

113. Differing views on "race-based nullification" are available: compare Paul Butler, "Racially Based Jury Nullification: Black Power in the Criminal Justice

System," *Yale Law Review* 105 (1995): 677, with Marder, "The Myth of the Nullifying Jury," 937–43.

114. See, generally, J. J. Prescott and Sonja Starr, "Improving Criminal Jury Decision Making after the *Blakely* Revolution," University of Michigan Olin Center for Law and Economics, Paper #05-004 (2005): http://papers.ssrn.com/sol3/papers.cfm?abstract_id=680682.

115. See discussion of *Blystone v. Pennsylvania,* text accompanying footnotes 48–51 *infra.*

116. Thought to be rare historically, recent decisions and legislative developments injecting juries more into sentencing proceedings (e.g., *Blakely v. Washington,* 124 S. Ct. 2531 [2004]) may result in increased nullifications for reasons relating to the potential sentence. Compare Kamipono David Wenger and David A. Hoffman, "Nullificatory Juries," *Wisconsin Law Review* (2003): 1115, and Prescott and Starr, *supra* n. 114.

117. For a discussion of the potential of jury nullification to work to the detriment of crime victims, see Schopp, "Verdicts of Conscience," 2103–10.

118. See *United States v. Navarro-Vargas,* __ F. 3d __, 2005 WL 1206632 (9th Cir. May 23, 2005) (no error in instructing grand jurors that they "must" indict upon showing of probable cause); but see Susan W. Brenner, "The Voice of the Community: A Case for Grand Jury Independence," *Virginia Journal of Social Policy and Law* 3 (1995): 67 (such instructions negate the grand jury's constitutional nullification power).

119. E.g., Arizona's jurors' oath, Rule 18.6(b), *Arizona Rules of Criminal Procedure* (required to swear or affirm that they will "abide by the court's instructions . . . and render a verdict in accordance with the law").

120. See Landsman, "The Jury's Role in Administering Justice in the United States," 75–76 ("The basic thrust of [the reforms] is the empowerment of the jury . . . [helping] jurors become more deeply engaged in each step of the fact gathering and decision making process.").

121. See B. Michael Dann, "'Learning Lessons' and 'Speaking Rights': Creating Educated and Democratic Juries," *Indiana Law Journal* 68 (1993): 1229.

122. Conrad, *Jury Nullification,* 297. See, generally, Marder, "The Myth of the Nullifying Jury" (one's view of the jury, "conventional" or "process," affects how one approaches jury nullification).

123. Dann, "'Learning Lessons' and 'Speaking Rights,'" 1231–36.

When Ethics and Empirics Are Entwined: A Response to Judge Dann's Nullification Proposals

Shari Seidman Diamond

Jury nullification, defined as occurring when a jury acquits "in the teeth of both law and facts,"[1] has stimulated both enthusiastic praise[2] and harsh condemnation.[3] Although there is no clear account or tabulation of how often juries nullify, the effect when a jury nullifies is unambiguous: It ends the case. A court, even if convinced that the jury ignored or misinterpreted the facts or the law, cannot reverse an acquittal. It is indisputable that, whether nullification promises justice beyond the law or merely represents lawlessness, juries possess significant power in their ability to nullify.

The controversies about nullification then lie not in the question of whether juries actually have this power, but in whether they have the right to nullify and whether they should be informed about their power to nullify. Courts uniformly reject requests to instruct juries about their nullification power.[4] Some legal scholars take a more benign view of nullification,[5] but the academic community—with some notable exceptions—generally resists such explicit instruction.[6] Against this background, is Judge Dann tilting at windmills to advocate that judges should inform jurors about their undisputed power, recognizing nullification as a right?

Courts sometimes suggest discomfort with the directions they give to jurors about the jury's obligation to follow the law. Thus, courts have occasionally rejected explicit instructions that seem to deny that juries have any discretion.[7] Nonetheless, despite that discomfort, courts consistently balk at explicitly describing that discretion.[8] Some scholars have argued in favor of instructing the jury on nullification,[9] and Dann has recently added his distinctive voice in favor of straight talk on nullification to jurors. And Dann is no Don Quixote.[10] He has shown that, in other areas, courts will significantly change the way they handle jurors and jury trials when they are led by someone who provides the thoughtful leadership he supplied in Arizona.[11] His chapter in this volume is appropriately viewed as an opening shot in what it likely to be a serious and focused attack. Grounding his argument in both constitutional and ethical terms, he forcefully argues that judges not only are constitutionally permitted to tell jurors about their nullification power, but also that they are ethically required to tell jurors that they are entitled to acquit on grounds of conscience.[12]

The thrust of my alternative perspective here is both ethical and empirical. One aspect of this ethical perspective shares Dann's vision: We should not lie to jurors, as we regularly do now, about what they must do. I also put myself in the camp of those who celebrate occasional instances of jury nullification as a crucial safety valve in the criminal justice system.[13] Other ethical concerns, however, are introduced by Dann's proposal to instruct explicitly on nullification. We have an ethical obligation to consider proposed changes in light of the unintended costs they may produce. Based on an analysis of the empirical evidence on nullification, I am not sanguine about embarking on a path of dramatic reform grounded on what we currently know about the potential effects of instructions on nullification. To anticipate the potential costs of explicitly informing jurors about their nullification role, I analyze the empirical evidence we currently have and what we still need to know in order to justify a radical change in our treatment of jury nullification. I also suggest an alternative strategy that in the end may accomplish much of what Dann advocates without entangling the judiciary in an awkward and potentially harmful role.

Before turning to the potential results of a nullification instruction, it is important to have a clear picture of the idealized version of nullification that is under discussion here. With characteristic care, Dann is aiming at a specific and limited form of nullification. It occurs when the jury follows the judge's instructions in applying the law until their final decision: After determining that all of the elements of the crime have been proved beyond a reasonable doubt, the jury nonetheless decides to acquit on the basis of conscience.[14] Under this formulation, nullification would never *increase* the likelihood of a conviction. Nor would it give the jury a license to decide what the law should be. It would only produce an acquittal in exceptional cases in which the jury finds the application of the law to the particular offender/offense to be unjust. It is against this standard that we are evaluating whether a carefully crafted instruction can achieve the desired result.[15]

I. LYING TO JURORS

We often try to prevent jurors from obtaining information they would like to have (for example, does the non-testifying criminal defendant have a criminal record; does the defendant in a civil case have insurance?). The rules of evidence are designed to control what jurors learn in an attempt to channel and control the decisions they reach. Instructions about the law are similar constraints, although scholars have often complained that instructions fail to inform jurors fully and clearly about the law they are expected to apply.[16]

These complaints are quite different from an objection that may be raised when an instruction explicitly tells jurors a lie. Yet lying clearly occurs when a judge says: "If you are satisfied that the defendant's guilt has been proven beyond a reasonable doubt, then you *must* find the defendant guilty" (emphasis added). This last step, as Dann accurately observes, is a lie because in the American legal system a jury can acquit at this point and that decision cannot be overturned by any court.[17] As an ethical matter, such a blatant lie delivered to the citizens who serve as jurors by the state's official representative in the courtroom seems unconscionable.[18] The difficult question that remains is: What *should* courts say in light of the effects that these various alternative formulations are likely to have?

II. ALTERNATIVES TO THE LIE

The simplest approach would be merely to omit the lie. Simply excising the lie, however, would leave the instruction incomplete. The jury instruction must connect the jury's determination of the defendant's guilt to the verdict if the jury is to be informed about how to reach its verdict. Of course, the jury may simply equate a finding of guilt with a guilty verdict, but that also would leave no room under any circumstances for nullification. Alternatively, the instruction could accurately substitute: "Before returning a verdict of guilty, all of you must agree that the guilt of the defendant for the crime charged has been proven beyond a reasonable doubt." Such an instruction—outlining the necessary, but not sufficient, ground for a conviction—avoids an explicit effort to block the door to nullification with deceit. But it is admittedly minimalist, and Dann believes that we should go further in instructing juries if jurors are constitutionally entitled to nullify.[19]

Indeed, some empirical evidence suggests that more drastic steps are required if the intent is to share useful information about nullification with the jury. In a classic nullification study by Irwin Horowitz, jury-eligible respondents heard evidence in one of three criminal cases (a standard robbery-murder, a drunk driving case involving vehicular homicide, and a euthanasia case in which a sympathetic nurse was tried for the mercy killing of a terminally ill cancer patient). The jurors were instructed one of three ways. They either received no instruction on nullification, heard an instruction concerning nullification that informed the jurors that they could reject the judge's instruction to reach a just verdict (Moderate Nullification Instruction),[20] or heard a nullification instruction that explicitly told jurors that they had the authority not to apply the law and that nothing would bar them from acquitting if they felt the law would produce an unjust result (Radical Nullification Instruction).[21] The Moderate Nullification Instruction had no effect on juror or jury verdicts in any of the three cases. In contrast, the more radical instruction significantly reduced guilty verdicts in the euthanasia case. Moreover, a content analysis of the deliberations indicated that the juries in the moderate instruction condition, unlike those who received the radical instruction, seemed hardly aware of the nullification possibility. Thus, Horowitz's results suggest that in order to increase juror awareness of their power to nullify, instructions must contain a strong and explicit message. Indeed, a strong message is what Dann advocates.

III. THE POTENTIAL BENEFITS AND COSTS OF A POTENT NULLIFICATION INSTRUCTION

If we grant that an acquittal in a mercy killing may be a justifiable use of jury nullification, the lower rate of conviction by jurors in that case in Horowitz's study demonstrates a potential benefit of the potent nullification instruction. A cost of the instruction would arise if it induced increased acquittals more generally, in less morally defensible situations. Horowitz showed, however, that jurors who received the radical nullification instruction in a case involving the killing of a grocery store owner during a robbery were just as likely to convict the defendant as those who received no instruction on nullification. These results suggest that an instruction on nullification would be unlikely to open the floodgates and produce a mass of unwarranted acquittals.[22]

Another cost emerged, however. The third case in Horowitz's study involved a vehicular homicide resulting from drunk driving. The defendant hit and killed a pedestrian walking along the shoulder of the road on a freeway exit. It was 1 A.M. and there was some fog. Jurors who received the radical nullification instruction were *more* likely to convict than those who did not receive the instruction. Recall that the instruction explicitly told the jurors that "nothing would bar them from acquitting the defendant if they felt that the law, as applied to the fact situation before them, would produce an inequitable or unjust result." The instruction said nothing that would justify harsher treatment for a defendant whom the jurors found to be particularly morally reprehensible. Why then were the jurors harsher on the drunk driving defendant when they received the radical nullification instruction? One likely explanation is that the nullification instruction implicitly released the jurors from the yoke of legal obligation that ordinarily tied their decisions closely to the legal requirements outlined in the other jury instructions.

Courts regularly use jury instructions in an attempt to control and direct jury behavior, but they have generally used a minimalist approach that appears to prefer obscurity to clarity. Why have the courts been so hesitant to say what they mean? One explanation is that typical jury instructions are the products of compromises between adversarial constituencies: Both prosecutors and defense attorneys as well as judges sit on the committees that write the pattern jury instruction in most states—a useful way to ensure balance, but not a recipe for clear and unambiguous communication.

Another more benign explanation may be a recognition that the jury's good judgment is often a reasonable alternative to an instruction that must necessarily lack nuance or invite unjustified reactions, like the increased conviction rate that Horowitz's research suggests might be the product of a nullification instruction. Before advocating an instruction on nullification, it makes sense to evaluate whether it is likely to confuse or otherwise cause mischief.

IV. DANN'S NULLIFICATION INSTRUCTIONS

In his attempt to provide clear guidance on nullification, Dann suggests two jury instructions, a short form and a second more elaborate version.[23] The suggestions are somewhat different from those tested by Horowitz, so it is possible that the Dann instructions would produce a different pattern of results. The Dann instructions both appeal to the jurors to do justice with a reference to conscience and community (in the longer version, "as representatives of the public") after the jury has considered the evidence and the law. While the references to justice, conscience, and community were present in the radical instruction that Horowitz and his colleagues tested, Horowitz's jurors were not told that they should first consider the evidence and the law. In addition, Dann's instructions include an admonition to exercise caution in acquitting if guilt has been proven. Horowitz did not include an explicit appeal to restraint. How would these differences affect juror reactions? We cannot tell without testing them.

Moreover, an additional ethical problem lurks in the instruction systems that Horowitz tested, as well as in the proposed instruction approaches recommended by Dann. Both appeal to conscience and community. The concerns that arise here stem from the less benign aspects contained in such appeals. Consider as an example a defendant who is on trial for the murder of a physician at an abortion clinic. The evidence strongly supports a conviction. For jurors who believe that abortion is tantamount to murder, would an instruction that authorizes them to acquit based on conscience make them more likely to acquit the defendant? Should we encourage that form of nullification? Note that the juror might believe in advance that she is willing to convict based on the evidence, that she rejects murder as an appropriate form of activism, and that she will follow the law, so that she could justifiably survive any challenge for cause during jury selection. Nonetheless, in response to a nullification instruction that appeals to her conscience and legitimates an acquittal, she would presumably be authorized—even invited—*under the law* to acquit the otherwise guilty defendant.

The proposed nullification instructions also invite the jurors to use their community as a reference point in deciding whether to nullify. The radical instruction used by Horowitz refers to the "feelings of the community" and

Dann's proposed short-form instruction calls on the jurors to rely on "your knowledge of your larger community" as well as your conscience and common sense. If we consider again our hypothetical juror deciding whether to nullify by acquitting the defendant on trial for murder of the abortion clinic doctor, the reference to community may further validate nullification if the juror considers her community to be composed of like-minded members. I suspect that Dann attempts to avoid this definition of community by referring to the "larger" community.[24] Even if the larger community is in fact generally opposed to nullification as an appropriate response in this situation, a juror in this scenario may succumb to the false consensus effect— the tendency for people to overestimate the extent to which others share their opinions.[25] Ordinarily the other members of the jury should eliminate or at least reduce that effect if they do not share the juror's position because the views of the other jurors are more available during deliberations than those of any non-jurors, but the proposed instructions provide a counter-weight to that dynamic. The reference to community invites a group reference to those outside the jury. The false consensus effect does not occur when people are asked about members of groups other than their own.[26] Thus, the nullification reference to community encourages the juror to search for support from his own community outside the jury room, giving less weight to the reactions of his fellow jurors.

How often would such a circumstance arise? Would the occasional occurrence be rare enough to be overshadowed by the benefits associated with encouraging the more celebratory instances of nullification? Here again empirical input would assist in informing ethical decision making.

V. THE IMPACT ON CONSISTENCY

Nullification instructions pose another ethically significant question in making their appeal to conscience. Do they invite unwarranted variation in jury decision making? A similar question arose in *Sandoval v. California* (1994) when the U.S. Supreme Court considered a set of disputed instructions about the definition of "beyond a reasonable doubt."[27] The definition equated lack of "reasonable doubt" with "moral certainty." Sandoval argued, among other things, that jurors might be "morally certain" that a defendant is guilty even when the government has not proved the defendant's guilt beyond a reasonable doubt. The Court found that any error stemming from the phrase "moral certainty" was corrected by other language in the instructions, but acknowledged that the "moral certainty" language was not optimal. We lack empirical evidence on how people actually understand and apply the phrase, but the appeal to moral certainty, like an appeal to conscience, appears to encourage the use of a person's individual moral standards. The important difference is that the nullification appeal to conscience logically should encourage only acquittal,[28] while moral certainty as a definition for lack of reasonable doubt can stimulate unwarranted convictions as well as acquittals. Both, however, may invite inconsistency, that is, treating similar cases differently depending on the particular consciences or moral preferences of the jurors deciding the case.

Should inconsistency trouble us? A common image of an ideal legal system would treat all similarly situated defendants the same. Thus, any system that encourages or even permits instances of nullification allows that power to undermine the desirable consistency of that ideal legal system. It is important, however, to distinguish among various types of inconsistency. Some inconsistency will arise in any human decision-making process. Jurors differ in the way they judge credibility and evaluate evidence, based on their backgrounds and life experiences. So do judges. When the variations are substantial, however, the legal decisions appear arbitrary and that inconsistency can undermine the sense of order and equal treatment that contributes to the legitimacy of the law. At this point, it appears unlikely that nullification, even authorized with a jury instruction, would affect most garden-variety criminal offenses.[29]

A second type of disparity can arise if decisions are influenced by legally impermissible characteristics, such as the race of the defendant. That systematic inconsistency, or bias, is the kind of discrimination that the legal system attempts to discourage. If, for example, a nullification instruction increased acquittals for sympathetic white defendants, but had little or no effect on the acquittals of minority defendants, it would encourage impermissible discrimination.

We have some limited evidence that such systematic bias in nullification rates is unlikely from a series of four studies by Keith E. Niedermeier, Irwin Horowitz, and Norbert L. Kerr.[30] In the first three experiments, they studied the effects of a defendant's ethnicity, gender, and professional status (hospital medical director versus resident) on the willingness of mock jurors to acquit a sympathetic physician who was technically guilty of the crime of transfusing a patient with blood unscreened for the HIV virus under extenuating circumstances. They varied whether the jurors were or were not instructed on nullification and found, as expected, that the extralegal characteristics of the defendant affected verdicts and the nullification instruction reduced the overall rate of convictions. Importantly, however, the extralegal characteristics in all but one instance did not influence the effect of the nullification instruction.[31] Moreover, in their fourth study, involving an ordinary case of assault in a bar, they found that a nullification instruction did not affect verdicts either overall or as a function of the defendant's ethnicity. These results provide some support for predictions that nullification instructions would not promote inconsistency in the form of discrimination, but none of these studies examined race, the most common and arguably the most pernicious form of discrimination.

VI. BALANCING INTERESTS

If we agree that some occasions ought to invite jury nullification to temper the hard edges of the law, Dann offers an appealing way to make it easier for jurors to use their power to nullify. His proposals set a challenging research agenda because they suggest a set of important and intertwined normative and empirical questions that need to be addressed in order to inform any drastic change. First, how often and under what circumstances does nullification occur, and how often and under what circumstances should it occur? Second, how can we best produce optimal exercise of the nullification power? As my review of the limited empirical literature on nullification indicates, we have only begun to address the relevant empirical questions.

What I want to suggest here is that if we have concerns about overuse of nullification and about the danger of increased convictions for unsympathetic defendants when judges signal to jurors that they can base their verdicts on conscience to achieve justice, there is an alternative to judicial instructions. The alternative would be to modify judicial instructions in the minimalist way so that courts do not explicitly mislead jurors, and then to permit defense attorneys to make nullification arguments to the jury. In most courts, nullification arguments are not currently permitted. By permitting defense attorneys to argue for nullification, judges would not undermine their legitimacy by deceiving jurors, and would avoid explicitly encouraging nullification.

We have some evidence for what the effect of this approach would be. In a follow-up study to his earlier work on nullification instructions, Horowitz tested the impact of defense attorney arguments for nullification in the presence or absence of a court instruction sanctioning nullification.[32] The nullification arguments of the defense attorney did increase the tendency of the juries to nullify in the two cases involving a sympathetic defendant, but defense attorney arguments had a more modest effect than did a judicial instruction on nullification.

The second advantage of permitting attorney-generated nullification arguments is that they would be tailored to the circumstances of the particular case. If we were to adopt Dann's position that jurors should be told about a right to nullify, the nullification instructions he has proposed would be given as a matter of course in all criminal trials. If, instead, only defense attorneys (and not prosecutors) were given the opportunity to address the subject of nullification, they would be able to decide whether the case for the defense made a nullification plea advantageous, and to argue for nullification only when it appeared likely to assist rather than harm their client. That option may be crucial. In Horowitz's third case, the unsympathetic defendant fared worse when the issue of nullification was raised, whether it was raised by the court or by his defense attorney.[33] In light of the fact that the accused generally is permitted to decide whether or not to have a jury trial, perhaps it is appropriate that the accused retain control over whether the jury will be primed to go beyond the evidence and the law.

In 1986, Stephen J. Herzberg filmed the deliberations of an actual deliberating jury in the case of *Wisconsin v. Leroy Reed.*[34] The case had been selected for filming because the facts indicated it might be a good candidate for nullification. The mentally deficient defendant was on trial for illegally possessing a weapon. The evidence clearly indicated that he possessed a gun in direct violation of the terms of his parole, but there were clear extenuating circumstances that troubled all of the jurors. The judge permitted the defense attorney to make an argument in favor of nullification. After a vigorous and contested deliberation that included discussion about nullification and the jury's role, the jury acquitted. The last juror who agreed to acquit did so with the greatest difficulty. It seems likely that a nullification instruction would have made it easier for him to agree to an acquittal in the case. Yet the struggle to arrive at the verdict appeared to satisfy even this juror. The jury as a whole, assisted by the defense attorney's argument, balanced respect for rule application and attention to the virtues of mercy. As a result, it provided an impressive example of the cautious application of nullification.

VII. CONCLUSIONS

If, as Dann argues, we currently violate the Constitution through judicial efforts to prevent verdicts of conscience, some change in current jury instructions is legally required. Even in the absence of constitutional mandate, Dann persuasively argues that some alteration is warranted to avoid judicial deception. What remains unclear at this point is how to achieve an optimal pattern of jury nullification.

As the analysis here reveals, explicit jury instructions may in some cases legitimize undesirable juror responses and we do not know how often such occasions arise under current conditions and how much more frequently they would arise if, as Dann recommends, jurors were instructed on nullification. We also know that juries occasionally nullify in the absence of explicit permission from the court and even when the court explicitly discourages nullification. Yet we have no estimate of how often nullification actually occurs and we have only a beginning sense of the conditions under which it is most likely to occur.

Before adopting a strategy of explicitly inviting nullification, it is worth learning more about the likely impact of such a dramatic change across a range of cases. In addition, we ought to consider the potential benefits and costs of a nullification instruction in comparison with less radical adjustments, such as permitting defense attorneys to argue for nullification. Finally, it is important in our assessments of what may assist jurors that we recognize the value of simply removing obstacles and depending on the common sense of jurors who are not actively discouraged from doing justice.

NOTES

I am indebted to James P. Levine and John Kleinig, who organized the September 2003 conference at John Jay College of Criminal Justice, "Jury Ethics: Juror Conduct and Jury Dynamics," and to Judge B. Michael Dann, whose thoughtful paper for the conference stimulated this chapter. I am also grateful to the other conference attendees for the lively exchange that contributed to my thoughts on this topic. Of course, none of these scholars is ultimately responsible for the lessons I drew from their ideas.

1. *Horning v. District of Columbia*, 254 U.S. 135, 138 (1920).

2. Jeffrey Abramson, *We, the Jury* (New York: Basic Books, 1994), chap. 2; Akhil Reed Amar, *The Bill of Rights: Creation and Reconstruction* (New Haven, CT: Yale University Press, 1998), 110; Daryl Brown, "Jury Nullification within the Rule of Law," *Minnesota Law Review* 81 (1997): 1149; Jack B. Weinstein, "The Many Dimensions of Jury Nullification," *Judicature* 81 (1998): 168; Nancy S. Marder, "The Myth of the Nullifying Jury," *Northwestern Law Review* 93 (1999): 877.

3. *Strickland v. Washington*, 466 U.S. 668, 695 (1984); *U.S. v. Thomas*, 116 F.3d 606 (2d cir. 1997).

4. *U.S. v. Dougherty*, 473 F.2d 1113 (D.C. Cir. 1972); see also *U.S. v. Thomas*, "Accordingly, criminal defendants have no right to a jury instruction alerting jurors to this power to act in contravention of their duty" (n. 9).

5. See David C. Brody, "*Sparf* and *Dougherty* Revisited: Why the Court Should Instruct the Jury of Its Nullification Right," *American Criminal Law Review* 33 (1995): 89.

6. See Richard R. St. John, "License to Nullify: The Democratic and Constitutional Deficiencies of Authorized Jury Lawmaking," *Yale Law Journal* 106 (1997): 2563.

7. *United States v. Hayward*, 420 F.2d 142 (D.C. Cir. 1969).

8. *U.S. v. Dougherty*.

9. For example, Alan Scheflin and Jon Van Dyke, "Jury Nullification: The Contours of a Controversy," *Law and Contemporary Problems* 43 (1980): 52.

10. B. Michael Dann, "The Constitutional and Ethical Implications of 'Must-Find-the-Defendant-Guilty' Jury Instructions," in this volume, 93–117.

11. For a characteristically modest description of Judge Dann's accomplishments in Arizona, see B. Michael Dann and George Logan II, "Jury Reform: The Arizona Experience," *Judicature* 79 (1996): 280.

12. Although the text reflects the general idea of Dann's proposed jury instructions, the wording that Dann suggests is more elaborate and includes an admonition that the power should be exercised with great caution. For further discussion, see *infra* at note 23.

13. Shari S. Diamond and Jason Schklar, "The Jury: How Does Law Matter?" in *How Does Law Matter?* ed. Bryant Garth (Evanston, IL: Northwestern University Press, 1998), 119, 211.

14. Dann, "The Constitutional and Ethical Implications of 'Must-Find-the-Defendant-Guilty' Jury Instructions," 94.

15. See Alan W. Scheflin, "Mercy and Morals: The Ethics of Nullification," in this volume, 131–72.

16. See Shari S. Diamond and Judith N. Levi, "Improving Decisions on Death by Revising and Testing Jury Instructions," *Judicature* 79 (1996): 224.

17. Dann, "The Constitutional and Ethical Implications of 'Must-Find-the-Defendant-Guilty' Jury Instructions," 104 (Dann actually uses gentler terminology; he says that such instructions are "affirmatively misleading.").

18. Courts have sometimes, but not always, disapproved the "must" language in the instruction, but even Judge Weinstein, a judicial supporter of jury nullification, has merely advocated the substitution of "should" for "must." Weinstein, "The Many Dimensions of Jury Nullification," 168–71.

19. Dann, "The Constitutional and Ethical Implications of 'Must-Find-the-Defendant-Guilty' Jury Instructions," 104.

20. The instruction was: "This is a criminal case and under the constitution and laws of the state of Maryland in a criminal case the jury are the judges of law as well as the facts in this case. So that whatever I tell you about the law while it is intended to be helpful to you in reaching a just and proper verdict in the case, it is not binding upon you as members of the jury and you may accept or reject it. And you may apply the law as you apprehend it to be in the case." Irwin Horowitz, "The Effect of Jury Nullification on Verdicts and Jury Functioning in Criminal Trials," *Law and Human Behavior* 9 (1985): 25.

21. This instruction, based on Jon Van Dyke's proposal ("The Jury as a Political Institution," *Catholic Law Review* 16 [1970]: 224), told jurors they had the final authority to decide whether or not to apply a given law to the acts of the defendant, that they should bring the feelings of the community and their own feelings of conscience to their deliberations, and that nothing would bar them from acquitting the defendant if they felt that the law as applied to the fact situation before them would produce an inequitable or unjust result. Horowitz, "The Effect of Jury Nullification on Verdicts and Jury Functioning in Criminal Trials," 30–31.

22. The murder case in Horowitz's study provided strong evidence of guilt. It would be useful to know whether the nullification instruction would affect the standard of proof applied in a case in which the evidence was somewhat weaker.

23. Dann, "The Constitutional and Ethical Implications of 'Must-Find-the-Defendant-Guilty' Jury Instructions," 107.

24. Dann, "The Constitutional and Ethical Implications of 'Must-Find-the-Defendant-Guilty' Jury Instructions," 107.

25. L. Ross, D. Greene, and P. House, "The False Consensus Phenomenon: An Attributional Bias in Self-perception and Social-perception Processes," *Journal of Experimental Social Psychology* 13 (1997): 279; Joachim Krueger and Russell Clement, "The Truly False Consensus Effect: An Ineradicable and Egocentric Bias in Social Perception," *Journal of Personality and Social Psychology* 67 (1994): 596.

26. B. Mullen, J. E. Davidio, C. Johnson, and C. Cooper, "In-group and Out-group Differences in Social Projection," *Journal of Experimental Social Psychology* 28 (1992): 422.

27. 511 U.S. 1 (1994).

28. But see Horowitz, "The Effect of Jury Nullification on Verdicts and Jury Functioning in Criminal Trials."

29. See Horowitz, "The Effect of Jury Nullification on Verdicts and Jury Functioning in Criminal Trials."

30. Keith E. Niedermeier, Irwin Horowitz, and Norbert L. Kerr, "Informing Jurors of Their Nullification Power: A Route to a Just Verdict or Judicial Chaos?" *Law and Human Behavior* 23 (1999): 313.

31. Jurors, but not juries, were more influenced by a physician's status when they were instructed on nullification.

32. Irwin Horowitz, "Jury Nullification: The Impact of Judicial Instructions, Arguments, and Challenges on Jury Decision Making," *Law and Human Behavior* 12 (1988): 439.

33. Horowitz, "The Effect of Jury Nullification on Verdicts and Jury Functioning in Criminal Trials," 446.

34. Alan M. Levin and Stephen J. Herzberg, *Inside the Jury Room* (Alexandria, VA: PBS Video, 1986). Available through the University of Wisconsin-Madison Law Library.

5

Mercy and Morals:
The Ethics of Nullification

Alan W. Scheflin

Shortly before he was elevated to the highest judicial office in the land, the late Warren Burger kindly appeared in one of my law school classes to talk about the philosophy of judging cases.[1] His central point to the students was that the judicial system could function only on the basis of respect because it had no real enforcement authority. Its prestige had to be its power.

The virtually unanimous rejection by judges of a nullification instruction to jurors[2] creates a serious problem of prestige for the courts. Everyone agrees that juries have the *power* to exercise mercy on the basis of conscience. Opponents of nullification believe that this power is a necessary though unfortunate by-product of the jury's nonreviewable authority to acquit, and it is tolerated only because of this historical or procedural anomaly. Proponents disagree and argue that the power to nullify is beneficial and, because that power exists, jurors should have the *right* to be instructed about it.[3] In that way, of course, there would be no dispute that jurors would be obeying the judge's instructions, and judges could fairly and clearly articulate the difference between valid nullification and impermissible emotion, bias, or sympathy.

The judicial attitude toward nullification has been bipolar, a point eloquently made by Chaya Weinberg-Brodt:

> At the same time courts characterize nullification as wrongful, they also characterize juries as "the conscience of the community," "instruments of public justice," and a "safeguard against arbitrary law enforcement." In their attack on any and all incidents of jury nullification, judges miss the justification for juries even as they pronounce it. Jury independence ensures that the presumptions and perceptions of individual jurors, not judges, are controlling.[4]

In recent years, perhaps due to increasing public knowledge about nullification, judges have felt it necessary to do more than simply tolerate nullification. Toleration has been replaced by active suppression, thereby sending judges, and all of the participants in the legal arena, on an unfortunate and dangerous slippery legal and ethical slope. The debate over the *power* versus the *right* of juries to nullify is not a matter of semantics. In the balance hangs juror respect for the system of justice, as well as the ability of juries to deliver fair verdicts. My intent in this chapter is to identify some of the legal difficulties and ethical dilemmas that necessarily ensue from the judicial decision to deny jurors the instruction that they have the power or the right to nullify in cases of conscience. The efforts to eliminate nullification have the effect of diminishing the prestige of the judicial system, thereby placing in jeopardy the justice it must be capable of delivering in order to earn the respect of the community it serves.

I. JUDGE

Judges have always had an uneasy relationship with juries, who may see cases differently from the way in which judges do.[5] Some judges have urged the abolition of the jury system; others have sought more modestly to reduce the jury's influence by limiting the types of cases brought before them. Still others have advocated that jury size be reduced, and the requirement of a unanimous verdict be abolished. As commentators universally have recognized, the jury system entered the nineteenth century with enormous law-making powers, but left that century substantially more subservient to judicial control.[6] Judges' refusal to offer a nullification instruction may be seen as a continuation of this process of the emasculation of the independence of juries from governmental control.

One commentator has stated that "even if jury nullification is not a 'right' whose exercise is encouraged and protected, it is still something more than a power. Indeed, it is not true that nullification is a completely lawless act: it is neither punished nor controlled in the American legal system. . . . Courts have upheld trial judges' refusals to sanction nullification but have been unwilling to go any further, so as not to invade the secrecy of jury deliberations."[7] There is increasing evidence that this judicial restraint is no longer practiced, and that judges are now quite willing to "go further."

A. Intrusion into Jury Deliberations

Judicial inquiry into jury deliberations is a delicate subject. Courts have a duty to investigate allegations of juror misconduct or incapacity,[8] but they cannot impermissibly intrude into the process by which a jury reaches its verdict. Intrusion could be viewed as an attempt to shape or unduly influence the contours of the way in which jurors decide cases, thereby interfering with their privacy and their freedom to engage in unfettered discussions leading to rendering a verdict. The concern with impermissibly influencing or shaping the way jurors deliberate arose in *United States v. Spock* (1969),[9] where the court concluded that the judge's use of a special verdict in a criminal case—which required jurors to answer specific questions rather than return a general guilt or innocence verdict—was held to be an improper attempt to guide the manner in which jurors reached their conclusions.[10] While refraining from examining juror deliberations is an important virtue, a rule prohibiting any inquiry might result in prejudiced or biased jurors infecting the deliberation process and violating the defendant's constitutional right to a fair trial.

During the course of jury deliberations, may a judge ask about whether a juror is expressing beliefs about nullification or deciding the case on that basis? In *United States v. Thomas* (1997),[11] the prosecutor unsuccessfully attempted to use a peremptory challenge against a person later empanelled as Juror No. 5, who became the only African American juror in a case involving African American defendants.[12] As discussions proceeded in the jury room, several jurors sent notes to the judge that Juror No. 5 was the lone holdout for acquittal. Upon inquiry, the judge discovered a conflict among the other jurors about Juror No. 5's position. One juror thought Juror No. 5 favored acquittal because the defendants were his "people," whereas another juror believed Juror No. 5 thought the defendants were good people. Two jurors understood Juror No. 5 to have said that drug dealing is commonplace, and another two jurors expressed the view that Juror No. 5 favored acquittal because the defendants committed the crime out of economic necessity. Five jurors told the judge that Juror No. 5 argued his view for acquittal in terms of the evidence, believing that the evidence presented by the prosecution was insufficient or unreliable. Speaking for himself, Juror No. 5 "said nothing in his interview with the court to suggest that he was not making a good faith effort to apply the law as instructed to the facts of the case. On the contrary, he informed the court that he needed 'substantive evidence' establishing guilt 'beyond a reasonable doubt' in order to convict."

Based on these facts, the judge removed Juror No. 5 on the grounds that he was ignoring the evidence in favor of his own preconceived ideas about the case, which were that "these folks have a right to deal drugs, because they don't have any money, they are in a disadvantaged situation and probably that's the thing to do." The judge said he doubted that Juror No. 5 "would convict them no matter what the evidence was." The defendants were convicted by the remaining eleven jurors, but not on all of the charges against them.

On appeal, the issue was "whether the district court's primary basis for the dismissal—the juror's intention to disregard the applicable criminal laws—constitutes 'just cause' for his removal under [Federal Rules of Criminal Procedure,] Rule 23(b)." The court held that a juror's intent to nullify constitutes "just cause" and a trial judge "has a duty to dismiss a juror who purposefully disregards the court's instructions on the law." A juror who intends to nullify is no different from a juror "who disregards the court's instructions due to an event or relationship that renders him biased or otherwise unable to render a fair and impartial verdict." However, before a juror may be removed during deliberations, there must be proof "beyond doubt" that the juror intended to disregard the court's instructions.[13] If there is any possibility that the juror was attempting to apply the law but was unpersuaded by the evidence, the judicial inquiry into the deliberations must cease.[14]

In *Thomas*, the court held that the trial judge erred in concluding that Juror No. 5 was purposefully disregarding the court's instructions on the law. Because there was evidence that Juror No. 5 had serious doubts about the defendants' guilt, rather than an intent to nullify the law, he had a valid motive to question whether the defendant should be found guilty.

Thomas at first blush may appear to be a reasonable accommodation between nullification and jury deliberation secrecy.[15] In fact, however, despite its cautious language, it opens the door too widely into the jury room. In a commentary on the case by an author who does not favor nullification, the view is expressed that the *Thomas* court "went too far in identifying the intent to nullify as just cause for dismissal," and too far in "imposing an affirmative duty on judges to use dismissal to prevent nullification."[16] According to the commentator: "Although judges may not and should not encourage nullification, they should not be required actively to prevent it. Such a requirement will result in excessive intrusion into the domain of jury deliberations and will disturb the traditional balance between the competing goals of accurate verdicts and jury secrecy." The *Thomas* decision, by permitting a judge to question jurors about the deliberations, and to remove a juror who might nullify, invites an intense scrutiny of what jurors say and do in the jury room. *Thomas* puts additional, and perhaps irresistible, pressure on jurors who disagree with the majority of their colleagues. And it puts a weapon in the hands of majority jurors to claim that the minority juror is engaging in nullification, thereby effectuating that juror's dismissal.

Thomas involved dismissal of a juror who allegedly engaged in jury nullification. May a trial judge go further and hold this juror in *contempt* for refusing to follow the court's instructions?

In February 1997, Laura Kriho became the first juror in more than 300 years to be convicted of contempt of court based on statements she made during sequestered jury deliberations.[17] Kriho served as a juror in a case involving three alleged violations of the drug laws. The jurors were unanimous that the defendant was guilty on one count and innocent on another count. However, Kriho was the lone holdout for acquittal on the third count. Kriho expressed the opinion to her fellow jurors that the sentence the defendant would face if convicted was excessive. A fellow juror then sent a note to Judge Nieto, who was presiding over the trial. Nieto had instructed the jurors not to consider the possible sentence in their deliberations. A mistrial was declared even though the jurors had reached a verdict on two of the three counts.

Following the mistrial, Kriho, outside the courthouse, handed one of the other jurors a pamphlet that supported jury nullification. The juror receiving the pamphlet gave it to the judge who spoke with several of the jurors. A few of the jurors contacted the prosecutor and he initiated a contempt action against Kriho claiming she disobeyed an order of the court, obstructed the administration of justice, and committed perjury by lying under oath during voir dire. The prosecution alleged that Kriho failed to reveal that she had previously pled guilty to a felony drug charge, that she opposed the enforcement of drug laws through the courts and was actively involved in an organization desiring to modify drug laws, and that she did not intend to follow the judge's instructions on the law. During voir dire, the trial judge had asked if any of the prospective jurors thought they would have problems following the law or if they had any bias regarding the drug laws. They were asked if they had any experiences with the criminal justice system, and they were also asked:

> Would all of you agree to follow my instructions on the law even if you don't agree with them or you don't think that they are what the law is or should be?
>
> * * * * *
>
> What I need from you is a commitment that you will follow my instructions even if you don't agree with them. And you all agree to do that? Follow the instructions on the law? My job is to tell you what the law is, and will you all agree to follow my instructions? Will you all agree? Anyone saying no?[18]

The contempt case was heard by another judge and, over Kriho's objection, a bench trial rather than a jury trial was conducted. The judge found no disobedience and no perjury, but found that Kriho had intended to obstruct the judicial process by preventing the seating of a fair and impartial jury. A prospective juror commits a crime by failing to bring political beliefs or historical knowledge to the attention of the court, even if prosecutors do not ask any specific questions about these topics. Kriho was ordered to pay a $1200 fine.

During oral argument to the Court of Appeals, Colorado Assistant Attorney General Roger Billotte told the judges Kriho had obstructed justice by failing to mention that she favored the legalization of hemp, and that she "hoped to win a slot on the jury to push her political agenda."[19] In fact, as Billotte was aware, Kriho had called the clerk of the court that morning to try to get out of jury service—only to be told she was expected to hitchhike to the courthouse if she did not have a car. Interestingly, while the prosecution argued that Kriho had a political agenda and used deception to secure a place on the jury, Kriho's attorney, Paul Grant, also chose to place politics in the forefront of his argument:

Jurors cannot be told what they must do in the deliberative process. . . . You
can't have trial by jury where you throw out jurors who are independent
thinkers.

＊＊＊＊＊

The jury system was created as a means for citizens to check the power of
their government. . . . Punishing jurors for their beliefs and speech will
destroy the jury system, as will purging juries of all independent-minded
jurors.[20]

The appellate judges expressed concern about the use of information
from jury deliberations as a basis for holding a juror in contempt. In response,
Billotte told the court that Kriho had failed to disclose that she was arrested
when she was nineteen for possession of LSD, a charge that was later
expunged from her record. The judges then asked if there was any other
evidence not related to deliberations to support affirming the conviction.
Billotte responded: "Well, she didn't disclose that she's been active in the
hemp legalization movement." When the judges inquired as to the
prosecutor's voir dire question that should have elicited this answer, Billotte
said, "When she was asked about her hobbies."[21]

Kriho's contempt citation was ultimately reversed on the grounds that
"evidence of jury deliberations should not have been, but was considered
by the trial court in finding Kriho in contempt. Hence, reversal is required
and the cause must be remanded for a new trial."[22] The court approvingly
cited the "*Thomas* court's almost *per se* rule prohibiting intrusions into the
secrecy of the deliberative process." Does this mean that nullification beliefs
expressed by a juror during deliberations are free from judicial punishment,
and that what is said in the jury room cannot be used by the prosecutor as
proof that the juror lied or was not forthcoming during voir dire?

B. Instructions on Nullification[23]

Judges who oppose nullification, such as Judge Harold Leventhal,
acknowledge that although "[t]he pages of history shine on instances of the
jury's exercise of its prerogative to disregard uncontradicted evidence and
instructions of the judge . . . [t]he way the jury operates may be radically
altered if there is alteration in the way it is told to operate."[24] Leventhal
believed that jurors already know of their power to nullify through "informal
communication from the total culture," including literature, television,
newspapers, conversations, and readings of history. These informal sources
convey the idea that jurors are free to depart from the judge's instruction in
rare cases. But, Judge Leventhal's analysis, even if accurate,[25] is ultimately
based on two troublesome propositions. First, it is better for jurors to be
informed, or misinformed, by the media and their friends than to be informed
by the carefully worded and cautious instructions from judges. Second, it is

better for judges to tell jurors a partial truth about their deliberative powers than to tell them the whole truth.

Judges universally fail to inform jurors of their power or right to exercise mercy in cases in which law and justice may be in conflict. May judges go further and instruct a jury *not* to nullify, and instruct the jury to report nullification arguments that occur in deliberations?

1. Anti-Nullification Instruction

In 1998, a new section was added to the California Jury Instructions regarding a juror's obedience to the judge's instructions. Instruction No. 17.41.1 provided: "The integrity of a trial requires that jurors, at all times during their deliberations, conduct themselves as required by these instructions. Accordingly, should it occur that any juror refuses to deliberate or expresses an intention to disregard the law or to decide the case based on . . . any . . . improper basis, it is the obligation of the other jurors to immediately advise the Court of the situation."[26]

Does this jury instruction impermissibly intrude on the deliberations of jurors and adversely impact on their power to nullify? In general, the jury must follow the court's instructions. As stated in California Penal Code section 1126, the jury "receives as law what is laid down as such by the court." A juror who actually refuses to deliberate is subject to discharge by the court,[27] as is a juror who proposes to reach a verdict without respect to the law or the evidence.[28]

The California Supreme Court in *People v. Engelman* (2002)[29] held that an instruction pursuant to section 17.41.1 did not violate the constitutional right to trial by jury. However, according to the court, although giving the instruction did not constitute error in this case, because section 17.41.1 has the potential to encourage unnecessary intrusions into jury deliberations, the instruction should not be given in future trials.

2. Responding to Juror Inquiries

Trial judges do not instruct jurors that they have the power to nullify, and may not tell jurors that they are obligated to report nullification arguments to the trial judge. But what if the jury specifically asks about its authority to nullify? Say, for example, a jury has received the judge's instructions and retires to deliberate its verdict. During the discussions, some jurors express concerns about the potential punishment if the defendant is convicted, or about the justice of stigmatizing the defendant as a criminal. To assist their discussions, the jurors send a note to the judge requesting information about their power to nullify. Should the judge answer truthfully, or should the judge withhold this information?

People v. Nichols (1997) raised, and answered, this question.[30] Although Justice Kaus's concurring opinion in *People v. Dillon* (1983)[31] argued that the judge must answer truthfully that the jurors do have the power to nullify, the majority in *Dillon* expressly rejected disclosure by holding that "in California, trial courts are not required to instruct on the power of jury nullification even if the jury asks whether it has that power."

While *Nichols* involved the refusal to respond to the jury's request for nullification information, some judges have gone further and endorsed the right of trial judges to misinform jurors. In *United States v. Krzyske* (1988), the trial court denied defendant's request for a nullification instruction, but it also denied the government's motion to prohibit the use of this term during the proceedings.[32] The defendant mentioned the doctrine of jury nullification in his closing argument. During its deliberation, the jury asked the court what jury nullification meant. The trial judge said: "There is no such thing as valid jury nullification. Your obligation is to follow the instructions of the Court as to the law given to you. You would violate your oath and the law if you willfully brought in a verdict contrary to the law given you in this case."

On appeal, defendant claimed that the court went too far by specifically telling the jury that there is no such thing as valid jury nullification and failing to inform the jurors of their inherent power to nullify. The appellate court, in refusing to accept this argument, explained that the "right of a jury, as a buffer between the accused and the state, to reach a verdict despite what may seem clear law must be kept distinct from the court's duty to uphold the law and to apply it impartially."[33]

The court's reasoning in *Krzyske* is faulty. The jury could consistently be informed by the judge of the correct law and also informed of its authority to nullify. This instruction would protect both the right of the jury to act as a buffer and the responsibility of the court to instruct on the law. Instead, however, the court misstated the issue by saying that "we are compelled to approve the district court's refusal to discuss jury nullification with the jury. To have given an instruction on nullification would have undermined the impartial determination of justice based on law." The trial court did not simply refuse to discuss nullification, as in *Nichols*, but instead affirmatively distorted the law concerning the jury's authority.

In his dissenting opinion in *Krzyske*, Judge Merritt disagreed with the trial court's handling of the nullification issue, and urged reversal:

> The jury returned to the courtroom concerned about the issue of "jury nullification." The jury wanted to know to what extent it had the right to acquit the defendant because it disagreed with the government's prosecution. It wanted to know what was meant by the idea of "jury nullification." The Court responded by telling the jury that it had no power to engage in jury nullification and that was the end of the matter. It told the jury in effect that it had no general authority to veto the prosecution. This is simply error. The Court should have explained the jury's function in our system. Our Court has made it clear in the past that the jury does have veto power and the jury should have been so instructed.

Judge Merritt lamented the failure to "explain to the jury its historical role as the protector of the rights of the accused in a criminal case." He believed trial courts should "advise the jury, if requested, concerning the jury's 'general veto power,' in accordance with the . . . historical prerogatives of the jury to return a general verdict of not guilty."[34]

Withholding information initially from jurors during the instructions raises substantial legal concerns. Responding incompletely or untruthfully to the jury's direct question, an act of *commission* rather than *omission*, is even more ethically troubling. Judicial failure to give honest and accurate information about nullification, especially when such information is directly requested by the jury, contributes to contamination of jury deliberations.[35] It is a sad irony that while judges continue to refuse to give honest jury nullification instructions, they may be replacing the anarchy they fear with the tyranny the jury system was created to avoid.

C. Dismissal of Prospective Jurors

If intrusion into jury deliberations is impermissible, at least in the absence of extreme circumstances, may prospective jurors be asked about their knowledge or beliefs concerning nullification? When the modern nullification debate began in the 1960s, few people had ever heard of it. Today, by contrast, jury nullification has been the subject of hundreds of media stories, television shows, documentaries, and legal articles. It is taught in various college courses. Some potential jurors may be aware of the nullification power, though they may be mistaken as to its scope. What should the judge do about the fact that jurors may know something accurate or inaccurate about nullification? Will judges purge from jury service every potential juror who states that he or she has heard of nullification?[36]

Judges face a tough issue in regard to what jurors may know, or be mistaken about, concerning nullification. Failure to permit voir dire on this topic may in fact allow jurors to bring their views, mistaken or not, about nullification into the jury room. On the other hand, allowing the defense lawyer or prosecutor to ask questions about nullification on voir dire may alert all of the prospective jurors to this power. The trial judge may decide to give an anti-nullification instruction, but this, of course, may then become a topic of discussion in the jury room.

People v. Merced (2001)[37] raised the question of whether a prospective juror could be dismissed for believing in jury nullification. Question No. 64 on the jury questionnaire asked: "Is there any matter that *has not* been covered by this questionnaire that you feel that you should mention at this time that might affect your ability to be a fair and impartial juror in this case?" A prospective alternate juror (Andrew B.) answered this question as follows: "I recognize and believe in jury nullification where it's appropriate." When Mr. B. was called into the box, the judge stated he appreciated the juror's candor "particularly . . . about jury nullification. I mean, that's your right. I have no problem with that. My question is this: If you are selected on this jury, and if I instructed you as to the law that implies [*sic:* applies] in the state of California and it went against your conscience for whatever reason, is it reasonable for me to assume that you would not follow the law as I dictate it to you?" After Mr. B. responded "It's reasonable for you to assume that," the judge excused him from the jury panel, and later provided the following explanation:

> First of all, Mr. B____, on Line 64, says: [']I recognize and believe in jury nullification where it's appropriate.['] One would never know when in his judgment it's appropriate.
>
> So that's the first thing, he's not inclined to follow the Court's instructions that he must follow if he's selected as a juror. He has a right not to, but I have a right not to let him sit if he's going to engage in jury nullification. So I excused him for that.
>
> The second reason I excused him, if he was selected on this jury I can see down the line four, five weeks from now we would have an issue then where somebody will report to the Court one juror is not following the instructions of the Court, which leads to more issues and more problems. So in order to avoid that issue down the line, if this man is up there and refuses to follow the Court's instructions, then we'd have to go . . . and bring the foreman down, you know, the whole nine yards, the objections. Again, that's a hot-button issue in the Appellate Court. I'm not going to lay the foundation for this happening. The fact that he believes in jury nulli- fication is enough for me as a challenge for cause. That's my justification.

Defense counsel objected to the removal of Mr. B., claiming it violated the defendant's right to a jury of his peers and to due process of law: "Because the jury is the conscience of the community, if one or more jurors simply feel that they do not wish to return a verdict, or that they cannot in good conscience follow the law as the Court gives it, that is the ultimate right of the juror." The trial court overruled this objection based on *People v. Williams* (2001)[38] and *People v. Cleveland* (2001),[39] which held that a juror may be removed from a jury if it appears as a "demonstrable reality" that "the juror is refusing to deliberate or follow the law in an effort to exercise the naked power commonly known as jury nullification." The California Supreme Court in these two cases concluded that such a juror is "unable to perform his duty" within the meaning of Penal Code section 1089. In *People v. Merced*, defense counsel argued that the "demonstrable reality" standard, which applies to sitting jurors, should also apply to prospective jurors, but this argument did not persuade the court, which noted that this standard had never been so applied. Instead, the excusal of a *prospective* juror for cause is reviewed under the far less rigorous "abuse of discretion" standard. Defense counsel then argued that Mr. B.'s general statement about nullification made no reference to the issues or the law in the pending case, and therefore excusal for cause was inappropriate. However, the *Merced* court held that the trial judge was reasonable in construing Mr. B.'s response to Question No. 64 "as fair warning that the prospective juror might not follow the law as instructed by the court. That answer, on top of Mr. B.'s volunteered belief in jury nullification, was more than an adequate basis on which the court could decide that seating Mr. B. would present an unacceptable risk that yet a third trial might be required. Mr. B.'s answer is more than an adequate basis for finding no abuse of discretion."[40]

The court also rejected defendant's argument that the trial judge should have made a further inquiry to determine Mr. B.'s views about this particular case, especially whether Mr. B. had a problem applying the penal laws that the defendant was accused of violating. According to the court:

> To require such an inquiry would be contrary to law and fraught with practical perils.
>
> First, to give a prospective juror a thumbnail sketch of the case—based on evidence not yet heard and often not known to the court at that time—and then ask whether that scenario would cause the person to nullify is in plain effect asking a juror to prejudge the case. That is not only contrary to statute and entrenched practice . . . , it amounts to misconduct for a sitting juror [to prejudge the case]. Second, we believe the logic of defendant's argument would not long be limited to questioning about statutory law. Many other factors would likely be just as influential to a person who believes in jury nullification. . . . The information required could be substantial, for no court would want to face the situation where, during deliberations, it becomes apparent that the jury has a nullifier who is motivated by a factor not mentioned during voir dire. Such an approach could take no account of considerations that emerge only during trial. It is too much to expect every individual's hot-button issues could be identified with questionnaires or during voir dire. No one wants a criminal trial to come to a frustrating non-decision because of a nullifying juror telling the court, "Well, you didn't ask about that." Finally, because nullification is such a controversial subject, it might appear that examination would best be conducted individually and in sequestration . . . in order to minimize impact on other prospective jurors. However, this is not an option since passage of Code of Civil Procedure section 223, which directs that "[v]oir dire of any prospective jurors shall, where practicable, occur in the presence of the other jurors in all criminal cases. . . ." . . . . It is for these reasons of law and practicality that we reject defendant's argument that a trial court must determine the precise basis for, or likelihood of, a prospective juror exercising the power of nullification.[41]

As an increasing number of people learn about nullification, an increasing amount of attention will have to be paid to it on voir dire, which will mean that even more people hear about it. Will knowledge of nullification in fact disenfranchise a growing number of potential jurors from serving on juries?

D. Judicial Nullification

Although judges have been quite insistent that juries should not be instructed about nullification, and that jurors who seek to nullify be removed from jury deliberations, they have been less critical when exercising nullification powers themselves. The story of *judicial* nullification sheds significant light on our understanding of *jury* nullification. After all, the ability of juries to exercise their nullification authority is heavily dependent on judges.

1. Refusal to Follow the Law

Is it ethical for a judge to refuse to follow the law when justice and fairness demand disobedience? May a judge exercise a power or right of nullification?[42] Should the arguments opposing the right of juries to nullify also apply to judges? These questions have hardly ever been asked because virtually all of the discussions of nullification pertain to the conduct of jurors, and when judicial nullification occurs, it is usually hidden.[43] A rare instance of overt judicial nullification arose in *Morrow v. Hood Communications, Inc.* (1997),[44] where presiding Justice J. Anthony Kline, in an extraordinarily frank admission, began his dissent with the following language: "There are rare instances in which a judge of an inferior court can properly refuse to acquiesce in the precedent established by a court of superior jurisdiction. . . . This is, for me, such an instance."[45] Kline acknowledged that prevailing law disagreed with his position, but he could not "as a matter of conscience" apply that law because he felt it was "destructive of judicial institutions." The majority shared Kline's belief that the law should be changed, but it felt bound by the rulings of higher courts that upheld the law. Ultimately, the law was changed by legislation.

Kline's act of conscientious disobedience led the Commission on Judicial Performance to file charges against him for misconduct in violating two provisions of the Code of Judicial Ethics. Kline was accused of failing to "respect and comply with the law" and of failing to "be faithful to the law."[46] Thus, for the first time, a judge faced discipline for what he wrote in a court opinion.

The charges "unleashed a firestorm of protest from judges, attorneys and lawmakers throughout the state." Even the American Bar Association (ABA), in a rare move, came to Kline's defense by urging that the charges be dismissed. ABA President Jerome Shestack, in a letter to the Commission, wrote: "It is difficult to understand how a reasoned, measured, rational dissent can become the subject of a disciplinary inquiry."

Kline's defenders argued that the charges threatened judicial independence and should not be brought in the absence of any corruption, dishonesty, or other malfeasance. A judge should be entitled to freedom of expression in a judicial opinion. According to J. Clark Kelso, "This clearly has the potential, and in some cases probably already has had, a real chilling effect on an appellate judge who may be considering or writing concurring or dissenting opinions." Kelso also expressed the view that the idea that judges should follow the law is a "simplistic syllogism." The real question is "what is the law?"[47]

Kline's refusal to follow the law not surprisingly attracted some negative comment from attorneys. John B. Lawrence wrote that there was no difference between Kline's conduct and jury nullification.[48] Wayne Cantero rebuked the ABA and Kelso for failing to understand the difference between expression and conduct: "What the honorable justice did was to refuse to apply precedential case law solely because he disagreed with it. This constitutes a clear violation of his oath of office. It is not his opinion that is called into question, but his action . . . his refusal to apply valid law."[49] In language echoing the objections to jury nullification, Cantero said: "If judges are allowed to pick and choose which laws they will recognize and apply, and which they will simply disregard, we will no longer be a nation of laws rather than men." Another California lawyer posed the rhetorical question: "If Justice Kline does not have to follow the laws with which he disagrees, then why should anyone else?"[50]

Should judges and jurors take an oath not to follow their consciences? Is it worse for a jury to nullify or for a judge to do so?[51] Kline's view of the law ultimately prevailed in the legislature and all charges against him were dropped by the Commission on Judicial Performance.

2. Nullifying the Constitution
The U.S. Supreme Court, in *Duncan v. Louisiana* (1968),[52] penned this important interpretation of the relationship between citizens accused of a crime and the juries and judges who must decide their fate:

> Those who wrote our constitutions knew from history and experience that it was necessary to protect against unfounded criminal charges brought to eliminate enemies and against judges too responsive to the voice of higher authority. The framers of the constitutions strove to create an independent judiciary but insisted upon further protection against arbitrary action. Providing an accused with the right to be tried by a jury of his peers gave him an inestimable safeguard against the corrupt or overzealous prosecutor and against the compliant, biased, or eccentric judge. If the defendant preferred the common-sense judgment of a jury to the more tutored but perhaps less sympathetic reaction of the single judge, he was to have it. Beyond this, the jury trial provisions in the Federal and State Constitutions reflect a fundamental decision about the exercise of official power—a reluctance to entrust plenary powers over the life and liberty of the citizen to one judge or to a group of judges. Fear of unchecked power, so typical of our State and Federal Governments in other respects, found expression in the criminal law in this insistence upon community participation in the determination of guilt or innocence.[53]

Putting aside the observation that these glorious words could hardly refer to a jury told to obey the judge's instructions on the law and merely find the facts to fit the law, historians have demonstrated that until the mid-1800s, juries traditionally decided questions of law as well as questions of fact. While judges have altered this traditional role of juries, three states— Georgia,[54] Maryland,[55] and Indiana[56]—continue to maintain provisions in their constitutions expressly supporting the right of the jury to declare the law. Ironically, in order to suppress the constitutional right of juries to nullify, judges in these states have nullified their state constitutions.[57] The most recent illustration occurred in Indiana.

Article I, Section 19, of the Indiana Constitution provides: "In all criminal cases whatever, the jury shall have the right to determine the law and the facts." The jury's right to determine the law has been enshrined in the constitution for well over a century.[58] In *Holden v. State* (2003),[59] the defendant (Holden) was convicted on four counts of forgery. The trial judge denied the defense request to instruct the jury that "[w]hile this provision does not entitle you to return false verdicts, it does allow you the latitude to refuse to enforce the law's harshness when justice so requires." Holden's request for the jury instruction was based on a law review article authored by Indiana Supreme Court Justice Robert D. Rucker, who wrote that "an instruction telling the jury that the constitution intentionally allows them latitude to 'refuse to enforce the law's harshness when justice so requires' would be consistent with the intent of the framers and gives life to what is now a dead letter provision."[60] Cases in Indiana had upheld the right of the jury to decide the law as well as the facts. Armed with Rucker's seemingly favorable article, with over a century of favorable precedent, and with the clear language of the constitution, Holden was surprised when the trial judge refused to give the jury the proffered instruction.

On appeal, the Supreme Court of Indiana held that the trial judge was correct in refusing to instruct the jury as the defense requested. According to the court, the Indiana Constitution does *not* provide the jury with the latitude to refuse to enforce the law's harshness when justice so requires. To make matters worse for Holden, the court's unanimous opinion was written by Judge Rucker. In discussing his law review article, Rucker said: "The general thrust of the article is that Article I, Section 19 amounts to a constitutionally permissible form of jury nullification. That is, under the Indiana Constitution the jury has the right to return a verdict of not guilty despite the law and the evidence where a strict application of the law would result in injustice and violate the moral conscience of the community. Although jury nullification has been variously defined, this is its central tenet."[61]

In an interesting tap dance to distinguish his own law review article, Rucker made the following argument interpreting Indiana's constitutional provision:

> It is historically accurate to say that a jury's right in a criminal case to "determine the law and the facts" has a long and distinguished history that can be traced from medieval England through the seditious libel trial of

New York publisher John Peter Zenger. . . . It is also true that early case authority in this state stood for the proposition that the jury's law determining function meant that the jury could "disregard" the instructions of the trial court. However, on closer examination it appears that the right to disregard the trial court's instructions has never been equated as a right to disregard "the law." This point is best illustrated by a case decided forty-one years after Article I, Section 19 was ratified. The trial court gave the following instruction:

> You, gentlemen, in this case, are the judges of law as well as of the facts. You can take the law as given and explained to you by the court, but, if you see fit, you have the legal and constitutional right to reject the same, and construe it for yourselves. (*Blaker v. State,* 130 Ind. 203, 29 N.E. 1077 [1892].)[62]

On appellate review the Supreme Court approved the instruction but admonished, "[T]he Constitution gives to juries in criminal cases the right to *determine* the law as well as the facts. It does not, however, give to them the right to *disregard* the law." How can the jury determine the law, which is its constitutional right, and yet be required to follow the judge's instructions? Rucker appears to be saying that the jurors may disregard "the law," but may not disregard the judge's instructions. How is this possible? Rucker's brief explanation simply adds further confusion:

> [R]ecent scholarly literature . . . sheds light on the meaning and scope of a jury's right to determine the law in criminal cases. For example one commentator has observed, "Although Eighteenth Century juries were invited to find both law and facts and not feel bound by the interpretation of the law offered by trial judges, they were admonished to apply the law as they understood it. The independence of jurors in this regard did not countenance deciding disputes in total disregard of the applicable common or other law." Lars Noah, "Civil Jury Nullification," 86 *Iowa L.Rev.* 1601, 1620 (2001). . . . Another commentator noted "the right to decide the law was neither equivalent to today's proposed right to nullify, nor did it encompass the right to nullify. To the contrary, the right to decide the law swept narrowly, placing a clear duty on juries to follow the law as they saw it, rather than reject the law as pro-nullification scholars would have them do." (David A. Pepper, "Nullifying History: Modern-Day Misuse of the Right to Decide the Law," 50 *Case W. Res. L.Rev.* 599, 609 [2000].)

In the final analysis, the Indiana Supreme Court upheld the constitutional language, but interpreted it out of existence. Here is how the justices reached that conclusion:

> Although there may be some value in instructing Indiana jurors that they have a right to "refuse to enforce the law's harshness when justice so requires," the source of that right cannot be found in Article I, Section 19 of the Indiana Constitution. This Court's latest pronouncement on the subject

is correct: "[I]t is improper for a court to instruct a jury that they have a right to disregard the law. Notwithstanding Article 1, Section 19 of the Indiana Constitution, a jury has no more right to ignore the law than it has to ignore the facts in a case." (*Bivins v. State*, 642 N.E.2d 928, 946 [Ind.1994].)

Thus, Indiana juries have the right to determine that the law given to them by the judge is correct. Judge Rucker, writing for the Indiana Supreme Court, has not only nullified the Indiana Constitution, but he has nullified his own law review article, which concludes with the following sentence: "Preserving to the jury the right to determine the law in criminal cases is consistent with the historical function of an ancient institution."[63]

And so in Georgia, Maryland, and Indiana, judges have chosen to disregard their respective state constitutions in order to uphold the law, while juries are forced to uphold the constitutions by violating the law.

II. JUROR

What are the ethical duties of jurors, and prospective jurors, in nullification situations? What should happen when the conscience of a juror meets the duty to obey the oath?

A potential juror with knowledge about nullification appears for jury duty and is asked about it during voir dire. What should the prospective juror do? Two options are available. First, tell the truth. The consequence of doing so is the virtual certainty of being dismissed from the jury panel. Even if the potential juror expresses the opinion that he or she can deliberate fairly, it is not likely that both sets of lawyers will be willing to take the chance, or even that the judge will let them do so. Thus, knowledge of nullification may disenfranchise that person from ever serving on a jury. The other option is concealment or lying. If this option is chosen, and the truth is later discovered, the juror may be held in contempt for obstruction of justice. Concealment or deliberate deception by a juror upon voir dire examination can constitute contempt if its tendency and design are to obstruct the administration of justice.[64] A juror who misrepresents or conceals relevant information impairs the right of the parties to challenge for cause or to exercise a peremptory challenge.[65]

The lack of candor of judges in informing the jury about nullification has produced an equal and opposite reaction. There is increasing evidence that potential jurors may be concealing their knowledge of nullification from judges. Evidence supplied by myself and Jon M. Van Dyke[66] includes several illustrations of advocacy groups urging potential jurors to refrain from providing complete answers,[67] or even to lie.[68]

There are only five reported cases in which jurors were held in contempt for failing to disclose information during voir dire.[69] Deception during voir dire does a disservice to the legal system. Judicial rules that increase the likelihood of such deception must be carefully scrutinized to determine that they do not do more harm than good.

III. PROSECUTOR

Should the prosecution strike from the jury panel anyone who has heard of jury nullification? The prosecutor appears in court as the representative of the people. The jury appears as the conscience of the community. In theory, these affiliations are in harmony. Why then should conscience be abolished from the jury?

Berger v. United States (1935) provides the classic statement about the ethical responsibility of prosecutors.[70] Justice Sutherland, writing for a unanimous Court, succinctly observed that the duty of the prosecution "is not that it shall win a case, but that justice shall be done."[71] Is it ethically consistent for a prosecutor to see that justice is done by challenging any juror who is willing to obey his or her conscience to do so? Is it proper for a prosecutor to urge the court to withhold information from the jurors about their power to nullify?

Assuming that it is proper for the prosecutor to inquire into a potential juror's knowledge of jury nullification, should it also be proper for a prosecutor to argue to potential or actual jurors that if they do nullify (refuse to follow the law as given to them by the judge) they will be committing a crime for which they will be prosecuted and punished?[72]

IV. DEFENSE COUNSEL

Courts have uniformly held that a criminal defendant is not entitled to a jury instruction explaining the jury's power to nullify.[73] Similarly, courts generally prohibit counsel from making a *direct* appeal to the jury that it has the power to nullify.[74] May defense counsel argue *indirectly* to the jurors that they have the right, or the power, to nullify—to acquit on the basis of conscience?[75]

If a judge directly orders counsel not to argue nullification to the jury, counsel risks contempt of court by disobeying the court. The proper response for counsel is to appeal the ruling. Of course, preserving counsel's objection for appeal is largely a symbolic gesture because appellate courts will not hold that defense counsel may argue nullification directly to the jury. Arguing nullification against the judge's order can be the basis for a disciplinary hearing against the attorney or result in a citation for contempt.[76]

Is it legitimate for a judge to order counsel to refrain from making a nullification plea to the jury? In order to become a member of the State Bar of California, every lawyer must swear an oath which includes the obligation to employ "those means only as are consistent with truth, and never to seek to mislead the judge or any judicial officer by an artifice or false statement of fact or law."[77] The Supreme Court of California has indicated that an attorney who pursues a nullification argument violates the Rules of Professional Conduct.[78]

By contrast, the District of Columbia Bar Association has suggested that nullification arguments may be part of the advocacy mandated by the Sixth Amendment guarantee of effective assistance of counsel.[79] After noting that zealous advocacy mandates that counsel make any "evidentiary argument for which he has a reasonable good faith basis," the D.C. Bar Association made it clear that counsel may not *directly* urge the jury to "nullify" or "disregard" the law.[80] However, unless otherwise specifically prohibited by the trial judge, counsel may argue *indirectly* that jurors are permitted to acquit on the basis of conscience:[81]

> Good-faith arguments with incidental nullification effects do not violate the Rules of Professional Conduct. . . . So long as the power to acquit in disregard of the evidence exists, we do not believe that the Rules of Professional Conduct prohibit zealous advocacy by a criminal defense lawyer that appeals indirectly to that power. Unless prohibited by the presiding officer of a tribunal, arguments that have a good-faith evidentiary basis ought not to be deemed violations of the Rules of Professional Conduct, even if those same arguments also have the potential for enhancing the jury's exercise of its power of nullification.[82]

Judges have repeatedly affirmed their belief that the jury has the *power* to acquit against the evidence, but not the *right* to do so. While judges may prohibit counsel from telling jurors they have the *right* to acquit, should judges also prohibit counsel from telling jurors the judicially affirmed truth— that the jury has the *power* to acquit? Given the fact that defense lawyers know that the law prohibits informing jurors about their power to nullify, any argument to encourage jurors to exercise this power might be construed as an artifice to mislead the court, or as an attempt to encourage disobedience of court rulings. Should the following defense arguments to the jury be permissible or impermissible?

"Jury Verdicts and Appeal"—Counsel tells the jury that if they convict, the defendant may appeal, but if they acquit, the prosecutor may not appeal and the defendant will be free. Furthermore, the jurors cannot in any way be punished for their verdict.

"You May Find My Client Innocent"—In the *Kriho* case, during oral argument to the Colorado Court of Appeals, Judge Sandra Rothenberg asked Assistant Attorney General Billotte whether jury nullification is a right in Colorado. Billotte responded that it was not. Rothenberg then asked "Would it be inappropriate for a defense attorney to argue that, even if you find the evidence against my client overwhelming, you may find him innocent?"[83] Billotte answered that it would not be an appropriate argument.

"The Punishment Does Not Fit the Crime"—In general, punishment is not supposed to enter into the jury's deliberations.[84] In *People v. Nichols* (1997), the trial judge cautioned defense counsel against mentioning the application of the "three strikes" law.[85] The appellate court upheld this ruling on the grounds that "informing the jury appellant was subject to three strikes would in effect be 'inviting' the jury to exercise its power of jury nullification."[86]

The most interesting, and controversial, ruling is *United States v. Datcher* (1993), because the trial court permitted the defendant to argue the issue of punishment to the jury. As the court pointed out, the defendant hoped the jury, upon learning "of the draconian sentence hanging over his head," would acquit because the penalty was too harsh for the crime.[87] The court made a distinction between a jury instruction on nullification, which the court found impermissible,[88] and an "argument for the right of the jury to have that information necessary to decide whether a sentencing law should be nullified." The basis for the court's analysis was respect for the purpose of the jury system and a desire to be honest in permitting jurors to perform their political function:

> [I]f community oversight of a criminal prosecution is the primary purpose of a jury trial, then to deny a jury information necessary to such oversight is to deny a defendant the full protection to be afforded by jury trial. Indeed, to deny a defendant the possibility of jury nullification would be to defeat the central purpose of the jury system.
>
> Argument against allowing the jury to hear information that might lead to nullification evinces a fear that the jury might actually serve its primary purpose, that is, it evinces a fear that the community might in fact think a law unjust. The government, whose duty it is to seek justice and not merely conviction . . . should not shy away from having a jury know the full facts and law of a case. Argument equating jury nullification with anarchy misses the point that in our criminal justice system the law as stated by a judge is secondary to the justice as meted out by a jury of the defendant's peers. We have established the jury as the final arbiter of truth *and* justice in our criminal justice system; this court must grant the defendant's motion if the jury is to fulfill this duty.
>
> * * * * *
>
> Mr. Datcher is entitled to have the jury perform its full oversight function, and informing the jury of possible punishment is essential to this function. The court finds no good reason for opposing candor.

Any hopes defendants might have had that the *Datcher* precedent would be accepted by other courts was soon dashed when the Sixth Circuit later found *Datcher* to be inconsistent with established law.[89]

"You Are the Law"—In the film *The Verdict*,[90] Paul Newman's client was suing a hospital and some doctors for medical malpractice. The judge expressed a strong bias for the defendants which hampered Newman's

ability to present the evidence essential to his case. As part of his closing argument, he told the jurors: "You are the law. Not some book. Not the lawyers. Not a marble statue or the trappings of the court. Those are just the symbols of our desire to be just. . . . If we are to have faith in justice, we need only to believe in ourselves and act with justice. I believe there is justice in our hearts."

"You Are the Conscience of the Community"—Courts and commentators have frequently described the jury as the "conscience of the community." Is it improper for defense counsel to use this expression in asking the jury to acquit the defendant?

"Convicting the Defendant Would Not Be Fair"—In *State v. Bjerkaas* (1991), prior to the closing arguments, defense counsel told the judge he intended to use "the word fair and concepts of fairness" in his argument.[91] He asked the court if he would be permitted to talk about fairness. The judge answered that counsel could "talk in terms of concepts of fairness in general terms," but he would not be allowed to argue "that [the jury] should discard the instructions and the law and find [the defendant] not guilty because it seems fair." The judge's ruling was upheld on appeal.

"Use Your Common Sense"—In *United States v. Rosenthal* (2003), the defendant was charged with violating federal drug laws by growing marijuana.[92] The judge refused to allow the jury to hear evidence that his motive was to make it available for medicinal purposes, and that he was growing the drug with the consent of the city government. The judge believed that the defendant's motive (*why* he acted) was not relevant to the issue of whether he had intended to commit the acts prohibited by the penal code. During closing arguments, defense counsel made the following statement to the jury:

> Nobody expects you to check your common sense at the door of the courthouse and come in with some kind of a blank slate. We can't expect you to do that. And we want you to use your life experiences to make judgments. It's unrealistic to think otherwise. You're well-equipped. Use your common sense. Use your life experiences when you judge this case.
>
> Likewise, we don't ask you to check your common sense of justice at the courthouse door when you judge this case. That would be asking far too much. And that we do not ask. We can't ask that. It's not realistic. So use your common sense. Use your common sense of justice and judge accordingly. We have to, I think, accept that as the stream of life flows along, our sense of what is just and unjust changes. And I can only hope that there are those among you and among all of us whose conception of justice.

The trial judge interrupted the argument at this point and told the jurors that "you cannot substitute your sense of justice, whatever that means, for your duty to follow the law, whether you agree with it or not. It's not your determination whether a law is just or whether a law is unjust. That can't be your task."

"Get It Right and Send a Message"—After the judge in *United States v. Rosenthal* interrupted defense counsel's closing comments, which were just quoted above, counsel continued the closing with the following language:

> Make your judgments carefully. Make your judgments considering all the tools that you bring to bear on this task. And remember that any decision you make, any decision that you make as far as the guilt or innocence is one that's going to last a very long time. This is your one opportunity to do it and get it right. And it's a crucial opportunity. Not only judge that, but as I mentioned earlier, to send a message about what you will expect and demand of the United States government when they prosecute cases like this. Send that message. You can do it. And you can acquit. . . . [W]e put our trust in your capacity to remember the evidence, and to interpret it accordingly, and to render a just result. Please do justice.

"Ask the Judge about Nullification"—During final argument in *United States v. Sepulveda* (1993), defense counsel invited the jurors to "send out a question" about jury nullification.[93] The government did not object, the trial judge did not interrupt the argument, and the instructions to the jury contained no reference to nullification. During deliberations, the jurors accepted counsel's invitation and asked the judge to clarify the law on jury nullification. The trial judge responded that "Federal trial judges are forbidden to instruct on jury nullification, because they are required to instruct only on the law which applies to a case." The jury was then reinstructed that the prosecution has the burden to prove each element of the offenses beyond a reasonable doubt for each defendant. "In short, if the Government proves its case against any defendant, you should convict that defendant. If it fails to prove its case against any defendant you must acquit that defendant." Defendants on appeal argued that the judge's instruction failed to inform the jurors of their power to nullify. Judge Selya, writing for the First Circuit, colorfully dispatched this defense contention:

> The applicable rule is that, although jurors possess the raw power to set an accused free for any reason or for no reason, their duty is to apply the law as given to them by the court. . . . Accordingly, while jurors may choose to flex their muscles, ignoring both law and evidence in a gadarene rush to acquit a criminal defendant, neither the court nor counsel should encourage jurors to exercise this power. . . . A trial judge, therefore, may block defense attorneys' attempts to serenade a jury with the siren song of nullification, . . . and, indeed, may instruct the jury on the dimensions of their duty to the exclusion of jury nullification.
>
> To the extent that appellants, during closing argument, managed to mention nullification, they received more than was their due. Having pocketed this gratuity, appellants now complain that they were not allowed

to capitalize on it. When the jurors rose to the bait, appellants say, Judge Devine should have assured them that nullification is an "historical prerogative" of juries from time immemorial. We disagree. Though jury nullification has a long and sometimes storied past, . . . the case law makes plain that a judge may not instruct the jury anent its history, vitality, or use. . . . This proscription is invariant; it makes no difference that the jury inquired, or that an aggressive lawyer managed to pique a particular jury's curiosity by mentioning the subject in closing argument, or that a napping prosecutor failed to raise a timely objection to that allusion. Thus, the district court appropriately scotched appellants' suggested jury instruction.

No cases have been found in which counsel's attempt to argue nullification indirectly has resulted in contempt or a disciplinary action.

V. COMMENTATORS

A. Leafleting

May judges prevent individuals from expressing their views about nullification in public forums where potential jurors may learn about this doctrine? On January 25, 1990, the *San Diego Reader* published a three-quarter-page advertisement telling present and future jurors that they may nullify the law. The advertisement was timed to influence jurors in trials that were beginning for Operation Rescue defendants accused of trespass and other offenses at the site of a medical clinic that performed abortions.[94]

Although the First Amendment most likely protects this general effort to influence jurors, a more difficult question is raised if leaflets are handed out in the courthouse, on the courthouse steps, or in the courthouse parking lot urging jurors to nullify in a specific case. If a potential or actual juror is handed such a leaflet, should it constitute jury-tampering or obstruction of justice?

Three weeks before the San Diego advertisement appeared, leaflets were distributed outside the courthouse in El Cajon, California. The demonstrators stopped when warned by the marshal that they could be arrested for felony jury-tampering. To combat the information being handed out, judges gave jurors special instructions to disregard the leaflets.[95]

Nancy J. King has persuasively demonstrated that these instances of attempts to influence actual jurors in particular cases have been increasing.[96] How much freedom of expression will be sacrificed to guard against potential jury nullification? While laws against jury-tampering and obstruction of justice are valid and important, no clear guidelines exist concerning whether leafleting at courthouses constitute violations of them. Further, if specifically handing leaflets to persons around or in the courthouse is prohibited because of the direct contact, especially if actual jurors are approached, may supporters wave signs and posters containing truthful information about nullification? These questions are not easily resolved because nullification is a significant part of American history; a history all citizens, including potential jurors, are entitled to know.

B. Jury Bashing—Scapegoating Nullification

After the O. J. Simpson criminal trial, where the jury returned a verdict of not guilty, public opinion turned not against the judge, not against the lawyers, but rather against the jury. Indeed, the father of one of the victims urged passage of a law that eliminated the requirement of jury unanimity. Gerald F. Uelmen, one of Simpson's defense counsel, noted that public opinion polls decrying the jury's verdict "demonstrate the perils befalling a jury that follows instructions."[97] Uelmen's view was that the jury did not engage in nullification, and his view is supported by the posttrial comments of the jurors themselves which indicate that they assessed the evidence and concluded that there remained reasonable doubt as to whether Simpson had committed the murders.[98]

Not surprisingly, cases in which unpopular defendants are acquitted have been addressed as jury nullification gone wild, and nullification has become the scapegoat for recent unpopular verdicts.[99] But many of these volatile verdicts are *not* examples of nullification. King correctly observes that "it seems wrong to classify the different judgments of black and white jurors as 'lawless' nullification rather than factfinding. It is especially difficult to separate the factfinding and law-applying functions of criminal juries from questions of intent."[100] Nancy S. Marder calls them "false claims of jury nullification."[101]

One intriguing idea is that of James P. Levine, who argues that jurors perceive and interpret the law and the facts through the prism of social policies and values prevalent at the time.[102] His study showed that juries tend to convict persons accused of evasion of selective-service laws at a higher rate during a time of war than during peacetime. An acquittal during a time of war could easily be perceived as nullification, whereas the same acquittal during a time of peace would draw no attention. Before nullification is condemned, or praised, we should be clear that a verdict is in fact the product of an act of conscience.

C. Misstating Nullification

Proponents of nullification have based their views on a reasoned discussion of the historical developments that created and shaped the jury system, on constitutional analyses of the Sixth Amendment guarantees of a fair trial, and on political science observations concerning the importance of citizen participation in democratic decision making. Opponents of nullification usually have been temperate in addressing their responses to these arguments.[103] Opposition to nullification is not unreasonable. There are strong and valid concerns about instructing jurors that they have the right to acquit on the basis of conscience even if the law would seem to indicate conviction, and there are sound legal arguments that have been made against the nullification position.

A frequent depiction of jury nullification is the claim, often by judges, that it will lead to "anarchy." However, it is a demonstrable fact that juries have been nullifying for centuries without legal chaos and the destruction of the government.[104] Furthermore, in those states that did instruct on nullification, at least for a time—Georgia, Indiana, and Maryland—anarchy has not been the adverse side effect.

Opponents of jury nullification generally define it in terms of defiance of the law and violation of the juror's oath. In *United States v. Thomas*, for example, the court said that nullification is "a practice whereby a juror votes in purposeful disregard of the evidence, defying the court's instructions on the law. . . . Nullification is, by definition, a violation of a juror's oath to apply the law as instructed by the court."[105]

The error in the argument that nullification is a defiance of the law and is inconsistent with the juror's oath to follow the judge's instructions on the law is eloquently addressed in Judge Dann's chapter. As he points out, the U.S. Supreme Court decision in *Sparf v. United States* (1895)[106] "cannot be read" to support the idea that the jury is limited to the single role as finders of fact. Dann quotes *United States v. Gaudin* (1995)[107] for the proposition that the jury is not a mere fact finder, and that *Sparf* "does not negate the separate responsibility of the jury to decide upon its verdict *after* applying the law in the judge's instructions to the facts found."[108]

Proponents of nullification do not see it in terms of anarchy, disobedience, or disrespect. For them, jury nullification is an act of discretionary mercy. The true question is: "May the jurors be instructed as to their power, in rare cases, to refuse to convict a defendant if, acting as the conscience of the community,[109] the jurors believe it would be unjust to punish that defendant?" Once the right question is asked, the right issue can be explored: Is it ever wise for a jury to exercise mercy?[110]

Indeed, the very term "nullification" distorts the power of juries to acquit on the basis of conscience. Opponents of jury nullification have argued that nullifying juries "ignore" or "disregard" the law, or return a verdict which may "fly in the face of both the evidence and the law." This rhetoric does nullification a disservice. As expressed by myself and Van Dyke: "Lawless 'Rambo' juries have no place in the legal system; the supremacy of the Rule of Law is essential in a constitutional democracy. Juries should not, and will not, act as mini-legislators waltzing through the statute books deciding which laws to incinerate."[111]

Juries do not "nullify" statutes or precedents.[112] The term "jury nullification," according to George Fletcher, "is unfortunate and misleading, because it suggests that when the jury votes its conscience, it is always engaged in an act of disrespect toward the law. The acquittal, supposedly, nullifies the law. In place of the law, it is said, the jury interposes its own moral judgment or political preferences."[113] For this reason Van Dyke and I prefer the term "jury mercy." Levine has written that "such altered terminology would also be more accurate in that juries cannot and do not strike laws from the books as is implied by the word nullification; they simply make an exception on the basis of the singular facts at hand."[114] Fletcher speaks in terms of the power to "complete" or "perfect" the law by permitting the jury that one last touch of mercy where it may not be appropriate and just to apply the literal law to the actual facts.[115] Does a police officer "nullify" the law by deciding not to arrest? Does a prosecutor "nullify" the law by deciding not to prosecute? Similarly, juries do not "nullify" by exercising discretion in favor of mercy. Jury nullification is not opposed to law; it is "an integral part of the law itself, serving the unique and vital function of smoothing the friction between law and justice, and between the people and their laws."[116]

The real issue is: Will a more democratic and just society be achieved by instructing juries on their power to nullify, or by denying them that information and systematically eliminating from jury service people who otherwise learn about nullification? According to Marder, "One of the most compelling reasons for judges to instruct the jury on nullification is that it allows the court to be candid with the jury. The jury has the power to nullify, and it should be told that it has this power. To do anything less is to reveal a certain distrust of the jury."[117]

D. Are Jury Advocates Hastening the Elimination of the Jury System?

It is no secret that attempts have been made in the last several decades, some of them successful, to weaken the jury system. Reduction of the size of juries—despite social science evidence that a smaller number will produce a different deliberative process—has received constitutional sanction. So too has the elimination of the requirement of jury unanimity. A significant literature has developed arguing that juries cannot understand the issues in complex cases and should not be asked to decide them. Recent high-visibility cases, especially the criminal trial of O. J. Simpson, have angered the public against the jury system. Will the fatal blow to juries be struck by those who desire to retain them the most?[118]

As a final irony—and ethical dilemma—proponents of jury nullification, by pushing the envelope concerning jury power, may push it in the opposite direction.[119] The stronger the plea for nullification, the greater the resistance to juries in general. After all, the issue of jury nullification is eliminated if juries themselves are eliminated.

Proponents must decide whether their cause is better advanced by strenuously arguing for direct recognition of the jury's right to nullify or by silently allowing juries to do what they have always done on their own—temper the law with mercy. The choice is not an easy one.

VI. CONCLUSION

Since the 1960s, and especially recently, the pros and cons of jury nullification have become part of a vigorous national debate in news reports, courts, classrooms, and legislatures. Proponents have pointed to juries protecting freedom of the press, such as in the *William Pitt* and *John Peter Zenger* cases, while opponents have pointed to civil rights–related decisions in the South acquitting white killers.[120] These cases that attract or repel us demonstrate that no system of law is perfect. It is foolhardy to think that one side has cornered the market on justice.[121]

One point is clear—the issue of jury nullification will never go away. Any time morality and law appear to be in conflict, jurors will feel the call to prevent the unfair or oppressive application of the criminal law upon a person the community is not prepared to condemn. The judicial refusal to instruct juries on the proper scope of nullification will not eliminate the phenomenon.[122] A legal system, in order to be perceived as a legitimate institution, must be respected by the community it serves. Law must be administered in the interests of justice by the community that assesses those laws and determines what justice means in a particular case.[123] Federal District Court Judge Nancy S. Gertner has written:

> The jury is a complex institution. It is an outgrowth of the democratic ideal of citizen participation in law enforcement. Although it is part of a rational system of general laws, it must also come to a just outcome in the individual case. It is to enforce the laws of the land, while, in its capacity as a "bulwark" between the individual and the state, it may be called upon to nullify those laws in the interest of a higher good. It is to make critical, and presumably accurate, decisions about central social issues, at the same time that it legitimizes those decisions by providing for the most representative lay participation. A truly representative jury runs the risk of being representative of all our biases, yet somehow must not fall prey to the community's irrational prejudices. Finally, the jury is to arrive at a fair outcome in the context of an adversary system in which each party is hell-bent to present only its side.[124]

For proponents of jury mercy, in order to ensure public respect for the judiciary, honesty must be the best policy.[125] Think about a juror, perhaps yourself, who did not know that he or she could vote on the basis of conscience and does not do so, only to learn later that the judge withheld this information. What juror, or citizen, will respect a judiciary that has turned jurors into handmaidens of injustice?[126]

The costs of maintaining an anti-nullification position are too high. The integrity of the judiciary and the legitimacy of the jury system are better preserved by addressing the jury's authority to nullify directly and honestly. As Sir Walter Scott wrote so many years ago:

> O, what a tangled web we weave,
> When first we practise to deceive![127]

NOTES

1. Alan W. Scheflin, "The Duty to Decide," *Catholic Lawyer* 18 (1972): 15.

2. A notable exception is Judge Jack B. Weinstein, "Considering Jury 'Nullification': When May and Should a Jury Reject the Law to Do Justice?" *American Criminal Law Review* 30 (1993): 239. According to Weinstein: "Nullification is but one legitimate result in an appropriate constitutional process safeguarded by judges and the judicial system. When juries refuse to convict on the basis of what they think are unjust laws, they are performing their duty as jurors. Once judges and courthouse personnel have set the stage and parameters for fair decision-making, the result is not nullification but vindication of the process." Another notable exception may be found in Judge B. Michael Dann's chapter, "The Constitutional and Ethical Implications of 'Must-Find-the-Defendant-Guilty' Jury Instructions," in this volume, 93–117.

3. In 1849, the Supreme Court of Vermont concluded that "when political power is conferred on a tribunal without restriction or control, it may be lawfully exerted; that the power of a jury in criminal cases to determine the whole matter in issue committed to their charge, is such a power, and may therefore be lawfully and rightfully exercised; in short, that such a power is equivalent to, or rather, is itself, a legal right." *State v. Croteau*, 23 Vt. 14, 54 Am. Dec. 90 (1849). The holding in this case, that jurors are judges of the law in criminal cases, was overruled in *State v. Burpee*, 65 Vt. 1, 25 A. 964 (1892). Discussion of whether the *jury* has the right to be instructed or whether the *defendant* has a right to have the jury instructed, or both, is beyond the scope of this chapter. Compare Eleanor Tavris, "The Law of an Unwritten Law: A Common Sense View of Jury Nullification," *Wayne State University Law Review* 11 (1983): 97, 104 ("power v. right issue remains significant; absent the jury's right to nullify the law, the defendant cannot rationally be entitled to a nullification instruction"), and Chaya Weinberg-Brodt, "Jury Nullification and Jury-Control Procedures," *New York University Law Review* 65 (1990): 825 (right to nullification instruction belongs to the defendant, not the jury).

4. Weinberg-Brodt, "Jury Nullification and Jury-Control Procedures," 844–45.

5. Valerie Hans and Neil Vidmar report on the results of a 1979 Canadian survey "where people were asked whether jurors should be instructed that they are entitled to follow their own conscience instead of strictly applying the law if it will produce a just result." The survey showed that "Over three-quarters of the respondents said yes. Furthermore, people who had actually served on a jury were even more supportive; 93% of them endorsed the idea of giving these instructions. (On the other hand, Canadian judges were overwhelmingly opposed; fewer than five percent agreed that jurors should receive such instructions.)" *Judging the Jury* (New York: Plenum, 1986), 158 citing A. N. Doob, "Public's View of Criminal Jury Trial," and A. N. Doob, "Canadian Trial Judges' View of the Criminal Jury Trial." Both of Doob's papers may be found in *Studies on the Jury* (Ottawa: Law Reform Commission of Canada, 1979).

158 *Alan W. Scheflin*

6. Mark DeWolfe Howe, "Juries as Judges of Criminal Law," *Harvard Law Review* 52 (1939): 582; Note, "The Changing Role of the Jury in the Nineteenth Century," *Yale Law Journal* 74 (1964): 170; Albert W. Alschuler and Andrew G. Deiss, "A Brief History of the Criminal Jury in the United States," *University of Chicago Law Review* 61 (1994): 867; Paul D. Carrington, "The Seventh Amendment: Some Bicentennial Reflections," *University of Chicago Legal Forum* (1990): 33 (civil juries).

7. Recent Case, "Criminal Law–Jury Nullification–Second Circuit Holds That Juror's Intent to Nullify Is Just Cause for Dismissal–*United States v. Thomas*, 116 F.3d 606 (2d Cir. 1997)," *Harvard Law Review* 111 (1998): 1347.

8. *People v. Diaz*, 95 Cal.App. 4th 695, 115 Cal.Rptr. 2d 799 (2d Dist. 2002), *cert. denied Diaz v. California*, 537 U.S. 907, 123 S.Ct. 242, 154 L.Ed. 2d 183 (2002).

9. *United States v. Spock*, 416 F.2d 165 (1st Cir. 1969).

10. According to *Spock*: "Uppermost of these considerations is the principle that the jury, as the conscience of the community, must be permitted to look at more than logic. . . . If it were otherwise there would be no more reason why a verdict should not be directed against a defendant in a criminal case than in a civil one. The constitutional guarantees of due process and trial by jury require that a criminal defendant be afforded the full protection of a jury unfettered, directly or indirectly." Similarly, in *United States v. Wilson*, 629 F.2d 439 (6th Cir. 1980), the court said: "In criminal cases, a jury is entitled to acquit the defendant because it has no sympathy for the government's position. It has a general veto power, and this power should not be attenuated by requiring the jury to answer in writing a detailed list of questions or explain its reasons. The jury's veto power was settled in Throckmorton's case in 1544 according to Professor Plucknett." The court quoted Theodore Frank Thomas Plucknett, *A Concise History of the Common Law*, 5th ed. (Boston: Little, Brown, 1956), 133–34: "From now onwards the jury enters on a new phase of its history, and for the next three centuries it will exercise its power of veto on the use of the criminal law against political offenders who have succeeded in obtaining popular sympathy."

11. 116 F.3d 606 (2d Cir. 1997). All quotations in this and the following paragraph are from *Thomas*.

12. The defense argued that the challenge was racially motivated, but the prosecutor claimed it was based on the fact that the juror failed to make eye contact. The judge ruled this to be an insufficient basis for removal.

13. The court, in creating this high evidentiary standard for the removal of a juror, highlighted the importance of the secrecy of jury deliberations: "The jury as we know it is supposed to reach its decisions in the mystery and security of secrecy; objections to the secrecy of jury deliberations are nothing less than objections to the jury system itself." See *United States v. Brown*, 823 F.2d 591, 596 (D.C. Cir. 1987) ("[A] court may not delve deeply into a juror's motivations because it may not intrude on the secrecy of the jury's deliberations.").

14. The court further said: "Where the duty and authority to prevent defiant disregard of the law or evidence comes into conflict with the principle of secret jury deliberations, we are compelled to err in favor of the lesser of two evils— protecting the secrecy of jury deliberations at the expense of possibly allowing irresponsible juror activity," *Thomas*, 623.

15. See *United States v. Rosenthal*, 266 F.Supp. 2d 1068 (N.D. Ca. 2003): "The sanctity of the deliberative process, however, does not give a jury license to flout

the court's instructions at will. . . . As such, the fact that juries *have* the power to nullify does not make the *exercise* of that power inherently legitimate or proper."

16. Recent Case, "Criminal Law," 1347.

17. Vin Suprynowicz, "Editorial: Denver Case Marks First in 300 Years of Convicting Juror of Contempt," *The Gazette*, 1998 WL 7992347 (September 1, 1998). Suprynowicz quoted *The Washington Times* (August 11, 1998) as follows: "Experts believe the last time jurors were charged with a crime for failing to issue a guilty verdict was in 1670, when a jury was imprisoned and fined for refusing to convict William Penn of unlawful preaching" in the streets of London.

In New York, a juror began to explain jury nullification to the other jurors, but they sent a note to the judge about him. The judge permitted the juror to continue to deliberate after telling him to "keep his politics out of the case and apply the law as given." The juror agreed, went back to the deliberations, and hung the jury. He was later threatened with perjury and contempt charges, but they were never brought. Larry Dodge, "A Complete History of the Power, Rights and Duties of the Jury System" (lecture, State of the Nation Conference, sponsored by the Texas Liberty Association, July 7, 1990).

18. *People v. Kriho*, 996 P.2d 158, 163 (Colo. App. 1999).

19. Valerie Richardson, "Hemp Activist Appeals Charge of Contempt While on a Jury," *Washington Times*, August 11, 1998, http://www.levellers.org/jrp/orig/jrp.appart.htm.

20. Both quotations are from Suprynowicz, "Editorial."

21. Grant also told the court that "the right of the jury amounts to more than just determining facts and taking the law as the judge gives it to them. Go back to the Revolution, they were not fighting for the right to apply British law as the British judges wanted it applied. That's why they denied us a right to trial by jury, because (colonial juries) were judging the law," Suprynowicz, "Editorial."

22. *People v. Kriho*, 996 P.2d 158 (Colo. App. 1999).

23. See, further, B. Michael Dann, "The Constitutional and Ethical Implications of 'Must-Find-the Defendant-Guilty' Jury Instructions," and Shari Seidman Diamond, "When Ethics and Empirics Are Entwined: A Response to Judge Dann's Nullification Proposals," in this volume, 93–117 and 119–30, respectively.

24. *United States v. Dougherty*, 473 F.2d 1113 (D.C. Cir. 1972). Judge Leventhal's thinking was very much influenced by the climate of the time. Political trials, disruptions in these trials, and verbal attacks on judges and the entire system of justice were on his mind. In discussions with him after his opinion in *United States v. Dougherty*, he expressed his grave concern that the law was no longer receiving the respect it deserved. We disagreed about whether the court's prestige was enhanced or diminished by the judicial refusal to give a nullification instruction. Candace McCoy has expressed a similar concern: "Personally, I fear that if we do give these explicit instructions, jurors will be encouraged to nullify not only in cases where they have a 'damn good reason' but also in cases in which their reasons might not be so damn good." Candace McCoy, "Hard Cases Make Bad Law, Easy Juries Make Bad Facts: A Response to Professor Levine," *Legal Studies Forum* 18 (1994): 497, 502.

25. Judge Leventhal's observation that jurors learn about nullification outside the courtroom was not accurate at that time. Information about nullification became slightly more widespread in later years. An empirical survey conducted in 1997 demonstrated that only about 5 percent of the population had some

awareness of the jury's power to nullify. David C. Brody and Craig Rivera, "Examining the *Dougherty* 'All Knowing Assumption': Do Jurors Know about Their Nullification Power?" *Criminal Law Bulletin* 33, no. 2 (1997): 151. Since 1997, information about jury nullification has become more publicly available.

26. 2 Cal. Jury Instr.—Crim. 17.41.1 (6th ed.) (July 2002 Pocket Part).

27. *People v. Cleveland*, 25 Cal. 4th 466, 21 P. 3d 1225, 106 Cal.Rptr. 2d 313 (2001).

28. *People v. Williams*, 25 Cal. 4th 441, 21 P. 3d 1209, 106 Cal.Rptr. 2d 295 (2001).

29. 28 Cal. 4th 436, 49 P. 3d 209, 121 Cal.Rptr. 2d 862 (2002).

30. 54 Cal.App. 4th 21, 62 Cal.Rptr. 2d 433 (1st Dist. 1997).

31. 34 Cal. 3d 441, 490, 668 P. 2d 697, 194 Cal.Rptr. 390 (1983).

32. *United States v. Krzyske*, 836 F.2d 1013 (6th Cir. 1988). All quotations in the next three paragraphs are from *Kryske*, 1021–22.

33. The court cited *Horning v. District of Columbia*, 254 U.S. 135, 41 S.Ct. 53, 65 L.Ed. 185 (1920) ("[T]he jury has the power to bring in a verdict in the teeth of both law and facts. But the judge always has the right and duty to tell them what the law is upon this or that state of facts."); *United States v. Burkhart*, 501 F.2d 993 (6th Cir. 1974) (approved a district court's instruction that the jury consider only the facts and law before them); *United States v. Avery*, 717 F. 2d 1020 (6th Cir. 1983), *cert. denied*, 466 U.S. 905, 104 S.Ct. 1683, 80 L.Ed. 2d 157 (1984) ("A jury's 'right' to reach any verdict it wishes does not, however, infringe on the duty of the court to instruct the jury only as to the correct law applicable to the particular case.").

34. Judge Merritt also dissented from the refusal to grant an en banc rehearing on the jury nullification issue:

> The law is settled that the jury has the power to decide against the law and the facts. The jury specifically asked about its power to do so, and was told by the District Court that it had no such power. The least that the jury should have been told was "the jury has the power to bring in a verdict in the teeth of both law and facts . . . the technical right, if it can be called so, to decide against the law and the facts . . . ." *Horning v. District of Columbia*, 254 U.S. 135, 138–39, 41 S.Ct. 53, 54, 65 L.Ed. 185 (1920). These were the words of Justice Holmes speaking for the Court. The Supreme Court has never taken these words back or indicated that they do not properly state the law. The District Court and our Court are simply refusing to apply these words because they do not agree with them. It is not our prerogative to overrule the Supreme Court.

35. A more reasonable instruction was provided in *State v. Weitzman*, 121 N.H. 83, 427 A. 2d 3 (1981), which involved defendant's participation in a demonstration at a nuclear power plant. According to the Supreme Court of New Hampshire, the defendant "during the trial stressed his moral conviction in committing the acts complained of in the indictment. Additionally, the judge correctly told the jury: '[Y]ou are entitled to act upon your own conscientious feeling about what is a fair result in this case.' The jury could have found the defendant not guilty had it wished to do so." I would question the second part of the court's additional statement that "jury nullification is an historical prerogative of the jury; it is not a right of the defendant." How can nullification be "an historical prerogative of the jury" if neither the jurors nor the defendant is entitled to a truthful instruction about it?

36. In describing his oral argument to the Court of Appeals in the *Kriho* case, defense attorney Paul Grant said: "I got into what judges want to use this decision for. What they're doing right now in Colorado is they're asking prospective jurors 'Do you know about jury rights?' and if you do then you're out. And I said that was just unacceptable," Suprynowicz, "Editorial."

37. 94 Cal.App. 4th 1024, 114 Cal.Rptr. 2d 781 (1st Dist. 2001). Quotations in this and the following paragraph are taken from *Merced*, 1028–29.

38. 25 Cal.4th 441, 21 P.3d 1209, 106 Cal.Rptr.2d 295 (2001).

39. 25 Cal.4th 466, 21 P.3d 1225, 106 Cal.Rptr.2d 313 (2001).

40. *People v. Merced*, 94 Cal.App. 4th 1030. The following quotation is also from *Merced*.

41. The court concluded that if the "defendant has no right to a nullifying juror . . . , it follows he has no right to a prospective nullifying juror." Under the federal standard, a prospective juror may be excused if the juror's voir dire responses convey a "definite impression" that the juror's views would "prevent or substantially impair the performance of his duties as a juror in accordance with his instructions and his oath." See the discussion in *People v. Holt*, 15 Cal. 4th 619, 937 P. 2d 213, 63 Cal.Rptr. 2d 782 (1997).

42. See M. B. E. Smith, "May Judges Ever Nullify the Law?" *Notre Dame Law Review* 74 (1999): 1657 (answering in the affirmative); Guido Calabresi, *A Common Law for the Age of Statutes* (Cambridge, MA: Harvard University Press, 1982) (defense of judicial nullification of obsolescent statutes); Michael J. Saks, "Judicial Nullification," *Indiana Law Journal* 68 (1993): 1281 ("The law's influence is mediated through the judge, and judges may recognize cases where following the letter of the law would lead to results contrary to the law's true intent. In such instances, judicial nullification is useful, because telling the jury explicitly about its nullification power would undercut some or much of the judge's control.").

43. William Simon, "Ethical Discretion in Lawyering," *Harvard Law Review* 101 (1988): 1083 ("while public general judicial nullification would not be feasible, low visibility ad hoc nullification at the enforcement level might be").

44. *Morrow v. Hood Communications, Inc.*, 59 Cal.App. 4th 924, 69 Cal.Rptr. 2d 489 (1st Dist. 1997).

45. Judge Kline cited Evan H. Caminker, "Why Must Inferior Courts Obey Superior Court Precedents?" *Stanford Law Review* 46 (1994): 817; Paul L. Colby, "Two Views on the Legitimacy of Nonacquiescence in Judicial Opinions," *Tulane Law Review* 61 (1987): 1041.

46. Nancy McCarthy, "Judge Faces Discipline for Opinion," *California Bar Journal* (August 1998), 1 and 22, at http://calbar.ca.gov/calbar/2cbj/98aug/index.htm. Quotations in this and the following two paragraphs are taken from McCarthy's article.

47. Kelso, quoted in McCarthy, "Judge Faces Discipline for Opinion,"22. Interestingly, though Professor Kelso provided a spirited defense for Judge Kline's act of judicial nullification, he is a strong opponent of permitting juries to nullify. J. Clark Kelso, "Jury Nullification Deprives the Accused and the State of Knowing What Is Legal, Violating Due Process," *California Bar Journal* (March 1999): 15. One would think that a judge's refusal to follow the law would be considered a more serious assault on justice than a single jury returning a verdict of acquittal based on conscience. Indeed, in his article, Kelso contradicts himself by saying: "I don't want judges or juries to pick and choose at their whim which laws they will or will not enforce."

48. John B. Lawrence, "Kline's Decision Amounts to Jury Nullification," Letter to the Editor, *California Bar Journal* (October 1998): 9–10.

49. Wayne P. Cantero, "Refusal to Apply Valid Law Violates Oath of Office," Letter to the Editor, *California Bar Journal* (October 1998): 9–10.

50. Douglas R. Thorn, "Kline's Bad Example Deserves Discipline," Letter to the Editor, *California Bar Journal* (October 1998): 9–10. Thorn continued: "I, for one, hope the disciplinary action against Justice Kline does have a chilling effect on any judge who would otherwise be inclined to so blatantly disregard the rule of law and his or her role in the hierarchy of our judicial system."

51. Paul H. Robinson, "Legality and Discretion in the Distribution of Criminal Sanctions," *Harvard Journal on Legislation* 25 (1988): 393, 404 ("Jurors may be in greater awe of their oath to uphold the law than judges are.").

52. 391 U.S. 145, 88 S.Ct. 1444, 20 L.Ed. 2d 491 (1968).

53. *Duncan v. Louisiana*, 391 U.S. 156.

54. Georgia Constitution, art. I, §1, para. XI states that "in criminal cases . . . the jury shall be the judges of the law and the facts." *Georgia Code Annotated*, §17-9-2 states: "The jury shall be the judges of the law and the facts in the trial of all criminal cases and shall give a general verdict of 'guilty' or 'not guilty.'" Despite the language in the constitution and statute, Georgia courts eliminated this jury power. *Harris v. State*, 190 Ga. 258, 9 S.E.2d 183 (1940) ("While the impaneled jurors are made absolutely and exclusively judges of the facts in the case, they are, in this sense only, judges of the law."); *Berry v. State*, 105 Ga. 683, 31 S.E. 592 (1898). Jurors are told that the judge has the responsibility to instruct the jury on the applicable law, and the jury has the responsibility to determine the facts of the case and apply the law given by the judge. *Parker v. State*, 270 Ga. 256, 507 S.E.2d 744 (1998).

55. Article 23 of the Maryland Declaration of Rights states: "In the trial of all criminal cases, the Jury shall be the Judges of Law, as well as of fact, except that the Court may pass upon the sufficiency of the evidence to sustain a conviction." In *Schanker v. State*, 208 Md. 15, 116 A. 2d 363 (1955), the Court of Appeals of Maryland said that "[u]nder our almost unique constitutional provision any instructions on the law which the court may give are purely advisory and the court must so inform the jury." The court in *Dillon v. State*, 277 Md. 571, 357 A. 2d 360 (1976), in reaffirming this point, further stated that defendants are entitled to have their counsel argue to the jury their legal theories, even when these theories may be contrary to the trial court's advisory instructions. Despite these holdings, the court in *Barnhard v. State*, 325 Md. 602, 602 A. 2d 701 (1992), held that the trial court did not err in instructing the jury that it was bound by the court's instructions as to the law to be applied in the case, and in preventing defendant's counsel from arguing an interpretation of the law to the jury. According to the court: "Since our decisions in those cases, our recent opinions have interpreted Article 23 in a less literal manner, and the language used in *Schanker* and *Dillon* has been eroded." Thus, judges have nullified the express language in the Maryland Declaration of Rights. As the court stated in *Sparks v. State*, 603 A. 2d 1258, 1277 (Md. App.), *cert. denied*, 610 A. 2d 797 (1992): "[C]ase law has made it clear that that curious constitutional relic has, through the interpretive process, been shrivelled up to almost nothing." According to *In re Petition for Writ of Prohibition*, 312 Md. 280, 539 A.2d 664 (1988): "As the Supreme Court has aptly observed, because of judicial narrowing, what is now Article 23 of the Declaration of Rights 'does not mean

precisely what it seems to say.' *Brady v. Maryland,* 373 U.S. 83, 89, 83 S.Ct. 1194, 1197–1198, 10 L.Ed.2d 215, 219 (1963). . . . What it all boils down to now is that the jury's right to judge the law is virtually eliminated; the provision, as we have construed it, basically protects the jury's right to judge the facts." This process of nullifying the state constitution occurred despite the belief of judges that giving the instruction that jurors may find the law as well as the facts "almost never" or "never" changed the outcome of cases. Gary G. Jacobsohn, "The Right to Disagree: Judges, Juries, and the Administration of Criminal Justice in Maryland," *Washington University Law Quarterly* 54 (1976): 571.

56. Indiana Constitution, art. I, §19. See Note, "The Jury's Role under the Indiana Constitution," *Indiana Law Journal* 52 (1977): 793.

57. Alschuler and Deiss, "A Brief History of the Criminal Jury in the United States," 867: "Today the constitutions of three states—Georgia, Indiana, and Maryland—provide that jurors shall judge questions of law as well as fact. In all three states, however, judicial decisions have essentially nullified the constitutional provisions."

58. However, jury instructions admonish the jurors not to arbitrarily and willfully disregard the law or substitute their own judgment for what they think the law should be in a particular case. See Rebecca Love Kourlis, "Not Jury Nullification; Not a Call for Ethical Reform; but Rather a Case for Judicial Control," *University of Colorado Law Review* 67 (1996): 1109, 1111.

59. 788 N.E.2d 1253 (Ind. 2003).

60. Robert D. Rucker, "The Right to Ignore the Law: Constitutional Entitlement versus Judicial Interpretation," *Valparaiso University Law Review* 33 (1999): 449.

61. Rucker, in *Holden v. State,* provided the following references:

Jeffrey Abramson, *We, The Jury* 57 (1994) (defining nullification as the jurors' "right to refuse to enforce the law against defendants whom they believe in good conscience should be acquitted"); Clay S. Conrad, *Jury Nullification: The Evolution of a Doctrine* 7 (1998) (defining nullification as the jurors' "right to refuse to convict if they believe that a conviction would be in some way unjust"); Irwin A. Horowitz, et al., "Jury Nullification: Legal and Psychological Perspectives," 66 *Brooklyn Law Review* 1207, 1208 (2001) (defining the term as the "power to acquit defendants despite evidence and judicial instructions to the contrary" and noting that its purpose is to "return an acquittal when strict interpretation of the law would result in an injustice and violate the moral conscience of the community").

62. *Holden v. State,* 788 N.E.2d 1254 (Ind. 2003). Quotations in the following two paragraphs are also from *Holden,* 1254, 1256.

63. Judge Rucker states that the historical function of the jury is to prevent government oppression and temper the rigors of the law (*Holden v. State,* 483).

64. *Clark v. United States,* 289 U.S. 1, 53 S.Ct. 465, 77 L.Ed. 993 (1933); *In re Mossie,* 768 F.2d 985 (8th Cir.1985); *In re Brogdon,* 625 F.Supp. 422 (W.D. Ark.1985); *United States v. Lampkin,* 66 F.Supp. 821 (S.D. Fla.1946); *Witherspoon v. Arkansas,* 322 Ark. 376, 909 S.W. 2d 314 (1995); *People v. Dunoyair,* 660 P. 2d 890 (Colo. 1983) (where a juror conceals or misstates important biographical information, "the juror's deliberate misrepresentation or knowing concealment is itself evidence that the juror was likely incapable of rendering a fair and impartial verdict on the matter").

65. *People v. Rael*, 40 Colo. App. 374, 578 P. 2d 1067 (1978).

66. Alan W. Scheflin and Jon Van Dyke, "Merciful Juries: The Resilience of Jury Nullification," *Washington and Lee Law Review* 48 (1991): 165.

67. In 1988, an Oregon group called Advocates for Life suggested that potential jurors refrain, during voir dire, from revealing that they have strong feelings about abortion, and that they "refrain from elaborating on answers to questions asked by attorneys. . . . This does not mean that you would be untruthful in answering questions. Simply keep your answers brief if you would like to improve your chances of serving on a jury" (quoted in Scheflin and Van Dyke, "Merciful Juries," 181).

68. A published advertisement in a San Diego newspaper stopped just short of advocating outright lying. The ad suggested that potential jurors should not let the "judge and prosecutor know that you know about this right [to nullify]. . . . Give them the same answer you would have given if you were hiding fugitive slaves in 1850 and the 'slave catchers' asked if you had runaways in your attic. Or if you were hiding Jews from the Nazis in Germany"(quoted in Scheflin and Van Dyke, "Merciful Juries," 182). This concept of "pious dishonesty" was followed by a recommendation that the other jurors be educated about nullification.

69. Two of the cases involved failures to disclose personal knowledge about the cases during voir dire and refusal to deliberate with the other jurors: *Clark v. United States*, 289 U.S. 1, 53 S.Ct. 465, 77 L.Ed. 993 (1933); *In re Brogdon*, 625 F.Supp. 422 (W.D. Ark.1985). The third case involved a juror who failed to disclose his felony conviction. *United States v. Lampkin,* 66 F.Supp. 821 (S.D. Fla.1946). The fourth case involved failure to reveal a prior felony conviction and independent outside knowledge of the case. The juror used the outside knowledge in an attempt to influence the verdict. *Witherspoon v. Arkansas*, 322 Ark. 376, 909 S.W. 2d 314 (1995). The fifth case is *Kriho*, discussed earlier in this chapter.

70. 295 U.S. 78, 55 S.Ct. 629, 79 L.Ed. 1314 (1935). In *Berger*, the prosecutor "was guilty of misstating the facts in his cross-examination of witnesses; of putting into the mouths of such witnesses things which they had not said; of suggesting by his questions that statements had been made to him personally out of court, in respect of which no proof was offered; of pretending to understand that a witness had said something which he had not said and persistently cross-examining the witness upon that basis; of assuming prejudicial facts not in evidence; of bullying and arguing with witnesses; and, in general, of conducting himself in a thoroughly indecorous and improper manner. . . . The prosecuting attorney's argument to the jury was undignified and intemperate, containing improper insinuations and assertions calculated to mislead the jury."

71. The full quotation is:

The United States Attorney is the representative not of an ordinary party to a controversy, but of a sovereignty whose obligation to govern impartially is as compelling as its obligation to govern at all; and whose interest, therefore, in a criminal prosecution is not that it shall win a case, but that justice shall be done. As such, he is in a peculiar and very definite sense the servant of the law, the twofold aim of which is that guilt shall not escape or innocence suffer. He may prosecute with earnestness and vigor—indeed, he should do so. But, while he may strike hard blows, he is not at liberty to strike foul ones. It is as much his duty to refrain from improper methods calculated to produce a wrongful conviction as it is to use every legitimate means to bring about a just one.

72. Lillian B. Hardwick, "Juror Misconduct or Juror Accountability?" *Litigation* 22, no. 4 (1996): 19.

73. *Washington v. Watkins,* 655 F. 2d 1346 (5th Cir. 1981); *United States v. Wiley,* 503 F. 2d 106 (8th Cir. 1974); *United States v. Dougherty,* 473 F. 2d 1113 (D.C.Cir. 1972); *United States v. Dellinger,* 472 F. 2d 340 (7th Cir. 1972), *cert. denied,* 410 U.S. 970, 93 S.Ct. 1443, 35 L.Ed. 2d 706 (1973); *United States v. Simpson,* 460 F. 2d 515 (9th Cir. 1972); *United States v. Boardman,* 419 F. 2d 110 (1st Cir. 1969), *cert. denied,* 397 U.S. 991, 90 S.Ct. 1124, 25 L.Ed. 2d 398 (1970); *United States v. Moylan,* 417 F. 2d 1002 (4th Cir. 1969), *cert. denied,* 397 U.S. 910, 90 S.Ct. 908, 25 L.Ed. 2d 91 (1970).

74. *United States v. Desmarais,* 938 F. 2d 347 (1st Cir. 1991); *United States v. Boardman,* 419 F. 2d 110 (1st Cir. 1969), *cert. denied,* 397 U.S. 991, 90 S.Ct. 1124, 25 L.Ed. 2d 398 (1970); *United States v. Garcia-Rosa,* 876 F. 2d 209 (1st Cir. 1989), *vacated on other grounds,* 498 U.S. 954, 111 S.Ct. 377, 112 L.Ed. 2d 391 (1990); *United States v. Dougherty,* 473 F. 2d 1113 (D.C. Cir. 1972); *United States v. Moylan,* 417 F. 2d 1002 (4th Cir. 1969), *cert. denied,* 397 U.S. 910, 90 S.Ct. 908, 25 L.Ed. 2d 91 (1970). As stated by the court in *United States v. Trujillo,* 714 F. 2d 102 (11th Cir. 1983): "While we recognize that a jury may render a verdict at odds with the evidence or the law, neither the court nor counsel should encourage jurors to violate their oath."

75. The commentary to *ABA Standards for Criminal Justice, Prosecution Function and Defense Function,* 3rd ed. (1993), Standard 4-7.7, states that defense counsel may argue for "jury nullification" in jurisdictions that permit such arguments.

76. American Law Institute, *Restatement of the Law Governing Lawyers* (2000), §105 ("a lawyer must comply with applicable law, including rules of procedure and evidence and specific tribunal rulings").

77. *California Business and Professions Code* § 6068(d). Similar laws and ethical rules apply in every state.

78. *People v. Williams,* 25 Cal. 4th 441, 448, 21 P. 3d 1209, 1212, 106 Cal.Rptr. 2d 295, 298 (2001).

79. "Jury Nullification Arguments by Criminal Defense Counsel," D.C. Bar Opinion 320 (May 2003). In *United States v. Sams,* 323 U.S. App. D.C. 59, 104 F.3d 1407 (Table), 1996 WL 739013 (D.C. Cir. 1996) (unpublished), the court said: "It may be possible for a defense lawyer to satisfy the *Strickland* standard [governing the effective assistance of counsel] while using a defense with little or no basis in the law if this constitutes a reasonable strategy of seeking jury nullification when no valid or practicable defense exists."

80. According to the D.C. Bar Opinion, "substantive law appears to preclude express advocacy of the jury nullification power":

> The District of Columbia has no rule or statute authorizing jury nullification. Both the local courts and the federal courts have rejected assertions that juries are entitled to an instruction apprising them of their "right" to nullify the law. See *United States v. Washington,* 705 F.2d 489 (D.C. Cir. 1983) (fact that juries can abuse their power and return verdicts contrary to the law does not mean that courts must give such instruction); *Reale v. United States,* 573 A.2d 13 (D.C. 1990) (trial court not required to instruct jurors about their power of jury nullification). Indeed, both federal and local courts in this jurisdiction have

endorsed jury instructions that are designed to discourage jury nullification. See, e.g., *United States v. Pierre*, 974 F.2d 1355 (D.C. Cir. 1992) (approving jury instruction that jury "should" return a guilty verdict if the government has proven its case beyond a reasonable doubt); *United States v. Braxton*, 926 F.2d 1180 (D.C. Cir. 1991) (same); *Watts v. United States*, 362 A.2d 706 (D.C. 1976) (en banc) (jury instruction may discourage nullification).

Moreover, the standard jury instruction given in District of Columbia courts contains this express admonition to the jury: "You may not ignore any instruction, or question the wisdom of any rule of law." Criminal Jury Instructions for the District of Columbia, Instr. 2.01 (Bar Assn. of D.C. 4th ed 1993). Within this jurisdiction express exhortations to ignore the law are, therefore, likely to be deemed prohibited by law and may, therefore, result in violations of the D.C. Rules of Professional Conduct by lawyers who advocate such a course. See D.C. Rule 8.4.

81. According to Opinion 320: "The legal system continues, however, to permit juries to exercise the power to nullify. A lawyer may, therefore, within the bounds of zealous advocacy, advance arguments that have a good faith evidentiary basis even though those same arguments may also heighten the jury's awareness of its capacity to nullify."

82. Opinion 320 provided the following hypothetical: "Counsel wishes to argue that the police investigation of and testimony about a crime is not credible because it is biased by animus toward the political viewpoint of the defendant. At one level this is a straightforward argument based upon reasonable inferences from the evidence—officers with political bias might, indeed, fabricate evidence. At another level, however, the same argument may also be characterized as a call for the jury to acquit based not on the evidence but on the political viewpoint of the defendant. It is in practice often impossible to distinguish between these two forms of argument. Counsel may often be able to make good-faith evidentiary arguments that have the collateral effect of heightening the jury's awareness of its capacity to nullify."

83. Suprynowicz, "Editorial."

84. In *State v. Burr*, 2003 WL 21448555 (Wis. App. 2003) (unpublished), Burr's counsel attempted to cross-examine a key prosecution witness by asking whether the witness was aware that first-degree intentional homicide, the crime Burr was charged with committing, carried a life sentence. The key witness had traded immunity for his testimony. The State objected, claiming that Burr was attempting to introduce evidence of his potential sentence by asking the witness about the homicide charge he avoided in exchange for his testimony. The trial judge sustained the prosecutor's objection, ruling that the question was an attempt at jury nullification: "Arguing jury nullification, or that the jury should acquit a defendant based on the fairness of the conviction rather than the law, is not permitted in Wisconsin."

85. 54 Cal.App. 4th 21, 62 Cal.Rptr. 2d 433 (1st Dist. 1997).

86. However, in *People v. Baca*, 48 Cal.App. 4th 1703, 56 Cal.Rptr. 2d 445 (2nd Dist. 1996), the trial judge informed the jury that it was a "three strikes case" involving prior convictions. In summation, defense counsel referred to this point by arguing that because of that law, the case was "not only serious, it's about as serious as it gets in a courtroom. And I assume you will agree with me that any

case that involves those kinds of consequences deserves or warrants pretty careful conscientious consideration and deliberation." The prosecutor reminded the jurors that they had been instructed not to consider punishment or penalty, and he said that the only reason the defense mentioned "three strikes" was because "they want someone to throw them a life preserver. That's not your job." The appellate court held that defendant had no right to have the jury informed of the penalty, though the court did not adversely comment on the judge's mention of the "three strikes" law or the arguments of the lawyers about it.

87. 830 F.Supp. 411 (M.D. Tenn. 1993). Other quotations in this paragraph are also from *Datcher*, 415.

88. "This court would not consent to abdicating its role as impartial giver of the law. This court would not engage in behavior before the jury that in any way encouraged nullification of a law. This court consents only to allowing the defendant to argue those facts that could lead a jury, *sua sponte*, to nullify a particular law."

89. In *United States v. Chesney*, 86 F. 3d 564 (6th Cir. 1996), *cert. denied*, 520 U.S. 1282, 117 S.Ct. 2470, 138 L.Ed. 2d 225 (1997), defendant claimed his Fifth Amendment right to a fair trial was violated by the trial judge's refusal to permit him to argue to the jury about the punishment he would receive if convicted. The *Datcher* decision was held to be contrary to Supreme Court rulings that the jury should not be instructed to consider a defendant's possible sentence during deliberations, and should be admonished to reach a verdict without regard to what sentence might be imposed. *Shannon v. United States*, 512 U.S. 573, 114 S.Ct. 2419, 2424, 129 L.Ed. 2d 459 (1994); *Rogers v. United States*, 422 U.S. 35, 95 S.Ct. 2091, 45 L.Ed. 2d 1 (1975). *Chesney* was reaffirmed in *United States v. Stotts*, 176 F. 3d 880 (6th Cir. 1999), *cert. denied*, 528 U.S. 1127, 120 S.Ct. 961, 145 L.Ed. 2d 833 (2000).

90. Twentieth Century-Fox, 1982, dir. Sidney Lumet.

91. 163 Wis. 2d 949, 472 N.W. 2d 615 (App. 1991).

92. 266 F.Supp. 2d 1068 (N.D. Ca. 2003). The quotations in this and the following paragraph are from *Rosenthal*, 1084–85.

93. 15 F. 3d 1161 (1st Cir. 1993), *cert. denied, Sepulveda v. U.S.*, 512 U.S. 1223, 114 S.Ct. 2714, 129 L.Ed. 2d 840 (1994). Quotations in this paragraph are from *Sepulveda*, 1190.

94. In fact, the publisher of the *Reader* was one of the defendants and his lawyer told the press that he was aware the ad would be run. Brooks Jackson, "DA's Office Decries 'Jury Nullification' Ad," *San Diego Union*, January 26, 1990, B1.

95. Operation Rescue adherents in Jackson, Mississippi, distributed leaflets urging jurors to "nullify every rule or 'law' that is not in accordance with the principles of Natural, God-given, Common, or Constitutional Law." The leaflet was sponsored by the Christian Action Group of Jackson, Mississippi.

96. Nancy J. King, "Silencing Nullification Advocacy Inside the Jury Room and Outside the Courtroom," *University of Chicago Law Review* 65 (1998): 433.

97. Gerald F. Uelmen, "Jury Bashing and the O.J. Simpson Verdict," *Harvard Journal of Law and Public Policy* 20 (Winter 1997): 475.

98. Tony Perry, "Snubbing the Law to Vote on Conscience," *The Los Angeles Times*, October 5, 1995. Jon Van Dyke, on the other hand, has written that the Simpson verdict was an act of jury nullification. Van Dyke, "Juries *Do* Work; We Must Listen to Their Message," *Honolulu Advertiser*, October 8, 1995, B1. On this point, I must disagree with Van Dyke based on the jurors' own assessment of their deliberations.

99. See Nancy S. Marder, "The Myth of the Nullifying Juror," *Northwestern University Law Review* 93 (1999): 877.

100. Nancy J. King, "Postconviction Review of Jury Discrimination: Measuring the Effects of Juror Race on Jury Decisions," *Michigan Law Review* 92 (1993): 63, 124 n. 234.

101. Nancy S. Marder, "The Interplay of Race and False Claims of Jury Nullification," *University of Michigan Journal of Law Reform* 32 (1999): 285.

102. James P. Levine, "The Legislative Role of Juries," *American Bar Foundation Research Journal* (1984): 605.

103. Steven M. Warshawsky, "Opposing Jury Nullification: Law, Policy, and Prosecutorial Strategy," *Georgia Law Journal* 85 (1996): 191. One notable exception is J. Clark Kelso: "Listen to a proponent of jury nullification for more than five minutes, and you'll likely discover a person who is upset about something; a person who feels put upon by society's injustices; who's mad as hell and isn't going to take it anymore. . . . When all the rhetorical dust has settled, we come back to the fundamental reality that jury nullification happens only when one or more members of a jury is so disaffected with conditions in society and so angry about the result which the law appears to require in a particular case, that the juror is willing to ignore the law as given to the jury by the court and cast his or her vote contrary to law. I am against having jurors make decisions based on anger, fear, resentment or pique." "Point Counter Point: Is it Ever Proper for Juries to Ignore or Reinterpret the Law?" *California Bar Journal* (March 1999): 14.

104. The claim that a nullification instruction would lead to anarchy is rhetorical, not empirical. In fact, in most cases juries and judges agree. Research on the effects of an explicit nullification instruction demonstrates that whether informing the jury of its power to nullify influences the jury's verdict depends on the wording of the instruction and the type of case involved. Irwin A. Horowitz gave experimental juries three different instructions in a felony murder case, a euthanasia case, and a vehicular homicide case involving a drunk driver. The first instruction contained no mention of nullification. The second instruction informed jurors of their power to decide the law. The third instruction told jurors to appreciate their power to express community sentiment or their own conscience, and encouraged them to exercise their historic power to set aside the law. The first and second instructions produced similar verdicts in all three cases. The third instruction produced more acquittals in the euthanasia case, but more convictions in the drunk driving case. See Horowitz, "The Effect of Jury Nullification Instructions on Verdicts and Jury Functioning in Criminal Trials," *Law and Human Behavior* 9 (1985): 25; Horowitz, "Jury Nullification: The Impact of Judicial Instructions, Arguments, and Challenges on Jury Decision Making," *Law and Human Behavior* 12 (1988): 439; Irwin A. Horowitz, Norbert L. Kerr, and Keith E. Niedermeir, "Jury Nullification: Legal and Psychological Perspectives," *Brooklyn Law Review* 66, no. 4 (2001): 1207.

105. *United States v. Thomas*, 116 F.3d 606, 614 (2d Cir. 1997).

106. *Sparf v. United States*, 136 U.S. 31, 15 S.Ct. 273, 39 L.Ed. 343 (1895).

107. *United States v. Gaudin*, 515 U.S. 506, 115 S.Ct. 2310, 132 L.Ed.2d 444 (1995).

108. Dann, "The Constitutional and Ethical Implications of 'Must-Find-the Defendant-Guilty' Jury Instructions," 96. A related point is also raised by Dann. While courts have been adamant in preventing *acquittals* that might result from a nullification instruction, they have been quite willing to instruct juries to facilitate *convictions*. According to Dann: "Most state and federal trial judges use the strongest term 'must'

when instructing the jury on its duty to convict if all the jurors agree that the law's definition of the crime has been met by proof beyond a reasonable doubt," 96.

109. The phrase "conscience of the community" comes from *United States v. Spock*, 416 F.2d 165 (1st Cir. 1969).

110. Letter from Alan W. Scheflin to Deputy Attorney General Gregory Gonot, February 14, 1994:

> I do not believe that juries have the right to rewrite laws, or to discard laws they don't like. Juries don't do that, as the major jury studies demonstrate. . . . General laws need particularized justice. In rare cases, where laws are being used oppressively or unfairly, the jury may say "no."
>
> * * * * *
>
> My reasons for supporting "jury nullification" are based on historical research (which demonstrates that juries did not abuse their power), pragmatic values (which suggest that better jury verdicts will come from juries that are given the option to nullify in tough cases) and democratic principles (which teach that jury nullification is directly linked to participatory government of, by and for the people).

111. Scheflin and Van Dyke, "Merciful Juries," 165.

112. According to Stephen J. Herzberg: "We use a shorthand when we talk about this concept. The shorthand often uses jury nullification. I don't buy the terminology, because there's nothing nullified. I think it's a pejorative term, and that when you start to argue, or if you go in and say you would like a jury nullification instruction, that you have lost half the fight. There's really nothing nullified. The law stays on the books. It's just a question of how it's applied in a particular case." Annual Judicial Conference Second Judicial Circuit of the United States, *F.R.D.* 141 (July 1992): 573, 662.

113. George Fletcher, *A Crime of Self-Defense: Bernhard Goetz and the Law on Trial* (Chicago: University of Chicago Press, 1988), 155.

114. James P. Levine, "The Role of the Jury Nullification Instructions in the Quest for Justice," *Legal Studies Forum* 18 (1994): 473, 491.

115. "[T]he function of the jury as the ultimate authority on the law [is] not to 'nullify' the instructions of the judge, but to complete the law, when necessary, by recognizing principles of justification that go beyond the written law. It would be better if we abandoned the phrase 'jury nullification' and spoke instead of the jury's function in these cases of completing and perfecting the positive law recognized by the courts and the legislature." Fletcher, *A Crime of Self-Defense*, 155.

116. Scheflin and Van Dyke, "Merciful Juries," 165.

117. Nancy S. Marder, *Jury Process* (New York: Foundation Press, 2005), 199.

118. A related issue is addressed by Valerie Hans, who examines ethical problems arising from the study of jury deliberations. Hans asks: "Are [we] damaging the jury as an institution by [our] intrusive inquiries or by taping jury deliberations?" "Jury Research Ethics and the Integrity of Jury Deliberations," in this volume, 250.

119. Similarly, advocates for the use of jury consulting services may in fact persuade judges and legislators that because juries appear to be easily manipulated, their authority should be curtailed.

120. In *United States v. Thomas*, 116 F. 3d 606 (2nd Cir. 1997), the court provided the following illustrations:

Moreover, although the early history of our country includes the occasional *Zenger* trial or acquittals in fugitive slave cases, more recent history presents numerous and notorious examples of jurors nullifying—cases that reveal the destructive potential of a practice Professor Randall Kennedy of the Harvard Law School has rightly termed a "sabotage of justice." Randall Kennedy, "The Angry Juror," *Wall Street Journal*, Sept. 30, 1994, A12. Consider, for example, the two hung juries in the 1964 trials of Byron De La Beckwith in Mississippi for the murder of NAACP field secretary Medgar Evers, or the 1955 acquittal of J. W. Millam and Roy Bryant for the murder of fourteen-year-old Emmett Till. . .—shameful examples of how nullification has been used to sanction murder and lynching.

Similarly, federal District Court Judge Peter C. Dorsey has observed that nullification is "a romantic idea in many respects. I'm sure that Robin Hood would never be convicted." However, if judges fail to "control what the jury does, . . . we end up in the kind of situation in which nullification was employed which I'm sure none of us would accept." Dorsey cites southern juries who nullified in cases involving killings of civil-rights workers. Annual Judicial Conference Second Judicial Circuit of the United States, *F.R.D.* 141 (July 1992): 573, 666. Herzberg has answered this point: "It is not a defense of the current system to say that it's a danger to tell people their power, because look what happened in the South. There were no instructions in those cases. This power, telling people they have the power, doesn't deal with underlying problems of racism, except it certainly would acknowledge it by saying to you, 'You do have this power, but you shall not allow feelings such as racism affect your deliberations or your exercise of the power.'" Annual Judicial Conference Second Judicial Circuit of the United States, *F.R.D.* 141 (July 1992): 573, 669. Additionally, Clay S. Conrad argues that nullification is not a proper interpretation for the southern acquittals. ("Scapegoating the Jury," *Cornell Journal of Law and Public Policy* 7 [1997]: 7)

121. As argued by Jeffrey Abramson:

Trial by jury is about the best of democracy and about the worst of democracy. Jurors in Athens sentenced Socrates to death for religious crimes against the state, but in England jurors went to prison themselves rather than convict the Quaker William Penn. Juries convicted women as witches in Salem, but they resisted witch hunts for communists in Washington. Juries in the American South freed vigilantes who lynched African-Americans, but in the North they sheltered fugitive slaves and the abolitionists who helped them escape. One jury finds the Broadway musical *Hair* to be obscene, another finds Robert Mapplethorpe's photographs to be art. The names of the Scottsboro Boys and of Emmett Till, Viola Liuzzo, Lemuel Penn, and Medgar Evers mark the miscarriages of justice perpetrated by an all-white jury system that was democratic in name only. The names of John Peter Zenger, John Hancock, Angela Davis, Father Philip Berrigan, and the Oakland Seven mark the courage of jurors willing to protect dissenters from the orthodoxies of the day. In short, the drama of trial by jury casts ordinary citizens as villains one day, heroes the next, as they struggle to deal justly with the liberties and properties—sometimes even the lives—of their fellow men and women. (*We, the Jury: The Jury*

System and the Ideal of Democracy [Cambridge, MA: Harvard University Press, 2000], 1.)

122. According to a poll taken in 1999, approximately 75 percent of the people polled said they would act on their own beliefs regardless of the judge's instructions to follow the letter of the law. Joan Biskupic, "In Jury Rooms, Form of Civil Protest Grows," *The Washington Post*, February 8, 1999, A1.

123. John H. Wigmore writes:

Law and Justice are from time to time inevitably in conflict. That is because law is a general rule (even the stated exceptions to the rules are general exceptions); while justice is the fairness of this precise case under all its circumstances. . . . [L]aw and justice every so often do not coincide. Everyone knows this, and can supply instances. But the trouble is that Law cannot concede it. Law—the rule—must be enforced—the exact terms of the rule, justice or no justice. . . .

[T]he judge must apply the law as he finds it alike for all. . . . The whole basis of our general confidence in the judge rests on our experience that we can rely on him for the law as it is. But, this being so, the repeated instances of hardship and injustice that are bound to occur in the judge's rulings will in the long run injure that same public confidence in justice, and bring odium on the law. We want justice, and we think we are going to get it through "the law," and when we do not, we blame "the law."

Now this, is where the jury comes in. . . . The jury, and the secrecy of the jury room, are the indispensable elements of popular justice. "A Program for the Trial of a Jury Trial," *Journal of the American Judicature Society* 12 (1929): 166, 170.

124. Nancy S. Gertner, "Is the Jury Worth Saving? Book Review of Stephen J. Adler, *The Jury: Trial and Error in the American Courtroom*," *Boston University Law Review* 75 (1995): 923.

125. Paul H. Robinson, "Legality and Discretion in the Distribution of Criminal Sanctions," *Harvard Journal on Legislation* 25 (1988): 393, 403–4:

Studies on jury nullification indicate that jurors frequently exercise their nullification power to circumvent specific rules when they believe that applying them would conflict with broad normative notions of justice. For example, patterns of nullification have been identified in cases involving self-defense, trivial harms, accidental or inadvertent conduct, and extreme intoxication. It is just these factors . . . that thoughtful code drafters have chosen to express as abstract concepts rather than as specific rules. The correlation is no accident. Presumably, the code drafters saw the strong moral component of these issues and sought to preserve and incorporate, rather than override, the jury's moral judgment.

A drafting approach that allows juries to exercise their judgment in cases that involve moral issues is not only insightful but also practical. If the criminal code fails to permit moral judgments where appropriate, the system risks being ignored or subverted on these issues and, after losing credibility here, is likely to be ignored or undermined in other instances, as well.

172   *Alan W. Scheflin*

126. For example, a California jury returned a guilty verdict against a defendant who was found with a rock of cocaine. The defendant stood up and told the jury that under California's "three strikes" law, the sentence would be twenty-five years to life imprisonment. Two jurors immediately changed their votes and the case ended in a hung jury. According to Harriet Chiang, "Some Jurors Revolt over Three Strikes/ Penalty Prospects Sway Their Verdicts," *San Francisco Chronicle,* September 24, 1996, jurors "have been outraged to learn their guilty verdict for criminals caught with a few dollars worth of drugs or a stolen six-pack of beer has meant penalties of 25 years to life behind bars."

In a medical marijuana case, the jurors became angry after their guilty verdict when they learned that significant information had been withheld from them that would have encouraged them to acquit. The strident remarks of the jurors, that they were "railroaded" into the guilty verdict, and that the result was a "kangaroo court," are quoted in Dennis Rockstroh, "Federal War on Marijuana Is Misguided," *San Jose Mercury News,* February 6, 2003. See also Dean E. Murphy, "Jurors Who Convicted Marijuana Grower Seek New Trial," *New York Times,* February 5, 2003, A13, reporting that five jurors, also speaking for two others, issued a public apology to the defendant they convicted and urged that a new trial be granted. The jurors were not allowed to hear that the defendant was growing the marijuana so that it could be used for medicinal purposes. The prosecution argued, and the trial judge agreed, that the defendant wanted to prove his motive in order "to encourage the jury to disregard the controlling law." The defense claimed that because the jury has the power to acquit notwithstanding the facts and established law, the jury was entitled "to receive evidence upon which it could choose to exercise its power." In *United States v. Rosenthal,* 266 F.Supp.2d 1068 (N.D.Ca. 2003), the trial judge rejected this argument. Compare Jack B. Weinstein, "Considering Jury 'Nullification,'" 239; Todd E. Pettys, "Evidentiary Relevance, Morally Reasonable Verdicts, and Jury Nullification," *Iowa Law Review* 86 (2001): 467.

127. Sir Walter Scott, "Marmion," (1808), canto vi, stanza 17.

The Truth of Nullification: A Response to Professor Scheflin

Candace McCoy

"One point is clear," says Alan W. Scheflin, "the issue of jury nullification will never go away."[1] Good! But is it not time that the issue of giving nullification instructions went away? I say this because, while we scholars obsess about whether appellate case law has set the correct standard about notifying jurors of their right (yes, *right)* to nullify, the real work of trial courts grinds onward without much use of juries at all. While we debate the finer points of whether jurors should be told they can nullify, or even more arcane questions about whether *judges* can nullify through "stipulated reversals," or the more common quandary of whether prospective jurors such as Laura Kriho must state during *voir dire* that they know what nullification is, the jury is, in fact, "vanishing."[2] In state courts today, fewer than 5 percent of indicted felony cases are resolved through jury trial. Of these, only an infinitesimal number acquit because they are nullifying.

Under these conditions, we might instead be asking ourselves why the professionals of the criminal justice system so profoundly distrust the American citizens who serve as jurors. After all, if the trial rate is so low, it is due to the fact that prosecutors and defenders strive to prevent cases from going to trial, which in turn could be attributable not only to the reasons of efficiency and economy usually offered to support plea bargains, but also to lawyers regarding juries as wild cards. Juries set the standard under which "bargaining in the shadow of the law" is possible; guilty plea agreements are made with reference to what jurors will probably do.[3] A major goal of plea bargaining is to eliminate the uncertainty about what might happen if cases were to be tried before juries.[4] Nullification represents the ultimate in jury unpredictability. Under these conditions, do we want to *encourage* the uncertainty of the jury system by telling jurors they may nullify if they choose? The result, unfortunately, might be that prosecutors will turn the screws even tighter in forcing pleas from defendants.

Admittedly, such consequentialist predictions are insufficient to counter all arguments for instructing jurors of their right to nullify. After all, we do

173

not really know what would be the impact of such instructions on pretrial processes, and in any event the advisability of openly informing jurors that they can nullify should stand on its own ethical grounds. Let us then be clear about the ethical issue at stake here: truth. How can jurors make choices that are based on the truth? Furthermore, if they are not openly informed of their right to nullify, has the court lied to them? And finally, does the "lie of omission" in not giving a nullification instruction somehow conflict with the possibility of mercy?

I doubt that any serious scholar of the jury system thinks that nullification is a bad thing or that mercy has no place in court. As Portia reminds us, "The quality of mercy is not strained. It droppeth as the gentle rain from heaven upon the place beneath. It is twice blest: It blesseth him that gives and him that takes."[5] But it is important to remember that Portia's plea for mercy in the trial of the Venetian merchant does not, in fact, prevail. She has to fall back on a legalistic strategy—it is impossible for Shylock to extract his pound of flesh as his contract requires without also taking blood, and, therefore, the merchant's execution cannot proceed. Shakespeare's insightful tale about mercy directs attention to the process by which the law is *interpreted*, not ignored.

Jurors may nullify, but more commonly they "interpret." The distinction between "hard" and "soft" nullification needs to be kept in mind. In the incredibly rare circumstance in which jurors determine what the facts are and then consciously decide to reject the law that applies to them, hard nullification occurs. Much more common is soft nullification, in which jurors filter the facts through their own experiences, attitudes, and beliefs, and strive to acquit if—for sociopolitical reasons—the defendant is sympathetic and the facts may be interpreted in a way that does not prove guilt beyond a reasonable doubt. Soft nullification is not nullification at all, but is, rather, jurors' agreement about the meaning of social and political phenomena— in other words, it is ordinary jury decision making that produces a result with which prosecutors or judges disagree. This process of interpretation and consensus-building is entirely the reason we have the jury system, since laypeople have different experiences, knowledge, and beliefs from those of the professional representatives of the state. The jury is supposed to check governmental power, and nowhere is power more palpable than in cognitive frameworks—how people think.

The epistemological underpinnings of jury decision making are post-modern in the sense that they do not presume that an absolute "truth" about the facts of any particular case can exist.[6] The truth is constructed by group deliberation and consensual decision. When jurors decide the meaning of facts in evidence, they do so through a cognitive process of applying the lessons of their own experiences and community knowledge to the arguments the parties present to them, and the outcome is the truth of the matter. Perhaps it is not what other people might think the truth is, but as long as the democratic political structure wisely requires local knowledge of community members to counter the professional worldviews of judges and prosecutors, it is the truth as the Sixth Amendment would regard it.

When prosecutors scream "nullification," they are frustrated that jurors have not interpreted facts the same way that they did. They assume that there is one truth of the case, and that if a jury verdict does not agree with it, the jurors are ignoring the truth and lying—that is, nullifying—even though they recognize the truth about the defendant's guilt. These "hard nullification" cases happen rarely, and even then, the jury is not lying. Usually, the hung jury or even the unanimously acquitting jury has deliberated about the evidence produced at trial and come up with a socially constructed version of the events that is congruent with juror values, attitudes, and political beliefs—including the moral value of mercy. That is not lying; that is social epistemology—the process by which we recognize the truth, which is more than mere facts.

Why is the concept of "truth" so important to the question of jury decision making? Because those who oppose nullification are angry that juries "lie" when they acquit in the face of solid evidence of guilt, while those who support the idea that juries should be told of their right to nullify believe that the court lies by omission in not informing them of that right. Either way, if court processes are tainted by falsehoods, justice will be seen to have been compromised. But both camps are mistaken. Neither jurors nor judges are lying under the structure that currently prevails in trial courts. In *U.S. v. Thomas* (1997), nullification was defined as a jury's refusal to "render a true verdict *according to the law and the evidence*."[7] But whereas the court focused on *"according to the law and the evidence"* as the important consideration, I prefer to emphasize the word "true."

To recap the argument set out above, when a jury looks at the evidence that the parties have produced in court, the jurors must determine the meaning and import of each piece of evidence, whether it is testimonial, forensic, inferential, or some other kind. This is an interpretive process, and the way that the jury regards the evidence may not be the same way that the prosecution or the defense regards it. Does this mean that the interpretation is not "true"? No. It means that the jury confers different meaning, or import, on the evidence from that of the court. That becomes the truth of the matter because, under the Constitution, the jury has the final say. Injecting this commonsense, community-oriented interpretive process into the criminal justice system is the very reason we have the jury system. To define nullification as a situation in which the court (lawyers and judge) knows an objective "truth" to which a jury verdict must correspond, but the maverick nullifying jury nevertheless ignores "the law and the evidence," is to misunderstand the process by which the great majority of jury verdicts are achieved. Jurors interpret the facts because that is what we ask them to do, and their decisions are not untrue if they do not correspond to the "truth" as understood by the court professionals. They are just differ-ent—and they are following the law, just as Portia did in finding her own way to arrive at mercy through a legal interpretation. In the extremely rare case of "hard nullification," in which jurors' interpretations of the facts *do* correspond to the truth as understood by court professionals, but are nevertheless ignored for reasons of mercy, I would venture to say that the truth has been served— mercy has its own logic, and the truth may be that the defendant does not deserve to suffer the full brunt of the law.

The merciful, nullifying jury is extremely rare, and it is probably prized partly for its very rarity. Scheflin's desire to inform jurors of their right to nullify would probably make it less rare.[8] If the nullification instruction would cause more juries to be merciful, this might be a good thing. But it is equally possible that it would cause more juries to be hateful, as in the cases of acquittal of the murderers of civil rights workers in the South in the 1960s. Scheflin bases his demand for open nullification instructions on ethical grounds—that is, that by not speaking, the court lies. By not telling the jurors they may nullify, jurors will believe they have no such power or right, and therefore the court has used silence to lie.

This is another important point at which the question of "truth" in jury decision making arises—this time from the view of the judge rather than the jury as the purported liar. Of course, judges—and more broadly, the entire system of the rules of evidence—lie to jurors through silence all the time. The rules of evidence include many prohibitions against letting the jury hear certain facts—the most obvious that springs to mind is the privilege against self-incrimination and thus the exclusion of the defendant's testimony from jury scrutiny. Indeed, it could be said that the rules of evidence are nothing more than an elaborate framework for setting out the standards by which juries will hear certain things and not hear other things. By keeping some facts out of jurors' purview, does the court lie to them?

Generally, the answer to that question is that the rules of evidence forbid giving some facts to jurors when an important policy goal overrides the jury's "need to know." For example, the Fifth Amendment's prohibition of self-incrimination is said to uphold a policy against forcing defendants to testify. Forcing testimony tends to devolve into state-sponsored coercion or even torture, and the policy against self-incrimination is more important to the sound administration of justice than is the need to hear the defendant's version of events. Thus, the defendant's silence is not regarded as a lie of omission, but simply as silence that occurs because of pragmatic and human rights–based considerations. We could trot through the rules of evidence and set out the policy behind each one, noting why that policy overrides the need for full disclosure of all relevant facts, and the exercise would take quite some time because there are so many examples of such rules.

Commentators such as Akhil Reed Amar believe that these evidentiary rules amount to a requirement that judges lie through omission, and that a better approach would be to adopt a "truth-telling" procedure by repealing most of them.[9] More traditional scholars are willing to accept that the greater good of upholding the policies for exclusion of evidence justifies these "lies of omission." From a utilitarian standpoint, this may be so, assuming one believes that the omissions are lies at all. But there is not complete agreement about the nature of the court's silence. By not telling jurors every fact of a case, or by not explicitly telling them that they have the right to nullify, has the court lied to them? Utilitarians think so, but believe the lies are justified by the greater good. In the case of refraining from nullification instructions, the evils that would result from encouraging the unpredictable and disparate exercise of jury discretion outweigh the evil of telling a lie of omission.

Deontological philosophers might answer differently, but I believe they would still disapprove of telling jurors they have the right to nullify.[10] Briefly, the argument runs like this: If we are to act always with respect for other persons, we will not lie to deceive. We ourselves would not want to have people deceive us. Immanuel Kant has said that we lie because we wish to conceal our faults: "Our proclivity to reserve and concealment is due to the will . . . that the defects of which we are full should not be too obvious. Many of our propensities and peculiarities are objectionable to others, and if they became patent we should be foolish and hateful in their eyes."[11] The essence of lying, then, is willfully deceiving the hearer so as to cover up some weakness or fact that the hearer can expect to know. Such expectation comes from the hearer's status of being a person accorded respect under the Categorical Imperative. Kant goes on to point out that some people are not accorded that respect if they themselves are ignoring the duty to respect others. For instance, a thief demanding that a victim tell where money is hidden has no right to expect the victim to tell the truth, because he is making his demands with no respect for the victim's personhood in intending to misuse the information. The victim may ethically give a false statement (*falsiloquium*) which is not the same as a lie (*mendacium*). Kant states that "not every untruth is a lie; it is a lie only if I have expressly given the other to understand that I am willing to acquaint him with my thought. Every lie is objectionable and contemptible [when] we purposely let people think that we are telling them our thoughts and do not do so."[12]

Kant was not thinking particularly about judges and juries when he gave this lecture, but insofar as truth in adjudication is the issue in matters of jury nullification, these principles of truthfulness can apply to our debate. Let us begin by admitting that the court's silence on the matter of the right to nullify could perhaps be considered a "lie of omission." Silence itself is an act, but of a different sort than oral statements. In the context of a judge refraining from telling jurors something is this act a lie? I think not.

First, silence about the right to nullify is not intended to deceive the hearer into believing something about the court that the court wishes to cover up, that is, some imperfection or wrongdoing. Second, the judge is not lying because of disrespect for the juror's personhood, only omitting to say something because the logic of the trial requires jurors to pay primary attention to whether the evidence meets the standard of proof of guilt "beyond a reasonable doubt." Third, the omission may be a *falsiloquium*, but not a *mendacium*, because the court has not indicated to the jurors that they can expect to be "acquainted with the thought" of every procedure or every piece of evidence. Paraphrasing Kant, the court has not purposely let jurors think that we are telling them our thoughts when every evidentiary objection in the trial has led them to understand that they are not to be privy to all the "thoughts" the court has.

Trial jurors know that they are watching a highly stylized dance in which some movements are not permitted, and that they are judging the quality of the movements that they see, not the ones that might have been danced but were not. This logic of evidentiary proof carries over to the logic of judges' instructions: Jurors follow the instructions they are given and understand that the judge is presenting them with a set of rules and standards that they are told to follow. They understand that if a rule is not mentioned in the instructions they will not follow it, even though it is possible to imagine using it. If the jurors feel so very strongly about something that they are willing to add their own rule—nullification being the metaphoric equivalent of substituting different movements in the dance's established choreography—they will do so only for extremely compelling reasons.

Put bluntly, silence is not a lie unless the hearer has a right to expect the speaker to say the truth. Jurors are not disrespected because they are not told every fact or law; if the judge was a juror, he or she would expect to be treated the same way, because that is the nature of the jury system. Anybody who is a juror should know that a trial is an adversarial match in which lawyers are going to try to emphasize some facts and downplay others, and that the role of the juror is to use his or her own interpretive skills to sort through it all. If jurors understand this about the lawyers, why would they expect the judge to tell them every legal standard applicable to the case, including that of nullification, and to have them find the facts in a mechanical, noninterpretive way? They would not and they should not. If they want to nullify, it will be done because they have a passionate need to do mercy, and we will know of that passion because it will emerge whether a judge tells them about it or not.

I have great sympathy for merciful jurors, and I, like Scheflin, want to support them. I hope they nullify often and well. But if reformers want to help jurors do mercy, I suggest that they look carefully at the example in Scheflin's paper of jurors who refused to convict because they found out the defendant was eligible for a third-strike mandatory life sentence. Why is there no outcry about the court's silence as to the sentencing implications of conviction, while the problem of silence about nullification gets all the ink? It is quite possible that jurors really expect that the punishments that result from criminal convictions are reasonable and proportionate to the severity of the crimes. If that is what they expect, the court's silence on these matters does indeed amount to deceit. This is not a call to inform jurors about what the likely sentence will be should they convict, although this is an intriguing idea that I thank Scheflin for raising. It is simply an observation that giving nullification instructions is not the only way to encourage jurors to use their common sense in interpreting facts to find the truth, or to reach for a higher truth by bestowing mercy. Rather than obsessively analyzing the extremely rare specimen of justice called hard nullification, legal reformers might do well to broaden their vision to the everyday impact of jury decisions on the operations of the entire case disposition process, and suggest how laypeople in general can be more involved in it.

NOTES

1. Alan W. Scheflin, "Mercy and Morals: The Ethics of Nullification," in this volume, 156.

2. See, for example, Marc Galanter, "The Vanishing Trial: An Examination of Trials and Related Matters in Federal and State Courts" (American Bar Association, 2004) available at http://www.abanet.org/litigation/vanishingtrial (accessed 5/31/05).

3. Robert H. Mnookin and Lewis Kornhauser, "Bargaining in the Shadow of the Law: The Case of Divorce," *Yale Law Journal* 88 (1979): 950–77. See also Candace McCoy, "Bargaining under the Shadow of the Hammer: The Trial Penalty in the USA," in *The Jury Trial in Criminal Justice,* ed. Douglas Koski (Durham, NC: Carolina Academic Press, 2003), 23–29.

4. Celesta Albonetti, "Criminality, Prosecutorial Screening, and Uncertainty: Toward a Theory of Discretionary Decision-making in Felony Case Processing," *Criminology* 24 (1986): 623–44.

5. William Shakespeare, *The Merchant of Venice,* act IV, scene I.

6. See Richard Rorty, *Objectivity, Relativism, and Truth* (Cambridge, UK: Cambridge University Press, 1991). Rorty's consensus-based definition of truth continues to be contested in philosophical circles, but its foundational assertion that there is no "correspondence" between the truth that people perceive and some absolute truth that exists somewhere independent of these perceptions is by now well understood—although not entirely embraced by more traditional rationalists.

7. *U.S v. Thomas,* 116 F. 3d 606, 614 (2nd Cir. 1997). The court was quoting from widely distributed jury instructions contained in the Federal Judicial Center, *Benchbook for U.S. District Court Judges,* 4th ed. (1996), 225, but the emphasis is the court's.

8. See B. Michael Dann, "The Constitutional and Ethical Implications of 'Must-Find-the-Defendant-Guilty' Jury Instructions," in this volume, 93–117.

9. Akhil Reed Amar, *The Constitution and Criminal Procedure: First Principles* (New Haven, CT: Yale University Press, 1997). See also "Against Exclusion (Except to Protect Truth or Prevent Privacy Violations)," *Harvard Journal of Law and Public Policy* 20 (1997).

10. One important exception to this would be the situation in which jurors explicitly inquire of the court whether they have the right to nullify. In this situation, the judge must tell them that they have that right, as the Kantian logic described here would require.

11. Immanuel Kant, "Ethical Duties to Others: Truthfulness," from *Lectures on Ethics*, trans. Louis Infield (Indianapolis: Hackett Publishing, 1981), reprinted in Daryl Close and Nicholas Meier, *Morality in Criminal Justice* (Belmont, CA: Wadsworth, 1991), 222.

12. Kant, "Ethical Duties to Others," 224.

6

Jury Deliberation: Fair and Foul

Jeffrey Abramson

In this chapter, I address a series of ethical issues raised by political behavior inside the jury room. Outside the jury room, in the halls of Congress, for instance, we take it for granted that legislators will and ought to engage in all sorts of political stratagems in search of votes on a pending bill. They will broker compromises; put together coalitions based on race, gender, region and the like; engage in trade-offs and vote-swapping; lobby and pressure holdouts; filibuster or go on vacation; read the polls and papers, and otherwise consult the interests of their constituents. This is not to say that legislative strategies know no moral limits. But who would want to be represented by a legislator opposed in principle to winning support through the normal favors, promises, and pressures of politics?

To what extent should jurors follow these standard norms of politics when deliberating toward a verdict? Elsewhere, I have argued that the jury is a fundamentally different kind of institution from a legislature, notwithstanding the fact that both juror and legislator are said to represent their communities.[1] A legislature is openly a forum of competing interests and factions: Senators from New England states, for instance, have particular interests of constituents to represent on fishing boundary questions and they are rightly expected to give voice and vote to constituent interests even against the interests of other regions of the nation. Clearly, jurors are not representatives of this sort. Their allegiance is to the truth and not to the interests of any one group.[2] Deliberation on a cross-sectional jury ideally serves the truth by drawing on the diverse experiences and views linked to demography in America, pushing all to consider how the evidence looks to those with different backgrounds. But jurors are not there to vote the static preconceptions of their own kind or to be loyal to the views popular or prevalent in their section of town. In other words, in whatever ways the jury may be a political as well as a legal institution, it is not just another embodiment of interest-group politics. We do well to consider the kind of behavior we want to encourage from jurors in light of these general considerations.

On the other hand, jurors should hardly approach deliberation as if they were students in a seminar. Power may ultimately flow to the persuasive on the jury, but it takes political skill to emerge persuasive in cases in which divisions on evidence or the law are deep. We should expect passion, yelling, argument, vehemence, pressure, strategy, and leadership.[3] The classic film *Twelve Angry Men* may be a naïve fictional account of one holdout juror turning around eleven others initially bent on conviction, but the movie does have merit for studying the small strategies through which persuasion occurs on juries.[4] Consider just one example. Early on, having expressed his reasons for casting the sole not-guilty vote on an open ballot, Henry Fonda realizes his arguments have swayed no one. So he takes a gamble: In exchange for an agreement from the eleven others to switch from open to secret balloting, Fonda agrees to vote to convict if even on a secret ballot he remains the only vote for acquittal. Fonda's sense that he needs an ally and his attention to the difference between open and secret ballots are strategic details that almost all students of the jury can appreciate.[5]

In what follows, I discuss three particular issues involving the politics of jury deliberation. The first has to do with the holdout juror in criminal trials and the permissible limits of majority pressure on those in the minority. The second has to do with compromise verdicts, including conviction on lesser included charges. The third is the issue of bloc voting on a jury.

I. THE HOLDOUT JUROR

In all U.S. jurisdictions save two, criminal juries must render a unanimous verdict either to convict or to acquit.[6] This two-way unanimity rule obviously gives power to even one juror to hang or deadlock a jury. How much pressure should majorities bring upon the recalcitrant juror or jurors and what responsibility do holdouts have to defer to the dominant view?

A. *Allen* Charges

The infamous "Allen" or "dynamite" charge, dating back to 1896, instructs seemingly deadlocked juries to return to their task and try to reach agreement. Much of the charge is unobjectionable, telling juries that "although the verdict must be the verdict of each individual juror, and not a mere acquiescence in the conclusion of his fellows, yet they should examine the question submitted . . . with a proper regard and deference to the opinions of each other."[7] But as originally approved by the Supreme Court, the *Allen* charge was deliberately one-sided: "if much the larger number were for conviction, a dissenting juror should consider whether his doubt was a reasonable one which made no impression upon the minds of so many men, equally honest, equally intelligent with himself."[8]

Since the *Allen* charge did not impose a mutual obligation on the majority to reconsider their views in light of the failure of the evidence to convince all, critics have complained that the instruction is inherently coercive. These criticisms have led a number of courts to prefer a modified *Allen*-type charge, in line with model American Bar Association standards that stress that (i) the majority has a reciprocal obligation to heed the views of the minority; (ii) no juror should surrender honest convictions arrived at through reasoning satisfactory to him or her; (iii) the jury has a right not to agree; and (iv) the burden remains on the government to prove the charges beyond a reasonable doubt.[9]

In their pioneering study of the American jury, Harry Kalven and Hans Zeisel presented evidence showing that "where there is an initial majority either for conviction or for acquittal, the jury in roughly nine out of ten cases decides in the direction of the initial majority." Kalven and Zeisel interpreted these data to mean that deliberation changes votes less through the force of reason and more through the peer pressure and intimidation that an initial majority musters against holdouts.[10] Numerous studies since have confirmed that an initial one- or two-member holdout group rarely hangs a jury, much less succeeds in turning it around.[11]

The wisdom of giving *Allen*-type charges should be considered in light of the empirical evidence showing the power majority jurors already exercise over holdouts. Insofar as an *Allen* instruction merely prods jurors on both sides of a divide to revisit respectfully the reasons dividing reasonable people, the charge is unobjectionable. Nor is there anything inherently coercive in pointing out to jurors that there is no reason to believe any subsequent jury could decide the case more accurately than the current jury.

What we want to guard against are admonitions that imply to holdouts that a hung jury is a failure or that, in the face of disagreement, the majority ought ultimately to rule on juries as it does in other institutions. The original *Allen* charge came close to blessing the majority side with the imprimatur of the judge, and courts do well today to give the modified, mutual instruction. The Ninth Circuit's *per se* rule against repeating the *Allen* charge if the jury continues to be deadlocked is also a necessary reform, since sending the jury back repeatedly does suggest an obligation to reach a unanimous verdict rather than remain deadlocked.[12]

B. Pressure Tactics

How much pressuring, bullying, pulling rank, and the like should jurors feel free to visit upon holdouts? As indicated above, courts have proved reluctant to overturn jury convictions on the basis of postverdict juror testimony about threats and intimidation during deliberation.[13] Moreover, recall the way in which the first trial of Erik Menendez, charged with joining with his brother in murdering their parents, ended in a mistrial when the jury split evenly between six women favoring a verdict of voluntary manslaughter and five of six men leaning toward first-degree murder (the sixth favored second degree). Some of the women interviewed after the hung jury was dismissed complained that "it was hostile in there. There were insults, sexual comments. [The men] tried to outshout us." Apparently, the men called some of the women "ignorant asses and empty-headed and 'those women.'" One male juror "would put on his sunglasses and be balancing his checkbook when the women were talking."[14]

It is difficult to judge categorically how much we should strive to turn the jury room into a zone free from group or ad hominem insults and bullying. On the one hand, there is something to be said for Justice Cardozo's remark that we should not design the jury for the comfort of "some timid soul who will take counsel of his fears and give way to their repressive power."[15] Standing in the way are also strong policies favoring jury secrecy and protecting juror verdicts from being impeached by any testimony that would require a judge to explore "any matter or statement occurring during the course of the jury's deliberation or to the effect of anything upon his or any other juror's mind or . . . concerning his mental processes."[16]

On the other hand, we certainly do not want death sentences imposed by juries where one juror threatened to kill another juror who voted for life.[17] Nor have we fought so many battles to treat all groups equally during jury selection only to permit persons selected to be baited on the basis of their race, religion, ethnic background, or gender. In one reported arson and insurance fraud case, male jurors apparently pressured three women jurors into a guilty verdict through relentless harangues against "stupid females" who "didn't have minds." In postverdict interviews, the three indicated that they would have voted to acquit on several counts had they not given in to the pressure.[18] Although on these facts about sexism the appellate court did not find reason to reverse the verdict, a contrary conclusion is usually reached in cases involving offers to prove expressions of racism in the jury room. Indeed, courts have specifically held that Fed. R. Evid. 606(b)'s prohibitions on hearing juror testimony about the mental processes or thoughts of jurors did not apply to testimony about racial bias, since this was testimony about a "mental bias unrelated to any specific issue that a jury may legitimately be called upon to testify."[19] Thus, jurors cross an important line when their verbal abuses turn into expressions of prejudice inconsistent with a defendant's right to a trial before an impartial jury. [20]

In its 2002 term, the Supreme Court handed down a troubling decision about permission to pressure a lone holdout juror.[21] In the trial of a defendant accused of attempted murder, murder, robbery, assault with a deadly weapon, and numerous other firearms charges, after the jury had been deliberating twenty-eight hours, they returned a sealed verdict as to all charges except the murder and attempted murder charges. At this point a juror asked to be dismissed for "health reasons," telling the judge she was "feeling burned out."[22] The judge asked her if she felt she could try to continue and she agreed to return to the jury deliberations. After another day, the foreman sent out a note saying "Eve Radcliff does not appear to be able to understand the rules as given by you." The note continued "nearly all my fellow jurors questio[n] her ability to understand the rules and her ability to reason."[23] Interviewing the foreman, the judge asked to be told the numerical division on the jury, but not whether toward conviction or acquittal. He was told that the division was 11 to 1. In California, a judge is prohibited from giving the *Allen* charge and the judge did not give one here.[24] But he did call the jury in and talk to them about their role in deliberation, how they were to go about their task, and he summarized pattern California instructions that the jury finds the facts but they "must accept and follow the law as I state it to you."[25] He then gave the jury a day off, after which he received yet another note from Juror Radcliff. She stated she was "feeling . . . distrust and disrespect from the other jurors" and that she had "reached a point of anger."[26] The judge again asked her to return to deliberations, and subsequently the jury returned guilty verdicts of attempted murder and of second-degree murder. In its sealed verdict, the jury had acquitted the defendant on ten other counts of the indictment.

On appeal, the California Court of Appeal held that the judge's intervention did not unduly coerce the juror. On habeas corpus review, the United States Court of Appeals would have reversed that ruling but the Supreme Court overturned the Ninth Circuit's ruling, letting the California court ruling stand. But it is difficult to believe that a juror would not feel coerced when a judge thrice sends her back to deliberate despite her statements that the atmosphere was intolerable in the jury room. The judge in fact knew she was the lone dissenter and that she was experiencing trouble in maintaining her dissent in the face of what she described as behavior from others so disrespectful that it made her sick and angry. At some point, given the totality of the circumstances, the judge should have realized that a reasonable juror could well feel coerced by a judge's repeated insistence that, despite the length of her holdout, she should go back and try to reach a verdict with the majority faction. One is tempted to ask the Court of Appeal what it would take to show coercive impact on a juror if these sorts of instructions and acts by a judge, who knows the vote is 11 to 1, are not sufficient to show coercion.

C. Misleading Information

The Capital Jury Project has documented repeated instances in which a majority favoring a death sentence convinces one or two holdouts to vote for death by suggesting to them that the judge's instructions leave them no choice.[27] In one Texas case, a juror reports using "persuasive tactics" to turn around two jurors by suggesting to them that "the judge is the one who will pronounce the sentence."[28] In another case, the majority tries to relieve the holdouts of responsibility for a death verdict by "effectively us[ing] the argument that the jury was simply answering questions [about aggravating and mitigating circumstances] rather than imposing a death sentence."[29] In one interview, a juror describes "one lady [who] could not sentence anyone to death." The only way to get her vote was to assure her that "she wasn't pronouncing death," that "[t]he judge did [the] sentencing; the jury only had to say [the defendant] was guilty of capital murder."[30]

Most of the interviews reported by the Capital Jury Project admit of two different interpretations. In one, the majority believes what it tells the holdouts and all are equally misled by ambiguous and poorly worded instructions.[31] In the other, the majority puts any ambiguity in the instructions to strategic use by persuading holdouts they can vote for death without bearing any moral responsibility for a penalty the law demands and the judge will have to impose. The majority colors the law this way because it correctly senses that this is the key to turning around the holdout's psyche. In either interpretation, at least some jurors end up voting for the death penalty on the basis of a misunderstanding of the law. That is bad enough. But it is worse if the problem is not only poorly worded instructions but also a kind of ethical con game on the part of some jurors to trick others into unwittingly imposing a death sentence.

II. COMPROMISE VERDICTS

When, if ever, is it permissible for jurors to broker a compromise verdict? Ever since Lord Mansfield learned in 1785 that a jury had decided the case by a toss of the coin,[32] cases have been reported about jurors splitting the difference rather than ending in deadlock.[33]

A. General Considerations

Certain sorts of compromises we should discourage on a jury—those motivated merely by convenience, expediency, time-saving, or some mistaken notion that hung juries are necessarily a sign of failure. It is one thing for representatives from coal-producing states to reach a compromise on an energy bill with representatives from oil-producing states. It is quite another for one bloc of jurors to "represent" a murder conviction and another to "represent" the interests of those who favor manslaughter, each bloc approaching deliberation as a process of compromise. The difference is that the paramount and sworn duty of jurors is to serve the truth as a higher goal than even consensus or agreement.[34]

We should also disfavor jury compromises motivated by attention to how their verdict will play in the outside world. Suppose that a white police officer is charged with the murder of a fleeing black motorist who is found to be carrying a loaded handgun. Even without reading the papers, jurors may sense that their decision either way will be controversial, that it might even spark rioting. Still, it is not the job of a jury to calculate the political reactions or to try to keep the peace by giving each side some sense of victory, say by acquitting the defendant of the most serious charges but at least convicting him of some offense. However understandable, jurors ought to resist sacrificing the accuracy of their verdict in favor of how best to sell the verdict politically.

Or suppose two police officers were charged with the murder of the fleeing suspect. It would be worse still for a jury to split the difference by convicting one and exonerating the other. Each defendant has an absolute right to a fair trial before an impartial jury. In a case with multiple defendants, that right is violated if the jury "uses" one defendant merely to benefit or to punish another.

As morally troubling as compromises are that benefit one defendant at the expense of another, I am still uncertain we can entirely rule out their legitimacy. In the above case, I can imagine a juror convinced beyond a reasonable doubt that one police officer is not guilty, whereas the other officer is clearly implicated but the juror wavers as to whether to vote for manslaughter or second-degree murder. An offer to vote for second-degree murder against the one in exchange for the jury's acquittal of the other officer might be acceptable behavior, if indeed the juror is persuaded that the evidence rationally considered could support the second-degree murder conviction. But this is a close call.

For all these qualms about compromises, two aspects of criminal trials arguably encourage jurors to compromise. The first is the giving of *Allen* charges to deadlocked juries, an issue we discussed in the previous section of this chapter. The second is the practice of instructing jurors to consider so-called lesser included offenses. I turn now to this issue.

B. Lesser Included Offenses

Lesser included offenses are crimes that the defendant is not specifically charged with in the indictment but that a jury nonetheless may be instructed to consider in cases in which the evidence would justify a reasonable jury in concluding that the defendant was not guilty of the greater crime but was guilty of the lesser. For instance, voluntary manslaughter is a lesser included offense in the crime of murder, because all the elements of murder are also elements of manslaughter, except that murder requires proof of the additional element of malice. Therefore, in an appropriate case where a reasonable jury could read the evidence as establishing that the defendant killed another human being without legal excuse, but short of malice, the jury may be instructed to consider manslaughter as well as murder.[35]

Must the trial judge *sua sponte* instruct a jury on lesser included offenses in appropriate cases or should the judge leave the decision to the strategic thinking of one or other of the parties? This question goes to the heart of the jury's role at criminal trial. According to one view, the giving of lesser included instructions is necessary if jurors are to be in a position to render a truthful verdict. Thus, a judge should always instruct the jury on lesser included offenses in any case in which the evidence presented is sufficient to justify a conviction. In the competing view, instructing juries on lesser included offenses is an invitation to juries to compromise rather than seek the truth. Therefore, the decision should be left to the litigants, rather than the judge, as to whether, as part of trial strategy, one side or the other wishes to gamble on an "all-or-nothing decision."[36]

The doctrine of lesser included offenses received wide public debate in the wake of the so-called Boston "Nanny" case. Au pair Louise Woodward was charged with murdering eight-month-old Matthew Eappen, who was left in her care; the Commonwealth's evidence was that Woodward caused the baby's death by violent shaking and that the shaking was severe enough to warrant a jury finding that Woodward acted with the malice necessary for murder.[37] The defense decided to roll the dice and forego any instruction on man-slaughter; their fear was that a manslaughter verdict gave the jury too comfortable a compromise choice. Their hope was that, faced with an all-or-nothing decision, a jury would acquit rather than finding that a young au pair acted with the malice of a murderer. On the other hand, the prosecution objected to the defense strategy and requested the manslaughter instruction.[38]

The trial judge deferred to the defense's strategic calculus and refused the Commonwealth's requested manslaughter instruction. As it turned out, the jury thereupon convicted Woodward of second-degree murder. The trial judge then controversially invoked his discretion to reduce the murder conviction to manslaughter, after concluding that the "interests of justice are best served . . . by lowering the degree of guilt attributable to Defendant."[39]

On appeal, the Massachusetts Supreme Judicial Court ruled that it was an error for the judge to have withheld the lesser-included option from the jury, at least in a case in which one party (here the prosecution) had requested that the jury be informed of this option and where the evidence was sufficient to support a conviction on manslaughter rather than murder.[40] The high court stressed that "no jurisdiction that has considered the issue has allowed a defendant to veto a lesser included offense instruction properly requested by the prosecution."[41] The trial judge's mistake was to leave the jury improperly with an all-or-nothing decision that may have been strategically sought by the defense but which "with the judge's approbation transformed the trial from a search for the truth to a high stakes game of chance."[42]

The high court's decision in *Woodward* contains strong language disapproving of leaving juries with all-or-nothing decisions. Still, the court stopped short of answering the question of whether a judge should instruct a jury on lesser included offenses in a case in which the evidence warrants the charge but *neither* party, for strategic reasons, wants it given. Nor did the case directly address the sense of the defense that lesser included offense instructions are an open invitation to juries to compromise.

I am unaware of any empirical study that documents how often juries acquit of the greater charge but convict on the lesser included offenses. Even were there such data, they would not inform us of the motives of the jury, whether moved by the spirit of compromise or the force of reason. Putting aside empirical questions, therefore, how should we normatively judge the jury that does render a compromise verdict? Let me offer two general considerations. First, I suppose there are a great number of cases in which jurors could partly be moved by a motive to compromise but also by an honest sense that the evidence rationally considered supported the verdict anyway; in these kind of cases, not even the jurors themselves could report whether a compromise occurred. Second, in general I find little to fault in a jury that explicitly considers the possibility that a compromise verdict might be preferable to the looming alternative of a hung jury. Hard-and-fast rules are hard to announce; there are surely cases in which hanging a jury is preferable to compromising on matters of conscience and principle, but there are just as surely cases in which the issues dividing the sides are not matters of conscience. There are also cases in which the jurors disagree emphatically about the facts and there are cases in which the parties disagree but agree that the facts are murky at best. There are cases in which a juror could honestly believe that a compromise verdict is in the interest of justice. Consider some examples:

1. In *Inside the Jury*, Reid Hastie and his coauthors report on mock jury deliberations about a barroom brawl that ends in the defendant stabbing the victim to death.[43] The two had quarreled earlier in the day at the same bar and the victim had threatened the defendant with a straight razor. The defendant returns to the bar later that night, the quarrel reignites, and the two step outside into an alley. The defendant kills the victim with a fishing knife that the defendant says he always carries. The defendant claims self-defense and testifies that the victim drew his straight razor. But the medical examiner testifies that the razor was found folded and in the dead man's trouser pockets. On these facts, mock juries are instructed on first- and second-degree murder, manslaughter, self-defense, and reasonable doubt. Only a small percentage of mock jurors vote for either first degree (no convincing evidence of premeditation) or not guilty by reason of self-defense (the defendant could have safely retreated). The lasting split is between those leaning toward second-degree murder and those favoring manslaughter. Their disagreement tends to be over whether the defendant stabbed the victim with malice or whether it was a sudden act of passion, however unjustified. Even though jurors reach different judgments about whether the facts imply the malice needed for murder, they tend to admit that the legal line separating the elements of second-degree murder from manslaughter is murky in their minds and that they can appreciate why

fellow jurors reach opposite conclusions. In this kind of situation, reasonable jurors could well conclude a compromise was preferable to hanging the jury.

2. Some years back a husband killed his wife in a particularly gruesome fashion, dismembered her body, and impaled certain parts on the backyard fence. At trial, the defendant offered an insanity defense and introduced psychiatric testimony about long-standing treatment for mental illness. The prosecution rebutted the testimony and pressed for first-degree murder on grounds that the killing was done with extreme cruelty and atrocity. Imagine a juror who is convinced by the insanity defense but finds eleven other jurors pressing for first-degree murder. The juror tries to convince others of the insanity defense but fails and she is savvy enough to realize that the defendant is likely to fare no better before any subsequent jury, given the lurid details. Such a juror might reasonably press for a compromise verdict of manslaughter as the best practical justice she could accomplish. The eleven might then express a willingness to come down to second-degree murder, since perhaps the defendant's mental problems did diminish his capacity to appreciate the atrocity of his acts. The jury might then battle it out from there.

III. BLOC VOTING

I turn to one final example of how jurors might use political tactics to win the deliberation. Almost all jury studies confirm that an individual has little chance of exercising power in the jury room unless he or she finds an ally, and preferably more than one. It would be natural for a juror to turn to those with similar backgrounds in the search for an alliance. So imagine a jury deliberation that begins with remarks such as "As a woman, I . . . " or "As a Hispanic, I . . . " Imagine further these remarks being made in an attempt to "rally the troops," as it were, prodding fellow women and/or Hispanics to join the fray and back up the remarks. This kind of behavior is not only expected but is all to the good: Why else do we empanel cross-sectional juries unless we want the conversation at times to be a conversation that reflects the initial differences in the preconceptions that jurors bring with them into the jury room?

Still, we want it to be a conversation, and a dynamic one at that. Under rules such as the unanimous verdict requirement, the criminal jury is uniquely designed to be a deliberative body and not just a majority-rule voting machine. At some point, bloc voting on the basis of race, sex, and the like is destructive of the group deliberation, a sign that jurors view themselves as locked into an antagonistic contest to be politically settled by outvoting or outpressuring one another.

Suppose, in some future televised jury deliberation, we see the jurors recessing the group deliberation to give time to various groups to caucus in corners of the room: the black caucus here, the women's group there, maybe a gay and lesbian caucus, or a gathering of the faithful. I take it that most of us would not find this an especially pretty picture. We all know that race matters, as do gender, religion, national origin, sexual orientation, and the like. It would be naïve to think that jurors suddenly ceased to bear demographic baggage simply because they had checked into a jury room.[44] So some argue as follows: Why not accept the reality that there is no such thing as impartial justice in a nation as "diversely biased" as the United States, only the clash of competing interests and views anchored to demographic identity? According to this view, jurors behave properly when they understand their task as reflecting and representing the interests of their bloc as forcefully as they can.

I have argued elsewhere that serious practical and ethical problems are created by the image of the jury as just another forum for competition among factions and identities.[45] To begin with, we would have to entertain some system of quotas or proportional representation if we seriously think that impartiality is mythic and that everything depends on achieving an ever-precarious balance of biases. Leaving the representative integrity of the jury to the luck of the random draw hardly seems enough. But what groups need to be represented on a jury and how can a jury of twelve (or fewer) have seats enough for all the blocs that might clamor for representation? And how do we avoid insulting and stereotyping those seated by implying to them that they are there to vote as we expect the median African American to vote, or as Latinos "typically" vote? Which federal courts are correct, those that consider "Italian Americans" to be a discrete group in America or those that do not (the answer governs whether prosecutors can routinely strike Italian Americans from juries trying Mafia-related crimes)?

It is one thing to defend diversity on a jury as contributing to the fullness of deliberation by adding knowledge to the room, by checking expressions of prejudice against previously absent groups, and by forcing all who wish to be persuasive to express themselves in ways capable of carrying the argument across group lines. It is quite another thing to defend diversity as if jurors owed some static allegiance to the preconceptions of their "own kind." Bloc voting speaks to the narrow, static, and parochial view of jury behavior in ways that undermine the dynamic "mixing it up" that is the better contribution diversity can make to the accuracy of verdicts.

Consider, for instance, Paul Butler's well-known urging of African American jurors to form a bloc and openly nullify the conviction of African American defendants accused of certain nonviolent crimes, principally those involving drug dealing.[46] Butler is at his most persuasive in making the case that legislators from majority white districts have little incentive to worry about drug laws with racially disparate impacts on black communities. But his suggestion that the disadvantage of minorities in legislatures practicing the tactics of bloc voting should be compensated for by importing bloc voting onto juries (where blacks can at least form a nullifying bloc even if they are in a minority) is a self-defeating recommendation. If African Americans were to vote openly as a bloc on juries and if they were to start nullifying as an act of racial loyalty whatever the evidence, then judges would respond by disqualifying more African Americans during voir dire. White jurors might feel less obliged to weigh seriously the arguments of minority jurors, dismissing not-guilty sentiments as just nullification in disguise. In short, although bloc voting is frequently viewed as empowering minority views, it is likely to provoke counterreactions that play to the strength of the majority community.

Thus far, I have approached the issue of bloc voting as if it were a political behavior jurors could choose to engage in or not. For many empirical researchers, this misstates the problem. They argue that juror voting behavior is influenced by crucial predispositions, personality traits, deep attitudes, and demographic markers over which the average person exercises little conscious control. Moreover, against the view of reasoned deliberation that I have defended, they argue that the supposed rationality of deliberation is greatly overstated and that the jury room is a pressurized container for small group dynamics, resulting in bloc voting not for conscious reasons of political strategy but simply by virtue of the social and psychological influences at work.

Is an ethic based on an ideal of reasoned deliberation in the jury room simply at odds with the empirical realities? Let me begin by pointing out at least two ways in which empirical studies of jury decision making actually confirm the capacity of jurors to vote on the basis of evidence and the law rather than group identity. First, a recent survey of the literature concluded that the demographic factors which receive so much attention in media coverage of trials—race, gender, educational level, and socioeconomic status—"have been only weakly and inconsistently related to juror verdict preferences."[47] Although there are clearly some trials in which publicity or the nature of the crime itself splits jurors along demographic lines, voting patterns tied to demography are the exception rather than the rule.[48] In fact, the survey concluded, "it is now clear that few if any characteristics [of the individual juror] are good predictors of juror verdict preferences."[49]

A second area of empirical research, this time on the wording of judicial instructions, also shows that reasoned deliberation is an ideal that jurors can practice when given the tools to do so. In study after study, researchers confirm that instructions often confuse jurors and that the simple reform of expressing instructions in ordinary language would do much to end the confusion.[50] If jurors really voted their racial and ethnic loyalties in the end, then we would not expect the *wording* of instructions to matter to verdicts one way or the other. There is an old saw that courts need not fret much over whether jurors do or do not comprehend their instructions, since they disregard them anyway.[51] But here is one place in which empirical study of juror behavior shows that as simple a legal reform as rewriting key instructions in common language has a definite impact on juror comprehension of, and fidelity to, the instructions. In short, competence of jurors to deliberate according to the law is not some fixed, God-given talent; it depends on giving jurors the resources to be able to practice the ideal.

I do not mean to suggest for a moment that real jurors practice the ideals of deliberation perfectly or that the persistent ways in which they fall short are not deeply troubling. What I do argue is that the ideal is practicable even if we are bound to fall short of ever achieving it perfectly. The power of deliberation to change initial predispositions is as "real" as is the alleged power of demography to close jurors' minds prematurely.

The ethic of jury deliberation I describe is quite different from the disembodied sort of deliberation John Rawls called for in his influential theory of justice.[52] Rawls asked people to imagine themselves in a hypothetical "original position" deliberating over the basic principles of justice upon which to found a new society. Rawls suggested that a procedure could be devised that would generate fair results even if persons by nature sought to reason in their own self-interest. The procedural solution was to impose a "veil of ignorance" over persons, depriving them of any knowledge of what social position they would occupy in the new society—who they were by race, religion, gender, education, income, intelligence, talent, and the like. By virtue of the veil of ignorance, people would be forced to reason not on behalf of their own kind but more generally out of a concern that their life position, whatever it turned out to be in the new society, would be treated fairly and with equal respect.

We do not ask jurors to do the impossible and to reason as pure disembodied agents of the Rawlsian sort. To the contrary, the ideal of the cross-sectional jury seeks to mire jury deliberation in the full-bodied life of the community, recruiting jurors from all walks of life precisely so that the jury room will echo with remarks about what a police officer's word is worth to a black man or what attention a woman does and does not invite by the clothes she wears or the hours she keeps. While it does not take a woman or a black man to make these points, it helps. We should be capable of recognizing the important contribution diversity makes to the quality of deliberation without falling into the mistake of thinking that jurors are necessarily static spokespersons for their own groups. In this regard, it is buoying to find that one of the clearest effects of increasing representation of women on juries is to make the overall deliberation "less hostile and more supportive" and not necessarily a forum for antagonistic expression of interests tied to gender.[53] The evidence about the effects of racial diversity on deliberation is more difficult to summarize. Some studies show that racially balanced juries are more likely to hang than predominantly white juries in cases involving at least one African American defendant.[54] But before one interprets this as a sign of racial bloc voting, it bears noting that, in cases in which the evidence is strong, black-majority juries tend to be harsher on a black defendant than white-majority juries.[55] The fact that racial diversity increases incidence of hung juries in cases against black defendants based on weak evidence is a sign that "embodied" deliberation may be doing just the job we ask of it.

IV. CRYING WOLF: THE POLITICS OF FERRETING OUT JURY NULLIFICATION

Most discussions of jury nullification focus on the political behavior of the jurors doing the nullification. Here the ethical question is whether jurors commit misconduct if and when they refuse to enforce the law and acquit a guilty defendant in order to deliver some sort of political or moral protest. Sometimes the protest is aimed at the felt injustice of the law the jurors are being asked to enforce; in other cases, the jurors object to the particular or selective way in which an otherwise decent law is being enforced against a given defendant or defendants. In either form, nullification invites jurors to consult their own consciences and refuse to enforce the law so as to accomplish a result that is just or merciful in their eyes. Some argue that nullification is a violation of the instructions jurors receive in most jurisdictions to apply the law whether they agree with it or not, and that it threatens the very rule of law by liberating jurors to vote on the basis of political ideology and personal moral beliefs. Others argue that nullification to acquit is a historical part of the ethics of "verdicts according to conscience" and is vital to the ability of the jury system to ameliorate what would otherwise be overly severe and mechanically blind enforcements of the law.[56]

Since other contributors to this volume have written well and at length on the politics of practicing jury nullification,[57] I propose to discuss a reverse and more recent aspect of the politics of jury nullification—the politics of accusing holdout jurors of being closet nullifiers. I will argue that a whole new form of majority-faction pressure threatens the integrity of jury deliberation, sponsored by recent court cases announcing a crackdown on jury nullification and asking jurors to be on the lookout for, and even to report, the existence of nullifiers in their midst. The danger is that jurors will start crying wolf every time a juror steadfastly refuses to go along with the majority in favor of conviction.

Until recently, most trial judges and appellate courts held to a "don't tell, don't ask" policy toward jury nullification. While it might be a fact about our jury system that jurors enjoy the raw *power* to nullify and acquit even a guilty defendant,[58] courts have insisted that jurors do not have any lawful *right* to nullify and are duty-bound to apply the law whether they agree with it or not.[59] Applying this distinction between the power and rights of juries, trial judges routinely refuse defense counsel requests that jurors be told about their nullification prerogatives, on the grounds that such information would encourage jurors to do what they ought not to do.[60] Judges similarly rebuff any queries from jurors themselves seeking guidance as to whether they *must* convict a defendant as charged.[61] But until fairly recently, if a jury spontaneously decided to nullify, then appellate courts treated it with a kind of grudging respect. The classic statement of such a "don't tell, don't ask" policy came during the Vietnam War in the prosecution of a group of war resisters charged with ransacking a Dow Chemical headquarters during a protest against that firm's manufacture of napalm, a chemical agent used by the U.S. Army to defoliate areas of Vietnam.[62] In upholding the judge's refusal to instruct the jury about their power of nullification, the U.S. Court of Appeals stated that telling jurors about nullification would be an implicit encouragement for them to do what they did not have a right to do, namely refuse to enforce laws against malicious destruction of property out of sympathy for the protesters' conscientious motives.[63] However much jurors can nullify and get away with it, the court reasoned that we do not want to prompt or encourage jurors to routinely canvass the issue of nullification, as courts would be doing were they explicitly to draw attention to and sanction the use of nullification. But if a jury not told about nullification feels so strongly about an issue that it goes ahead and nullifies, then the very spontaneity of the nullification meant to the Court of Appeals that the jury's reservations about law enforcement are grave enough to be afforded respect.[64]

A series of factors have combined in recent years to increase judicial hostility toward jury nullification and to end the *modus vivendi* practiced under the "don't tell, don't ask" policy, as courts turn actively to policing for suspected nullifiers during voir dire and sometimes even in the midst of deliberations. The first factor was the emergence of an organized political group dedicated precisely to telling jurors about the secrets of nullification. Calling itself "The Fully Informed Jury Association" (FIJA), this group employs a host of informal, even guerilla-like tactics to bypass judicial restrictions and get the word out about jury nullification.[65] Its members leaflet courthouses, leave stacks of sheets about nullification in the corridors, and sometimes even place the information under the windshield wipers of parking lots used by persons summoned for jury duty. FIJA appears to be a loose confederation of persons from all over the political spectrum who share only some gripe against some law, be it gun laws for militia members, marijuana restrictions for the Hemp Society, or tax laws for tax resisters. Their leafleting does not appear to be generated by any particular trial but nonetheless some judges have considered an entire jury pool contaminated by its exposure to FIJA literature and have excused jurors en masse.[66]

As FIJA worked to let the cat out of the bag in violation of the "don't tell, don't ask" arrangements, another factor emerged to politicize jury nullification. To many observers, the jury's decision to acquit O. J. Simpson of double murder charges smacked of jury nullification by a predominantly African American jury that knew Simpson was guilty but preferred to acquit him as a way of sending a protest message against the racism of some of the investigating cops and against the glee of the white community in bringing down a powerful black icon.[67] On the day following the verdicts, *The Wall Street Journal* buttressed this fear of nullification by publishing an article on page one purporting to document widespread acts of nullification by predominantly African American juries in the Bronx, Washington, D.C., and Wayne County (Detroit), Michigan.[68] The *Journal* pointed to Paul Butler's *Yale Law Review* essay explicitly calling for blacks to nullify as further evidence of a mounting trend.[69] The combination of FIJA activity, the Simpson verdict, and the *Journal* accusations gave unprecedented publicity to jury nullification, the subject even making its way onto the CBS show *60 Minutes*.[70]

Courts responded to the avalanche of publicity by abandoning the "don't tell, don't ask" policy in three important regards. First, instead of maintaining silence on the subject of nullification, some judges began explicitly instructing jurors that nullification was misconduct and that they should report any jurors making nullification arguments during deliberation.[71] Second, in light of swirling publicity about nullification, some judges felt obliged to poll prospective jurors on the subject during voir dire,[72] disqualifying for cause not only persons who confessed a willingness to nullify but also sometimes persons who simply acknowledged that they had seen, and therefore been tainted by, FIJA literature or other information about jury nullification.[73] Third, and most ominously, courts began to investigate complaints coming out of the jury room during ongoing deliberations that one or more holdouts against conviction were advocating the jury's right to nullify.

These reports accusing holdouts of being nullifiers came, of course, from majority-faction jurors and it is here that the potential for shrewd jurors to artfully use judicial fear of nullification to pull the rug out from under holdouts came into view. Two leading cases, one federal and the other state, illustrate the dangers in the new enforcement regime.

In *United States v. Thomas* (1997), while the jury was still deliberating, several jurors complained to the judge that Juror No. 5 was simply unwilling to convict any of the defendants of conspiracy to possess and distribute cocaine.[74] After interviewing the complaining jurors as well as Juror No. 5, the trial judge concluded that Juror No. 5 was intent on nullifying and he dismissed the juror for just cause pursuant to Fed. R. Crim. P. 23(b). On defendant's appeal following his conviction, the court emphatically agreed with the trial judge that nullification was a form of misconduct subjecting an offending juror to discharge. But the difficulty was in devising procedures that would permit a judge to investigate what was being said during deliberations without unduly compromising the secrecy and privacy of jury deliberations. As the Court of Appeals noted:

As a general rule, no one—including the judge . . . —has a "right to know" how a jury, or any individual juror, has deliberated or how a decision was reached. . . . The secrecy of deliberations is the cornerstone of the modern Anglo-American jury system. . . . The mere suggestion that the views of jurors may be conveyed to the parties and the public . . . understandably may cause anxiety and fear in jurors, and distort the process by which a verdict is reached.[75]

Not only was there a need to balance the state's interest in preventing juror misconduct with the jury's interest in the secrecy of its deliberations, the Second Circuit also emphasized the difficulties inherent in distinguishing a holdout based on improper nullification from a holdout rooted in reasonable doubts about the evidence. In fact, in the particular case before it, the appellate court concluded that the trial judge had erred in concluding that the evidence established that Juror No. 5 was bent on nullification, a charge the juror himself rejected. But although wrong in his conclusions, the Court of Appeals stressed that the trial judge acted properly in seeking to investigate pre-verdict complaints about a juror's intent to nullify. It gave a cautious yellow light for such investigations to proceed in future cases, yet reminded trial judges not to probe more deeply than necessary into the thought processes of individual jurors.

It is still an open question what the practical effects on jury deliberation will be of the Second Circuit's approval of judicial interrogation of jurors accused of nullification. But there is a danger that majority-faction jurors can turn the new judicial vigilance to their advantage during deliberations. With good or bad intentions, the majority can report, or merely threaten to report, holdouts as a way of intimidating them into capitulation. Even in the best of circumstances, it is difficult for one or a small number of jurors to resist majority sentiment in favor of conviction but it becomes even more difficult when resistance could trigger a judge's investigation of the basis of the holdout.[76] The holdouts themselves may harbor confusion about the basis of their refusal to convict and may be susceptible to suggestions that they differ from the majority only because they are reasoning improperly.[77]

One court that has systematically explored these dangers is the California Supreme Court. A 2002 decision about the propriety of a jury instruction reads as follows:

The integrity of a trial requires that jurors, at all times during their deliberations, conduct themselves as required by these instructions. Accordingly, should it occur that any juror refuses to deliberate or expresses an intention to disregard the law or to decide the case based on [penalty or punishment, or] any [other] improper basis, it is the obligation of the other jurors to immediately advise the Court of the situation.[78]

Although the court held that this instruction was constitutionally permissible, it exercised its supervisory powers to disapprove of its continued use. The court specifically worried that "the instruction [could] be used by one juror as a tool for browbeating other jurors."[79] A shrewd juror "could . . . without ever actually communicating with the court, place undue pressure on another juror by threatening to accuse that juror in open court of reasoning improperly or of not following the court's instructions." In the same vein, the court went on to worry that "[t]he instruction could cause jurors to become hypervigilant during deliberations about *perceived* refusals to deliberate or other ill-defined 'improprieties' in deliberation."[80] In short, even though the instruction was correct in telling jurors that they were subject for dismissal for misconduct during deliberations, the court thought it was a bad idea to encourage jurors to report one another during the heat of deliberation battle. It would be difficult for even a well-intentioned juror to know whether another juror's holdout was motivated by nullification or by reasonable doubts about the evidence.[81] It would be easy for a less well-intentioned juror to jump to the conclusion that any opposition to conviction must be a form of nullification. And it would be difficult for a judge to investigate complaints without "chill[ing] the free exchange of ideas that lies at the center of the deliberative process."[82]

The California Supreme Court's decision in *Engelman* is notable for its sensitivity to the way the fight over nullification can recruit judges onto the majority faction's side during an ongoing jury deliberation. But, even though the court disapproved of this particular instruction, it noted with approval the position of the Second Circuit that nullification was misconduct and that judges should respond to complaints jurors might make about fellow jurors in future trials, even when not prompted by the disapproved instruction.[83] It remains to be seen how often such complaints will be made and how judges will neutrally investigate them without signaling to holdouts that the judge is on the side of the majority. But, as even one scholar who favors dismissing jurors for nullification has noted, there is every reason to fear that the search for nullifiers could degenerate into "one-sided favoritism" of the prosecution side.[84] She cautions against "mid-trial investigations of alleged nullifiers . . . becom[ing] so intrusive that they deprive a defendant of the Sixth Amendment right to a jury's independent view of the facts."[85] We can hope that such dangers do not come to fruition, but they seem inherent in the recent judicial overreaction to media-fed fears of rampant nullification.

V. CONCLUSION

In closing, it is worth mulling over Alexis de Tocqueville's well-known insistence that the jury is every bit as much a political institution as it is a legal one.[86] Tocqueville had a way of pressing his insistence without regard to the potential conflict between politics and law in the life of a juror. Yet much of American law has evolved around this conflict, trying to preserve the impartiality of juries even as juries become more representative of communities and the diversity within communities. Given what it sometimes takes to preserve the impartiality of jurors (screening for pretrial publicity, changes of venue, sequestration), Tocqueville's praise of the political nature of the jury often seems too relaxed. Perhaps this was because he was more interested in the contribution jury duty makes to the civic education of jurors than in the contribution of jurors to justice for litigants. Indeed, in a much neglected footnote, Tocqueville adds the thought that, were he to be called upon to defend the jury merely as a legal institution, he would be far less enthusiastic.[87] One of his favorite comparisons was between jury and primary school.[88] But the fact that jurists may learn the virtues of democratic self-government while serving on juries is hardly a benefit capable of inspiring confidence in litigants whose claims are being settled by those still in school.

This chapter has focused on politics writ small in the jury room—the pressures that jurors visit one on the other as they wrangle over the verdict. In law school, I once asked a professor why there were no courses on the jury, only abundant courses drawing on appellate case law. I was told that jurors are more properly subjects for a psychology course, since they are a prime example of small groups obedient to peer pressure. As an empirical observation, there is obviously much truth in this. But if "small group dynamics" is all there is to study about juries, then I see no way to defend the jury robustly as an institution serving justice. We should remain clear about the ideal that ought to inspire jurors to escape from the "usuals" of small group pressure—an ideal that makes the search for the truth the highest obligation of jurors. We know that jurors will constantly fall short of practicing the ideal, but this is no reason to abandon the ideal or to doubt our capacity to always do better.

NOTES

1. Jeffrey Abramson, *We, the Jury: The Jury System and the Ideal of Democracy* (Cambridge, MA: Harvard University Press, 2000), 99–142.

2. Some scholars deny that there is any objective standard of truth against which to measure the accuracy of jury verdicts. According to this way of thinking, even so-called facts are socially constructed and therefore "what happened" is relative to the observer and context. And what is true of the social construction of facts is even more the case with values that jurors bring to their understanding of the law. This is not the place for me to develop fully my views on these issues. Suffice it to say that in a great number of cases, there is a search for the truth that jurors can share regardless of background: the semen either did or did not come from the defendant; the bus hitting the pedestrian did or did not run the stop sign. However racialized or gendered our first perceptions of what happened might be, the purpose of a cross-sectional jury is still to escape those preconceptions in favor of a richer and fuller understanding of events when people try on one another's lenses.

3. "'[J]urors can be expected to disagree, even vehemently, and to attempt to persuade disagreeing fellow jurors by strenuous and sometimes heated means' . . . . During deliberations, expressions of 'frustration, temper, and strong conviction' may be anticipated." *People v. Engelman*, 28 Cal. 4th 436, 446 (2002).

4. *Twelve Angry Men* (1957), dir. Sidney Lumet, Twentieth Century-Fox.

5. Not all tactics of persuasion are equally egalitarian. In one Watergate-era prosecution, a vice president of a major bank who had strong Republican ties apparently lied in voir dire to stay in the pool of eligible jurors. Once on the jury, he used his bank connections to provide some entertainment benefits to the jury during the case. When it came time to deliberate, the social dominance he had achieved spilled over into parallel patterns of deference in argument and he was able to achieve the relatively rare feat of turning an initial eight to four vote for conviction into a unanimous vote of acquittal for two high-ranking former members of Richard Nixon's Cabinet. See Hans Zeisel and Shari Seidman Diamond, "The Jury Selection in the Mitchell-Stans Conspiracy Trial," *American Bar Foundation Journal* 1 (1976): 151–74, and Martin Arnold, "How Mitchell-Stans Jury Reached Acquittal Verdict," *New York Times*, May 5, 1974, A1.

6. Oregon and Louisiana are the only two exceptions to the requirement of unanimity in criminal cases.

7. *Allen v. United States*, 164 U.S. 492, 501 (1896).

8. *Allen v. United States*, 501. Likewise, if "the majority was for acquittal, the minority ought to ask themselves whether they might not reasonably doubt the correctness of a judgment which was not concurred in by the majority."

9. See, e.g., *United States v. Hernandez-Albino*, 177 F.3d 33, 38 (1st Cir. 1999); *Tucker v. Catoe*, 221 F.3d 600, 610–11 (4th Cir. 2000) (judge may not single out minority jurors). Some federal circuits and some states disfavor the use of *Allen*-type instructions altogether. See, e.g., *United States v. Quintero-Barraza*, 57 F.3d 836, 842 (9th Cir. 1995) ("*Allen* charge stands at the brink of impermissible coercion"); *United States v. Graham*, 758 F.2d 879, 883 (3d Cir. 1985) (charge suggests that a juror should mistrust his own judgment); *People v. Gainer*, 19 Cal. 3d 835, 852, 566 P. 2d 997, 1006 (1977) (specifically disapproving of the giving of the *Allen* charge in California and holding that no instruction may be given which either "(1) encourages jurors to consider the numerical division or preponderance of opinion on the jury . . . ; or (2) states or implies that if the jury fails to agree the case will necessarily be retried"). See also, Jeffrey C. Corey, "Thirty-First Annual Review of Criminal Procedure: III: Trial: Influences on the Jury," *Georgia Law Journal* 90 (2002): 1636, text accompanying notes 1665–1668.

10. Harry Kalven Jr. and Hans Zeisel, *The American Jury* (Chicago: University of Chicago Press, 1970), 487–88; Nancy S. Marder, "The Myth of the Nullifying Jury," *Northwestern Law Review* 93 (1999): 877, 951 (citing recent studies on difficulty of maintaining resistance to majority pressure on juries).

11. See Abramson, *We, the Jury*, 196ff.

12. See, e.g., *United States v. Seawell*, 550 F.2d 1159, 1163 (9th Cir. 1977) (reversible error to repeat *Allen* charge unless jury asks for the repetition).

13. See, e.g., *People v. Keenan*, 758 P.2d 1081, 1121 (Cal. 1988) (declining to hear evidence that a male juror threatened a holdout, an elderly woman, threatening even to kill her; remarks, while particularly harsh, could not be taken literally and inquiry into the demeanor, eccentricities, or personalities of individual jurors

would deprive jurors of free expression); *United States v. Kohne*, 358 F.Supp. 1046, 1047 (W.D. Pa. 1973) (threats and abusive language directed at holdout, including threats to get even, merely represented heated exchanges common in the jury room); *People v. Jacobson*, 440 N.Y.S. 2d 458, 464 (N.Y. Sup. Ct. 1981) (allegations about intimidation through obscenities, slamming of fists, and chair-throwing, even if true, do not impeach a verdict; although not to be encouraged, they are a reality of life); *People v. Reid*, 583 N.E. 2d 1 (Il. App. Ct. 1991) (threatening telephone call from male juror to female holdout juror, saying "you son of a bitch, we'll get you for that"). For these and other cases, see Denise M. O'Malley, "Impeaching a Jury Verdict, Juror Misconduct, and Related Issues: A View from the Bench," *John Marshall Law Review* 33 (1999): 145.

14. These comments are reported in Sandra Benlevy, "Venus and Mars in the Jury Deliberation Room: Exploring the Differences That Exist among Male and Female Jurors during the Deliberation Process," *Southern California Review of Law and Women's Studies* 9 (2000): 445, 452.

15. *Clark v. United States*, 289 U.S. 1, 16 (1933), quoted in *People v. Engelman*, 28 Cal. 4th 436, 453 (2002) (Baxter, J., concurring and dissenting).

16. Fed R. Evid. 606(b). Although this rule applies only to postverdict secrecy, the Supreme Court has reached similar conclusions about inquiries into misconduct by jurors even before deliberation begins. See *Tanner v. United States*, 483 U.S. 107 (1987) (refusing to consider evidence of juror use of drugs and alcohol during trial). Other courts have been equally wary of inquiring into alleged jury misconduct even when they become aware of complaints during deliberation and before a verdict is reached. See generally Alison Markovitz, "Jury Secrecy during Deliberations," *Yale Law Journal* 110 (2001): 1493. But see *infra*, Section IV for recent trends in favor of preverdict inquiries into alleged juror misconduct.

17. *People v. Engelman*, 28 Cal. 4th at 451, citing *Keenan v. Woodford*, No. 89-CV-2167 DLJ (N.D. Cal. Jan. 10, 2001).

18. Benlevy, "Venus and Mars," text accompanying n. 43.

19. *United States v. Henley*, 238 F.3d 111 (9th Cir. 2001) (error to reject without hearing African American defendant's offer to prove a juror had used the word "nigger" during deliberations). See also *Tobias v. Smith*, 468 F.Supp. 1287 (W.D.N.Y. 1979) (habeas corpus petition requesting hearing on jury conduct granted to investigate allegations of racist remark that "you can't tell one black from another"); *State v. Johnson*, 627 N.W. 2d, 2001 WL 694730 (S.D. June 20, 2001) (misconduct for one juror to say, during trial of black defendant, "I have a rope" and the other responding "I have a tree"); *United States v. Heller*, 785 F.2d. 1524, 1526–28 (11th Cir. 1986) (conviction reversed where juror said, supposedly in jest, "the fellow we are trying is a Jew, I say, let's hang him"). See generally, "Developments in the Law—Race and the Criminal Process: VII: Racist Juror Misconduct during Deliberation," *Harvard Law Review* 101 (1988): 1595.

20. For an interesting article showing emerging tensions between Anglo-American understandings of jury secrecy and the human rights decisions by the European Court on Human Rights protecting the right to trial before an impartial tribunal, see John D. Jackson, "Making Juries Accountable," *American Journal of Comparative Law* 50 (2002): 477.

21. *Early v. Packer*, 537 U.S. 3 (2002).

22. *Early v. Packer*, 4.

23. *Early v. Packer,* 4.

24. *Early v. Packer,* 5–6; for California ban on *Allen* charge, see *People v. Gainer,* 19 Cal. 3d 835 (1977).

25. *Early v. Packer,* 5–6.

26. *Early v. Packer,* 6.

27. Ursula Bentele and William J. Bowers, "How Jurors Decide on Death: Guilt Is Overwhelming; Aggravation Requires Death; and Mitigation Is No Excuse," *Brooklyn Law Review* 66 (2001): 1011, 1039–41. For a general description of the Capital Jury Project's interviews with capital jurors, see William J. Bowers, "The Capital Jury Project: Rationale, Design and Preview of Early Findings," *Indiana Law Journal* 70 (1995): 1043, 1079.

28. Bentele and Bowers, "How Jurors Decide on Death," 1039.

29. Bentele and Bowers, "How Jurors Decide on Death," 1040.

30. Bentele and Bowers, "How Jurors Decide on Death," 1040–41.

31. Bentele and Bowers, "How Jurors Decide on Death," 1039–41. For the general way in which death penalty instructions mislead jurors, see Peter Tiersma, "The Rocky Road to Legal Reform: Improving the Language of Jury Instructions," *Brooklyn Law Review* 66 (2001): 1081, 1092–99.

32. 99 Eng. Rep. 944 (K.B. 1785). The rule against permitting jurors to impeach their verdict dates back to this case. This rule is essentially codified in Fed. R. Evid. 606(b).

33. Once again, courts are loathe to violate jury secrecy by investigating allegations that the verdict was reached through compromise. In this vein, consider this exchange when a judge polled jurors individually, asking "was this and is this now your verdict?" One juror succinctly responded, "Compromise." Reviewing this exchange, the Illinois Supreme Court found that the juror's remarks were essentially unresponsive to the judge's question and did not amount to the required repudiation of assent to the verdict. *People v. Preston,* 391 N.E. 2d 359, 364–66 (Ill. 1979).

34. According to many studies, juries that begin by taking a straw vote ("verdict driven-juries") are more likely to deadlock than juries that begin by discussing the evidence without voting ("evidence-driven juries"). See, e.g., Reid Hastie, Steven D. Penrod, and Nancy Pennington, *Inside the Jury* (Cambridge, MA: Harvard University Press, 1983). It is a reasonable surmise that verdict-driven juries may therefore think more in terms of compromising than evidence-driven juries.

35. For a review of various statements of the doctrine of lesser included offenses, see Catherine L. Carpenter, "The All-or-Nothing Doctrine in Criminal Cases: Independent Trial Strategy or Gamesmanship Gone Awry?" *American Journal of Criminal Law* 26 (1999): 257, 263–74 and accompanying notes.

36. For an excellent discussion of the tension between these two positions, see Carpenter: "The All-or-Nothing Doctrine in Criminal Cases."

37. *Commonwealth v. Woodward,* 694 N.E. 2d 1277 (Mass. 1998).

38. *Commonwealth v. Woodward,* 1277 and 1281 n. 1.

39. Memorandum and Order, *Commonwealth v. Woodward,* No. Crim 97-0433 (Mass. Super. Nov. 10, 1997), 6–7. It is not clear on what grounds the trial judge substituted his reading of the evidence for the jury's. But, ironically, after having refused to instruct the jury on manslaughter, the trial judge then used his own refusal to let the jury consider manslaughter in order to enter a manslaughter verdict on his own. He reasoned that "had the manslaughter option been available

to the jurors, they might well have selected it, not out of compromise, but because that particular verdict accorded with at least one rational view of the evidence." Memorandum and Order, *Commonwealth v. Woodward*, 6.

40. *Commonwealth v. Woodward*, 694 N.E.2d 1284.

41. *Commonwealth v. Woodward*, 1283.

42. *Commonwealth v. Woodward*, 1299 (Greany, J., dissenting). Notwithstanding the error, the high court ruled that the judge's subsequent decision to reduce Woodward's conviction to involuntary manslaughter rendered the error harmless. *Commonwealth v. Woodward*, 1284.

43. Hastie, Penrod, and Pennington, *Inside the Jury*.

44. See n. 48, *infra*, for citations to studies showing case-specific influence of gender and race.

45. *We, the Jury*, chap. 5.

46. Paul Butler, "Racially Based Jury Nullification: Black Power in the Criminal Justice System," *Yale Law Journal* 105 (1995): 677.

47. Dennis J. Devine, Laura D. Clayton, Benjamin B. Dunford, Rasmy Seying, and Jennifer Price, "Jury Decision Making: 45 Years of Empirical Research on Deliberating Groups," *Psychology, Public Policy, and Law* 7 (2001): 622, 673–75. See also Edith Greene, Sonia Chopra, Margaret Bull Kovera, Steven D. Penrod, V. Gordon Rose, Regina Schuller, and Christina A. Studebaker, "Jurors and Juries: A Review of the Field," in *Taking Psychology and Law into the Twenty-First Century*, ed. J. R. P. Ogloff (New York: Kluwer, 2004), 227 ("researchers have found few demographic characteristics that consistently predict juror verdicts"; the article cites studies that found that occupation, gender, income, religion, and age of jurors did not significantly predict verdicts).

48. The influence of juror gender or race on verdict preferences is quite case-specific. On gender, see, e.g., Benlevy, "Venus and Mars in the Jury Deliberation Room," 449–55 (women more sympathetic to rape victims, more sympathetic to children as victims, less tolerant of the use of force); Greene, Chopra, Kovera, Penrod, Rose, Schuller, and Studebaker, "Jurors and Juries," 228 (citing studies showing that women more likely than men to convict defendant of incest, more likely to convict of sexual crimes against women and children); Nancy S. Marder, "Juries, Justice and Multiculturalism," *Southern California Law Review* 75 (2002): 659, 688 (juries balanced on gender lines exhibit less hostile and more supportive deliberations). On race, Greene, Chopra, Kovera, Penrod, Rose, Schuller, and Studebaker, "Jurors and Juries," 228 ("researchers have also shown that the effects of juror race tend to depend on the particulars of the case being tried"). But cf. Theodore Eisenberg, Stephen P. Garvey, and Martin T. Wells, "Forecasting Life and Death: Juror Race, Religion and Attitude toward the Death Penalty," *Journal of Legal Studies* 30 (2001): 277, 279 (black jurors more likely than white jurors to vote for life on the first ballot, but not on the final one; jurors identifying themselves as Southern Baptists also more likely to cast their first vote for death); Kenneth S. Klein and Theodore D. Klastorin, "Do Diverse Juries Aid or Impede Justice?" *Wisconsin Law Review* (1999): 553 (summarizing conflicting studies on demographic influences on jurors but noting a relationship between racial diversity and likelihood that a jury will hang).

49. Although the demographic characteristics of the individual juror standing alone have not proven to be important influences on verdicts, researchers have documented that demography does lead to bias when there is a similarity between

the group identity of defendant and juror, triggering a kind of invisible solidarity or loyalty. The most disturbing instance of this kind of bias comes in death penalty cases, in which (mostly white) juries are more likely to impose the death penalty when the victim is white like them and the defendant is not. See David C. Baldus, George Woodworth, and Charles A. Pulaski Jr., *Equal Justice and the Death Penalty: A Legal and Empirical Analysis* (Boston, MA: Northeastern University Press, 1990), 42–46, 140–97, 306–69; Arthur L. Rizer III, "Justice in a Changed World: The Race Effect on Wrongful Convictions," *William Mitchell Law Review* 29 (2003): 845, 865–66 (citing study showing that both black and white students in mock juries convict more often when they share racial affinity with the victim). In regard to the topic of this chapter, what is especially alarming about the race-of-victim bias in death penalty deliberations is that it seems to occur not out of deliberate political choice but rather from an invisible bias.

50. See, e.g., Stephen P. Garvey, Sheri Lynn Johnson, and Paul Marcus, "Correcting Deadly Confusion: Responding to Jury Inquiries in Capital Cases," *Cornell Law Review* 85 (2000): 627, 635–36, 643; Tiersma, "The Rocky Road to Legal Reform," 1089–92 (describing Illinois research showing failure of jurors to understand instructions on several points of law); Shari Seidman Diamond and Judith N. Levi, "Improving Decisions on Death by Revising and Testing Jury Instructions," *Judicature* 79 (1996): 224.

51. In *Weeks v. Angelone*, 528 U.S. 225, 229 (2000), a Virginia jury deliberating over whether to sentence the defendant to death sent a note out to the judge, stating they were confused by instructions on the crucial issue of whether, once they found the presence of an aggravating circumstance, they *had* to impose the death sentence or whether they had a choice (they did). Rather than answering the question in plain language, the judge just told them to reread the instruction that confused them. The Supreme Court affirmed. It is difficult to believe a case would have come out the same way if judges truly believed that jurors at least tried to abide by their instructions and acted accordingly.

52. *A Theory of Justice* (Cambridge, MA: Belknap/Harvard University Press, 1972), 11–21.

53. See, e.g., Marder, "Juries, Justice and Multiculturalism," 688 (juries balanced on gender lines exhibit less hostile and more supportive deliberations).

54. See Klein and Klastorin, "Do Diverse Juries Aid or Impede Justice?" 553.

55. Devine, Clayton, Dunford, Seying, and Price, "Jury Decision Making," 630.

56. For a general review of jury nullification, see Abramson, *We, the Jury*, 57–95; Alan W. Scheflin and Jon M. Van Dyke, "Jury Nullification: The Contours of a Controversy," *Law and Contemporary Problems* 43 (1980): 51.

57. See the contributions by Alan W. Scheflin, B. Michael Dann, Shari Seidman Diamond, and Norman J. Finkel to this volume.

58. The power to nullify to acquit flows from two sources. First, the constitutional protection against double jeopardy means that a criminal jury's verdict of not guilty is final and not subject to appeal, no matter how obvious it might be that the decision goes against the law and the evidence. Second, criminal juries pronounce just the general verdict of guilty or not guilty; they provide no explanation of their reasoning and thus can nullify without ever admitting as such and without fear of ever being held to account. Jurors no doubt also sometimes nullify the

law or disregard the evidence in order to convict. But, unlike the finality of a not-guilty verdict, convictions against the law or evidence are subject to appeal and hence jurors do not enjoy a parallel power to nullify and make it stand.

59. From the colonial era until the twentieth century, many American jurisdictions did recognize that jurors had the right to decide the law as well as the facts of the case and hence gave at least limited recognition to jury nullification. It was not until 1895 that the Supreme Court expressly disapproved of jury nullification in *Sparf and Hansen v. United States*, 156 U.S. 1 (1895). For a review of the history of nullification, see Abramson, *We, the Jury*, 57–95.

60. See, e.g., *United States v. Dougherty*, 473 F. 2d 1113 (D.C. Cir. 1972); *People v. Cleveland*, 25 Cal. 4th 466 (2001); *People v. Williams*, 25 Cal. 4th 441 (2001).

61. See, e.g., *People v. Dillon*, 34 Cal. 3d 441 (1983).

62. *United States v. Dougherty*, 473 F. 2d 1113.

63. *United States v. Dougherty*, 1137–38, n. 4.

64. *United States v. Dougherty*.

65. See generally *FIJActivist*, the organization's newsletter. See also Clay S. Conrad, *Jury Nullification: The Evolution of a Doctrine* (Durham, NC: North Carolina Academic Press, 1998), 158–66.

66. See examples cited in Nancy J. King, "Silencing Nullification Advocacy Inside the Jury Room and Outside the Courtroom," *University of Chicago Law Review* 65 (1998): 435, 438–43 (trial judge in Dayton, Ohio, disqualified the entire jury pool appearing in court upon learning that a man was distributing pro-nullification pamphlets; when one person in jury pool of seventy passed around a FIJA brochure, Colorado trial judge disqualified all seventy).

67. For the debate over whether the Simpson jurors nullified or acquitted on the basis of having reasonable doubts about the evidence, given the racial prejudice of some of the investigating officers, see Jeffrey Abramson, ed., *Postmortem: The O. J. Simpson Case: Justice Confronts Race, Domestic Violence, Lawyers, Money, and the Media* (New York: Basic Books, 1996), 12–18, 33–45.

68. Benjamin A. Holden, Laurie P. Cohen, and Eleena de Lisser, "Color Blinded? Race Seems to Play an Increasing Role in Many Jury Verdicts," *Wall Street Journal*, October 4, 1995, A1.

69. See, *supra*, text accompanying note 46 for a discussion of Professor Butler's views on racial nullification.

70. See Marder, "The Myth of the Nullifying Jury," 938.

71. See *infra*, text accompanying notes 78–85, for a discussion of a California jury instruction explicitly asking jurors to report suspicions of nullification to the presiding judge. Such instructions arguably override the traditional concession that jurors have the power to nullify. Essentially, courts began to try to nip nullification in the bud before the power was exercised. The new position depended on distinguishing the situation when judges hear reports of nullification only after a verdict has been reached and read (in which case it remains true that jurors have the power to nullify and there is no judicial remedy), and situations where judges learn of potential nullification while deliberations are still ongoing (in which case nullification can be considered misconduct and grounds for removing a juror who is trying to exercise a power to which he has no lawful right). For the distinction between preverdict and postverdict judicial inquiries into juror misconduct, see Markovitz, "Jury Secrecy during Deliberations."

206 *Jeffrey Abramson*

72. In one infamous Colorado case, juror Laura Kriho was convicted of contempt of court for expressing nullification views during jury deliberation in a drug case and for failing to disclose her nullification views during voir dire. The jury on which Kriho served hung on the drug charges. When the judge learned that she had expressed hostility toward enforcing drug laws during deliberation, and had not disclosed her views on drug laws during voir dire (she was a founder of a local group in favor of legalizing marijuana) nor her own drug conviction history (she had been charged with possession of LSD and received a deferred judgment), he ordered her arrested and charged with contempt of court. At her subsequent contempt trial, a second judge found her guilty but the Colorado Court of Appeals overturned her conviction. The appeals court noted that Kriho had never been directly asked about her views on drug laws and had no obligation to volunteer her views at voir dire. The court remanded the case for a new trial on the one issue of whether Kriho's failure to disclose her prior LSD arrest and deferred judgment was contemptuous. She was asked during voir dire whether she had ever been accused of a crime. But the appeals court noted that her apparent failure to answer the question accurately would constitute contempt only if it could be proven at retrial that her omission was a deliberate attempt to obstruct justice, rather than understandable confusion about whether a "deferred judgment" and eventual dismissal of the LSD charges meant she had ever been accused of a crime. *People v. Kriho*, Case No. 96-CR-91 (Division 1, Gilpin County, February 10, 1997), rev'd. and remanded, *People v. Laura J. Kriho*, No. 97CA0700, 1999 Colo. App. Lexis 101, petition and cross-petition for writ of certiorari denied, No. 99SC766, 2000 Colo. Lexis 465.

73. See note 65, *supra*.

74. 116 F.3d 606 (2d Cir. 1997).

75. *United States v. Thomas*, 618–19. See also *People v. Cleveland*, 25 Cal. 4th at 481–82; *People v. Engelman*, 28 Cal. 4th 436, 443 (2002).

76. Marder, "The Myth of the Nullifying Jury," 951 ("Research has shown that when there are only one or two holdouts, they have a hard time maintaining their position in the face of pressure from other jurors. The position of holdouts has become even more precarious now that the majority can threaten to describe any holdouts as potential nullifiers, even if they are not.").

77. In *United States v. Brown*, 823 F.2d 591 (D.C. Cir. 1987), the appellate court found the trial judge erred in removing a juror who himself asked to be dismissed and said he was unable to continue deliberating; the record left open the possibility that his refusal to deliberate was based on honest convictions about the insufficiency of the evidence. *United States v. Brown*, 597.

78. *People v. Engelman*, 28 Cal. 4th 436, 441–42 (2002), quoting CALJIC No. 17.41.1(2).

79. *People v. Engelman*, 445.

80. *People v. Engelman*, 447.

81. In *United States v. Symington*, 195 F.3d 1080 (9th Cir. 1999), jurors complained that one juror was unable to comprehend the evidence and engage in deliberation. The trial judge dismissed the juror after finding that he was unable or unwilling to deliberate. But since the record was ambiguous as to why the juror had withdrawn from deliberation, the appellate court found it was possible that the withdrawal

spoke to views on the insufficiency of the evidence and therefore it was error to dismiss the juror.

82. *People v. Engelman*, 447.

83. *People v. Engelman*, 442. In two decisions in the years immediately prior to *Engelman*, the California Supreme Court had held in no uncertain terms that jurors do not have any right of nullification. *People v. Cleveland*, 25 Cal. 4th 466 (2001) and *People v. Williams*, 25 Cal. 4th 441 (2001). While the *Engelman* court disapproved of the particular instruction calling on jurors to report suspected nullifiers, it quoted with approval the pattern instructions informing the jury that "you must accept and follow the law as I [the judge] state it you, regardless of whether you agree with the law." CALJIC No. 1.00 and CALJIC No. 0.50.

84. King, "Silencing Nullification Advocacy Inside the Jury Room and Outside the Courtroom," 482. See also Ran Zev Schijanovich, "Note, The Second Circuit's Attack on Jury Nullification in *United States v. Thomas*: In Disregard of the Law and the Evidence," *Cardozo Law Review* 20 (1999): 1275 (criticizing judicial attempts to detect and stamp out expressions of nullification during deliberation as threatening judicial control of juries in deprivation of jury's historic power to nullify).

85. King, "Silencing Nullification Advocacy Inside the Jury Room and Outside the Courtroom," 482.

86. Alexis de Tocqueville, *Democracy in America*, trans. George Lawrence (New York: Harper and Row, 1966), I: 271–72.

87. Tocqueville, *Democracy in America*, 272.

88. Tocqueville, *Democracy in America*, 274.

The Ethics of Jury Room Politics: A Response to Jeffrey Abramson

James P. Levine

The title of Jeffrey Abramson's chapter, "Jury Deliberation: Fair and Foul," is elegant in its simplicity. It gets to the heart of a critical question: In the face of virtually no guidance about proper jury behavior, how should jurors conduct themselves in trying to reach a verdict? Which approaches to reaching agreement are legitimate, and which ones are beyond the pale?

Unfortunately, posing the question adroitly is easier than answering it. It is well and good to state that jurors should confine themselves to rational discourse about the law and the evidence in trying to convince each other about the proper verdict, but the sociodynamics of the collective choice process normally entail much greater complexity. Political ploys, histrionics, pejorative language, bloc formation, peer pressure, and bargaining are standard elements of decision making by groups. Should such behavior be off-limits for jurors?

An old film classic, *Twelve Angry Men*, aptly cited by Abramson at the outset of his chapter, illustrates the dilemma. Recall that in the movie Henry Fonda plays a juror who finds himself a minority of one voting for not guilty after the first show of hands by a jury deliberating a murder case. He then proposes a "deal" to his fellow jurors: If after a secret ballot the vote remains eleven in favor of conviction and one against, he will capitulate and go along with the guilty verdict. However, if anyone else joins him in dissenting, discussion will continue. The jury accepts this proposal, and someone else does in fact change his mind, resulting in two not-guilty votes. This sets the stage for the rest of the film which results in the other ten ultimately changing their minds and acquitting the defendant.

Abramson uses the film as an example of the use of clever strategy to persuade co-jurors—a recognition that politics "writ small" occurs in the jury room. But the deeper issue that *Twelve Angry Men* raises is a serious ethical question: Had the juror played by Fonda strongly believed that guilt had not been proven beyond a reasonable doubt, should he have agreed to yield? Was this being open-minded, or was this a cowardly yielding to the pressure to conform? Was this a brilliant gamble that demonstrated respect for his colleagues, or was this a reckless act that might well have doomed an innocent man? The ploy used by this fictitious juror creates a host of ethical dilemmas.

Tough as these questions are, imagine a different scenario that presents an even more problematic tactic: The secret ballot is taken, the dissident juror portrayed by Fonda remains the sole vote for not guilty, and he reneges on his promise. He adamantly refuses to go along with the majority, resulting in a hung jury. Had this juror's conscience truly precluded voting to convict and subjecting the defendant to the death penalty, would there have been anything wrong about lying to the other jurors about his intentions?

The above hypothetical may be a bit far-fetched, but the quandaries discussed by Abramson most assuredly are not. He identifies some of the most perplexing moral conundrums confronting deliberating jurors and presiding judges, and he posits sensible tenets that he thinks should guide their behavior. Although I have no substantial disagreement with Abramson, the ethical terrain of rightful jury deliberations is somewhat bumpier than he indicates. As is so often the case when normative standards are put forth, Abramson's code of conduct for jurors has penumbras in which the distinctions between right and wrong may be more shadowy than he suggests.

I. THE HOLDOUT JUROR

Abramson is rightly concerned that holdout jurors will be improperly bulldozed into subscribing to a verdict with which they actually disagree. Because the coercive power of the majority is inherently strong and the urge to conform is quite palpable, the legitimacy of *Allen* changes ought to be reconsidered. Dissent from the prevailing sentiment within the jury is an honorable position if it is based on reason and fact, so it is problematic whether judges ought to "dynamite" a jury stalemate by coaxing the minority to reconsider their stance. Moreover, because the issuing of such instructions is discretionary rather than mandatory, this practice really requires that judges inject themselves into the fact-finding process which is supposed to be the jury's exclusive province. Juries should have carte blanche to engage in extended debate without interference by judges until it is virtually certain that a verdict is unattainable.

Abramson correctly decries a related phenomenon: the wearing down of a holdout's resistance that can result from a judge's control over the duration of deliberations. No matter how committed a juror may be to the correctness of his opinion, being subjected to long, protracted deliberations can erode a juror's autonomy. To cite an extreme example, in 1987 an Illinois judge kept a jury deliberating two months (!) after a lengthy civil trial of the Monsanto

Company for a railroad tank spill in Sturgeon, Missouri, that had contained the toxic chemical, dioxin. The sole juror who had held out against awarding $16 million in punitive damages ultimately gave in, despite the fact that he had not really changed his mind. He later stated: "I was really tired. I just wanted peace of mind. . . . I agreed because I wanted to get out of there."[1] At some point, subjecting the jurors to such torment becomes a dubious means of forcing nay-saying jurors to agree with the majority.

The issue of jurors pressuring one another, a routine part of jury deliberations, is a different matter. The stakes of jury decision making are quite high, so it would be unrealistic to limit jurors to discourse that is rational and temperate. Some emotionalism and manipulation are inescapable. Having said that, jurors *do* have a moral obligation to engage in respectful treatment of one another. While debating legislation or the confirmation of appointments, U.S. senators often refer to colleagues whose views they detest as the "distinguished" senator from the "Great State" of such-and-such rather than disparaging them with vitriolic epithets. The protocol of addressing people honorifically works well in Congress as a means of furthering the business of passing laws, and the exercise of such decorum is equally desirable in the jury room as a means of defusing passions and facilitating the reaching of verdicts. Although appellate courts may countenance highly disrespectful and even threatening remarks by jurors to one another (as Abramson rightly points out), such abusive discourse is nonetheless ethically dubious.

Thus, it is just plain wrong for jurors to bully or insult their peers. Not only do ad hominem attacks violate manners that are an accepted part of civil society, but they can impugn the validity of verdicts if judges conclude that such torment intimidated jurors who had been slurred into compromising their convictions. Such verbal abuse is especially pernicious when it degenerates into name-calling based on race, ethnicity, gender, or sexual orientation. On the one hand, jurors who react to prejudiced personal attacks may well reach decisions on verdicts out of defensiveness and pride rather than conscientious examination of the evidence at hand; face-saving concerns may interfere with thoughtfulness. On the other hand, they might succumb to such ill treatment, capitulating to the majority to end the antagonistic onslaught.

Yielding as a means of ending abuse is not idle speculation. A New York City jury verdict was overturned in 2001 in a defamation case because three black women and one Hispanic woman continuously used curse words and racial slurs to denigrate the white foreman; they also kept referring to a male black juror who sided with the foreman as an Uncle Tom. Said the judge who overturned the verdict: "These invectives were more than vulgarities of personal animus; they were involved with the purpose to malign [the dissenting jurors'] view of the evidence and compel their uniformity."[2] The judge's condemnation is well taken: Robust debate and forceful argumentation should never deteriorate into inflammatory personal attacks. Abramson is correct: forceful advocacy has its ethical limits, which may well be narrower than the legal ones.

II. COMPROMISE VERDICTS

Abramson takes a balanced view on compromise verdicts whereby "hardliners" who favor "throwing the book" at defendants and "softies" favoring leniency meet halfway to achieve unanimity. The jury's task often entails much more than determining "who done it"—not infrequently it involves determining the degree of culpability of those implicated in illegal acts. In deciding on a verdict between conviction on the worst charges and total exoneration as a means of coming to agreement, juries may be groping for levels of guilt commensurate with the moral opprobrium of the crime. The middle ground, Aristotle's "golden mean," may well be the just result.

But, as Abramson notes, some compromises have greater ethical probity than others. Cynical deals completed only for the sake of ending deliberations quickly are indubitably contrary to the jurors' sworn duty to get things right to the best of their ability. To be legitimate, compromise verdicts must have a defensible legal and moral foundation. Compromises that *clearly* contravene the facts are out of order. Consider the case of El Sayyid Nosair, a radical Muslim accused of killing Rabbi Meir Kahane, head of the fanatical Zionist Jewish Defense League which advocated Jewish vigilantism against Arabs (among others). Kahane was shot to death on November 5, 1990, in a crowded New York City hotel meeting room after delivering an inflammatory and provocative speech. Nosair, who attended the speech, was apprehended by a postal service officer about a block away. A gun was discovered nearby that ballistics experts subsequently linked to bullet fragments found in the meeting room in which Kahane was killed. Eyewitness testimony was inconsistent, and Nosair had an explanation for running from the hotel: He was afraid (as an Arab) that he would be attacked by vindictive Jews had he remained at the scene of the crime. Nosair denied knowing anything about the gun found in his vicinity, and he claimed that he peacefully surrendered to the arresting police.

The jury acquitted Nosair of murder but convicted him for gun possession and assault against the postal officer. The split verdict, which had all the markings of a compromise, was deemed "strange, irrational, inconsistent, and repugnant" by Nosair's lawyer.[3] It was said to be "devoid of common sense and logic" by the sentencing judge who stated that the "overwhelming weight of evidence" cast Nosair as the killer.[4] Such a verdict smacks of injustice—either the conviction of an innocent man or the indulgence of a murderer.

What this suggests is a categorical imperative about jury-room compromises: Defendants thought to be innocent of all charges against them (that is, where guilt has not been proved beyond a reasonable doubt) should *never* be convicted of anything no matter how tempting a compromise is. Scaling down convictions to lesser included offenses because of mitigating factors is a permissible way of helping make the punishment fit the crime, but upward scaling that convicts people of things they apparently did not do is unacceptable.

It is therefore all right to let off minor figures in a criminal operation ("small fry") to get everyone on the jury to agree to convict the central figures ("kingfish"), a gambit routinely undertaken by prosecutors who dismiss charges against the former in order to get them to testify against the latter. Indeed, under federal sentencing guidelines accused persons who cooperate with the prosecution may receive "departures" which spare them from the prison sentences that the circumstances of their crime and their criminal history would otherwise warrant. The cardinal rule is relatively simple: Showing leniency toward those who are presumably guilty can be ethically tolerable, but negotiations that sacrifice those who are truly innocent are ethically out of line.

This brings me to one modest disagreement with Abramson—the issue of compromises that consider how verdicts "will play in the outside world."[5] He argues that potential reactions of the community ought to be entirely disregarded by jurors. How verdicts might be received by partisans, the press, politicians, and the vox populi should be outside the purview of jury deliberations. Yet the community *does* have a legitimate interest in trial outcomes—like the litigants, it too deserves justice. Might there not be instances in which taking account of popular sentiment in fashioning verdicts in order to heal aggrieved communities and keep the peace can be accomplished without subjecting defendants to injustice? I suggest that where levels of culpability are unclear, a bargained verdict that achieves *some* accountability for crimes committed, even if short of that which may be truly deserved based on the facts, might be ethically acceptable.

The two Rodney King cases are illustrative. It will be remembered that on March 3, 1991, King, an African American, was beaten severely by four white Los Angeles police officers after having been stopped for a traffic violation—a beating that was videotaped by a bystander and subsequently televised repeatedly around the world. Although the tape showed the nonstop beatings in gruesome detail, it also showed that King was resistant and aggressive after the police officers stopped him. The officers were charged with aggravated assault in state court, and the trial was moved from Los Angeles to suburban Simi Valley. An all-white jury exonerated all four defendants, leading to massive rioting in black neighborhoods in Los Angeles that resulted in thirty deaths, hundreds of serious injuries, and billions of dollars in property damage. Subsequently, the officers were charged with the federal offense of violating King's civil rights. The second jury's verdict seemed to reflect a compromise (although there is no concrete evidence that this occurred). Two of the officers whose conduct was less egregious were acquitted whereas the two whose behavior seemed to be more nefarious were convicted, but not of the most serious charges. Although many considered the verdict far from perfect (too tough or too soft depending on one's perspective), calm prevailed and a sense of cloture was achieved.

More recently a Mississippi jury in June 2005 convicted 80 year old ex-Klansman Edgar Ray Killen of being the ring leader who plotted the killing of James Earl Chaney, Andrew Goodman, and Michael Schwerner, three civil rights workers killed in 1964.[6] The jury found him guilty of manslaughter but not of murder. The jurors had been evenly split between acquittal and conviction on the murder charge but ultimately agreed to convict on the lesser charge. The verdict smacks of compromise, because if the defendant indeed had planned the slayings it would seem that premeditation was involved and a murder conviction in order. But it is certainly arguable that such a diluted conviction was an appropriate means of getting resolution of a long-festering matter which for over four decades had tormented Philadelphia, Mississippi, where the crimes took place. A compromise verdict that contributes peace and reconciliation has much to recommend it.

I suggest that as long as no one gets wrongly convicted for a crime, it is not improper that jurors take into account, consciously or even subconsciously, how the verdict will play out. Mollifying the community can be a legitimate function of jury decision making so long as guilt has been proved beyond a reasonable doubt. As I wrote in *Juries and Politics*: "Many of those on trial are neither paragons of virtue nor evil incarnate, and the positions that the jury takes between the two extremes is therefore quite appropriate. Justice comes in many shades of gray."[7]

III. BLOC VOTING

Psephologists have long observed that voters of like background tend to have rather similar electoral preferences. Although Richard Scammon and Ben Wattenberg certainly exaggerated when they wrote that "demography is destiny" in the polling place,[8] it is doubtless true that one's race, ethnicity, religion, economic status, and sexual orientation (among other things) may have enormous impact on how candidates are evaluated. Put colloquially, birds of a feather (often) flock together.

What does this have to do with juries? Jurors, like voters, invariably bring to the table the experiences and attitudes garnered over a lifetime; they are not tabulae rasae. To be sure, personal characteristics of jurors do not *determine* verdicts, but there can be little doubt that they affect them. Abramson rightly objects to jurors aligning themselves into factions based solely on their identities; verdicts should *not* be based on which demographic group is dominant in the jury room. On the other hand, it is unrealistic and unreasonable to expect jurors to dissociate themselves from compatriots with whom they are likely to share much in common. For example, although there is no single "black" view on police brutality, there is no gainsaying the fact that because police-community relations in black areas have been more turbulent than those in white areas, black jurors may well be more skeptical of police testimony that denies police improprieties. Just as African Americans tend to be overwhelmingly Democratic in their political party preference and voting behavior because of common interests, there is nothing wrong with their clustering together in the jury room because of common perceptions. People will often cling together in the jury room not because they want blacks to prevail, Jews to prevail, women to prevail, or gays to prevail—but because they are like-minded in their appraisal of the evidence.

The O. J. Simpson case exemplifies this. The largely black jury that acquitted the former star athlete and television sportscaster of murdering his wife and his wife's friend was very skeptical of the evidence. The predominantly white jury that ruled against Simpson in the civil case thought the evidence against Simpson was more than sufficient.[9] Some argued that the verdicts were based on sheer racial bias (racial favoritism in the criminal case, racial hostility in the civil case), but the reality is that blacks and whites simply disagreed in their interpretation of the evidence.[10] Police testimony in particular was viewed dimly by black jurors in light of the overt racism of Mark Fuhrman, one of the chief detectives in the case, though white jurors had fewer reservations.

So how do we resolve the dilemma posed by Abramson? He asserts that the jury *is* an inherently political institution but it needs to be much more than that. The answer was nicely put by Alan W. Scheflin: Jurors, within the limits of their capabilities, need to go "from me to we."[11] Although jurors can never leave behind the built-in prism through which they see the evidence, we can expect them to transcend their roots by listening attentively and responsively to fellow jurors with different backgrounds and persuasions. At times they will undoubtedly be more comfortable siding with jurors with whom they share much in common, but their challenge is to resist the temptation to look at the facts in a uniform way simply because of the ties that bind.

Although jurors are entitled to establish connections with those with whom they share common origins and circumstances, they ought to bring their individuality to bear in the application of the law and the assessment of the evidence. Each of us has a unique persona, and that persona ought to inform the judgment process. It is not race alone that defines us but a host of other attributes such as education, occupation, place of birth, marital status, travel experiences, and so forth. Perhaps too quickly, Abramson dismisses the propensity for demographic commonalities to result in like-mindedness,[12] but he is right on target in urging that jurors try hard to resist rigid bloc formation based exclusively on the coalescence of kindred spirits. The body of twelve (or whatever) should be more than the sum of its parts.

IV. SQUELCHING SO-CALLED NULLIFIERS

Jury nullification has been examined extensively in this volume and elsewhere. Is it good or is it bad? Is it a valid means of constantly assessing the wisdom of laws on the books or contextualizing allegedly illegal behavior, or is it an invitation to anarchy? Should judges encourage it, discourage it, or keep their mouths shut? Should jurors who subscribe to it be allowed on the jury, kept off the jury, or even removed from the jury while trials are in progress?

What is striking about the debate about nullification is how much of it is divorced from reality. Only rarely do jurors purposefully and consciously set the law aside or ignore the evidence.[13] Even the examples often put forth to show juries blatantly disregarding the law (such as opting not to convict those accused of harboring fugitive slaves during the antebellum era) are few and far between.[14] The fact is that jurors en masse conscientiously try to put aside personal prejudices and beliefs, try to heed the judge's instructions, and try to determine the facts objectively.

But the very nature of the adversary system creates two points of view in every case, and the ambiguous, probabilistic standard that is necessary to convict ("guilt beyond a reasonable doubt") often puts jurors at odds with one another. Jurors, being sensate beings rather than robots, divine their own understandings of the law and their own construal of the facts. Truth does not emerge from trials and announce itself; it must be found. In the face of uncertainty, honest, dutiful jurors can see things differently. As Jerome Frank so succinctly put it over a half-century ago: "Facts are guesses."[15] Moreover, at times it is the minority that may get things right and the majority that errs. In cases in which the defendant is accused of a particularly heinous offense that creates the potential for scapegoat justice, the majority may well jump to the wrong conclusions because of a desire to avenge the crime.

Abramson is therefore most assuredly correct in sternly cautioning against labeling dissidents as nullifiers whose behavior cannot be tolerated. In the 2004 case of two Tyco executives accused of defrauding the company of millions of dollars, one juror steadfastly refused to join her eleven peers in a conviction.[16] Although she was accused by fellow jurors of "poisoning deliberations"[17] and publicly excoriated, *she* claimed later that she was simply unable to conclude that criminal intent had been proved.[18] Although the case ended in a mistrial because she was personally threatened (as the result of having been identified in the press prior to a verdict being reached), she had every right to stand her ground and adhere to her understanding. Indeed, one virtue of the unanimity rule is the extra protection against wrongful conviction that it gives the accused, a safeguard for those tried for corporate skullduggery as well as defendants accused of other kinds of crimes.

Just as it is arguable that groups such as the Fully Informed Jury Association are in a sense tampering with the jury when they inform jurors of their power to nullify despite lacking the right to do so, a case can be made that judges who raise the specter of nullification are undermining the independence of jurors and the integrity of the fact-finding process. Mischaracterizing jurors' dissenting opinions as nullification can have a stigmatizing and coercive effect, making them feel that they are acting improperly when all they are doing is "calling it as they see it." There is a real danger, forcefully articulated by Abramson, that judges may lose their neutrality and wittingly or unwittingly become allies of the prosecution as they endeavor to ferret out nullification. The jury, for all its flaws, is the body entrusted with fact-finding; they should be allowed to do their job.

V. CONCLUSION

Politics is a ubiquitous and normal part of the collective choice process—whether in legislatures, college governance bodies, or juries. "Politicking," the art and science of influencing people, can be an honorable part of achieving agreements—despite the negative connotation of the word. Passionate advocacy, peer pressure, coalition formation, and even bargaining can play an appropriate role in jury deliberations, as long as they are kept within bounds.

Abramson does a fine job of giving politics (broadly construed) its proper due while also recognizing its perils. He rightly condemns a no-holds-barred state of affairs in the jury room. My response is but a codicil to his carefully nuanced positions—a recognition that the very humanity of jurors that justifies their role in the judgment process will sometimes prompt them to politicize their interactions more than Abramson would endorse. Jury rooms cannot and should not be forums for sterile intellectual exchanges; they are appropriately the loci of robust give-and-take. Political machinations can enable jurors to forge consensus out of conflict and, while doing so, reach just verdicts. Such practices, with necessary caveats and restrictions, should get the ethicist's blessing as juries struggle to do the very difficult job that confronts them.

NOTES

1. "Dioxin Case Juror Acted to Go Home," *New York Times*, October 25, 1987, 26.

2. Barbara Ross and Don Singleton, "Jury's Hatred Kills Verdict," *New York Daily News*, September 8, 2001, 8.

3. Selwyn Raab, "Jury Selection Seen as Crucial to Verdict," *New York Times*, December 23, 1991, B8.

4. Ronald Sullivan, "Judge Gives Maximum Term in Kahane Case," *New York Times*, January 30, 1992, A1.

5. Jeffrey Abramson, "Jury Deliberations: Fair and Foul," in this volume, 186.

6. Shaila Dewan, "Ex-Klansman Guilty of Manslaughter in 1964 Deaths," *New York Times*, June 22, 2005, 1.

7. James Levine, *Juries and Politics* (Belmont, CA: Wadsworth, 1992), 84.

8. Richard Scammon and Ben Wattenberg, *The Real Majority* (New York: Coward-McCann, 1970), 45.

9. An exact comparison of the two verdicts is not possible because the burden of proof was lower in the civil case, the lawyers were not the same, and there were evidentiary differences.

10. M. Gottleib, "Racial Split at the End as at the Start," *New York Times*, October 4, 1995, A11.

11. This was part of Scheflin's response to Abramson during the conference that gave rise to this volume.

12. See James Levine, "The Impact of Racial Demography on Jury Verdicts in Routine Adjudication," *Criminal Law Bulletin* 33 (1997): 523–42. By most observers' reckoning, the race of the jurors had much to do with the acquittal of four white police officers accused of murdering African immigrant Amadou Diallo in New York City in 1999. Diallo, who was unarmed and innocent of any wrongdoing when accosted by police on the lookout for a rapist, was killed around midnight by a fusillade of forty-one shots by the officers who thought he was reaching for a gun when he in fact was reaching for his wallet to show identification on the steps of his own apartment building. Because of adverse publicity in the largely non-white Bronx where the shooting occurred, the trial was moved to upstate Albany where the jury wound up being overwhelmingly white. It is hard to imagine that a jury selected from the Bronx (which would most likely have comprised a majority of people of color) would have reached a similar verdict.

13. James Levine, "The Role of Jury Nullification Instructions in the Search for Justice," *Legal Studies Forum* 18 (1994): 473–96.

14. J. Pease and W. Pease, *They Who Would Be Free: Blacks' Search for Freedom, 1830–1861* (Urbana: University of Illinois Press, 1990), 232.

15. Jerome Frank, *Courts on Trial: Myth and Reality in American Justice* (New York: Atheneum, 1967), 14.

16. Andrew Ross Sorkin, "Jury Is in Turmoil over Tyco Case," *New York Times*, March 26, 2004, C1.

17. Sorkin, "Jury Is in Turmoil over Tyco Case," C1.

18. The juror's own words defending her decision not to yield to the majority poignantly describe the ethical basis of her behavior: "If I had voted against my conscience and said, 'All right, they're guilty,' when I don't believe it, then why can't anybody else do the same thing? And that's an absolute destruction of what the jury system is all about." Andrew Ross Sorkin, "Juror No. 4 Says No. O.K. Sign and No Guilty Vote," *New York Times*, April 7, 2004, C2.

7

Ethics for the Ex-Juror: Guiding Former Jurors after the Trial

Nancy J. King

I. INTRODUCTION

When the trial judge has polled the jury and accepted its verdict, the trial may be over but the experience of being a juror is not. Ex-jurors may face decisions about what to say or do about the trial for weeks, months, or even years after they are discharged from jury service. Some jurors may receive advice from their judge about this, but there is little agreement on what advice should be given.[1] Contributing to the lack of consensus is the uncertain legality of restrictions on the speech and conduct of ex-jurors. In the United States, attempts to ban ex-jurors from speaking about their experience are rarely enforceable through contempt or other formal sanctions, and vigilant media advocates allow few such attempts to go unchallenged.[2] To fill this void, a set of advisory guidelines, conveying clear and simple principles safe from First Amendment attack, could prove to be a particularly useful tool for jurors. This chapter, then, picks up where the law leaves off, addressing what ex-jurors *should* do, regardless of what they must be allowed to do under existing legal rules.

II. FIRST PRINCIPLES

In searching for ethical principles to guide juror behavior, it makes sense to look in two directions: first, toward the functions of the jury itself, and second, to the ethical principles governing people who fill similar roles. As to jury function, most would agree that settling disputes using trial by jury rather than bench trials promotes the following ends: (1) it protects litigants from abuse of judicial power; (2) it brings community-based sense to fact-finding and to the application of law to facts; (3) it helps to promote acceptance of case outcomes and the legitimacy of the justice process; and (4) it increases lay participation in our democracy and provides a firsthand

219

civic education to jurors.[3] Of these four aims, the third, involving the public's view of the legitimacy of the justice process, is most affected by the post-verdict conduct of jurors. Turning to the ethical principles that regulate other analogous actors, two parallels are instructive: voter ethics and judicial ethics. A common theme in each is independence of mind and freedom from corrupt influence. Building on these themes, this chapter proposes several principles to help guide ex-jurors through the questions that they may face after they complete their jury service. It then describes how these principles might be applied in particular situations that often occur, and concludes with a sample set of instructions to be given to the jury at the end of trial.

A. Limited Accountability: The Juror as Decision Maker

At first glance it is not at all obvious which postverdict behavior by ex-jurors would strengthen or weaken the integrity of the jury system. Is this aim advanced, for example, by greater public exposure of information about juror deliberations, or by less? The answer in the judicial realm is clear—some formal justification for decisions is essential. But trust in the jury system has never depended upon an adequate explanation for each jury verdict. Unlike the tradition of written judicial findings and conclusions—considered essential to the legitimacy of judicial decision making—there is currently no regular posttrial process to verify that the rationale underlying the verdict is sound. The double jeopardy bar, the practice of returning general verdicts, and a varied collection of rules promoting deliberation secrecy do not permit such oversight. This is as it should be. The freedom of jurors to decline to explain their verdicts does not undermine, but indeed fosters, confidence in jury decisions.

Freedom from "reason-giving," or from the formal "evaluation"[4] of jury verdicts by non-jurors, furthers the legitimacy of jury decisions in two ways. First, when existing assumptions about jury decisions are already positive, deliberation secrecy promotes after-the-fact acceptance of verdicts by minimizing debate over the propriety of the rationale underlying the verdict. So long as the jury is generally given the benefit of the doubt, jury legitimacy is strengthened by the absence of evidence that jury decisions are tainted by biased or uninformed inferences. On the other hand, should jury verdicts be generally suspect in the public's eye, the gap in information about deliberations would become a powerful tool for critics who could point to the lack of proof that jurors are actually conscientious, impartial, and competent. This brings me to the second reason that protection from external accountability promotes juror legitimacy—without it, jurors might not receive the benefit of the doubt in the first place.

Research suggests that trust in the jury system, or in any given verdict, is promoted by a complex combination of features: how well the jury represents the community; the assurance of group deliberation and consideration of differing points of view compelled by the unanimity rule; and the extent to which the adversaries participate in the selection of the decision maker.[5] One reason that juries may be given higher fairness ratings than judges (although not specifically tested in the growing body of social-science literature on procedural justice) is that jurors, unlike elected judges, are *not* politically accountable for the outcome or rationale of their decisions. Historically, a juror's freedom to decline to explain or justify her verdict has been a constant feature of the jury trial in the United States. Seeking to improve the caliber of trial jurors, Thomas Jefferson once called for their election, but his idea fell on deaf ears.[6] Jurors today remain free to fade into obscurity after the trial, to refuse to talk, and to simply state "no comment." To critics of the verdict, they can and do say, "You weren't there, I was," or, "We did our best to follow the instructions," and leave it at that, without repercussion. This freedom helps to *empower* jurors during deliberations to resist pressure that they may feel from the public, the media, the litigants' supporters, or even the judge to decide the case one way or the other for reasons unrelated to the strength of the evidence. The public understands what researchers have documented: Anticipation of the need to defend one's decision to an audience that has expressed its preference warps decision making.

Indeed, researchers on accountability and decision making have noted "[t]he falsity of the conventional wisdom—often born out of frustration at irrational, insensitive, or lazy decision makers—that accountability is a cognitive or social panacea: 'All we need to do is hold the rascals accountable.' Two decades of research now reveal that (a) only highly specialized subtypes of accountability lead to increased cognitive effort; (b) more cognitive effort is not inherently beneficial, it sometimes makes matters even worse; and (c) there is ambiguity and room for reasonable disagreement over what should be considered worse or better judgment when we place cognition in its social or institutional context."[7]

Importantly, the relatively little *public* accountability that jurors experience does not leave them unaccountable for the reasons for their decisions. Instead, jurors are accountable to each other. Each juror is required to deliberate, and when she does so, her reasoning is evaluated by the other jurors. Jurors must persuade each other, for consensus and unanimity is required. This, researchers have concluded, "induces people to think more deeply and critically about their own views and other criteria for decision making."[8] Put slightly differently, because jurors must deliberate, the jury itself is an expression of democratic accountability.[9] It is a careful balance, then, that affirmatively promotes legitimacy. Internal accountability to other jurors is enforced through unanimity rules, while external accountability is reduced by secrecy during the trial and the option for secrecy afterward.

B. Constructive Disclosures: The Juror as Watchdog

The voluntary nature of jury secrecy is also a key feature of the public respect for the jury system. Jurors can speak out if they choose to, despite their qualified "right to remain silent." The U.S. system is not one in which jurors' deliberations are kept secret by threat of contempt. Given that the law permits jurors to voluntarily report bribery, corruption, or other serious misconduct, and it requires them to do so if asked to testify in postverdict hearings under oath, the fact that jurors seldom report occurrences of misconduct promotes public confidence.

Jurors in this country know that if they speak truthfully about what occurred in the jury room, they will suffer no penalty for speaking. Even confessing their own indiscretions typically will not lead to punishment, and this knowledge further encourages disclosure. Because jurors are not *forced* to hide their process or their discussion, and are free to inform the public when the process falters, the relative infrequency of such disclosures enhances the acceptance of jury decisions. It may be no coincidence that in other countries such as Canada and Great Britain, where it is a punishable offense for jurors to disclose deliberations,[10] there may be less public confidence in the competence of the jury in general, and there are ongoing and continuing efforts to second-guess and restrict its power.[11]

Thus, while the limited accountability of jurors is the first principle that jurors should turn to for guidance after trial (i.e., the freedom to choose not to explain their decision to anyone, now that they have persuaded each other), a secondary consideration is that not all disclosures are undesirable. Just as the option not to talk about one's jury service enhances legitimacy, the option to discuss one's jury service should be exercised with legitimacy in mind. When deciding if a particular situation is one that calls for revelation, a juror should ask himself or herself, "Are my disclosures constructive? Do they serve a public purpose? Is what I have to say likely to further improvements in the justice system or to correct injustice?"

C. Tell the Truth

If an ex-juror does choose to discuss her jury experience, she should consider another key principle: Be truthful. The juror's duty to truth is captured in the Latin term describing the jury's most vital function—*verdict*, a declaration of truth. Truth does not lose its importance once the jury is discharged. Jurors who discuss their jury service should relate accurately what took place at trial or in the jury room, whether asked to testify under oath as a witness in a posttrial hearing, or in making voluntary disclosures about the trial experience. If jurors misrepresent their experiences after the fact, their representations before and during trial, and even the verdict itself, also lose credibility. Should a juror choose to embellish her story, she has a responsibility to label her tale as fiction.

D. Respect the Confidences of Fellow Jurors

An ex-juror making statements about her jury service should also attempt to preserve the confidences of her fellow jurors. If information about deliberations and conduct in the jury room is revealed, a juror should avoid identifying which juror engaged in what conduct. The most common argument in support of jury secrecy, often raised by opponents of post-verdict revelations, is consequentialist. The fear is that "jurors are being taught that their deliberations will not be secret at all,"[12] leading to lower participation rates, less candor in deliberations, and less accurate verdicts. Courts have also noted that not only "freedom of debate" is threatened, but "independence of thought checked if jurors were made to feel that their arguments and ballots were to be freely published to the world."[13]

Secrecy also protects against influence and its appearance. Just as the key weapon against influence and corruption in the election context is the secret ballot, in the jury context the same function is served by the jurors' privilege to decline to explain the jury's decision to those outside the jury. Partisans have more difficulty influencing individual jurors when they cannot learn the identity or number of jurors voting for conviction or acquittal if a jury deadlocks, and when they can never be sure on what basis any given juror joined the verdict. While a formal prohibition on revealing the votes and statements of fellow jurors is probably as unenforceable as a ban on lying about one's jury experience, ex-jurors would benefit from a reminder that betraying confidences carries the risk that in the long run fewer jurors will speak honestly, and more jurors may be pressured by partisans to the dispute.

Apart from the consequentialist justifications for confidentiality, there is an independent, moral basis for protecting fellow-jurors' confidences. Jurors accept as part of their duty as jurors an obligation *to each other* to deliberate in good faith. Along with this obligation is a unique trust, a duty to respect each other's privacy. As one of my colleagues observed, ex-jurors "should follow the Golden Rule just like everybody else," and not reveal anything about the deliberations of fellow jurors that they might want to keep confidential if they were in the other jurors' shoes. This principle is, like the others in this chapter, not absolute. As with any privilege, an ex-juror's duty to protect the confidences of fellow jurors should yield to prevent a miscarriage of justice, such as when a ex-juror is asked about deliberations under oath in a postverdict hearing.

E. Avoid the Appearance of Bias

Finally, ex-jurors should avoid conducting themselves in ways that suggest the appearance of bias toward one adversary or another. The integrity of the jury system, like the integrity of elections and judicial decisions, depends in part on the independence of jurors from influence, both real and perceived. Judges, like jurors, are bound by their oaths to act impartially between parties. Most of the ethical proscriptions that judges follow are designed to help judges maintain neutrality, and to preserve the confidence of the public, parties, and the profession in that impartiality.[14] Just as a judge must avoid bias and its appearance even after a case has ended, ex-jurors should continue to avoid any conduct that would suggest partiality. Suspicions concerning corruption can arise from postverdict payoffs as well as from preverdict promises.

III. APPLICATION TO SPECIFIC CONTEXTS

How do these platitudes—"You need not explain your decision ever to anyone, but you may discuss your experience, so long as you keep disclosures constructive, truthful, and respectful of the confidences of your fellow jurors, and avoid the appearance of bias"—help guide jurors through a range of potentially troubling dilemmas after the verdict is announced? A juror may be uncertain how to respond in several recurring scenarios. The trial judge may in his jury debriefing invite the jurors to speak about deliberations. In a jurisdiction where attorney contact is not heavily regulated, a juror may be tempted by an invitation to talk with the attorneys or consultants in the case who, like himself or herself, were immersed in the drama of a particular trial for days. Media representatives—with fewer legal restrictions on their access to ex-jurors than lawyers—may contact a juror for an interview about the case. Researchers may seek information for a study of jury behavior. A grateful litigant may seek to express appreciation for the juror's decision. Each of these situations is addressed below.

A. Debriefing by Trial Judges

Judges often debrief their jurors, with or without attorneys present. To thank jurors for their service and help jurors with concerns they may have, juror debriefings are common in several jurisdictions.[15] As an Illinois court explained, many judges take this time to "assure [jurors] that they did a good job." Some judges, however, do not share the understanding, expressed by the same court, that debriefing "offers an opportunity for the trial court— *not* the jurors—to answer questions."[16] A judge may question jurors about their experience, even ask them about their decision making. This information may be sought in good faith. For example, a judge may wish to learn ways to improve jurors' experiences or minimize deadlock in future cases. How should jurors respond? Returning to the principles that should guide jurors in their decisions whether to disclose deliberation information, jurors should understand that they are off-duty during these judicial debriefings, and are free to decline to answer a judge's questions about deliberations if they choose to do so. Jurors have no obligation to explain their decision to anyone, and that includes the judge. Because the judge has been in authority throughout the trial, and the jurors have obediently answered the judge's questions and spent hours or days watching everybody else behave the same way, it may be difficult for some jurors to change gears and simply decline politely to respond. But it is their privilege nonetheless. If a juror does have a suggestion to make, or a revelation that the juror considers is necessary to set the record straight (for example, the unlikely case where a juror made a false statement under oath during trial or when polled about her agreement with the verdict), jurors should not hesitate to disclose truthful information to the judge, protecting fellow jurors' confidences where possible.

B. Interviews by Attorneys

Jurisdictions vary in the regulation of attorney contact with jurors following a trial.[17] In some states, attorneys are permitted to question jurors after trial, with only limited restrictions.[18] A juror should not hesitate to decline such interviews. Talking about the jury's decision-making process to attorneys and consultants[19] so that they can refine their trial techniques for the next client does little to improve the overall integrity of the justice system. Attorneys are able to use alternative means to discover better ways of teaching and communicating with jurors. A juror's duties are to the public and to her fellow jurors, not to the clients or the attorneys. If a juror decides that an occurrence during deliberations or trial requires disclosure, in most instances the appropriate recipient of that information is the judge, who will be able to share the information with the parties or the public if necessary.

C. Media, Press, Publication

The higher the popular interest in a trial, the more effort reporters will make to discover and then tell the story of jury deliberations. While the First Amendment clearly bars legislation similar to Great Britain's Contempt of Court Act criminalizing postverdict discussions, U.S. courts have a range of options for regulating communications between jurors and the press, including counseling jurors not to talk, encouraging them to report harassment, limiting questioning of jurors, and insisting that all contact be channeled through a court-appointed liaison. In litigation over who can ask what and when, the judge is typically portrayed as either the benevolent or overprotective parent, the media as either greedy meddlers or courageous whistleblowers. The juror is relegated to the status of a child in a custody battle. This is unfortunate, for ultimately it is the juror who must decide if and when to say anything. When should she answer? And what of the juror who is not sought out for her story, but decides on her own that it is worth telling? Should this be discouraged?

Again the first principle guiding jurors when faced with the decision whether or not to speak publicly about jury deliberations should be the option to remain silent. No explanation or comment at all is expected, to anybody, for any reason. Also, if a juror simply wants to make a buck or gain attention, or if her commentary is more sensational than educative, she should refrain from speaking out. When jurors profit from selling their stories, the integrity of the justice system suffers. Even if the prospect of a lucrative tell-all deal does not actually affect a juror's behavior in a given case, the public may suspect that it has, or that in future cases jurors might be more interested in publicity than justice.[20]

The more difficult decisions arise when a juror has an incentive to speak out, and that motive is based on her perception that (1) sharing her experience will improve the public's understanding of the workings of the jury system generally, (2) remaining silent about the process would leave the public with an inaccurate impression of the decision, or (3) continuing to be silent would leave uncorrected a verdict that the juror has come to believe is fundamentally unjust.

Take the first situation, where the juror considers that discussing her experience is useful commentary on the justice system as a whole. Ours is a country in which censorship of criticism of public institutions is prohibited due to the corrosive effects of censorship on democracy and freedom. There is no exception to this rule that would allow for the silencing of ex-jurors. If an ex-juror in good faith believes her commentary will contribute to the ongoing public evaluation of the jury system as a whole, no ethical principle should stand in her way, so long as she is truthful and protects the confidences of fellow jurors.

Consider now the second situation, where the juror hopes that by speaking out she will help set the record straight. In her survey of media reports of postverdict juror interviews, Nancy S. Marder reported that in cases of media interest, jurors will sometimes justify their decision to talk publicly by explaining that their comments are necessary to correct a false impression about the jury and its deliberations that was left by other commentary on the case. So long as a juror is truthful, and preserves the confidences of her fellow jurors when possible, this sort of defensive disclosure is harmless.[21] Comments such as, "I don't recall it the same way," "That isn't necessarily the view held by all of the jurors," "There were twelve of us. That's his take on it. There may be others," all fall into this category. Again, a juror should not feel as if she is doing anything wrong if she chooses to make such defensive disclosures, so long as she is truthful, and does her best to preserve the confidences of fellow jurors.

Defensive disclosure is not limited to those comments that tend to justify a verdict. Should one juror decide that another juror has been less than truthful about what happened— for example, claiming that the jurors never conducted an experiment with the exhibits when they actually did—she might choose to counteract the impression. A juror should bring this type of concern to the attention of the judge by volunteering to make a statement under oath in the context of posttrial proceedings in the case.

Generally, explanations that a juror feels are necessary to prevent a miscarriage of justice are more appropriately directed not to the media, but to the judge. If a juror's conviction that the jury made the wrong decision is so strong that she is willing publicly to disavow her verdict and explain why, and if her motivation for making these views public is not to profit or to draw attention to herself but to prevent an unjust outcome, she should feel free to make truthful disclosures to those who are in a position to correct the verdict, carefully limited to protect the confidences of fellow jurors.[22] Statements of this sort should be offered under oath to the judge, who will be able to share the information with parties and the press as appropriate. Of course, if the perceived source of injustice is the judge's own behavior, then the proper audience for a juror's complaint may be the attorneys, a judicial oversight body, or the media.

A particular problem arises when, following the discharge of one jury, a new trial is imminent. The former jurors are likely to be besieged by questions from attorneys or the media seeking a window on the trial-to-be. A decade ago, Abraham Goldstein argued that in this situation the judge should have the power to limit reports of the first jury's deliberation until after the second jury has been selected.[23] This same problem arose in November 2001 in the New Jersey case against Rabbi Fred Neulander for the capital murder of his wife when the first jury was dismissed after it could not reach a verdict. The New Jersey Supreme Court upheld the trial judge's order forbidding the media from contacting the jurors who had been dismissed after the first trial ended without a verdict. The court even extended the trial judge's order to bar "communications between the media and the jurors that are initiated by the jurors."[24] Neulander was later convicted by a new jury, and in 2003 the Supreme Court declined to review the media's First Amendment challenge to the state court's ruling. What is relevant here is not the legality of these restrictions under the First Amendment, which is certainly subject to dispute.[25] Even if such restrictions are invalid, it is important to examine if there is something about this scenario concerning disclosure that warrants extra care by jurors.

Two separate rationales were advanced for the extraordinary restrictions imposed in the *Neulander* case. The defendant raised the familiar claim that disclosures by the former jurors would chill participation by the next set of jurors who might anticipate that their deliberations would not remain confidential either. Perhaps because this same argument would warrant gag orders in nearly every trial, completed or not, the New Jersey high court did not rely on this argument. Instead it decided that the gag order was appropriate due to the possibility that "such disclosures could provide the prosecution with an undue advantage in the retrial proceeding."[26] The risk that one party or another would be able to take advantage of juror disclosures also follows, of course, whenever an additional trial is anticipated in another jurisdiction on the same incident, or whenever a retrial is granted on appeal. But the probability of a second try in these contexts tends to be lower than the probability of a second trial after mistrial. As a general rule, when retrial is certain, a former juror should be even more wary of revealing information about deliberations in the first trial.

D. Researchers

Special mention should be made of efforts by jury researchers to find out from jurors what went on behind the jury-room door. Once again, my premise is that a juror is accountable to no one other than his fellow jurors and the public at large. He has no duty whatsoever to speak to those of us who study juries for a living. He should never feel pressured into participating in any sort of posttrial study, and should feel free to decline for any reason or no reason. In exercising the option to speak or not speak, jurors should extend to researchers no special accommodation that they would not extend to a journalist who promises anonymity.[27]

To be sure, researchers seek to advance general knowledge by sharing their findings publicly, and their questions and conclusions are typically screened by scholarly norms. But the line between inquiries by media and by academics can be quite indistinct, as demonstrated, for example, by some of the work of journalist Mark Curriden.[28] Like jury researchers, the press can promise anonymity, conduct in-depth investigations, and perform a valuable public service in disseminating information about governmental institutions. Generally, reporters and publishers attempt to follow professional standards to ensure accuracy and integrity, just as researchers do. (Both academicians and reporters bristle at accusations that their work is influenced by its potential to generate income, although neither group is entirely free from suspicion on this score.) Simply put, the juror's public duty does not extend to advancing scholarly understanding of the jury system or group decision making. It is complete when the verdict is delivered. Any further participation may well be a laudable contribution to a body of knowledge that could eventually help to strengthen the justice system, but it remains optional from an ethical standpoint, and must be undertaken with honesty and respect for the confidences of fellow jurors.

E. Confiding in Friends, Family, and Counselors

Fortunately most jurors find jury service to be a rewarding experience in which they would willingly participate again. They move from jury service back into their daily routine with little effort. Some, however, continue to feel anxiety or to suffer other effects after trials that involved disturbing evidence or difficult deliberations.[29] For many of these jurors, talking through aspects of the deliberations with family, friends, or professionals is essential to restoring peace of mind after the trial is over.[30] The advice some judges give at the close of jury service—"I urge you to respect the secrecy of the jury room and not discuss what went on there"—may create even greater anxiety for some jurors, as they feel caught between following the judge's instructions and the lingering emotional burden of their experience. As we have emphasized, ex-jurors should understand that they need not discuss the case with anyone. But ex-jurors should not hesitate to talk through their experiences with individuals who can be trusted to keep their confidences. They should realize, however, that as with any confidential information, the degree to which secrets of the jury room remain secret depends entirely on the trustworthiness of the confidant. If a conversation is overheard by others, or if a confidant carelessly or recklessly betrays a confidence, what was once secret may end up in the news.

F. Accepting Favors from Litigants

Former jurors may find themselves the object of gift-giving by litigants who prevailed. For example, after the verdict in one case, tobacco industry attorneys reportedly accepted the judge's invitation to meet with the jurors while they were sitting in the jury box, and after meeting with the jurors for about forty-five minutes, the attorneys invited all the jurors to a postverdict party at a nearby Hyatt hotel where they arranged for subsequent individual interviews of jurors.[31] How should a juror respond to expressions of gratitude after the trial? Here the problem is not a choice of speaking out versus keeping confidences. It is instead a situation in which following one's interest in personal gain may raise the appearance of bias. No one would doubt that for a juror to accept gifts from a litigant before or during a trial is illegal. Accepting gifts after the trial raises the suspicion of the same sort of corruption. As one court said, "[I]mpartial jury decisions may be endangered by events taking place after the jury has rendered its verdict, as well as before."[32]

The appropriate response when offered a gift by a litigant or by a litigant's supporter is for the juror either to decline the gift or to insist that any benefit be bestowed on the jury system in general. For example, a donation could be made to the juror-transportation fund or child-care fund, so long as no part of that benefit is enjoyed directly by the juror herself. Juror fees in many jurisdictions are already donated by jurors toward general jury funds or charity. If invited to a celebration party, a juror should decline.[33] (Incidentally, just as jurors should not accept gifts from trial participants, they probably should not bestow them either. What may be an entirely innocent gesture by a juror[34] could be interpreted by a verdict opponent as proof confirming suspicions of favoritism.)

IV. CONCLUSION AND RECOMMENDATIONS

Judicial instructions should include information about the decisions an ex-juror may face. Drawing upon a previous effort to construct an instruction along these lines by Arthur Murphy and Christine Kellett,[35] I propose that the following model jury instruction be given to jurors as they are discharged from service:

A. You may find that others are interested in learning from you what you have to say about your experience as a juror. Remember this: **You do not have to answer anyone's questions.** You have no obligation to talk to anyone about the trial or deliberations if you don't want to. You do not have to explain your verdict, or discuss what took place in the jury room, with anyone—neither with me, nor with the attorneys, nor the press, nor your friends or family. You can always say "No comment." Nothing else is expected of you. If anyone persists in pestering you with questions after you have asked them not to, please let me know.

B. Although you do not have to answer questions about the trial, you may find that you do want to talk about it. No one will stop you if you do; **you have a right to free speech.** However, I'm going to give you four guidelines that you should keep in mind before you decide to voluntarily reveal what happened in the jury room during your deliberations. These should help you as you decide whether to talk, who to talk to, and what to say:

1. **Don't talk about deliberations unless you believe that some public good will come of it.** What was said in the jury room is known only to each of you. Do not reveal what happened in deliberations merely because you hope for money or fame, or for some personal benefit. As jurors you have served in the public's interest, not your own. If you believe that by disclosing information about deliberations you could improve the justice system or help prevent a miscarriage of justice, then disclosure to a trusted source—me, or your own lawyer, for example—might be warranted.

2. **Respect the confidences of your fellow jurors.** If you do choose to discuss your deliberations, try not to divulge anything said or done in the jury room by any of the *other* jurors that might indicate his or her thinking about the case. This means that you should not disclose opinions expressed or votes cast by your fellow jurors, even if you disclose your own opinions and votes. If you are persuaded that it is important to reveal the opinions or votes of jurors other than yourself, try to protect their anonymity. Do not reveal the identity of any other juror or information that could be used to identify any other juror. There are three reasons for respecting the confidences of your fellow jurors. First, it is the right thing to do—just as you hope they will respect your privacy, you should respect theirs. Second, disclosure could mean that future

jurors may think that what they say will be made public. Thus they might be more reluctant to participate and speak their minds in jury deliberations. Third, such disclosures may encourage those who might seek to influence jury decisions to monitor which jurors joined or opposed their side. Keeping deliberations confidential helps to ensure that future juries remain independent decision makers.

3. **Always tell the truth** when you discuss your jury service. If you stretch the truth after the trial, people will have less confidence that you were truthful during the trial, for example, when you were answering questions during jury selection, or when you were making statements to your fellow jurors.

4. **If you are unsure about whether or not to talk or what to say, it is a good idea to talk first to me or to someone you can really trust to keep a confidence, such as your spouse, counselor, religious advisor, or your own attorney.**

C. I've mentioned so far that you have no obligation to talk about the trial, and have given you a few pointers to help you decide what, if anything, to say about your jury service. Finally, it is important to avoid conduct that might inadvertently lead others to conclude that you were biased toward one side or the other. So **it is not a good idea to accept gifts or favors from parties, attorneys, or supporters in this case.** Likewise, it is unwise to give gifts *to* parties, attorneys, or supporters of one side or the other. Giving or receiving gifts might create suspicion that you were biased in favor of one side or the other.

NOTES

1. Compare *Passantino v. Johnson & Johnson Consumer Products, Inc.*, 982 F.Supp. 786 (W.D. Wash. 1997) (refusing to allow losing party to interview jurors) with California pattern jury instructions quoted at note 18 below. See generally, Alison Markovitz, "Jury Secrecy during Deliberations," *Yale Law Journal* 110 (2001): 1493, 1515 nn135–37; Nancy S. Marder, "Deliberations and Disclosures: A Study of Post-Verdict Interviews of Jurors," *Iowa Law Review* 82 (1997): 465, 487.

2. See generally Marcy Strauss, "Juror Journalism," *Yale Law & Policy Review* 12 (1994): 389.

3. See *Duncan v. Louisiana*, 391 U.S. 145 (1968); Harry Kalven Jr. and Hans Zeisel, *The American Jury* (Boston: Little, Brown and Co., 1966), 7; Charles Nesson, "The Evidence of the Event? On Judicial Proof and the Acceptability of Verdicts," *Harvard Law Review* 98 (1985): 1357, 1368; Alexis de Tocqueville, *Democracy in America*, ed. Phillips Bradley, ed. and trans. Henry Reeve and Francis Bowen, 8th ed. (1835; New York: Alfred A. Knopf, 1960), 282.

4. See Jennifer S. Lerner and Philip E. Tetlock, "Accounting for the Effects of Accountability," *Psychological Bulletin* 125 (1999): 255–56. Lerner and Tetlock break down accountability into four different phenomena: "mere presence of another

(participants expect that another will observe their performance)"; "identifiability (participants expect that what they say or do in a study will be linked to them personally)"; "evaluation (participants expect that their performance will be assessed by another according to some normative ground rules and with some implied consequences)"; and "reason-giving (participants expect that they must give reasons for what they say or do)".

5. Robert J. MacCoun and Tom R. Tyler, "The Basis of Citizens' Perceptions of the Criminal Jury," *Law and Human Behavior* 12, no. 3 (1988): 333–52 (finding that "the probability of convicting the guilty, community representation, and minority representation are each independent predictors of the perceived fairness of a jury procedure"); E. Allan Lind and Tom R. Tyler, *The Social Psychology of Procedural Justice* (New York: Plenum Press, 1988) (discussing the value of participation).

6. See Daniel D. Blinka, "'This Germ of Rottedness': Federal Trials in the New Republic, 1789–1807," *Creighton Law Review* 36 (2003): 135, 178–80. Blinka quotes Jefferson as warning in 1798 that a "'germ of rottedness' . . . had infected trial by jury because the people had no control over the selection of jurors" and notes that Jefferson argued that the election of jurors would end the corruption that was made possible because jury boxes were filled with "'accidental bystanders,' 'foreigners,' and 'idle persons collected for purposes of dissipation,' 'whose ignorance or dependence render them pliable to the will and designs of power.'" For more on jury trials in Virginia during this period, see Nancy J. King, "The Origins of Felony Jury Sentencing in the United States," *Chicago Kent Law Review* 78 (2003): 937.

7. Lerner and Tetlock, "Accounting for the Effects of Accountability," 255, 270.

8. "In trying to arrive at a unanimous group verdict, jurors must justify their opinions to fellow jury members. In other words, they are accountable to each other, a state of affairs that induces people to think more deeply and critically about their own views and other criteria for decision making. . . . [By contrast to the single juror simulation] jurors who are accountable to their peers should feel compelled to view their task in a more complex way—that is, to recognize that any personally appealing verdict that rests on evidence that they have been instructed to ignore may be difficult to justify to fellow jury members, who have heard the same instructions and may believe that proper legal procedure must be followed." David R. Shaffer and Shannon R. Wheatman, "Does Personality Influence Reactions to Judicial Instructions? Some Preliminary Findings and Possible Implications," *Psychology, Public Policy, and Law* 6 (2000): 655, 657–58; Shaffer and Wheatman cite P. E. Tetlock, "Accountability and Complexity of Thought," *Journal of Personality and Social Psychology* 45 (1983): 74–83.

9. Lind and Tyler, *The Social Psychology of Procedural Justice*, 91–92 (jury increases legitimacy of justice system by allowing community participation and representation in legal decision making).

10. See Jury Act, 1977 (New South Wales) §§ 68A and 68B (it is an offense for jurors to disclose information without the consent of the judge or coroner); Canada, Criminal Code § 649 (it is an offense for a juror to disclose any information relating to the proceedings of a jury when it was absent from the courtroom); Contempt of Court Act 1981 (United Kingdom) § 8 (it is an offense to disclose any particulars of statements made, opinions expressed, arguments advanced, or votes cast by members of the jury during deliberations). In Scotland, for example, even inquiry into confidential deliberations in connection with an attack on the verdict

is banned. These restrictions are designed to prevent juror tampering and to preserve the finality of verdicts.

11. In countries in which juror speech is suppressed, there have been recent calls to change the rules to allow judicial inquiry into alleged impropriety by a jury. See John Robertson, "Judge Moves to End Jury Room Confidentiality," *The Scotsman*, December 7, 2002 (the article notes that Lord Reed had called for reform in the Lord Upjohn Lecture at the Inns of Court School of Law in London); Department for Constitutional Affairs, Consultation Paper, "Jury Research and Impropriety: A Consultation Paper to Assess Options for Allowing Research into Jury Deliberations and to Consider Investigations into Alleged Juror Impropriety" (January 21, 2005), available at http://www.dca.gov.uk.

12. Abraham S. Goldstein, "Jury Secrecy and the Media: The Problem of Postverdict Interviews," *University of Illinois Law Review* (1993): 296–97.

13. *United States v. Cleveland*, 128 F.3d 267 (5th Cir. 1997) (upholding an order limiting the press from inquiring about deliberations, quoting *United States v. Harrelson*, 713 F.2d 1114, 1118 (5th Cir. 1983), and noting that order "does not prevent jurors from speaking out on their own initiative").

14. See, e.g., *Model Code of Judicial Conduct* (Chicago: American Bar Association, 1990); Cynthia Gray, *Ethical Standards for Judges* (Chicago: American Judicature Society, 1999).

15. For a recent study collecting research and recommendations on this topic, see Roi Holt, Janvier Slick, and Amy Rayborn, "Understanding Jurors, Jury Debriefing in Yamhill County," *Oregon State Bar Bulletin*, July 2003, available at http://www.osbar.org/publications/bulletin/03july/understanding.html. See also Judge Eugene A. Lucci, "Jury Management Procedures," 6, available at http://web2.lakecountyohio.org/courts/images/Jury%20Management%20 (LLV%2005-2002).pdf. Judge Lucci states that he debriefs jurors before they leave the courthouse "not necessarily about how or why they reached their verdict, but rather about how well the learning process met their expectations." Compare "Recommendations of the Jury Innovations Committee, Response by the Supreme Court Committee on Standard Jury Instructions in Civil Cases" (2001), at 21 para. 42, available at http://www.wfsu.org/gavel2gavel/briefs/01-1226_responseSC Committee.pdf: "Post verdict discussions with jurors can inadvertently affect the trial court's ability to rule on post-trial motions. There are other ways to obtain input from jurors about the trial process without encouraging a conversation between the trial judge and the jurors about a case that is still pending." The same concern was expressed by members of the Maryland Council on Jury Use and Management, while others objected to the proposed rule change concerning jury debriefing on a different ground, arguing that instead of insisting that judicial debriefing take place in the courtroom with the parties present, judges should be able to speak in private with the jurors. See Standing Committee on Rules of Practice and Procedure, "Minutes of Meeting May 18, 2001," available at http://www.courts.state.md.us/rules/5-18-01.pdf. Other jurisdictions have provided jury-support personnel to perform similar functions. See Daniel Wise, "Kaye Institutes Juror Ombudsman Program," *New York Law Journal* 213 (April 13, 1995): 1.

16. *People v. Peck*, 674 N.E. 2d 440, 444 (Ill. App. 1996), emphasis added.

17. See "Propriety of Attorney's Communication with Jurors After Trial," A.L.R. 4th 19 (2000): 1209; Jennifer Adair, "Post-Verdict Contacts with Jurors by Attorneys," *Journal of the Legal Profession* 23 (1998/1999): 337. In many federal

courts, jurors may not be questioned by the parties or their lawyers without the permission of the court, which is granted only in extraordinary situations. See, e.g., "Jury Selection, Instruction and Verdict Process for the District of Maine in Portland and Judge Hornby's Practices in Impaneling a Jury" (July 2004), available at http://www.med.uscourts.gov/practices/DBH%20Jury%20Process.pdf; "Judge Echols usually does not allow interviewing of jurors immediately after the trial unless he is notified in advance and the jurors have agreed to be interviewed. Many jurors don't want to answer questions about their vote, the jury's verdict, the position of fellow jurors, or justification of their decision. Jurors take their jobs seriously and most are mentally drained after the verdict is rendered. Judge Echols has allowed attorneys to submit proposed written jury questions to him with copies to the other side, and he has forwarded the approved questions to the jurors. Answers received are furnished to both sides" (*Practice and Procedure Manual*, U.S. District Judge Robert L. Echols, Middle District of Tennessee, available at http://www.tnmd.uscourts.gov/echospractice.html). See also Karlene S. Dunn, "When Can an Attorney Ask: 'What Were You Thinking?'—Regulation of Attorney Post-Trial Communication with Jurors after *Commission for Lawyer Discipline v. Benton*," *South Texas Law Review* 40 (1999): 1069 (collecting authority governing attorney interviews of jurors).

18. For example, see the recommended instructions in California contained in "Bench Handbook: Jury Management" issued by the California Center for Judicial Education and Research: "Throughout this trial I have admonished you not to discuss the facts and issues of this case with anyone. I am now releasing you from that order. You have an absolute right to discuss or not to discuss this case, including your deliberations or verdict, with anyone you choose. It is appropriate for the parties, their attorneys, or their representatives to ask you to discuss your deliberations or verdict with them. The discussion must take place at a reasonable time and place" (San Francisco: California Center for Judicial Education and Research, 2001). See also *Commission for Lawyer Discipline v. Benton*, 980 S.W.2d 425, 433 (Tex. 1998), cert. denied, 526 U.S. 1146 (1999): "We have long concluded that communication between parties, counsel, and discharged jurors can be a valuable experience for all concerned. In particular, a lawyer. . . who has lost at trial may respectfully ask the jurors to tell him why they were not persuaded by his case, and thus learn something that will help him serve his clients better in the future. . . . Texas trial judges in civil cases are required to instruct jurors after the verdict that once they are discharged they are free to discuss the case with anyone, including the attorneys and parties, and that the attorneys may question them about their deliberations"; *Lind v. Medevac, Inc.*, 219 Cal. App. 3d 516, 268 Cal. Rptr. 359 (Cal. Ct. App. 1990): "An attorney who wins a trial by jury should not be barred from writing jurors post verdict, thereby requesting that he be notified of any posttrial contact with the jurors by the adverse side; and requesting that he be further allowed either to be present for any interviews granted the adverse side, or to discuss with the juror any telephonic or written communications received from the adverse side."

As for limitations, see *Benton*. *Benton* upheld the constitutionality of a disciplinary rule barring an attorney from "ask[ing] questions of or mak[ing] comments to a member of that jury that are calculated merely to harass or embarrass the juror or to influence his actions in future jury service." In the case, an attorney was disciplined for writing a letter to jurors that included statements such as, "I was so angry with your verdict that I could not talk with you after the trial. I could not believe that 12 allegedly, good people from Cameron County, who swore to return a verdict based on the evidence, could find that the [plaintiffs] were not damaged," and "maybe someday you will need the aid of our civil justice system and it will be as corrupted for you as you made it for the Salases." See also *In re Berning*, 468 N.E.2d 843 (Ind. 1984), upholding the discipline of a prosecutor for writing to jurors after acquittal in a domestic violence case. The prosecutor had questioned their decision, suggesting it tells him he shouldn't bring domestic violence cases, and stating, inter alia, "everyone involved in the prosecution of the case was terribly upset and shocked at the verdict of not guilty. Marilyn Martin had the difficult task of trying to explain to her children why Mr. Martin was able to get away with such an act without being punished for it. The victim was in tears because the finding of not guilty meant to her that the jury felt that she was a liar."

19. Cathy E. Bennett & Associates, Inc., jury consultants, list the cost of post-verdict interviews as running between $1,000 and $5,000 plus expenses, and summarize, "We have found the postverdict interview to be the most humbling and insightful of all the lessons learned in our 20-plus years in this profession. . . . Postverdict interviews consist of a trial consultant contacting the jurors and asking a variety of questions about the case, the lawyers, the evidence and the witnesses. This is a particularly helpful tool if counsel has a series of cases involving the same type of litigation." From Cathy E. Bennett & Associates' Web site, http://www.CEB jury.com.

20. Strauss, "Juror Journalism," 405–6.

21. See Marder, "Deliberations and Disclosures."

22. This sort of protest sometimes follows when the jurors learn of key information denied them during the trial. For example, one jury in a federal prosecution petitioned the governor and judge after finding out that the defendant they convicted of illegally growing marijuana was authorized to do so by the state government. Dean E. Murphy, "Jurors Who Convicted Marijuana Grower Seek New Trial," *New York Times*, February 5, 2003, A14.

23. Goldstein, "Jury Secrecy and the Media."

24. *State v. Neulander*, 173 N.J. 193, 801 A.2d 255 (2002).

25. Around the same time, the Supreme Court of Ohio struck down an order suppressing the names, addresses, and questionnaire responses of jurors in a high-profile murder case that had ended in a mistrial. The defendant was facing retrial. The court dismissed the argument that the jurors in the next trial would be chilled from responding candidly, reasoning that in-camera voir dire is an option for those concerned about privacy, and concluding that trial court authority to inform jurors of their right not to respond to media inquiries and to bar repeated media requests is a sufficient protection against the harassment of jurors. Unlike the *Neulander* court, the Ohio court seemed to accept the likelihood that some of the jurors would "rather enjoy" the opportunity for "the disclosure of secrets." *State ex rel. Beacon Journal Pub. Co. v. Bond*, 98 Ohio St. 3d 146, 781 N.E.2d 180 (2002).

26. *Neulander*, 219.

27. See Valerie P. Hans, "Jury Research Ethics and the Integrity of Jury Deliberations," in this volume, 247–64.

28. See his award-winning sixteen-part series, "Juries on Trial," *Dallas Morning News* in 2000, see http://www.abanet.org/media/jul01/silvergavel.html. Curriden's series was honored by the ABA. The first in the series is available at http://www.geocities.com/bigbro_arizona/ib2253.html. Curriden served on the ABA's panel on the American Jury.

29. See Leigh B. Bienen, "Helping Jurors Out: Post-Verdict Debriefing for Jurors in Emotionally Disturbing Trials," *Indiana Law Journal* 68 (1993): 1333. See generally Tori DeAngelis, "Juror Stress Can Influence Final Verdict," *American Psychological Association Monitor on Psychology* 26 (June 1995): 5–6; Theodore B. Feldmann and Roger Bell, "Crisis Debriefing of a Jury after a Murder Trial," *Hospital and Community Psychiatry* 42 (1991): 79. Nor is the need for counseling or professional support limited to trials in the United States. A study of jurors in New Zealand recommended that some sort of debriefing by judges and support services be provided after finding that for one-third of the trials examined, there were jurors who felt that "their own methods of release and debriefing ['talking it through with their partner, laughter, and having a cry'] were not adequate, and that they would have appreciated at least the availability of a support service." Warren Young, Neil Cameron, and Yvette Tinsley, "Juries in Criminal Trials," Part Two, Nov. 1999, available at http://www.lawcom.govt.nz/documents/publications/PP37 Vol2.pdf.

30. See Marianne Meadahl, "Jury Secrecy Harmful, Researchers Find," *Simon Fraser University News*, no. 20 (Jan. 25, 2001), available at: http://www.sfu.ca/mediapr/sfnews/2001/Jan25/ogloff.html. Meadahl reports on research by James Ogloff and Sonia Chopra, "Evaluating Jury Secrecy: Implications for Academic Research and Juror Stress," *Criminal Law Quarterly* 44 (2000), noting that unlike in the United States, where "the main buffer is social support," Canadian jurors "don't have access to that" (190).

31. See http://www.smokefree.net/doc-alert/messages/246782.html.

32. *Benton.*

33. See, e.g., *United States v. Mangano*, 1992 U.S. Dist. LEXIS 2128 (E.D.N.Y.). A dinner party celebrating the verdict was held at the Steakout Restaurant in Little Italy. Among those present at the party were trial counsel to the defendant, a private investigator hired by the defense team, and Juror No. 6. Later that same evening, these three moved to Ruggiero's, a restaurant owned by one of the five acquitted defendants. Celebrations continued the next evening, at another dinner party, with Juror No. 6 and two other jurors.

34. *Hernandez v. State*, 50 P.3d 1100 (Nev. 2002) (three jurors purchased "cute" outfit for three-year-old daughter of murder victim in death penalty case); *Beemer v. Town of Portville*, 2003 N.Y. Misc. LEXIS 776 (2003) (after the jury was dismissed, one of the jurors gave the plaintiff a gift). See also *People v. Hardy*, 2 Cal. 4th 86; 825 P.2d 781; 5 Cal. Rptr. 2d 796 (1992) (during trial, one of the jurors gave a gift of some fruit cocktail to Detective Bobbitt, one of the investigating police officers and a prosecution witness due to his "attractiveness").

35. See Arthur Murphy and Christine Kellet, "Meet the Press: How the Court Can Prepare Jurors," *Criminal Justice* 11 (1996): 8, 49–50.

When Jurors Talk about Their Verdict

Neil Vidmar

American jurors, as Nancy J. King reminds us, are often under pressure from media reporters and lawyers to explain why they decided trials as they did, and King proposes ethical guidelines to assist them.[1] In the first part of this response I provide three examples of jurors who offered comments on the jury deliberation. The first two examples resulted in the kinds of problems that her guidelines hope to avoid, that is, individual juror comments that brought the jury verdict into disrepute. The third example is one in which jurors' explanation of their deliberation process arguably helped vindicate and legitimize a controversial verdict. I then briefly discuss why these issues about juror interviews seldom arise in other common law countries such as Canada, England, and Australia, and I reflect on the relative advantages and disadvantages of juror interviews in helping to legitimize controversial verdicts.

I. THREE AMERICAN CASE EXAMPLES

In August 2003, Omar R. Ali was put on trial for the 1980 slaying of a male high-school guidance counselor in Burlington, Connecticut, after police finally linked twenty-year-old fingerprints and a bloody palm print to Ali.[2] Defendant Ali exercised his constitutional right not to testify and the defense called no witnesses. After two days of deliberation the jury convicted Ali of the crime. A reporter for the *Hartford Courant* described a posttrial interview with the jurors:

> "Once we put all the pieces together, there was no more doubt in anyone's mind," said juror Michael Martel. "It fit together too good."
>
> The jurors also said they might have had more doubt if Ali had taken the stand to explain why he was in Ashton's home, a fact they definitely concluded.
>
> "He needed to say, 'I went there with someone else,'" juror Bonnie Allen said. "If he took the stand and said it, it would have raised questions."[3]

On October 2, 2003, the trial court ordered a special preliminary inquiry to determine if those juror comments indicated that "juror misconduct, i.e., consideration of the defendant's decision not to testify, may have occurred during the deliberations leading to the verdict in the case."[4]

Did the jury actually engage in misconduct, or was this a passing thought by juror Allen that was ascribed to the jury deliberations by her or by the newspaper reporter? Was this an after-the-verdict musing about what additional evidence would have been required—another person being responsible for the killing—to cast doubt on the prosecution's charge since, juror Martel is quoted as saying, "all the pieces" of evidence convinced the jurors that Ali was at the crime scene? If the reporter had interviewed other jurors about this matter, would they have denied that it was a part of their deliberations? Would they have said that Ms. Allen raised the issue but the rest of the jurors admonished her that such musings were inappropriate under the judge's instructions? Or ignored her? In the Arizona Jury Project we documented a substantial number of instances in which an individual juror made a comment that went beyond what the judge had instructed the jurors to do.[5] Sometimes the other jurors admonished that juror by indicating that the comment was inappropriate. In other instances, they just appeared to ignore the comment. We found no significant evidence that such a comment affected final verdicts. The newspaper report does not tell whether the jurors were interviewed separately after the verdict or all together. In the latter case, the other jurors could have taken issue with or elaborated on the context of juror Allen's comment.

In any event, the quotation ascribed to juror Allen raised the concern of the trial judge about the appropriateness of the jury's guilty verdict. In the special inquiry he asked juror Allen if the quotation was accurate. According to a subsequent article in the *Courant,* juror Allen purportedly testified that the "gist" was correct, but added, "I don't exactly remember what I said to the reporter."[6] She then answered affirmatively to another question by the judge inquiring if all his instructions had been followed. A second juror who was quoted in another newspaper story as saying that the jury had followed the judge's instructions was also questioned by the judge.[7] This juror affirmed his quotation to the judge.[8] The judge concluded there was no juror misconduct,[9] but juror Allen's comment had created a temporary problem that could have been avoided, and in any event probably caused her anxiety and inconvenience.

In a second example, O'Keefe, a Mississippi funeral home business, went to trial in 1995 against Loewen, a Canadian-based funeral home corporation, in a dispute involving claims of breach of contract, intentional interference of contract, tortious breach of contract, willful breach of contract, antitrust violations, and fraud. The jury returned a verdict for the plaintiff in the amount of $100 million in compensatory damages and $400 million in punitive damages. In Mississippi, the agreement of ten of twelve jurors is sufficient for a legal verdict in a civil trial. Eleven jurors agreed on the O'Keefe verdict.[10]

Shortly after the verdict two lawyers for Loewen interviewed four of the jurors, including the lone dissenting juror, to determine why the jury decided as it did. After a complicated appeals process, Loewen eventually settled the case for $85 million. However, Loewen then sued the United States under a provision in the North American Free Trade Agreement (NAFTA), claiming that U.S. courts failed to provide fair and equitable treatment of a foreign litigant.[11] In its NAFTA appeal, Loewen produced two experts who offered opinions on the Mississippi jury's behavior: Sir Robert Jennings and Sir Ian Sinclair, English experts on international law.[12] At paragraph 7 of his expert submission, Mr. Jennings ascribed the jury verdict as a result of the

> latent prejudice of a small, remote and not well-off, African-American community against strangers from a strange land many hundreds of miles to the north of even the north of the United States, and who were moreover, "Canadians;" and the gratifying self-importance it might lend a jury from such a community if they were given to believe from the outset that this was a very special case involving unimaginable sums of money and that their gratifying role in the matter was to realize and experience their potential powers to award damages of such amounts as had hitherto been wholly beyond their experience and even their most unlikely fantasies.[13]

Mr. Sinclair echoed this view in his submission.[14]

These invidious comments about the jurors, suggesting expert opinions based upon racial and socioeconomic stereotypes, appear to have ignored the following facts: while the trial judge was African American, both litigants were white; both had racially mixed litigation teams; the jury was racially mixed with four white and eight black jurors; the jury contained college-educated persons; and the foreman of the jury was a former Canadian with an advanced college degree.

Apparently the expert opinions were based, at least in part, on the post-trial juror interviews undertaken by the defense team. The foreperson was not one of the interviewees. The principal juror around whom Loewen's experts drew their conclusions was the lone dissenter. She was an older, highly religious person who held a pre-burial insurance contract with the Loewen group. She was quoted in the lawyers' interviews as saying that she "wished the jury had been composed of persons with 'a little education'" and had "more white jurors." Despite her other comments the dissenting juror conceded in the interview that some of the African American jurors favored a lesser damage award than was eventually rendered. The interview with her and the other three interviewees indicated that the other three whites who served on the jury voted for liability, and that a white female juror initially advocated for a $3 billion award. As the case progressed through the NAFTA dispute process, an affidavit by the jury foreperson solicited by the U.S. defense team refuted the views provided by the dissenting juror.[15]

Even considering the fact that the lawyers and experts for Loewen in the NAFTA claim were acting in the context of an adversary system—the racial stereotyping notwithstanding—it is fairly apparent that their impressions of the jury's deliberations were drawn primarily from one juror who interpreted the process through a racially colored lens. Had that juror refused to be interviewed, had all the jurors been systematically interviewed, or had they been interviewed as a group, the picture of the jury deliberations would likely have been very different. Like the Ali trial in Connecticut, one juror created a lot of mischief.[16]

A third example involves the trial of novelist Mike Peterson for the December 9, 2001, murder of his wife, Kathleen Peterson, in Durham, North Carolina.[17] Kathleen Peterson, a Nortel executive, was found dead in a pool of blood at the bottom of the stairs in their Durham mansion. The prosecution charged Mike Peterson with first-degree murder but did not seek the death penalty. The defense claimed that her death was the result of an accident, a fall partly resulting from an imbalance due to pain pills and alcohol that she had ingested. The case garnered a great deal of pretrial and trial publicity because of the couple's social prominence in Durham, Mike Peterson's controversial political views on Durham city politics, rumors of his homosexual liaisons, and the fact that a close female friend had died in similar circumstances almost sixteen years before at an army base in Germany. The fifteen-week trial was covered daily from opening to adjournment on nationwide Court TV as well as by local television media. Later, NBC's *Dateline* aired a two-hour documentary of the trial.[18] ABC produced a two-hour documentary entitled *The Staircase* with filming by award-winning French director Jean-Xavier de L'Estrade.[19] Awareness of national and international attention increased local interest in the proceedings.

In opening trial statements the prosecution conceded that it had found no murder weapon, but believed that the weapon was probably a fireplace tool called a "blowpoke." The prosecution called experts to testify about autopsy findings and technical evidence about blood spatter and accident reconstruction. The prosecution considered, but then rejected, a motion asking the judge to allow the jurors to view the actual scene of the death rather than have the jurors rely exclusively on photographs and drawings. The prosecution persuaded the judge to allow the testimony of a male escort who had been contacted by Mike Peterson as evidence bearing on motive. The judge also allowed testimony about Peterson's female friend who was found dead in Germany on the legal ground that it was evidence showing Peterson had gained knowledge that might have assisted him in staging an accidental death scene.

Mike Peterson's defense lawyers produced experts—including the famous forensic specialist, Dr. Henry Lee, of the O. J. Simpson trial fame—who offered opinions opposing those of prosecution experts. Surprising the prosecution, Peterson's lawyers requested that the jurors be taken to the death scene. The judge granted the request. In a "Perry Mason" maneuver near the closing of their defense, Peterson's lawyers produced a blowpoke that they claimed was the missing tool that police had overlooked in their search of the Durham mansion and that was such an important part of the prosecution's opening address. It showed no physical traces of being a weapon. Mike Peterson exercised his constitutional right not to testify.

In the end, the prosecution's case was based on circumstantial evidence. After several days of deliberation the jury returned a verdict, finding Peterson guilty of first-degree murder. The jurors were under great pressure from television and newspaper media to explain their verdict. However, rather than grant individual interviews, eleven jurors and an alternate (who was dismissed on technical grounds near the very end of the trial) gathered in the courthouse grand-jury room. With television and documentary cameras operating, the jurors answered questions from the news media.[20] They explained that at the beginning of deliberations they were divided, with five jurors undecided, four favoring guilt, and three favoring a not-guilty verdict. During their week-long deliberations they considered the death of the woman in Germany and the homosexual evidence as insignificant. However, while they disregarded the prosecution's blowpoke theory, none of them believed Kathleen Peterson accidentally fell down the stairs because the blood stains were so extensive and the lacerations on the back of her skull and other bruises on her body were inconsistent with a fall. They devoted substantial discussion to the prosecution's medical testimony indicating that the woman had bled to death over a protracted period of time, suggesting a discrepancy between the time of Mike Peterson's 911 call and the time of Kathleen's death. They believed that the police and the state's forensic examiners could have done a better job and they were skeptical of some of those forensic experts' attempts to re-create blood spatter by beating on a Styrofoam head topped with a bloody sponge. However, they also gave little weight to the opinions of the defense's Dr. Henry Lee because he did not actually conduct any tests. The jury foreperson emphasized that they examined the autopsy photos of Kathleen Peterson's head many times. The jurors reported that they argued vigorously with one another and that they carefully considered all five aspects of the instructions on the law that the judge provided them.

In contrast to the possibly distorted views of one or two jurors giving individual interviews, the group interview very arguably presented a detailed picture of the deliberation process. The comments made by individual jurors were made in the presence of the other jurors, providing the others an opportunity to correct any misstatements and to clarify ambiguous utterances. Both the newspaper accounts and the television programs resulting from the group interview produce an impression of a group of citizens who did their very best in arriving at a difficult verdict. The Mike Peterson jury's interview serves as a model way of responding to media or lawyer pressures and stands in stark contrast to the results of individual juror interviews in the *Ali* and *Loewen* cases.[21]

II. CANADIAN, ENGLISH, AUSTRALIAN, AND NEW ZEALAND JURORS DO NOT GRANT INTERVIEWS

None of the three interview examples described above could have occurred in Canada, England, Australia, or New Zealand. Although each of these countries values a free press, restrictions are placed on what the press may report before, during, and after trial.[22] Sometimes proscriptions on publishing trial proceedings are delayed even after the trial if the judge concludes that the publication would jeopardize a future trial involving the defendant or a co-defendant. One purpose of these restrictions is to preserve the right to a fair trial defined as one as free as possible of facts or misrepresentations that might taint the jury—before, during, or after the trial. In Canada, for example, section 649 of the Criminal Code prohibits jurors from ever disclosing anything about their deliberations under the threat of a summary conviction (that is, by a judge deciding alone) that could result in a sentence of six months in jail or a fine of Can$5,000 or both. Moreover, under similar threat of contempt proceedings, news reporters and their publishers would not approach jurors for the scoop on jury deliberations.

One result of these proscriptions is that jurors in these countries do not serve on the jury with the thought that they might sell the story to a newspaper, as has happened in some cases in the United States. Nor are they placed in a position to offer comments on their verdict even when it is controversial.

The legal development of contempt proceedings for publishing material that might jeopardize a trial occurred in mid-eighteenth-century England. Their original purpose was to prevent pre- and mid-trial prejudice by pamphleteers—the forerunners of today's tabloid press—but the basic concept has evolved into judicial reasoning that disclosure of the jury's deliberation process will destroy the mystique of the jury, open it to second-guessing, and affect the perceived legitimacy of the verdict.[23] There are additional concerns. Jurors in England are chosen without either challenges for cause or peremptory challenges. New Zealand and Australia allow each side a few peremptory challenges and Canada allows very restricted challenges for cause under special circumstances. The assumption is that any juror as called is "indifferent between the Queen and the accused." Under these constraints that inhibit inquiries into potential prejudices, judges worry about whether a future jury would be prejudiced by juror interviews if there is a mistrial or a future trial of a co-defendant.

Contempt and the threat of contempt are just part of a more general judicial philosophy in these countries that mandates closer supervision of the trial process. For instance, in contrast to the American system, a lawyer or barrister must be very circumspect in what he or she says to the press about the trial—before or after—out of fear of censure by the judge and probably fellow members of the law society. Cameras are never allowed in courts. At the end of evidence, the trial judge "sums up" the evidence to the jury as part of final instructions before they are sent back to deliberate. If jurors have questions during deliberation, the judge will typically consult with both sides and attempt to clarify the law, whereas the American judge usually just reads back the original instructions verbatim.

It is probably not excessive rhetoric to say that judges in these other countries are appalled by the intrusive practices of the American media and lawyers regarding jury deliberations. On the other hand, some controversial verdicts in these countries have caused judges and others to argue that the right to trial by jury should be abolished for "complex cases."[24] Perhaps if juror interviews similar to those in the Peterson case were allowed, the critics and the general public would have a different perspective on juries.

III. JUROR INTERVIEWS IN PERSPECTIVE

Although it is only an academic argument since American law is quite settled on the rights of media to inquire and the rights of jurors to speak,[25] the merits of American practice versus the practices in these other countries can be debated. Postverdict intrusions into jury decisions by the press and by lawyers and jury consultants can be annoying to individual jurors and can occasionally cast doubts on the legitimacy of jury verdicts as the first two of my case examples indicate.

Yet, when criminal or civil disputes are of great interest to the community, disclosure by jurors of how they reasoned and reached their verdict can possibly increase acceptance of that outcome. King provides important guidance for jurors when they are approached as individuals, but the best option is to speak as a group. Some members of the Durham community are still convinced that Mike Peterson did not kill his wife,[26] but the posttrial interview with the jurors certainly produced an image of a jury that took its job seriously. In this important instance I submit that the fairness and legitimacy of this controversial trial verdict by the jury were enhanced.

NOTES

1. Nancy J. King, "Ethics for the Ex-Juror: Guiding Former Jurors after the Trial," in this volume, 219–36.
2. Katie Melone, "Verdict Brings Family Justice: Jury Convicts Suspect in 1980 Murder Case," *Hartford Courant*, August 20, 2003, B1.

3. Melone, "Verdict Brings Family Justice, B1.

4. *State of Connecticut v. Omar Ali*, No. CR 00 11174, Order of Superior Court, Judicial District of New Britain, October 2, 2003; Roberto Gonzalez, "Judge Will Question Juror on Deliberations," *Hartford Courant*, October 22, 2003, B4.

5. Shari Seidman Diamond, Neil Vidmar, Mary Rose, Leslie Ellis, and Beth Murphy, "Juror Discussions during Civil Trials: Studying an Arizona Innovation," *Arizona Law Review* 45 (2003): 1–81.

6. Gonzalez, "Judge Will Question Juror on Deliberations."

7. Gonzalez, "Judge Will Question Juror on Deliberations."

8. Roberto Gonzalez, "Judge Queries Two Jurors," *Hartford Courant*, October 29, 2003, B3.

9. Robert Gonzalez, "Judge Finds No Misconduct in Ali Trial," *Hartford Courant*, October 29, 2003, B6.

10. Many of the details of the case are contained in a lengthy article in the *New Yorker* magazine and need not concern us here. Jonathan Haar, "The Burial," *New Yorker*, November 1, 1999, 70–95.

11. *The Loewen Group Inc. and Raymond Loewen, v. The United States of America*, NAFTA Arbitration, ICSID Case No. ARB (AF)/98/3. See also http://www.state .gov/s/l/c3755.htm.

12. For a discussion of these matters see, Opinion of Neil Vidmar in *The Loewen Group Inc. and Raymond Loewen, v. The United States of America*, NAFTA Arbitration, ICSID Case No. ARB (AF)/98/3.

13. Sir Robert Jennings, opinion dated October 26, 1998, at Paragraph 7 in *The Loewen Group Inc. and Raymond Loewen, v. The United States of America*, NAFTA Arbitration, ICSID Case No. ARB (AF)/98/3.

14. Memorial of Sir Ian Sinclair in Loewen Reply in *The Loewen Group Inc. and Raymond Loewen, v. The United States of America*, ICSID Case No. ARB (AF)/98/3, June 8, 2001.

15. See http://www.state.gov/s/l/c3755.htm.

16. On June 26, 2003, the tribunal dismissed the claims against the United States in their entirety, see http://www.state.gov/s/l/c3755.htm.

17. See http://newsobserver.com/peterson for full coverage of the trial.

18. *Mystery on Cedar Street*, aired on February 13, 2004.

19. A longer eight-part documentary by L'Estrade began airing on the BBC on January 10, 2005, http://www.bbc.co.uk/bbcfour/documentaries/storyville/ death-on-the-staircase.shtml.

20. Anne Saker, "A Complex Drama Ends with a Simple Conclusion," *Raleigh News and Observer*, October 15, 2003, A1; John Stevenson, "Anatomy of a Conviction," *Durham Herald Sun*, October 12, 2003, A1.

21. To be sure, a group interview might reveal jury misbehavior, sparking a judicial inquiry similar to the *Ali* case in Connecticut. If the misbehavior was serious, a judicial inquiry would be warranted, but, at least in contrast to the Connecticut case, the judge would know that the juror report appeared to be uncontradicted by the other jurors and would have more information to guide an inquiry.

22. See Sally Lloyd-Bostock and Cheryl Thomas, "The Continuing Decline of the English Jury," in *World Jury Systems*, ed. Neil Vidmar (New York: Oxford University Press, 2000), 53, 79; Michael Chesterman, "Criminal Trial Juries in

Australia: From Penal Colonies to a Federal Democracy," in Vidmar, *World Jury Systems*, 125, 162; Neil Cameron, Susan Potter, and Warren Young, "The New Zealand Jury: Towards Reform," in Vidmar, *World Jury Systems*, 167, 198; Neil Vidmar, "The Canadian Criminal Jury: Searching for a Middle Ground," in Vidmar, *World Jury Systems*, 210, 224.

23. Indeed, this reasoning is held so strongly that judges in England and Canada have forbidden researchers from interviewing jurors even under strict confidentiality conditions and when the research might answer important questions about how to improve the jury process. In Australia and New Zealand, judges have recently made some minor exceptions to the rule by allowing carefully controlled research, but generally the proscriptions regarding disclosure of jury deliberations remain in effect in those countries. See generally, Vidmar, *World Jury Systems*.

24. See, e.g., Lloyd-Bostock and Thomas, "The Continuing Decline of the English Jury," in Vidmar, *World Jury Systems*, 87–88; Terry Honess, Michael Levi, and E. A. Charman, "Juror Competence in Processing Complex Information: Implications of Simulation of the Maxwell Trial," *Criminal Law Review* (1998): 763–72.

25. See King, "Ethics for the Ex-Juror," 219.

26. John Stevenson, "Peterson Friends Say Owl Did It; Galifianakis, Pollard Say Gashes Are Talon Marks," *Durham Herald Sun*, December 13, 2003, A1.

8

Jury Research Ethics and the Integrity of Jury Deliberations

Valerie P. Hans

> We are intruding into the sanctity of the jury room. There was a fear that
> we might, by observing, change the process, change the result.[1]

This chapter discusses ethics relating to the jury, but takes a different
perspective from that of the other contributions to this volume. Instead of
focusing exclusively on the jury, the object of our collective study, I turn the
camera's eye around so that it points at those who observe, research, record,
and occasionally tinker with the jury. I consider and discuss particular
ethical issues that are implicated in jury research.

Facing questions about ethics, those who engage in social science research
on legal topics such as the jury have plenty to draw upon. Most social
science organizations, such as the American Psychological Association
(APA) and the American Sociological Association (ASA), have developed
and published codes of ethics.[2] These guidelines are directed to the proper
treatment of research participants, the analysis of data, and public comments
about research findings. The ASA, for example, urges sociologists to "rely
on scientifically and professionally derived knowledge; act with honesty
and integrity; and avoid untrue, deceptive, or undocumented statements in
undertaking work-related functions or activities."[3] The ASA Ethical
Standards insist that sociologists avoid or disclose conflicts of interest,
adhere to standards of informed consent and privacy rights of research
participants, and inform participants in advance of any potential limits on
the confidentiality of information obtained in research.[4] The APA Ethics
Code provides detailed guidance on what must be communicated to research
participants prior to their involvement, including the purpose of the research,
the exact procedures that will be followed, their right to decline to participate,
the consequences of withdrawing from the study, the confidentiality of the
data, and any anticipated costs and benefits to participation.[5]

The American Psychology-Law Society has developed guidelines
specifically for work in forensic and legal contexts that provide advice about

psycholegal research and other matters such as serving as expert witnesses, clinical examiners, or trial behavior consultants.[6] It describes "an aspirational model" for psychologists who provide their professional expertise to the judicial system.[7] Recognizing the adversary structure of the American legal system, it warns forensic psychologists to "take special care to avoid undue influence upon their methods, procedures, and products, such as might emanate from the party to a legal proceeding by financial compensation or other gains."[8] The U.S. government has a set of research guidelines as well, stressing informed consent, the safety of participants, and the confidentiality of research data.[9] All of these codes and guidelines can be very helpful.

But there are more particular ethical issues that arise in researching an existing yet controversial governmental institution such as the jury. Despite its long history, the jury is the subject of considerable debate, and there have been many efforts to eliminate the jury or reduce its role. The field of jury studies developed as a response to criticisms about the jury's functioning. The earliest systematic research project on the institution, reported in *The American Jury* (1966), began as a way to explore the merits of complaints about the jury system.[10] *The American Jury*'s largely favorable evaluation may have buttressed the institution against attacks and preserved it.[11] However, in the light of continuing criticisms, researchers now test the claims in the debates over the merits of the jury, examining the jury's functioning and measuring the impact of reforms.[12]

Ethical issues arise in undertaking research in this contested terrain. For instance, parties to litigation, or parties who anticipate litigation, may fund jury research that they hope will support their side of the dispute.[13] Litigants hire trial behavior consultants to conduct pretrial research to better assist the litigants in presenting their side of the case at a jury trial. It is rare for people who participate as subjects in pretrial jury research endeavors to learn which party is funding the work, though that is a typical requirement for scientific research with human subjects.

Another array of ethical issues arises because of the distinctive nature of the jury as a political body.[14] Despite decades in which other political institutions such as Congress and the courts have moved toward greater accountability and public scrutiny, the American jury remains an exception.[15] The jury normally deliberates in secret and need not provide reasons for its verdict. Judges rarely investigate or inquire into the content or process of the jury deliberation; if they do, their questions are carefully recorded, limited, and controlled. This secrecy, privacy, and lack of accountability, some commentators argue, are essential to the jury's proper functioning.[16] However, as Kate Stith-Cabranes observes, this secrecy is at odds with certain contemporary political values:

There is much about the jury . . . that does not fit comfortably into our modern constitutional and political culture. Many preeminent constitutional values of the founding period—private liberty, federalism, and local control—were well served by a requirement of jury verdicts in criminal trials. Over the past two hundred years, these values have been challenged, if not eclipsed, by competing values. Some essential characteristics of the jury—or, at least, characteristics that until recently we have believed essential to the jury—are difficult to reconcile with certain of the social and political values that characterize the latter half of the twentieth century. . . . The values that have become ascendant in the modern era, in constitutional decision making as well as the larger legal culture, are rationality, equality, and freedom of expression. Our legal system seems to value reason and complexity over intuition and emotion, diversity and representation over judgments of individual impartiality or special competence, and access and openness over confidentiality and secrecy.[17]

There is much evidence of a contemporary desire to open the jury-room door, if not all the way, at least part way. Jurors in high-profile trials often give media interviews or write books following their jury experiences.[18]

Jury scholars hold forth to news-media representatives on the merits of specific jury verdicts. The news media themselves make further incursions. Perhaps the most explosive in recent years was news coverage of a New York City jury hearing a criminal case against executives of Tyco International that ultimately led to a mistrial.[19] Trouble erupted in the jury room when jurors disagreed heatedly about the merits of the case, according to notes sent to the judge.[20] The judge urged them to continue deliberating. But the following day, as the jurors filed out of the courtroom, reporters observed Juror No. 4 make a hand motion that they interpreted as an "okay" sign to the defense team.[21] Both the *Wall Street Journal* and the *New York Post* then identified the juror by name in their publications.[22] Juror No. 4, her identity unmasked, received a hostile telephone call and a letter complaining about her apparent sympathy for the defendants in the trial, and the judge was forced to declare a mistrial.[23] Posttrial interviews with the Tyco jurors revealed a great deal about the identities and views of the members of the jury.[24]

Even more startling, news media have taken cameras into the jury room, recording actual jury deliberations, and included excerpts of those deliberations on prime-time television shows.[25] Media organizations have justified these recordings of jury-room behavior by arguing they have salutary educational and research benefits.[26] Jury researchers interview jurors after trial, get them to fill out questionnaires, and ask them the most private details about their own thinking and what went on in jury deliberations. One recent research project even taped the jury discussions and deliberations.[27]

All of these activities open the door of the jury room. Is that an ethical problem? Does the fact that research techniques such as taping may influence a specific jury's work raise ethical concerns? What if, in the process of doing research, researchers uncover evidence of injustice or substantial error? Are they ethically obligated to report it? What if reporting error or injustice violates the promise of confidentiality to research participants? What if researchers receive a court order—should they refuse, or how can they cope? Are they damaging the jury as an institution by their intrusive inquiries or by taping jury deliberations?

These are among the ethical questions that arise during the process of jury research. But they have rarely been debated or discussed in a systematic way by the research community. (Consider, in contrast, the extensive literature on the ethics of expert testimony.)[28] This volume, including contributions from a number of prominent jury researchers, provides a valuable opportunity to debate the ethics of jury research.

To illustrate ethical dilemmas in jury research, this chapter focuses on the ethical issues raised in two jury research projects: a hung jury research project I collaborated on with researchers from the National Center for State Courts[29] and a research project supervised by Shari Diamond and Neil Vidmar that included videotaping jury deliberations.[30] Analysis of the particular ethical problems confronted in undertaking these two research projects will show that jury researchers, as well as the jurors they study, must confront and resolve significant moral questions.

I. THE HUNG JURY PROJECT: ETHICAL ISSUES

Suppose that you are in the midst of conducting a juror interview study in your local jurisdiction. The study is ongoing, and involves interviews with jurors who have convicted in criminal cases. You've set the study up following the usual human subjects procedures, and assured your participants that what they say will be confidential. However, the interview you conduct today leaves you troubled. The juror admits that the evidence might have been shaky but that he convicted the defendant because he learned about the defendant's prior criminal record from one of the other jurors. Does your receipt of this information about the questionable basis for the jury's verdict create any ethical obligation at all to the defendant? Or, does your prior assurance of confidentiality to the participant trump the defendant's right to the information?[31]

This hypothetical yet troubling scenario raises the kind of ethical dilemma that could arise for researchers who open the jury-room door. When I presented the dilemma to a group of nationally prominent jury researchers assembled to discuss jury ethics, I obtained a range of responses.[32] Some researchers immediately took the position that the damaging information, although obtained with a promise of confidentiality, must be presented to the court. Some were torn between what they saw as twin obligations to the defendant and the juror, but reluctantly thought the information would have to be disclosed. A few insisted on complete confidentiality to study participants, with the exception of life-threatening information.

The dilemma presented in the hypothetical scenario was anticipated in a collaborative project in which I participated with colleagues from the National Center for State Courts. Our aim was to develop ethically and procedurally sound research techniques for studying hung juries. The hung jury research design, which we spent a great deal of time debating among ourselves and with a terrific advisory board,[33] included several different approaches to studying hung juries. The one that raised the most significant ethical issues was a posttrial questionnaire study of judges, jurors, and attorneys in criminal felony trials in four jurisdictions.

The purpose of the study was to determine the causes and correlates of hung juries, examining how case and evidence factors, individual juror factors, and deliberation factors were related to the jury's ability to reach a unanimous verdict. The National Center for State Courts obtained funding from the National Institute of Justice (NIJ) for such a study. The project was stimulated by concerns expressed by some state court judges, administrators, and prosecutors about an increase in or high numbers of hung juries in their jurisdictions. The policy-driven National Center for State Courts context and the NIJ funding shaped the nature of the questions we planned to ask.

Asking questions of hung jurors would usually not implicate a trial defendant's rights, since by definition no verdict was reached.[34] But we concluded after much discussion that the best research approach was to gather juror information from juries that reached verdicts as well as juries that hung, so that we could compare them. Therefore, many trials in our data set would have resulted in convictions on one or more charges.

One of the issues that arose was with the specific questions we wanted to ask. A good deal of commentary about hung juries attributes their cause to jury nullification, and we were eager to explore that issue.[35] However, taking a direct approach by asking jurors whether they thought the evidence merited a conviction but voted to acquit anyway, or vice versa, was problematic. From a Sixth Amendment point of view, it would be troubling to discover that a juror thought the evidence was inadequate but convicted anyway. Even if jurors were aware that the evidence did not support their ultimate verdict, even if they were willing to tell us, the inclusion of a direct question might have raised a serious ethical dilemma, for what would we do if jurors were to tell us "yes"?

We explain this situation in an article discussing jury nullification and the hung jury data:

> For a number of reasons, we had to approach the issue of jury nullification indirectly, rather than directly, in the juror surveys. First, the fact that we were conducting this research with actual jurors posed a challenge. To preserve the privacy of surveyed jurors and the confidentiality of the research data, we had to be cautious not to include any questions to which a particular response would provide a prima facie basis for an appeal,

which a direct question about jury nullification certainly would. We were also concerned that a direct question—such as, "In rendering your verdict, did you intentionally disregard the law and follow your own conscience about what was right?"—would be unlikely to generate a truthful response from jurors who had, in fact, done so. Indeed, some psychologists would argue that it is unlikely that the majority of jurors would be able to say with any certainty which specific factors led them to their decision.[36]

One of our solutions was to eliminate or modify the questions included in the study. Direct questions about jury nullification were not asked. Perhaps this cost us something in scientific accuracy, but we concluded it was more than balanced by other factors. We also limited our cases to noncapital trials. We estimated that the unusual and heavily litigated nature of death-penalty cases would make it more likely that at some point in the litigation some defense attorney would request the data.

Nonetheless, we did collect a fair amount of information that might have indicated that there was something awry in the basis for a jury conviction. We asked judges, jurors, and attorneys, for example, to rate the extent to which the evidence in the case favored one side or the other. We asked about whether jurors felt they understood the evidence in the case, and how much sympathy they had for the victim. We also obtained demographic information about jurors. However, individual jurors, particularly those with distinctive personal characteristics, might be identified, especially if the specific case name was known or could be traced. A good adversary who had full access to our data might conceivably have been able to make a convincing argument to a judge to inquire into the jury's verdict in more detail.

We also had to consider what to do about an apparent conflict between the requirements of the funding agency, the National Institute of Justice, and the Sixth Amendment right of the defendant to a jury trial. The NIJ specifically requires that researchers maintain the confidentiality of data and prohibits the use of data in adjudicative proceedings.[37] Since we were obtaining information from real jurors in real criminal cases, what if something we discovered indicated very strongly that the defendant had been wrongly convicted? Did we have an ethical obligation to search for such information? Or, should we be prepared to turn over data if asked, even if the NIJ regulations prohibit it?

We developed a set of procedures to try to minimize the likelihood of being placed in an ethically difficult position, and sketched out a protocol to follow should we land in one.[38] Following common procedures used in many sensitive studies today, questionnaires were identified initially only by case number and no names were provided on the surveys. Questionnaires were to be immediately sealed in an envelope and mailed to the National Center for State Courts from the trial court. Once the questionnaire data were entered in a data file, the case identification numbers that linked a particular set of questionnaires to a specific case name were eliminated and the raw questionnaires were destroyed. Thus, it would be difficult for us or anyone else to determine which questionnaires went with which case. However, especially if the case or the jury were unusual in some way, it was conceivable that a person with full access to the database, given enough detail about the jurisdiction, the case type, the evidence presented at trial, and the individual characteristics of jurors, might have been able to guess correctly which set of questionnaires corresponded to a particular case.

What if a defendant, believing that he or she had been wrongly convicted, asked for access to the full database?[39] Or asked the court to review the data for evidence that the defendant thought would show that the verdict was wrongly decided? In that event, we identified a number of strategies that Paula Hannaford presented to the Institutional Review Board that evaluated this proposal. In addition to reducing our and others' ability to identify individual cases and juror data, as explained above, we proposed several other options, including: legal remedies to challenge any subpoena for the data; juror consent to release the data; and procedures to minimize the invasion of jurors' privacy if ordered to produce the data, such as providing aggregate data for the case rather than individual juror data.[40] We were never in a position to select any of these options, as no defendant made a request for our data set.

In retrospect, an outside observer might criticize our proposals for resolving this issue on the ground that the individual rights of the study participants seem to be more important than the rights of an unjustly convicted defendant. Did we get the balance right? Did we have an obligation to set up periodic review of incoming data to determine whether any defendant might have a legitimate claim? In my view, the balance struck was a reasonable one, and can be justified. The jury system arguably provides one of our best chances to secure justice. The purpose of our jury research was to develop sound information about jury dynamics, thus to enable the jury to function better as an institution. It is also important to consider how the balancing act is affected by the broader legal context. For instance, the issue facing us in the hung jury research was a peculiarly American question in one way, because a U.S. defendant's right to a fair trial is protected by the Sixth Amendment.

Furthermore, the choice of individual participant rights over defendant consequences might be altered in, say, death-penalty cases where the consequences to the defendant are literally life-threatening. The presumption of confidentiality of client disclosures to psychologists and psychiatrists, for example, may be waived when the client threatens serious harm to another in the course of a therapeutic session.[41] However, even in death-penalty cases, the American courts provide no regular institutional method of certifying the propriety and soundness of jury deliberation.[42] And one of the best-known American death-penalty researchers, William J. Bowers, head of the Capital Jury Project, concluded that the promise of confidentiality to jurors should trump other important concerns:

> On the matter of the researcher's responsibility to jurors and to defendants whom they may have improperly convicted, I am an absolutist. . . . Ideally, I think social scientists trying to understand jury behavior from interviews with real jurors should promise and ensure absolute confidentiality and take steps to see that this cannot be breached, quite apart from the injustices that may have occurred in specific cases. To do otherwise compromises the integrity of the scientific enterprise of the particular study in question and jeopardizes the work of other scientific investigators in the field.[43]

Thus a strong argument can be made to privilege the confidentiality of juror-research participants even in cases where the consequences for doing so may cause serious injustice.

II. LIGHTS! CAMERA! ACTION! IS VIDEOTAPING JURY DELIBERATIONS ETHICAL?

Thus far I have discussed the ethical quandaries that researchers face when they interview jurors or collect other retrospective data from them after the trial has concluded. A second set of ethical issues arises when researchers and the media tape or film actual jury deliberations.

The first tape recording of jury deliberations within a research context is well known. It occurred in 1954 as part of the work of the Chicago Jury Project.[44] A federal judge in Witchita, Kansas—Judge Delmas C. Hill—agreed to permit Jury Project researchers to undertake audio recordings of civil jury deliberations in his courtroom.[45] The agreement required the permission of the attorneys, strict control over access to the taped deliberations, and editing of transcripts so that jurors, parties, and cases would be anonymous. Importantly, the jurors were not told about the fact that they would be recorded, because of concerns that it might affect the jury deliberation. Six civil jury deliberations were taped in 1954, without incident.

However, controversy erupted the following year after Judge Hill and one of the researchers made a presentation at the Tenth Circuit Judicial Conference describing the taping project and playing an excerpt of one of the deliberations. Three months after the Judicial Conference presentation, the *Los Angeles Times* carried a story about the taping, creating a firestorm of protest. Editorials and stories around the country denounced the "bugging" of the jury room. A congressional investigation followed. One of the researchers, Harry Kalven Jr., was asked by a subcommittee chair: "Now, do you not realize that to snoop on a jury, and to record what they say, does violence to every reason for which we have secret deliberations of a jury?" Subsequently, the federal government passed a law forbidding the recording of federal jury deliberations, and some thirty state legislatures followed suit.[46]

Nonetheless, over the past several decades, several courts have agreed to permit the taping of actual jury deliberations. Several broad social changes, including the emphasis on accountability for public institutions and the dominance of television news, are probably responsible for the fact that today, media and researchers' requests to videotape jury deliberations have met with some success.[47]

The first contemporary effort was a collaborative project between University of Wisconsin law professor Stephen Herzberg, producer Alan Levin, and PBS television. They taped deliberations in a Wisconsin criminal trial that involved potential jury nullification.[48] Certain conditions of the taping agreement differed from those of the Chicago Jury Project. Most significantly, jurors were informed in advance that they would be filmed. Furthermore they understood that excerpts from the deliberation might be shown on national television. A *Frontline* program subsequently showed excerpts of the case and the jury deliberation. The jury deliberation was also the subject of a PhD dissertation and several scholarly articles.[49]

In a more expansive project, CBS News obtained an administrative order from the chief justice of the Arizona Supreme Court, Stanley Feldman, to tape the trials and jury deliberations in a set of Arizona criminal trials. Justice Feldman explained that he had seen the *Frontline* program and was very impressed with it.[50] He believed that showing the jury at work was important both for educating the public about the jury process and for demonstrating the soundness of the institution. He also thought it would be helpful to examine how well Arizona's jury reforms, aimed at improving the justice system, were operating.[51] As Justice Feldman observed at the time of the taping request:

> There was at the time [1996], and still is, a lot of criticism of the jury system. I've always been a believer in it. Still am. So I thought, hey, okay, let's put it to the test, let's see how it works. . . . Let 'em see what goes on, and I think that'll be the answer to this criticism of juries. I think, if anything, televising it will make the jurors do better. I just don't understand how you could have any objection to people knowing how it works. I think they have the right to know that about the system they pay for.[52]

Recently, ABC News pushed the envelope even further with its *State v.* television series, which involves taping the trial proceedings, jury deliberations, and interviews with trial participants in a series of actual cases.[53] In programs shown in the summer of 2002, Arizona jury trials and deliberations were taped with the knowledge and permission of all participants, including jurors. In 2003, after Arizona prosecutors voiced concerns about the taping because of a high proportion of hung juries in the taped cases, ABC News moved to another venue, Colorado, where it did another series of tapings.[54]

Finally, in a research project testing the impact of jury reform, jury scholars Shari Diamond and Neil Vidmar obtained permission from the Arizona Supreme Court to videotape jury discussions and deliberations in a set of civil trials. Judges, the litigants, the attorneys, and all of the jurors had to consent to the taping. In contrast to the media efforts, which were intended for a wide television-viewing audience, the Arizona Supreme Court strictly limited the use of the taped deliberations:

> [T]he materials and information collected for the study, including audio and videotapes, may be used only for the purposes of scientific and educational research. The Court shall take all measures necessary to ensure confidentiality of all materials. . . . The materials and information collected for the study, including audio and videotapes, shall not be subject to discovery or inspection by the parties or their attorneys, to use as evidence in any case, or for use on appeal.[55]

Although the Arizona research study has received only modest public attention, the media forays into the jury room have met with substantial commentary, much of it critical. Barbara A. Babcock, for example, condemned the taping, arguing that juries needed privacy to engage in candid and robust debate, and that videotaping their discussions would undermine the jury's and the verdict's legitimacy.[56]

To examine ethical issues about videotaping jury deliberations, whether as part of a research project or a media story, Nancy King's approach is helpful. In examining how to address moral questions about juror behavior after the trial, she identified the multiple purposes of trial by jury, and asked how different behaviors either promoted or undermined these key functions.[57] So let us consider first how videotaping might affect the community-based, fact-finding function of the jury. Then we will consider broader potential effects on the jury's legitimacy as an institution.

First, taping could affect the composition of the jury, as citizens may be more likely to decline to serve (or, in some cases, more willing to serve!) if their deliberations will be videotaped. The problem appears most acute in the media projects. Diamond and Vidmar estimate that their juror participation rate was approximately 95 percent.[58]

The proportion of the jury pool that declined to participate in the media tapings was substantially higher, although hard to estimate exactly because of the jury selection procedure and the absence of records. According to Charles Brotherton, who interviewed Arizona participants in the CBS and ABC media projects, prospective jurors were informed about the taping and had the option of declining to participate prior to the traditional case-related questions of voir dire.[59] In the one Arizona case with complete records, the Chappell case, 12 of 62 potential jurors (19%) declined to participate because of the cameras.[60] However, several other court officials who spoke to Brotherton recalled that very few people declined to participate because of the media taping.[61] In the Harrison trial taped by ABC, 14 of 110 prospective jurors (13%) said that they might be affected by the presence of the camera, and were dismissed from service on the case.[62]

A prosecutor interviewed by Brotherton observed that during jury selection in the Macnab case, which was taped by ABC, citizens' responses were atypical. For instance, in typical DUI cases, the prosecutor observed that it is customary for a substantial number of prospective jurors to indicate that they or a close friend or family member had been involved in a collision with an impaired driver. However, during the Macnab jury selection, not a single person indicated any such involvement. The prosecutor concluded: "And so I think that we didn't lose good people because of the media, but what happened was, people were more concerned that they wanted to be on the jury. So they weren't going to do anything that would get them struck for cause. . . . They wanted to be on the jury . . . for the media."[63]

If significant numbers decline to serve on a taped jury or are removed because of their reluctance to be filmed, that lessens the representativeness of the jury and hence its ability to fulfill the community-based, fact-finding function. The unwillingness to be taped could be associated with demographic or attitudinal characteristics or other distinctive views that would be valuable to include on the jury. One remedy is to undertake for cause challenges prior to presenting information to the jury pool that the trial and deliberations will be taped, but this will reduce, not eliminate, the problem.

In addition to its impact on jury composition, the question arises about how the taping itself affects the behavior of the jury and the decision that the jury reaches. Justice Feldman observed that in the *CBS Reports* project, the fact that the media would be taping jury deliberations was "intruding into the sanctity of the jury room. There was a fear that we might, by observing, change the process, change the result."[64] One potential effect is that jurors will be less candid in their statements during deliberation and in their voting.[65] Cameras may have a chilling effect on frank and robust deliberation. Candor is critically important as it promotes the full and vigorous debate that is essential to high-quality jury deliberations.[66] I have noted previously that the jury trial is a context in which social desirability may be especially important as the judge and others continually emphasize the importance of adhering to legal principles. When jury deliberations are taped, jurors' enhanced social-desirability urges may be particularly strong and the normal dissipation pattern (in which people who are videotaped pay less attention to the camera over time) may be attenuated.[67]

Justice Feldman goes so far as to suggest that jurors may become more lawful and less biased as a result of cameras in the jury room.[68] Whether or not this eliminates our ethical concerns, if true it might suggest that jury deliberations should *always* be taped to promote public accountability, much as police interrogations may be taped to encourage fair questioning methods.

Diamond and Vidmar defend their research project on this score, saying that they have no reason to believe that the videotaping influenced juror behavior. They point to research studies that show that the impact of videotaping on human social behavior dissipates rather quickly, and that their taped discussions and deliberations provide many examples of frank talk.[69] A recent study of mock juror participants lends some support to the position advanced by Diamond and Vidmar.[70] The researchers surveyed participants in trial-consulting studies who were either videotaped or observed behind a one-way mirror with their knowledge. The mock jurors reported at the end of their experience about their awareness of being recorded and observed, and were asked for their personal judgment about how that awareness influenced their behavior. Awareness of being videotaped and observed was substantial, with about half the participants reporting that they were "very aware" of being watched.[71] However, the significant majority of participants (184 of 268, or 69%) claimed that being watched in this way had no impact at all on their behavior and the comments they made during the mock jury discussions.[72] While the authors of the study caution that their participants might have claimed little influence because of social desirability, or because they were not able to accurately gauge the effect of the one-way mirrors or cameras, the failure to find an impact in this study converges with the other work that Diamond and Vidmar cite.[73]

This brings us to a final set of issues, the broader social and political impact of showing videotapes of jurors making their decisions. Nancy Marder argues that postdeliberation disclosures may negatively affect the legitimacy of the jury system for several reasons. Her arguments can be easily extended to the taping of deliberations. She asserts that learning about how individuals on the jury reacted to the evidence detracts from the collective nature of the verdict, drawing attention away from the jury verdict as a group judgment.[74] Furthermore, jurors may make comments that reflect badly on themselves, and divisiveness in deliberation may undermine the legitimacy of the jury verdict.[75]

These effects remain speculative, as there are no systematic studies yet that have looked at how posttrial comments or taped jury deliberations influence perceptions of the institution. Should the potentially negative effects of the exposure of what once was a secretive process be taken into account as researchers consider embarking upon and conducting studies that include the recording of jury deliberations? More generally, do researchers have any moral responsibility for how research affects the functioning and credibility of the system that they study?

Ethical issues in jury research constitute new terrain. This chapter has raised more questions than it has answered. Jury researchers have devoted only modest attention to these questions to date, and they have engaged in few attempts to assess how incursions into the jury room, whether by the media or by researchers, affect the ability of the jury to achieve its multiple institutional purposes. As we consider the ethical dimensions of jury research, our discussions are sure to make us more sensitive to the many ethical issues that arise as research on this fascinating social and political institution is planned, carried out, and reported.

NOTES

An early version of this chapter was presented at the Jury Ethics Conference, John Jay College of Criminal Justice, New York: September 13, 2003. I appreciate the insightful comments about ethical issues in jury research made by the conference organizers John Kleinig and James Levine and the conference attendees. I also wish to thank William Bowers, Paula Hannaford-Agor, and Tom Munsterman for their comments on the original paper.

1. Arizona Chief Justice Stanley Feldman, interview by Ed Bradley, *CBS Reports: Enter the Jury Room*, April 1997.

2. The American Sociological Association's Code of Ethics, approved by ASA membership in 1997, available online at http://www.asanet.org/members/ecoderev.html; Ethical Principles of Psychologists and Code of Conduct 2002, available on the American Psychological Association's Web site: http://www.apa.org/ethics.

3. ASA Ethical Standards, Section 1. From http://www.asanet.org/members/ecostand.html#9.

4. ASA Ethical Standards, Section 9 (Conflicts of Interest), Section 11 (Confidentiality).

5. APA Ethics Code 2002, available from the APA Web site. Section 8.02 Informed Consent to Research reads as follows:

> (a) When obtaining informed consent . . . psychologists inform participants about (1) the purpose of the research, expected duration, and procedures; (2) their right to decline to participate and to withdraw from the research once participation has begun; (3) the foreseeable consequences of declining or withdrawing; (4) reasonably foreseeable factors that may be expected to influence their willingness to participate such as potential risks, discomfort, or adverse effects; (5) any prospective research benefits; (6) limits of confidentiality; (7) incentives for participation; and (8) whom to contact for questions about the research and research participants' rights. They provide opportunity for the prospective participants to ask questions and receive answers. . . . (b) Psychologists conducting intervention research involving the use of experimental treatments clarify to participants at the outset of the research (1) the experimental nature of the treatment; (2) the services that will or will not be available to the control group(s) if appropriate; (3) the means by which assignment to treatment and control groups will be made; (4) available treatment alternatives if an individual does not wish to participate in the research or wishes to withdraw once a study has begun; and (5) compensation for or monetary costs of participating including, if appropriate, whether reimbursement from the participant or a third-party payor will be sought (http://www.apa.org/ethics/code2002.html#8_02).

6. Committee on Ethical Guidelines for Forensic Psychologists, "Specialty Guidelines for Forensic Psychologists," *Law and Human Behavior* 15 (1991): 655.

7. "Specialty Guidelines," 656.

8. "Specialty Guidelines," 661.

9. U.S. Department of Justice, *Federal Policy for the Protection of Human Subjects* (Basic DHHS Policy for Protection of Human Research Subjects), 28 C.F.R. 46. A discussion of human subjects protection in research sponsored by the Department of Justice is available online at http://www.ojp.usdoj.gov/nij/humansubjects/hs_01.html.

10. Harry Kalven Jr. and Hans Zeisel, *The American Jury* (Chicago: University of Chicago Press, 1966), 5–9.

11. Valerie P. Hans and Neil Vidmar, *"The American Jury* at Twenty-five Years," *Law and Social Inquiry* 16 (1991): 323–51.

12. Valerie P. Hans and Neil Vidmar, "Jurors and Juries," in *Blackwell Companion to Law and Society,* ed. Austin Sarat (Oxford: Blackwell, 2004), 195–211.

13. This issue was discussed in some detail at a symposium, "Applications of Jury Research: A Debate on the Selection of Research Questions and Methods," organized by Steven D. Penrod for Psychology and Law International, Interdisciplinary Conference 2003, Edinburgh, Scotland, July 2003. Participants included Steven Penrod (chair), Brian Bornstein, Penny Darbyshire, Kerrie Dunn, Valerie Hans, Margaret Bull Kovera, Neil Vidmar, and Richard Wiener.

14. Nancy Marder, "Deliberations and Disclosures: A Study of Post-Verdict Interviews of Jurors," *Iowa Law Review* 82 (1997): 465–546.

15. Kate Stith-Cabranes, "Faults, Fallacies, and the Future of Our Criminal Justice System: The Criminal Jury in Our Time," *Virginia Journal of Social Policy and Law* 3 (1995): 133.

16. Marder, "Deliberations and Disclosures"; Nancy J. King, "Ethics for the Ex-Juror: Guiding Jurors after the Trial," in this volume, 219–36.

17. Stith-Cabranes, "Faults, Fallacies, and the Future of Our Criminal Justice System," 135, 136.

18. Abraham S. Goldstein, "Jury Secrecy and the Media: The Problem of Postverdict Interviews," *University of Illinois Law Review* (1993): 295.

19. Andrew Ross Sorkin and Jonathan D. Glater, "Fresh from Deliberations, Jurors Recall Pivotal Moments Leading up to Tyco Mistrial," *New York Times,* April 5, 2004, A21.

20. Andrew Ross Sorkin, "Jury Is in Turmoil over Tyco Case," *New York Times,* March 26, 2004, C1–C2. One note read in part, "The atmosphere in the jury room has turned poisonous" and another observed that "There is reason to believe that one or more Jurors do not have an open mind as to the possibility of the defendants' innocence" (p. C1).

21. Adam Liptak and Andrew Ross Sorkin, "Emergence of Juror Leaves Tyco Judge in Legal Quandary," *New York Times,* March 28, 2004, A1, A20.

22. Liptak and Sorkin, "Emergence of Juror Leaves Tyco Judge in Legal Quandary," A20.

23. Sorkin and Glater, "Fresh from Deliberations," A21.

24. Andrew Ross Sorkin, "No O.K. Sign and No Guilty Vote by Juror No. 4," *New York Times,* April 7, 2004, A1, C2. The Sorkin and Glater article in the *New York Times,* "Fresh from Deliberations," A21, named all of the jurors. Pete McEntegart,

"One Angry Man," *Time*, April 12, 2004, 47–48. Interview with Ruth Jordan (Juror No. 4), *60 Minutes II*, CBSNews.com, April 7, 2004. The full transcript of this interview is available on the CBSNews.com Web site at http://www.cbsnews .com/stories/2004/04107/6011/main610667.shtml.

25. Charles C. Brotherton, "Cameras in the Jury Room: The Arizona Experience" (Applied Project done in conjunction with master's degree work, Walter Cronkite School of Journalism and Mass Communication, Arizona State University, Tempe, Arizona, 2003).

26. The courts have similarly justified their willingness to permit such intrusions on educational grounds. See Justice Feldman's comments on why the Arizona Supreme Court allowed media access to jury deliberations, quoted in Brotherton, "Cameras in the Jury Room."

27. Shari Seidman Diamond, Neil Vidmar, Mary Rose, Leslie Ellis, and B. Murphy, "Juror Discussions during Civil Trials: A Study of Arizona's Rule 39(f) Innovation," *Arizona Law Review* 45 (2003): 1–81.

28. See, for example, Daniel W. Shuman and Stuart A. Greenberg, "The Expert Witness, the Adversary System, and the Voice of Reason: Reconciling Impartiality and Advocacy," *Professional Psychology: Research and Practice* 34 (2003): 219–24.

29. See Valerie P. Hans, Paula L. Hannaford-Agor, Nicole L. Mott, and G. Thomas Munsterman, "The Hung Jury: *The American Jury's* Insights and Contemporary Understanding," *Criminal Law Bulletin* 39 (2003): 33. Paula L. Hannaford-Agor, Valerie P. Hans, Nicole L. Mott, and G. Thomas Munsterman, "Are Hung Juries a Problem?" (Final Report, National Center for State Courts, to National Institute of Justice, September 30, 2002). The entire report is available online at the NCSC Web site at http://www.ncsconline.org/WC/Publications/ Res_Juries_HungJuriesPub.pdf.

30. Shari Seidman Diamond and Neil Vidmar, "Jury Room Ruminations on Forbidden Topics," *Virginia Law Review* 87 (2001): 1857.

31. The same problem might arise with clinical psychologists debriefing jurors who have served in notorious cases (see Timothy R. Murphy, Genevra Kay Loveland, and G. Thomas Munsterman, *A Manual for Managing Notorious Cases* [Williamsburg, VA: National Center for State Courts, 1992]); or with a judge who conducts a private posttrial discussion with jurors. In his book, *A Trial by Jury* (New York: Vintage, 2001), D. Graham Burnett reports on one extremely problematic juror. The question for people in all of these roles is: What, if anything, is your ethical duty when you learn about juror misconduct? The judge's duty is the clearest. The responsibility of the others seems more ambiguous.

32. Jury Ethics Conference, John Jay College of Criminal Justice, New York, NY, September 13, 2003.

33. The advisory board included: Judge Jacqueline Conner, Superior Court of California, County of Los Angeles; Judge Joseph Heilman, Superior Court of Arizona, Maricopa County; Professor Nancy King, Vanderbilt University School of Law; Judge Katherine Streeter Lewis, Pennsylvania Court of Common Pleas, Philadelphia; Professor Robert MacCoun, University of California-Berkeley; and Judge Edward Stern, New Jersey Superior Court, Appellate Division.

34. This turns out not to be completely true; many juries that hung on one or more charges convicted on others. Hans, Hannaford-Agor, Mott, and Munsterman, "The Hung Jury," 43.

35. Jeffrey Rosen, "One Angry Woman," *New Yorker*, February 24 and March 3, 1997, 55; California District Attorneys Association, *Non-Unanimous Jury Verdicts: A Necessary Criminal Justice Reform* (May 1995).

36. Paula L. Hannaford-Agor and Valerie P. Hans, "Nullification at Work? A Glimpse from the National Center for State Courts Study of Hung Juries," *Chicago-Kent Law Review* 78 (2003): 1249 (footnotes omitted).

37. 28 C.F.R. Sec. 22.

38. Memorandum from Paula L. Hannaford to Members of the Institutional Review Board, National Center for State Courts, December 14, 1999, RE: The Protection of Human Subjects in Research Concerning the Incidence and Causes of Hung Juries in Criminal Felony Cases; see also Minutes of January 10, 2000, Meeting, Institutional Review Board, National Center for State Courts. Hannaford's legal expertise and interest in ethical questions proved to be an invaluable resource as we attempted to develop alternatives that were responsive to the twin concerns of participants' and defendants' rights.

39. Most federally funded research databases are made public to allow other researchers to conduct further analyses. The hung jury database is now publicly available at Interuniversity Consortium for Political and Social Research (ICPSR), but no case identifying information is included.

40. Hannaford, Memorandum to IRB, 7–11.

41. *Tarasoff v. Regents of the University of California*, 108 Cal. Rptr. 878 (Ct. App. 1973); reversed and remanded, 13 Cal. 3d 177 (1974); modified, 17 Cal. 3d 425 (1976).

42. William J. Bowers, Benjamin Fleury-Steiner, Valerie P. Hans, and Michael E. Antonio, "Too Young to be Executed: An Empirical Examination of Community Conscience and the Juvenile Death Penalty From the Perspective of Capital Jurors," *Boston University Law Review* 84 (2004): 609.

43. William J. Bowers, e-mail correspondence with author, September 16, 2003, and April 22, 2004.

44. Hans and Vidmar, *"The American Jury* at Twenty-five Years," 325; Jay Katz, ed., *Experimentation with Human Beings* (New York: Russell Sage Foundation, 1972), 67–109; Valerie P. Hans and Neil Vidmar, interview with Hans Zeisel, February 5, 1991, cited in Hans and Vidmar, *"The American Jury* at Twenty-five Years," 323, 325.

45. Hans and Vidmar, *"The American Jury* at Twenty-five Years," 325.

46. Hans and Vidmar, *"The American Jury* at Twenty-five Years," 326; see also Kalven and Zeisel, *The American Jury*, xv.

47. See Stith-Cabranes, "Faults, Fallacies, and the Future of Our Criminal Justice System"; Goldstein, "Jury Secrecy and the Media."

48. *Frontline*, "Inside the Jury Room" (PBS television broadcast, 1986).

49. John Manzo, "The Social Organization of Talk and Experience in Jury Deliberations" (PhD diss., University of Wisconsin-Madison, 1993). See also John Manzo, "'You Wouldn't Take a Seven-Year-Old and Ask Him All These Questions': Jurors' Use of Practical Reasoning in Supporting Their Arguments," *Law and Social Inquiry* 19 (1994): 601–26; John Manzo, "Jurors' Narratives of Personal Experience in Deliberation Talk," *Text* 13 (1993): 267–90; Douglas W. Maynard and John Manzo, "On the Sociology of Justice: Theoretical Notes from an Actual Jury Deliberation," *Sociological Theory* 11 (1993): 171–93.

50. Brotherton, "Cameras in the Jury Room," 30.

51. Brotherton, "Cameras in the Jury Room," 29.

52. Brotherton, "Cameras in the Jury Room," 29.

53. ABC News, *State v.*, television series, June–July 2002.

54. Brotherton, "Cameras in the Jury Room," 63–64.

55. Supreme Court of Arizona Administrative Order 98-10 (February 5, 1998).

56. Barbara A. Babcock, "Preserving the Jury's Privacy," *New York Times*, July 24, 2002, A19. See also Editorial, "The 13th Juror," *New York Times*, November 27, 2002. But see Bruce Fein, "Thwarting a Useful Jury Experiment," *Washington Times*, February 18, 2003 [online].

57. King identifies important functions of the jury, including the following: "(1) it protects litigants from abuse of judicial power; (2) it brings community-based sense to fact-finding and the application of law to facts; (3) it helps to promote acceptance of case outcomes and the legitimacy of the justice process; and (4) it increases lay participation in our democracy and provides a firsthand civic education to jurors." Nancy J. King, "Ethics for the Ex-Juror: Guiding Former Jurors after the Trial," in this volume, 219.

58. Diamond and Vidmar, "Jury Room Ruminations on Forbidden Topics," 1857, 1922; Diamond, Vidmar, Rose, Ellis, and Murphy, "Juror Discussions during Civil Trials."

59. Brotherton, "Cameras in the Jury Room," 40.

60. Brotherton, "Cameras in the Jury Room."

61. Brotherton, "Cameras in the Jury Room,"40–42.

62. Editorial, "To Peer Inside the Jury Room," *San Francisco Chronicle*, December 12, 2002. Available online on SFGate at http://www.sfgate.com/cgi-bin/article.cgi?f=/chronicle/archive/2002/12/12/ED190741.DTL

63. Brotherton, "Cameras in the Jury Room," 42.

64. Arizona Chief Justice Stanley Feldman, interview by Ed Bradley, *CBS Reports: Enter the Jury Room*, April 1997.

65. Analyzing the potential consequences of posttrial disclosures of jury deliberations, Marder outlines several potentially negative effects. Her reasoning applies equally well to the videotaping of jury deliberations. See Marder, "Deliberations and Disclosures," 500–504.

66. Marder, "Deliberations and Disclosures," 503.

67. Valerie P. Hans, "Inside the Black Box: Comment on Diamond and Vidmar," *Virginia Law Review* 87 (2001): 1917, 1925.

68. Let's not forget the possibility that the cameras may affect judges, too, arguably by becoming more careful and attentive to the rights of various parties; see Brotherton, "Cameras in the Jury Room," 42. There is a lively literature discussing both positive and negative effects of cameras in the courtroom. See Jeffrey S. Johnson, "The Entertainment Value of a Trial: How Media Access to the Courtroom Is Changing the American Judicial Process," *Villanova Sports and Entertainment Law Forum* 10 (2003): 131–52; Joshua Sarner, "Justice, Take Two: The Continuing Debate over Cameras in the Courtroom," *Seton Hall Constitutional Law Journal* 10 (2000): 1053–83.

69. Diamond and Vidmar, "Jury Room Ruminations on Forbidden Topics," 1870 n. 49.

70. Dennis P. Stolle, Dennis J. Devine, and Amy H. Joliet, "Watching Mock

Jurors Deliberate: The Impact of Observation on Deliberations," poster presented at the Psychology and Law International: Interdisciplinary Conference, Edinburgh, Scotland, July 11, 2003.

71. Stolle, Devine, and Joliet, "Watching Mock Jurors Deliberate, 4–5.
72. Stolle, Devine, and Joliet, "Watching Mock Jurors Deliberate," 5.
73. Stolle, Devine, and Joliet, "Watching Mock Jurors Deliberate," 9.
74. Marder, "Deliberations and Disclosures," 470.
75. Marder, "Deliberations and Disclosures," 473.

What Price Knowledge? A Response to Professor Hans's Inquiry into the Ethics of Invading the Sanctity of the Jury Room

Maureen O'Connor

> Conscience and morality, Milgram teaches us, do not run in smooth, logical grooves but recede and advance according to the expectations and possibilities embedded in situations both more public and politicized than hypothetical moral dilemmas.[1]

The American Psychological Association recently launched a major initiative to promote the science of psychology, PSY21.[2] One of the three main themes for the initiative is the "responsible conduct of research." A worthy objective! In her article, "Jury Research Ethics and the Integrity of Jury Deliberations," Valerie P. Hans asks significant and difficult questions about the responsible conduct of research on/about/for/with the jury.[3] As one of the researchers who has spent as much if not more time with jurors and juries than other psychologists (all well represented in this volume), Hans has an excellent vantage point from which to raise her well-articulated questions. Her use of two actual studies to illustrate the array of ethical issues that might arise grounds the discussion in a "more public and politicized" context of real-world research and challenges social scientists with an interest in the jury to reflect, perhaps for the first time, on the ethical implications of their own efforts toward really understanding the jury.

Why is it so important to peer into that jury room? As an experienced criminal defense attorney said to me, there may be a reason we do not want to know how sausage is made, how bills are passed, or how juries reach their verdicts! Yet, we *do* want to know. Of course, perhaps preaching to the converted here, it is simply fascinating from a psychological perspective to imagine the dynamic that is occurring in such a vital, constitutionally compelled, yet commonplace activity—everyone who knows anything or cares at all about a particular case is on the <u>outside</u> waiting for a relatively random group of citizens on the <u>inside</u> to decide the fate of someone or some entity.

The original jury researchers may have been more interested in small group decision making and found the jury to be an intriguing example from which to test psychological theories. In most ways, though, such research could have comfortably remained in the laboratory and have relied on mock jurors and juries to explore the questions of interest.

Since Harry Kalven Jr. and Hans Zeisel's seminal work in the American jury project,[4] however, interest in the jury qua jury has been the focus of research by many scholars such as those represented in this volume. The explicit goal of that work has been to understand and improve the conduct and decision making of *real* juries. To attain that goal, it has become increasingly important to focus on and get as close as possible to real juries. Larry B. Heuer and Steven D. Penrod's seminal field experiment, in which judges agreed to assign cases randomly to varying jury conditions, is the prime early example of this effort.[5] But, with the exception of a number of recent studies discussed in this volume, gaining access to real juries has proven to be a difficult challenge.

Nevertheless, the drive toward external validity has potency despite fairly clear findings that mock jurors and real jurors do not actually differ much on responses of consequence.[6] Despite those findings, judges (and lawyers) resist the notion that any jury we might assemble in our laboratories acts, thinks, or decides like juries in real courtrooms. This point was made crystal clear to me when, as a graduate student, I was in a federal district courtroom in Arizona in one of the country's first *Daubert* hearings. Conference participant Steven Penrod was sitting in his office in Nebraska testifying via speakerphone about how his expertise on eyewitnesses would be beneficial to the jury in the case. After listening for a short while, the rather acerbic and blunt district court judge asked Penrod whether most of his research was done with real or mock jurors, and upon hearing the response ("mock jurors") essentially dismissed the testimony because the *real* jurors *in his courtroom* had no trouble recognizing the difficulties faced by eyewitnesses to crime. Faced with this rather characteristic response, social scientists have worked diligently on the external validity problem—if we could just get closer and closer to the real jury, we could say more about juries and ultimately, justice, and perhaps judges (and lawyers) would listen to us![7]

Beyond the question of why we would want to peek into the jury room, though, is the more challenging question—Do we have the right to do so? The questions raised by Hans, who concedes that she raises more questions than she answers, revolve around this issue.

Hans correctly observes that as other political institutions have moved toward "greater accountability and public scrutiny," the jury and its deliberations have remained cloaked in secrecy. And, that secrecy has long-standing potency. Described in a recent report from England as the "cornerstone of the legal system . . . seen as key to public confidence in the criminal justice system, . . . to frankness in the jury room and to the adequate protection of jurors,"[8] that secrecy has been closely guarded constitutionally as well.[9] U.S. courts refer to it as "a 'core principle' in the American system of justice."[10]

Yet, as Hans also observes, this cloak is becoming a bit threadbare in spots. She notes the media circus surrounding many cases. It is not uncommon to turn on the television to find a juror in one or another high-profile case talking about the jury and its deliberations. She also discusses the reality-type shows that have recorded and played actual jury trials and deliberations in prime time. She mentions the regular posttrial interviewing of jurors, especially in death-penalty cases, and the recent Arizona study that involved explicit taping of jury discussions and deliberations.[11]

There is, however, another relevant and seemingly growing incursion into the sanctity of the jury room that Hans alludes to but does not mention explicitly in discussing the Tyco case. It is different in kind from the examples just discussed—judicial examination of juror (mis)conduct inside the deliberation room.[12] And, because it may provide an important backdrop against which to consider Hans's ethical queries about research-based intrusions, it is worth a brief sidebar. Under Federal Rule of Criminal Procedure 23(b), the trial judge has some discretion to allow a criminal trial to proceed with fewer than the original twelve jurors in cases in which there is "good cause" to dismiss one of the jurors even after deliberations have begun. So, for example, if a juror has a heart attack during the second day of deliberations, the parties may themselves stipulate to proceed without that juror, or the judge may, in her discretion, elect to continue the deliberations with the remaining eleven jurors. In the present context this becomes relevant when the "good cause" is not as readily apparent as an illness or incapacitation of some kind, but derives instead from "misconduct" of a juror during the deliberations. In such circumstances, an inquiry into the content of the deliberations becomes essential at least to the extent that the judge must determine whether the recalcitrant juror is actually misbehaving (e.g., refusing to deliberate, relying on racial prejudice, explicitly nullifying) or has, instead, come to a different conclusion or understanding of the law and facts from that of his or her fellow jurors.[13] This is not a clear-cut determination.

What this raises, then, is official recognition by the legal system that the sanctity of the jury room is not absolute. Although Rule 23(b) does not give judges unfettered discretion to probe into jury deliberations, some inquiry into the deliberative process of the jury is appropriate under certain circumstances, especially where the legitimacy of the constitutional right to a fair and impartial jury could be compromised.

Given this inroad, then, it could be argued (though Hans stops short of making this argument) that gaining an empirically grounded perspective on the functioning of real juries is a worthy objective—sufficient to justify carefully crafted intrusions into the sanctity of the jury. It could even rise to the level of being constitutionally compelled *if*, as has happened for example in the area of misunderstanding jury instructions, the insights gained by our penetration preserve and protect the constitutional right to a fair and impartial jury. One of the unspoken concessions made by the courts in these juror misconduct cases is that, on occasions when jurors do not appear to be acting properly (e.g., by deliberating in good faith) it is incumbent on judges to ferret out these transgressions. This concession is or should be music to the scholar's ears as the work done by those social science and legal scholars participating in the symposium giving rise to this volume (among others) is aimed at precisely that target—unpacking and examining the behavioral assumptions made by the law, by judges, and by lawyers with respect to juries and jury behavior about their capabilities, the power of nullification, the pragmatics of jury service, their duties, the deliberation process, posttrial conduct, and the like.

For the sake of argument, then, let us assume that researchers have both an interest in and the legal right to peek into the jury room just as presiding judges do. That still does not answer another essential question raised by Hans's commentary—"[i]s [peeking into that room] . . . an ethical problem?"

Can this question be answered by resorting to codified ethics? Hans begins her chapter by reminding us (much as the APA is doing in its PSY21 campaign) that researchers as well as practitioners are governed by ethical codes. The American Psychology-Law Society's Specialty Guidelines are directed explicitly at work involving the judicial system.[14] Hans astutely recognizes that there are "more particular ethical issues that arise" for those who study the jury. She explicitly mentions two such issues. The first is a specific concern dealing with trial consultants who work with mock jurors or jury pool members and who, because of the adversarial nature of the work, fail to inform their participants about the partisan nature of the funding source for their work. Traditional protections for human subjects normally require such disclosure whereas the opposite is true for trial consultants. Of course, trial consultants are not required to submit their work to any institutional review board. In fact, under the Professional Code of Conduct of the American Society of Trial Consultants (ASTC), a trial consultant owes a duty to the client (i.e., the attorney or party who is paying for the consultant's work) *not* to disclose the identity of the client unless the client chooses to be so identified.[15]

This example is not quite as simple as Hans presents it, however. Nor does it provide us with much guidance on the more general topic of jury research methods. Although the ASTC Code does delineate certain duties owed to participants in their work (including duties to inform them that participation is voluntary, to treat them with respect and consideration, and to use best efforts to protect their anonymity), these duties are, of necessity, subordinate to the interest of the client in the particular lawsuit. By using this example, Hans perhaps unwittingly raises a question of jury research ethics that goes well beyond invading the jury deliberation room. Those experts conducting the most research with potential jurors and actual jurors (during jury selection, during trial, and in posttrial survey work) are not, generally, doing so as researchers. Though governed by their own discipline's code of conduct as well as the ASTC Code, they are not focused in the main on preserving the sanctity of the jury room or on the larger research enterprise. Although a more thorough discussion of ethical issues potentially raised by trial consulting is beyond the purview of this response,[16] suffice it to say that any thorough examination of encroachment into the sanctity of the jury should include a more thorough examination of the work being done by trial consultants. In any event, the ethical norms applicable to those who are part of the adversarial process are inapposite to the domain of scientific research.

Hans also raises ethical issues derived from the jury's distinctive nature as a political institution. Hans mentions in particular the issues of accountability and privacy as political variables that are not necessarily compatible values. But this tends to ignore one of the most challenging features of research on the jury as political institution—it is just that, an institution or collective, rather than an individual. It comes together for one purpose, it will disband after that purpose is finished, and it has meaning only in its group form.

To that extent, in both the specific and general, I believe Hans overestimates the extent to which existing professional ethical standards address the questions she is raising. The protection of human subjects literature focuses on the protection of individual research participants, not a group or institution. What is informed consent in this context? Jurors are told that no one will look over their shoulder, that deliberations are sacrosanct. When researchers want to do exactly that and look over their shoulder it is to look over their collective shoulders. Can the individual informed consent documents required in this context, signed by jurors, lawyers, and litigants, adequately anticipate how the collective might be affected by external scrutiny? Is it possible to be honest about what might happen with such scrutiny and in raising those contingencies not forever alter the dynamic of the group? Like Hans, I am not sure of the answers here, but I believe that our typical informed consent procedures are inadequate to this task.[17]

Assuming we have concluded that we have both an interest in and the right to penetrate the sanctity of the jury, we must then ask the final question: What is the consequence of doing so—first, on the jury itself, and second, on the rights of the defendant and the legal process itself? As for the first, do we alter the jury's meaning and effect merely by scrutinizing it, an inevitable

Hawthorne effect in a context in which people's rights and lives may be at stake? Or, contrariwise, do jurors take probing of outsiders for granted in the same way they ignore flies buzzing round the jury room? When we pick the jury apart in piecemeal fashion, do we undermine its totality?[18] As good empiricists, it bears mentioning that, to a large extent, many of the questions raised by Hans and in this response (including these latter ones) are empirical ones. Should we be required to have a research foundation about the effects of these techniques on juries and the jury process before we are allowed to make claims about them? Do we know enough from research on the shelf about group dynamics to be able to make empirically grounded predictions on these matters? If not, then it is incumbent upon jury researchers to include these methodological and ethical issues in their research programs. Developing a research agenda on the import of jury research is essential to grounding the ethics of such research in reality.

Hans asks whether she and her "hung jury" team got the balance right in privileging the individual rights of the study participants over the rights of a potentially unjustly convicted (or acquitted) defendant. As a civil libertarian and social scientist, I am not sure I can answer that question definitively.[19] I do, however, believe that, to a certain extent, Hans has overstated the prevalence or likelihood of the problem here. The courts are fiercely protective of a jury verdict once rendered. As any practicing attorney will attest, it is exceedingly difficult to impeach such a verdict. Though permitted under rules governing criminal law and procedure, posttrial or postconviction challenges to verdicts are few and far between. We should be at least as concerned about the ethics and standards of practice of others in the system as the jurors. I wish we had a system closer to that envisioned by Hans, in which lawyers would be so vigilant as to file requests to obtain research data that might benefit their clients. The reality is that, except in capital cases, few would do so.

Nevertheless, in theory at least, and perhaps increasingly in practice as discussed above, the presence of juror misconduct within the jury room is one of the grounds upon which a verdict can be set aside.[20] Hans correctly identifies this contingency—researchers should be concerned with the implications of uncovering misconduct in the course of their investigation. Yet she may paint the problem with too broad a brush. Issues and appropriate responses may vary significantly depending on the type of information uncovered. I am not convinced, for example, that evidence of nullification by a jury or juror (where one juror, perhaps, simply refused to deliberate) in a case in which the jury actually rendered an acquittal would be grounds for postverdict relief. Nullification seems to fall into the category of conduct which is within the jury's purview—although they do not have the right to do so, they certainly have the power. And, once a verdict is rendered, judges are reluctant to impeach it particularly if there are no obvious external influences (e.g., a juror went to the crime scene and, having seen it, decided not to deliberate; a juror was bribed; a juror slept during deliberations). Researchers could perhaps lessen the chance for problems here, even where deliberations are videotaped, by blind monitoring of the filming by an unaffiliated camera operator, and, thus, by not observing or inquiring into the deliberations prior to verdict.

Assuming the researchers did uncover something that might be grounds for juror misconduct and a reopening of the case, another approach would be to take affirmative steps to alert the juror to the problem as you see it and urge the juror to come forward with the information. This is analogous to attorneys' obligation to warn their clients not to commit perjury on the stand; the potential problem is identified by the professional, but the duty is on the person with direct knowledge to come forward. Here, the creative use of a multidisciplinary advisory board, as Hans described in her two examples, could be of enormous value to the researchers (and is analogous to the medical researchers' approach). The researcher could inform the juror that, as a researcher, she is not obligated to report this potential misconduct but would strongly suggest that the juror consult with an attorney or the judge about it. Of course, none of these Band-Aid approaches can provide the definitive answer.

Toward the end of her chapter, Hans eloquently phrases the key underlying question driving her inquiry, "[d]o researchers have any moral responsibility for how research affects the functioning and credibility of the system that they study?" The answer here is most certainly "yes"; the challenge, as I hope is clear from some of the issues raised by Hans and in this response, is to strike the proper balance between knowledge generation and fairness to all parties. If researchers writ large were as thoughtful and articulate about these matters as Hans and the other scholars represented in this volume, we could all rest assured that both values could and would be pursued with integrity and vigor.

We conclude by returning to psychologist Stanley Milgram, who was quoted at the outset of this essay. Milgram is most widely known for his book *Obedience to Authority*, which describes his experiments in which participants were induced through deception to administer what were thought to be electrical shocks to people who failed to perform certain tasks correctly.[21] As part of an elaborate research design intended to ascertain how far people would go in following orders from someone in a position of authority, the latter individuals were actually Milgram's confederates who feigned pain when in point of fact they were not being shocked at all. These shock studies may well have harmed participants (and they would certainly not receive IRB approval today!). But that research produced critically important findings about people's morality that are still relevant. It is inevitably a question of whether the ends justify the means. Does producing enlightenment about jury behavior and perhaps better process justify putting justice at risk? The conversation begun in this volume must surely continue.

NOTES

1. E. Cave and S. Holm, "Milgram and Tuskegee Paradigm Research Projects in Bioethics," *Health Care Analysis* 11 (2003): 27, citing A. J. Damico, "The Sociology of Justice: Kohlberg and Milgram," *Political Theory* 10, no. 3 (1982): 427.

2. L. Winerman, "APA Launches Campaign to Support Psychological Science," *APA Monitor Online* 35 (2004), available at http://www.apa.org/monitor/dec04/campaign.html.

3. Valerie P. Hans, "Jury Research Ethics and the Integrity of Jury Deliberations," in this volume, 247–64.

4. Harry Kalven Jr. and Hans Zeisel, *The American Jury* (Boston: Little, Brown, and Co., 1966).

5. See Larry B. Heuer and Steven D. Penrod, "Juror Note Taking and Question Asking during Trials: A National Field Experiment," *Law and Human Behavior* 18 (1994): 121–50; Larry B. Heuer and Steven D. Penrod. "Increasing Juror Participation in Trials through Note Taking and Question Asking," *Judicature* 79 (1996): 256–62.

6. See Kerri F. Dunn, "Assessing the External Validity of Jury Simulation Research: A Meta-Analysis," *Dissertation Abstracts International* 63 (2003): 6141; see also Brian H. Bornstein, "The Ecological Validity of Jury Simulations: Is the Jury Still Out?" *Law and Human Behavior* 23 (1999): 75–91.

7. Donald N. Bersoff, "Psychologists and the Judicial System," *Law and Human Behavior* 10 (1986): 151–65; Donald N. Bersoff, "Social Science Data and the Supreme Court: Lockhart as a Case in Point," *American Psychologist* 42 (1987): 52–58.

8. Department for Constitutional Affairs, *Jury Research and Impropriety: A Consultation Paper to Assess Options for Allowing Research into Jury Deliberations and to Consider Investigations into Alleged Juror Impropriety* (London, UK: Department for Constitutional Affairs, 2005), 4, available at http://www.dca.gov.uk/consult/juryresearch/juryresearch_cp0405.htm.

9. See, e.g., *Garcia v. People*, 997 P. 2d 1, 7 (Colo. 2000); *United States v. Thomas*, 116 F. 3d 606 (2d Cir. 1997).

10. *People v. Kriho*, 996 P. 2d 158, 167 (Colo. 1999); *United States v. Antar*, 38 F. 3d 1348, 1367 (3d Cir. 1994) (Rosenn, J., *concurring*) ("We must bear in mind that the confidentiality of the thought processes of jurors, their privileged exchange of views, and the freedom to be candid in their deliberations are the soul of the jury system."); for a more general discussion of the issue, see Note, "Public Disclosures of Jury Deliberations," *Harvard Law Review* 96 (1983): 886.

11. Shari S. Diamond, Neil Vidmar, Mary Rose, Leslie Ellis, and Beth Murphy, "Juror Discussions during Civil Trials: A Study of Arizona's Rule 39(f) Innovation," *Arizona Law Review* 45 (2003): 1–81.

12. Désirée Cassar, "To Dismiss or Not to Dismiss: Legal Issues and Psychological Factors Associated with Juror Misconduct and Dismissal," unpublished manuscript (available from the author) (2001).

13. See, e.g., *United States v. Thomas*, 116 F. 3d 606 (2d Cir. 1997); *People v. Metters*, Not Reported in Cal.Rptr.2d, 2002 WL 31106404, Cal.App. 1 Dist. (2002); *People v. Molina*, 82 Cal.App. 4th 1329 (2000). The *Thomas* court stated the issue quite clearly:

> Once a jury retires to the deliberation room, the presiding judge's duty to dismiss jurors for misconduct comes into conflict with a duty that is equally,

if not more, important—safeguarding the secrecy of jury deliberations. This conflict is especially pronounced here, where the alleged misbehavior is a purposeful disregard of the law, a particularly difficult allegation to prove and one for which an effort to act in good faith may easily be mistaken. (618)

14. Committee on Ethical Guidelines for Forensic Psychologists, "Specialty Guidelines for Forensic Psychologists," *Law and Human Behavior* 15 (1991): 655.

15. American Society of Trial Consultants, The American Society of Trial Consultants Professional Code (2005), available at http://astcweb.org/content/File/AboutUs/ASTC_Code_Full.pdf.

16. See, e.g., F. Strier. "Why Trial Consultants Should Be Licensed," *Journal of Forensic Psychology Practice* 1 (2001): 67–74; but see Rachel Hartje, "A Jury of Your Peers? How Jury Consulting May Actually Help Trial Lawyers Resolve Constitutional Limitations Imposed on the Selection of Juries," *California Western Law Review* 41 (2005): 479–506.

17. Medical researchers and ethicists have long faced these complicated research questions in the conduct of clinical trials. It is now part of the standard of care in such research to have a data monitoring and evaluation team that oversees the conduct and/or termination of research where literally people's lives can be at risk balanced against knowledge generation about a particular treatment. Barbara Stanley, personal communication, June 20, 2005; see also David L. DeMets, "Clinical Trials in the New Millennium," *Statistics in Medicine* 21 (2002): 2779–87. Franklin G. Miller and Henry J. Silverman, "The Ethical Relevance of the Standard of Care in the Design of Clinical Trials," *American Journal of Respiratory and Critical Care Medicine* 169 (2004): 562–64.

18. Nancy J. King's chapter, "Ethics for the Ex-Juror: Guiding Former Jurors after the Trial," in this volume, 219–36, confronts this issue as well.

19. In an analogous context, however, the rights of the individual defendant have been found to trump other considerations. Where laws or privileges might prevent a defendant from putting on a defense, for example, the right to put on that defense trumps other concerns; see, e.g., *Rock v. Arkansas*, 483 U.S. 44 (1987) (law prohibiting admissibility of hypnotically refreshed testimony must give way to defendant's right to put on a defense); see also *Washington v. Texas*, 388 U.S. 14 (1967).

20. See, e.g., Gary Muldoon and Hon. Sandra J. Feuerstein, *Handling a Criminal Case in New York* (St. Paul, MN: West, 2003), §§9:38–10:46.

21. Stanley Milgram, *Obedience to Authority: An Experimental View* (New York: Harper and Row, 1975).

Index

discretion, 64; and jury instruction problems, 94, 100–101; vs. local knowledge requirements of juries, 2; as political demand, 16n26; vs. politics of deliberation, 191; in selection process, 28, 30, 40, 43–44; and trial consultants, 47; and venue issues, 14n5–6

false consensus effect, 124

favors from litigants, ethics of accepting, 229, 231

The Federalist Papers (Madison), 55

Federal Judicial Center (FJC), 96–97

federal vs. state court systems, 2, 11, 50n22. *See also* Supreme Court, U.S.; *individual cases*

Feinberg, Joel, 76

Feldman, Stanley, 255, 257

felony convictions and jury eligibility, 16n19

FIJA (Fully Informed Jury Association), 87–88, 195

Finkel, Norman J., 55, 63–64, 83

Finkelman, Paul, 72

Finnis, John, 73

FJC (Federal Judicial Center), 96–97

Fletcher, George P., 66, 154

following the law issue, 38, 49n15, 54, 142, 148

former jurors, ethical conduct of, 219–31, 232n8, 233n42, 234–35n18, 237–43

Frank, Jerome, 14n8, 216

Franken, William, 75

freedom of expression: and judicial nullification, 142; and lack of restrictions on former jurors, 219, 220, 230; and leafleting near courthouses, 152–53, 195; and media interaction with former jurors, 225–26

freedom of religion, 72–73

Freedom's Law: The Moral Reading of the American Constitution (Dworkin), 69

FTA (failure to appear) rates, 32n8

Fuhrman, Mark, 215

Fully Informed Jury Association (FIJA), 87–88, 195

Furman v. Georgia, 61

Gates, Henry Louis, Jr., 88

Gathers, South Carolina v., 61

Gaudin, United States v., 154

gender issues, 15n17, 184, 193

Georgia courts, 144, 162n54

Gertner, Nancy S., 156

gifts from litigants, ethics of accepting, 229, 231

Goldstein, Abraham, 227

Goodman, Andrew, 214

Grant, Paul, 135–36, 161

Gregg v. Georgia, 61

guilty vs. innocent verdicts: and erroneous convictions, 87; and jury nullification powers, 121–22, 125

Hamilton, Andrew, 7

Hannaford-Agor, Paula, 35, 37, 253

Hans, Valerie, 169n118

hard cases, moral vs. legal analysis in, 53, 56, 66–69, 70–71, 84

hardship excuse, 38, 44, 49n11

hard vs. soft nullifications, 174, 176

Hardwick, Bowers v., 67, 68, 86

Hardwick v. Georgia, 67–68

Harlan, Justice, 86–87

Harris v. State (Georgia), 162n54

Hastie, Reid, 189–90

Herzberg, Stephen J., 127, 255

Heuer, Larry B., 266

Hill, Delmas C., 254

Holden v. State (Indiana), 144, 163n61

holdout jurors, 34n36, 182–86, 194, 196–97, 198, 210–12

Holmes, Oliver Wendell, 53, 55, 56, 64, 66–67, 98

honesty: and dismissal of jurors with nullification knowledge, 146–47; need for judicial honesty on nullification, 156, 175, 178–79; and recording of deliberations, 257; in selection process, 27, 29–30, 40–43; and ulterior motives of jurors, 37–39

Hood Communications, Inc., Morrow v., 142–43

Horning v. District of Columbia, 97–98, 160n33

Horowitz, Irwin, 121, 125, 168n104

hung juries: compromise verdicts as alternative to, 189; and dissenting

About the Contributors

Jeffrey Abramson is the Louis Stulberg Distinguished Professor of Law and Politics at Brandeis University. He received his PhD in political science and JD from Harvard University. He teaches political theory and law, including courses on civil liberties, constitutional law, and the history of political thought. His best-known book, *We, the Jury: The Jury System and the Ideal of Democracy*, first published in 1994, was reissued with a new introduction in 2000 by Harvard University Press. Professor Abramson served as law clerk to the late Rose Bird, Chief Justice of the California Supreme Court, and has also been an assistant district attorney and special assistant attorney general in Massachusetts.

B. Michael Dann received his undergraduate education at Indiana University and his law degrees at Harvard Law School (LLB) and University of Virginia Law School (LLM). For twenty years he was a Maricopa County (Phoenix) Arizona Superior Court judge (chief judge for five years). He chaired the Arizona Jury Trial Reform Committee and has spoken in over thirty states in support of the kinds of trial innovations adopted and used in Arizona. He received the 1997 Rehnquist Award for Judicial Excellence at the U.S. Supreme Court for his national work in jury trial reform. After retiring from the trial bench in 2000, he accepted a visiting fellowship at the National Center for State Courts, where his work focused on jury trial and judicial selection reforms and on science and law issues. In 2003, he began a fellowship at the National Institute of Justice, U.S. Department of Justice, where he conducted research on ways to improve juror comprehension of DNA trial presentations: (with Valerie P. Hans and Judith Kaye), *Testing the Effects of Selected Jury Trial Innovations on Juror Understanding of Contested mtDNA Evidence* (National Institute of Justice, 2004). He currently serves as a member of the American Jury Project of the American Bar Association which is revising ABA jury standards. His many articles on juries and jury trial innovations include "'Learning Lessons' and 'Speaking Rights': Creating Educated and Democratic Juries," *Indiana Law Journal* 68 (1993): 1229, and "Recent Evaluative Research on Jury Trial Innovations," *Court Review* 41 (2004): 12. He has also published on criminal justice, judicial selection, and judicial and lawyer performance review issues.

Shari Seidman Diamond (PhD, Northwestern University [social psychology]; JD, University of Chicago) is the Howard J. Trienens Professor of Law and Professor of Psychology at Northwestern University Law School, and a senior research fellow at the American Bar Foundation. She has conducted research and published extensively in law reviews and behavioral science journals, and has testified as an expert on juries, trademarks, and deceptive advertising. She also practiced law at Sidley and Austin (1985–1987), served as editor of the *Law and Society Review* (1989–1991), was president of the American Psychology-Law Society (1987–1988), and received the 1991 Award for Distinguished Research Contributions in Public Policy from the American Psychological Association. She has served on advisory groups for the National Center for State Courts, the Federal Judicial Center, the National Academy of Sciences, and the National Science Foundation. Her current research includes a study of actual jury deliberations in civil cases. She is a member of American Jury Project of the American Bar Association which is currently revising ABA jury standards.

Norman J. Finkel is professor of psychology at Georgetown University. He has published widely in the area of psychology and law, with a particular focus on how jurors' notions of "commonsense justice" (*Commonsense Justice: Jurors' Notions of the Law* [Harvard University Press, 1995]) and "commonsense fairness" (*Not Fair! The Typology of Commonsense Unfairness* [American Psychological Association, 2001]) may affect, nullify, or perfect black-letter law. He recently published an edited volume (with Fathali Moghaddam), *The Psychology of Rights and Duties: Empirical Contributions and Normative Commentaries* (American Psychological Association, 2004). He has also authored *Insanity on Trial* (New York: Plenum Press, 1988), and is coeditor of *Law and Public Policy/Psychology and the Social Sciences*, a book series published by the American Psychological Association. He is currently working on a new book, *Emotions, Culpability, and Law* (with W. Gerrod Parrott).

Paula L. Hannaford-Agor is a staff attorney and principal court research consultant with the research division of the National Center for State Courts. Her principal area of expertise is jury system management and trial procedure, and she has also conducted research on the topics of civil litigation, complex and mass tort litigation, access to justice for self-represented litigants, and legal and judicial ethics and discipline. In addition to conducting applied research on jury topics, she has authored or contributed to numerous books and articles on the American jury, including: *Jury Trial Innovations*, 2nd ed. (forthcoming, 2005), *The Promise and Challenges of Jury System Technology* (NCSC, 2003), and *Managing Notorious Trials* (NCSC, 1998). As an adjunct faculty member at William and Mary Law School, she teaches a seminar on the American jury. She received her law degree and a master's degree in public policy from the College of William and Mary.

Valerie P. Hans is professor of sociology and criminal justice at the University of Delaware, where she teaches courses on social science and the law, psychology and the law, jury decision making, and the courts. She is also a research affiliate with the National Center for State Courts. She received her PhD in social psychology from the University of Toronto in 1978. Professor Hans has conducted research and written widely about various aspects of the jury system, including jury selection, juror prejudice and bias, and the group decision-making process. Her coauthored book (with Neil Vidmar), *Judging the Jury* (Plenum, 1986) has been cited frequently by academics, lawyers, and the courts. *Business on Trial: The Civil Jury and Corporate Responsibility* (Yale University Press, 2000) examines how civil jurors decide the liability of business corporations. Her recent research projects have examined the causes of hung juries and the use and impact of jury trial reforms.

Julie E. Howe is president of J. Howe Consulting, a nationally recognized trial consulting firm based in New York City. She earned her doctorate in social psychology from North Carolina State University. She holds an MA in psychology from The College of William and Mary and a BA in psychology and political science from the University of Vermont. She has conducted and presented research on the bias of capital-sentencing instructions and her article (with James Luginbuhl), "Discretion in Capital Sentencing: Guided or Misguided?" *Indiana Law Journal* 70 (1995): 1161, is often cited in articles and legal pleadings regarding jurors' understanding of aggravating and mitigating circumstances. As a professional trial consultant, she applies social science theories, methodologies, and jury research to assist attorneys during all stages of litigation. She provides pretrial research and consultations including case analysis, venue analysis, focus group and mock jury studies, jury selection, in-court observations, and posttrial juror interviews in state and federal courts nationwide. Dr. Howe currently serves on the board of directors for the American Society of Trial Consultants. She is a member of the American Psychology-Law Society Division of the American Psychology Association, the New York Association of Public Opinion Researchers, and the Qualitative Research Consultants Association. She is a member of the National and New York State Associations of Criminal Defense Attorneys. She also serves as an invited speaker at national and local bar associations, and designs and participates in continuing legal education programs.

Nancy J. King is Lee S. and Charles A. Speir Professor of Law at Vanderbilt University Law School, where she has taught since 1991. A frequent contributor to conferences on jury reform, her research focuses on juries and on the post-investigative features of the criminal process including plea bargaining, trial, sentencing, double jeopardy, and postconviction review. Her articles on juries have included such topics as jury selection, anonymous juries, jury sentencing, nullification, and jury misconduct. She is coauthor of the two leading treatises on criminal procedure. With the late Charles Alan Wright and Susan R. Klein, she wrote *Federal Practice and Procedure, Criminal 3d* (Eagan, MN: West, 2003); and with Wayne R. LaFave and Jerold H. Israel, she wrote *Criminal Procedure,*

2nd ed. (West, 1999). With Yale Kamisar, Wayne LaFave, and Jerold Israel, she has also written the leading criminal procedure casebook, *Modern Criminal Procedure*, 10th ed. (West, 2002). Her work has been cited in decisions of the U.S. Supreme Court and lower courts. Professor King is a member of the advisory committee on the Federal Rules of Criminal Procedure.

John Kleinig is professor of philosophy at both John Jay College of Criminal Justice in New York and the doctoral programs in philosophy and criminal justice at the CUNY Graduate Center. He is also director of the Institute for Criminal Justice Ethics. In 2004, he accepted an appointment as the inaugural chair in policing ethics at Charles Sturt University, Australia, in which he was seconded as a professorial fellow in criminal justice ethics at the Centre for Applied Philosophy and Public Ethics in Canberra. In this latter position, he spends six months of each year in Australia. Since 1987 he has been editor of *Criminal Justice Ethics*. He has authored six books and edited several others, and written well over a hundred articles and book chapters. Among his books are: *Punishment and Desert* (Nijhoff, 1973); *Paternalism* (Rowman & Allanheld/ Manchester University Press, 1984); *Ethical Issues in Psychosurgery* (Allen & Unwin, 1985); *Valuing Life* (Princeton University Press, 1991); *The Ethics of Policing* (Cambridge University Press, 1996). He is currently working on three single-authored volumes, *Loyalty and Loyalties; Ends and Means in Policing*; and *Ethics and Criminal Justice*.

James P. Levine is dean of research and graduate studies at John Jay College of Criminal Justice where he is also a faculty member of the Government Department. From 1993 to 1999 he served as executive officer of the doctoral program in criminal justice of the City University of New York located at John Jay College. He received his doctorate in political science from Northwestern University in 1968. Prior to coming to John Jay he served on the faculties of Michigan State University, the University of Oregon, and Brooklyn College of the City University of New York. Dean Levine has published two textbooks on criminal justice (coauthored with Michael Musheno and Dennis Palumbo): *Criminal Justice: A Public Policy Approach* (Harcourt, Brace, Jovanovich, 1980) and *Criminal Justice in America: Law in Action* (John Wiley, 1986). He is the coauthor, with David Abbott, of *Wrong Winner: The Coming Debacle in the Electoral College* (Praeger, 1991), and sole author of *Juries and Politics* (Wadsworth, 1992). He has also published articles on criminal justice institutions and policy, jury behavior, and research methodology in scholarly periodicals and books.

Candace McCoy specializes in studying the operation of criminal courts, particularly pre-trial processes, from a social science perspective. Her most recent publication, "Plea Bargaining as Coercion: The Trial Penalty and Plea Bargaining Reform," *Criminal Law Quarterly* 50 (2005): 67–107, covers the jurisprudential underpinnings of plea bargaining and explains why the jury trial is endangered. McCoy has also published extensively on such topics as sentencing and criminal justice ethics. She is associate professor of criminal justice at Rutgers University–Newark, where she teaches graduate courses in law and society, prosecution and the courts, and sentencing. McCoy is a member of the Ohio bar, holding a law degree from the University of Cincinnati, and also has a PhD in jurisprudence and social policy from the University of California, Berkeley.

G. Thomas Munsterman is director of the Center for Jury Studies of the National Center for State Courts: http://www.ncsconline.org/Juries/index.html. He is author of *Jury System Management* (NCSC, 1996), coeditor (with Paula L. Hannaford and G. Mark Whittaker) of *Jury Trial Innovations* (NCSC, 1997), and coauthor (with Timothy R. Murphy and Genevra K. Loveland) of *A Manual for Managing Notorious Cases* (NCSC, 1991). He has written many papers, directed research, and spoken on many aspects of jury systems, ranging in topics from multiple source lists and juror attitudes to the impact of variations in jury size. He also has a column on "Jury News" in the quarterly publication *Court Manager*. He has served on the faculty for many state judicial education programs and has been a faculty member at the National Judicial College for twelve years. Munsterman was formerly with Bird Engineering Research Associates and the Applied Physics Laboratory, Johns Hopkins University. He holds a BSEE from Northwestern University and an MSE from George Washington University.

Maureen O'Connor is associate professor and chair of the Psychology Department at John Jay College of Criminal Justice and has appointments on the faculty of the doctoral programs in forensic psychology, social/personality psychology, and criminal justice at the Graduate Center of the City University of New York. She received her JD and PhD with specialization in law, psychology, and policy from the University of Arizona. Her research interests focus on the intersection of gender, psychology, and law, and include stalking and sexual harassment, with particular attention to lay and legal definitions of those concepts and juror reactions to them. One of her other primary areas of scholarly interest is the use of scientific information and expert testimony in the legal system. Dr. O'Connor was a law clerk for the Honorable Patricia M. Wald on the U.S. Court of Appeals for the D.C. Circuit, and she is a member of the bar in Arizona and Washington, D.C. She has served on the American Psychological Association's Committee on Legal Issues, and is on the governing council of the Society for the Psychological Study of Social Issues. She also serves on the editorial board of *Psychology, Public Policy, and Law*, and is a member of the Association of the Bar of the City of New York's Committee on Women in the Profession.

Alan W. Scheflin is a professor of law at Santa Clara University School of Law. He has authored 6 books and has written over seventy articles. In addition to teaching and publishing, Professor Scheflin has delivered over one hundred and twenty-five invited addresses and has been an expert or consultant in legal cases in fourteen states and Canada. He is the recipient of twelve awards from human rights and mental health associations, including the American Psychiatric Association and the American Psychological Association. Professor Scheflin began writing on jury nullification in the early 1970s, after serving on the defense team in the leading case of *United States v. Dougherty*.

Adina Schwartz received her PhD in philosophy from Rockefeller University in 1976, and was an assistant professor of philosophy at Yale University from 1975–1982. She received her JD from Yale Law School in 1985 and became a federal public defender. Since 1993, she has been an associate professor in the Department of Law and Police Science, John Jay College of Criminal Justice, City University of New York. Among her publications are "'Just Take Away Their Guns': The Hidden Racism of *Terry v. Ohio*," in *Fordham Urban Law Journal* 23 (1996): 317–75; "A 'Dogma of Empiricism' Revisited: *Daubert v. Merrell Dow Pharmaceuticals, Inc.* and the Need to Resurrect the Philosophical Insight of *Frye v. United States*," in *Harvard Journal of Law and Technology* 10 (1997): 149–237; "Homes as Folding Umbrellas: Two Recent Supreme Court Decisions on 'Knock and Announce,'" in *American Journal of Criminal Law* 25 (1998): 545–94; "A Market in Liberty: Corruption, Cooperation, and the Federal Criminal Justice System," in *Private and Public Corruption*, ed. William C. Heffernan and John Kleinig (Rowman and Littlefield, 2004), 173–223; and "A Systemic Challenge to the Reliability and Admissibility of Firearms and Toolmark Identification," *Columbia Science and Technology Law Review* 6 (March 28, 2005): 1–42, at http://www.stlr.org/cite.cgi?volume=6&article=2.

Neil Vidmar is Russell M. Robinson II Professor of Law at Duke University School of Law and holds a secondary appointment in the Psychology Department at Duke. He received his PhD in social psychology from the University of Illinois in 1967. He is coauthor with Valerie Hans of *Judging the Jury* (Plenum, 1986), author of *Medical Malpractice and the American Jury* (University of Michigan Press, 1995), and editor/author of *World Jury Systems* (Oxford University Press, 2000). He has testified or consulted as an expert on jury behavior for trials in the United States, Canada, England, Australia, and New Zealand. His national and international research on pretrial prejudice is documented in "Case Studies of Pre- and Mid-trial Prejudice in Criminal and Civil Litigation," *Law and Human Behavior* 26 (2002): 73, and in "When All of Us Are Victims: Juror Prejudice and 'Terrorist' Trials," *Chicago-Kent Law Review* 78 (2003): 1143.